STUDY GUIDE TO ACCOMPANY

Intermediate Accounting

VOLUME 2: CHAPTERS 13 – 23

Donald E. Kieso, PhD, CPA
KPMG Peat Marwick Emeritus Professor of Accounting
Northern Illinois University
DeKalb, Illinois

Jerry J. Weygandt, PhD, CPA
Arthur Andersen Alumni Professor of Accounting
University of Wisconsin
Madison, Wisconsin

Terry D. Warfield, PhD
Associate Professor
University of Wisconsin
Madison, Wisconsin

Nicola M. Young, MBA, FCPA, FCA
Saint Mary's University
Halifax, Nova Scotia

Irene M. Wiecek, FCPA, FCA
University of Toronto
Toronto, Ontario

Bruce J. McConomy, PhD, CPA, CA
Wilfrid Laurier University
Waterloo, Ontario

Study Guide prepared by
Bruce Wright, MBA, CPA, CA
Loyalist College
Belleville, Ontario

WILEY

Library and Archives Canada Cataloguing in Publication

Wright, Bruce, 1964-, author
    Study guide to accompany Intermediate accounting, eleventh Canadian edition / study guide prepared by Bruce Wright.

Supplement to: Intermediate accounting.
ISBN 978-1-119-27442-1 (v. 2 : paperback)

    1. Accounting–Problems, exercises, etc. I. Title. II. Title: Intermediate accounting, eleventh Canadian edition.

HF5636.K54 2016 Suppl.   657'.044076   C2016-902138-6

Production Credits
Executive Editors: Emily McGee and Zoë Craig
Senior Marketing Manager: Anita Osborne
Editorial Manager: Karen Staudinger
Developmental Editor: Daleara Jamasji Hirjikaka
Media Specialist, Content Management & Technology: Meaghan MacDonald
Cover and Interior Design: Joanna Vieira
Production Editing: Belle Wong
Typesetting: Thomson Digital
Printing and Binding: ePAC

Printed and bound in the United States of America
1 2 3 4 5 EP 19 18 17 16

John Wiley & Sons Canada, Ltd.
Suite 300, 90 Eglinton Ave East
Toronto, Ontario, Canada, M4P 2Y3

Visit our website at: www.wiley.ca

Preface

To the Student

The purpose of this study guide is to help you to improve your success rate in solving accounting homework assignments and in answering accounting exam questions. For each chapter we include the following:

OVERVIEW To briefly introduce the chapter topics and their importance.

STUDY STEPS To discuss the business transactions or issues pertinent to the chapter topics, including an analysis of key recognition, measurement, and disclosure issues.

TIPS To alert you to common pitfalls and misconceptions and remind you of important terminology, concepts, and relationships that are relevant to answering specific questions or solving certain problems.

EXERCISES To provide you with a selection of problems representative of homework assignments that an intermediate accounting student may encounter.

MULTIPLE CHOICE To provide you with a selection of multiple-choice questions that are representative of common exam questions covering topics in the chapter.

PURPOSES To identify the essence of each question or exercise and link it to the text material.

SOLUTIONS To show you the appropriate solution for each exercise and multiple-choice question presented.

EXPLANATIONS To give you the details of how selected solutions were derived and explain why things are done as shown.

APPROACHES To coach you on the particular model, computational format, or other strategy to be used to solve particular problems. To teach you how to analyze and solve multiple-choice questions.

This book will provide you with the opportunity to solve accounting problems in addition to the ones assigned by your instructor without having to rely on your teacher for solutions. Many of the exercises and questions contained herein are very similar to material in your intermediate accounting textbook; the difference is, the ones in this book are accompanied with detailed, clearly laid-out solutions.

The use of the multiple-choice questions in this volume and the related suggestions on how to approach them can easily increase your ability (and confidence in your ability) to deal with exam questions of this variety.

HOW TO STUDY ACCOUNTING

The successful study of accounting requires a different approach than most other subjects. In addition to reading a chapter, applying the material through completion of exercises or problems is necessary in developing a true and lasting understanding of the concepts introduced in the text chapter. The study of accounting principles is a combination of theory and practice; theory describes what to do and why, and practice is the application of guidelines to actual situations. We use illustrations to demonstrate how theory works and we use theory to explain why something is done in practice. Therefore, it is impossible to separate the two in the study of accounting.

Learning accounting is a cumulative process. It is difficult to master Chapter 4 until you are thoroughly familiar with chapters 1–3, and so on. Therefore, it is imperative that you keep up with class assignments. And, because accounting is a technical subject, you must pay particular attention to terminology.

Accounting is the language of business. It is an exciting subject that provides a challenge for most business majors. Your ultimate success in life may well depend on your ability to grasp financial data. The effort you expend now will provide rewards for years to come.

We encourage you to follow the four steps for study outlined below to give yourself the best possible chance for a successful learning experience and to make the most efficient use of your time. These steps provide a system of study for each chapter in your text.

Step 1

- Scan the learning objectives at the beginning of each chapter.
- Scan the chapter (or chapter section).
- Glance over the questions at the end of the chapter.

This first step will give you an overview of the material to be mastered.

Step 2

- Read the assigned pages slowly.
- Study carefully, and mark for later attention any sections requiring review.

- Pay particular attention to examples and illustrations.
- Try to formulate tentative answers to end-of-chapter questions.

During this phase, you will be filling in the chapter "outline" you formed in Step 1. Most of the details will fall into place during this phase of your study. The remaining steps are necessary, however, for a keen understanding of the subject.

Step 3

- Carefully read the **Overview**, **Study Steps**, and **Tips** sections of this study guide.
- Do the **Exercises** and **Cases** in this study guide that pertain to the same topics as your homework assignments.
- Review the relevant **Illustrations** in this study guide.
- Do the **Multiple-Choice Questions** in the study guide that pertain to the same topics as your homework assignments.
- Refer back to the text chapter sections that you marked for review, if any. It is likely that any confusion or questions will have been cleared up through your work in the study guide. If a section remains unclear, carefully reread it and rework relevant pages of the study guide.
- Repeat this process for each assigned topic area.

Step 4

- Write out formal answers to homework assignments in the text. This step is crucial because you can determine whether you can independently apply the material you have been studying to new situations. You may find it necessary to go back to the text and/or the study guide to restudy certain sections. This is common and a good indicator that the study assignments are working for you.

Here is some additional guidance to help you get the most out of this study guide:

The **Study Steps** and **Tips**, along with the **Illustrations**, will aid your understanding and retention of the material. Exercises provide examples of application of the text material. These should be very valuable in giving you guidance in completing homework assignments that are often similar in nature and content.

The **Approach** stated for an exercise or question is likely the most valuable feature of this study guide because it provides guidance on how to think through the situation at hand. This thought process can then be used in similar situations. It is impossible to illustrate every situation you may encounter. You can, however, handle new situations by simply applying what you know and making modifications where appropriate. Many students make the mistake of attempting to memorize their way through an accounting book. That, too, is an impossible feat. **Do not rely on memorization**. If this material is going to be useful to you, you must think about what you are reading and always be thinking of why things are as they are.

If you know the reasoning for a particular accounting treatment, it will be much easier to remember that treatment and reconstruct it even weeks after your initial study of it.

Explanations are provided for exercises and questions. These are very detailed so that you will thoroughly understand what is being done and why. These details will serve you well when you complete your homework assignments.

Always make an honest effort to solve the exercises and answer the questions contained in this study guide **before** you look at the solutions. Answering the questions on your own will maximize the benefits you can expect from this book.

The **Multiple-Choice Questions** are self-tests to give you immediate feedback on how well you understand the material. Study the **Approaches** suggested for answering these questions in the study guide. Practise the approaches when answering the multiple-choice questions in the text. Apply them when taking examinations. By doing so, you will learn to calmly, methodically, and successfully process examination questions. This will very likely improve your exam scores.

When you work through an **Exercise** or **Case** in the study guide or in the text, always read the instructions **before** you read all of the given data. This allows you to determine what is being asked of you and what you are to accomplish, before you read the given data. As you tread through the data, you can begin to process it because you can determine its significance and relevance. If you read the data before the instructions, you will likely waste time having to reread the data after you find out what you are to do with it. Also, more importantly, reading the data before the instructions will likely cause you to begin anticipating what will be asked of you, which will often cause you to do analysis other than what is required of you.

Good luck and best wishes for a positive learning experience!

Chapter 13

Non-Financial and Current Liabilities

OVERVIEW

Resources or assets of a business are financed either by the business's internal operations or by funds from entities external to the business. Two main external sources of funds are creditors, who are owed liabilities, and owners, who are contributors of equity capital. In this chapter, we begin our in-depth discussion of liabilities.

Due to the nature of business activities, it is common for goods and services to be received with the related payment to be made days or weeks later. Therefore, at a specific point in time, such as at a statement of financial position date, we may find that a business has obligations to pay for merchandise received from suppliers (accounts payable), salaries and wages incurred (salaries and wages payable), and interest incurred (interest payable). The business may also have obligations to remit amounts due to government agencies that are related to property tax incurred (property tax payable), sales tax charged to customers and not yet remitted to the government (sales tax payable), and other amounts due to government agencies in connection with employee compensation (such as withholding taxes payable). These current (short-term) liabilities are classified separately from non-current liabilities in order to provide information about obligations that will place a demand on the business's current assets.

Non-financial liabilities are more difficult to account for, because there may be uncertainty regarding the existence of a liability and/or measurement amount. Non-financial liabilities, including decommissioning and restoration obligations, product guarantees and customer programs, and contingencies and uncertain commitments, require extensive analysis of relevant facts to determine the proper accounting treatment.

Accounting for current liabilities and non-financial liabilities is discussed in this chapter.

STUDY STEPS

Understanding the Nature of Liabilities

Liabilities

The current definition of a liability is "an obligation that arises from past transactions or events, which may result in a transfer of assets." Current standards outline that liabilities have three essential characteristics:

- They embody a duty or responsibility.
- The entity has little or no discretion to avoid the duty. (For example, the company must pay vacation pay because an employee has earned it according to the law or the employment arrangement.)
- The transaction or event that obliges the entity has occurred. (For example, the act of the employee working causes the vacation pay obligation to arise.)

The definition of liabilities is being reviewed as a result of the May 2015 Exposure Draft *Conceptual Framework for Financial Reporting*. This study guide applies definitions being used when the study guide went to press.

Financial versus Non-Financial Liabilities

An important distinction is made between financial and non-financial liabilities. Under both IFRS and ASPE, a **financial liability** is a contractual obligation:

1. to deliver cash or other financial assets to another entity, or
2. to exchange financial assets or financial liabilities with another entity under conditions that are potentially unfavourable to the entity.

- A financial liability is both created by a contract and settled by delivery of cash or another financial asset or financial liability to another entity. Therefore, a key characteristic of a financial liability is the existence of a contract.

- Not all liabilities settled by delivery of cash, financial assets, or financial liabilities are considered financial liabilities. (For example, sales tax payable is a liability created by legislation, not a contract.)

A **non-financial liability** is often not payable in cash, but instead payable by delivery of goods or services (for example, dismantling and restoring an offshore oil drilling platform at the end of its useful life).

Financial liabilities are recognized initially at their fair value. After acquisition, most are accounted for at their **amortized cost**. When liabilities are short-term in nature, they are usually accounted for at their maturity value since the difference between fair value and maturity value is not material.

ASPE does not specifically address the measurement of non-financial liabilities. Under IFRS, non-financial liabilities are measured initially and at each subsequent reporting date at the best estimate of the amount the entity would rationally pay at the date of the statement of financial position to settle the present obligation.

Understanding the Accounting Issues related to Non-Financial Liabilities

This chapter discusses various types of non-financial liabilities, including decommissioning and restoration obligations, unearned revenues, product guarantees and customer programs, contingencies and uncertain commitments, financial guarantees, and commitments.

Decommissioning and Restoration Obligations

Accounting standards require companies to recognize, in the period when the obligation is incurred (usually in the period of asset acquisition), a liability for future costs of retiring the asset, even though payment for these obligations may be years away. Examples include decommissioning and/or restoration of nuclear facilities, oil and gas properties, mines, and landfills. With these types of assets, at the end of the asset's useful life, the company usually has a legal or constructive obligation to restore the asset and its surrounding area to a certain condition. The best estimate of the present value of the expenditure required to settle the present obligation at the reporting date is included in the cost of the asset. This cost is then depreciated over the asset's useful life. The offsetting liability (asset retirement obligation) remains on the entity's books and is increased to its future value over the asset's useful life. This provides better matching of costs with expected benefits, as well as better predictability of the future obligation to be paid.

Under **IFRS**, recognition of an obligation related to decommissioning and restoration of a long-lived asset is consistent with the proposed definition of a liability outlined above. Specifically, IFRS requires that the present value cost of both **legal and constructive obligations** related to decommissioning and restoration be included in the related asset's recorded acquisition cost, with an offsetting credit entry to a liability account (such as Asset Retirement Obligation). Under IFRS, the subsequent costs of producing inventory from the long-lived asset are not included in the asset's capital asset account.

In contrast, under ASPE, only the present value cost of **legal obligations** related to decommissioning and restoration are included in the asset's recorded acquisition cost (with a similar offsetting credit entry to a liability account such as Asset Retirement Obligation). Under ASPE, the subsequent costs of producing inventory from the long-lived asset are included in the asset's capital asset account.

Product Guarantees and Warranty Obligations

A warranty is a type of product guarantee used by a seller to promote sales. Under a warranty, the seller makes a promise to the buyer to correct certain problems experienced with the product after the point of sale. Because a warranty is a stand-ready obligation that will likely result in significant future costs, it is a liability that should be recorded.

For **assurance-type** warranties, the warranty is part of the sales price. In this case, the outstanding liability is measured at the cost of the economic resources needed to meet the obligation. This expense-based approach has historically been used under ASPE.

For **service-type** warranties, the warranty is sold as an additional service. In this case, the outstanding liability is measured at the value of the service to be provided, not at its cost. The revenue received in advance is recognized as unearned revenue (a liability) at the point of sale. The liability is reduced in future periods as revenue is earned. This revenue-based approach is accepted under IFRS 15 and parallels the contract-based approach to revenue recognition introduced in Chapter 6. This approach is also being increasingly used under ASPE with bundled sales.

Customer Loyalty Programs

A customer loyalty program offers award credits to the buyer at the time of sale, redeemable in exchange for future awards or benefits. Under IFRS, the revenue from the original sale transaction should be allocated between the award credits and the other components of the sale, and at the time of sale, the fair value of the award credits should be recognized as unearned revenue. The unearned revenue should be recorded as earned when the award credits are exchanged for the promised awards. Customer loyalty programs are not explicitly addressed under ASPE; however, under ASPE, the revenue recognition criteria should be applied similarly "to the separately identifiable components of a single transaction in order to reflect the substance of the transaction."

Contingencies and Uncertain Commitments

A **contingency** is "an existing condition or situation involving uncertainty as to possible gain or loss to an enterprise that will ultimately be resolved when one or more future events occur or fail to occur. Resolution of the uncertainty may confirm the acquisition of an asset or the incurrence of a liability." Contingent gains (gain contingencies or contingent assets) are not recorded.

Currently, both IFRS and ASPE require that only obligations of sufficient likelihood be measured and recorded. However, proposed revisions to the accounting standards for contingencies under IFRS favour recording of all events that represent **unconditional obligations** as liabilities (consistent with the definition of a liability), and incorporating uncertainty surrounding a particular liability in the measurement of the liability. See **Illustration 13-1** for a chart summarizing accounting standards for contingencies and uncertain commitments.

Understanding How Liabilities Fit into the Financial Reporting Model

Financial Statement Analysis

Proper classification of liabilities between current and long-term is very important, as it impacts key ratios such as the current ratio and the quick (or acid-test) ratio. There may be a bias to show liabilities as long-term (for example, to falsely increase the current ratio).

Key ratios are:

$$\text{Current ratio} = \frac{\text{Current assets}}{\text{Current liabilities}}$$

$$\text{Quick ratio} = \frac{\text{Cash} + \text{Marketable securities} + \text{Receivables (net)}}{\text{Current liabilities}}$$

$$\text{Days payables outstanding} = \frac{\text{Average trade accounts payable}}{\substack{\text{Average daily cost of goods sold or} \\ \text{Average daily cost of total operating expenses}}}$$

If a company's current ratio exceeds 2:1, it is normally considered acceptable. However, care should be taken to analyze the individual assets and liabilities included in current assets and current liabilities, how quickly the current assets can be realized (or converted into cash), and how quickly the current liabilities will need to be paid. Referring to industry "standards" may also be useful in evaluating a company's ratios.

The quick (or acid-test) ratio benchmark is generally below 2:1 since, by definition, the formula focuses on more liquid assets only.

The days payables outstanding ratio zeroes in on how long it takes a company to pay its trade payables. When cash is managed well, the payment of payables is delayed as long as possible, but not beyond the due date.

TIPS ON CHAPTER TOPICS

- **Current liabilities** are often called **short-term liabilities** or short-term debt. **Non-current liabilities** are often called **long-term liabilities** or long-term debt.

- The key to analysis of a potential liability is analysis of the transaction or event that gives rise to the obligation. If the obligation is **unconditional**, promised, or required, or if the entity has a **stand-ready** responsibility to satisfy the obligation as at the statement of financial position date, a liability should be recorded. Any uncertainty about the amount to be paid should be taken into account in the measurement of the liability (for example, by calculating the

(continued)

liability amount as an expected value or probability-weighted average of the range of possible outcomes).

- Standards for **classification of debt** between current and long-term are more stringent under IFRS than ASPE. For example, if long-term debt becomes **callable** due to a violation of a debt agreement, IFRS requires that the debt be reclassified as current. In the same situation, under ASPE, the debt may remain classified as long-term under certain conditions. As a second example, if short-term debt is expected to be **refinanced** (on a long-term basis) after the statement of financial position date but before the financial statements are released, IFRS requires that the debt remain classified as current as at the statement of financial position date, unless at the statement of financial position date, the entity expects to refinance it or roll it over under an existing agreement for at least 12 months and the decision is solely at its discretion. Under ASPE, however, as long as the short-term debt expected to be refinanced is refinanced on a long-term basis before the financial statements are released, the debt can be reclassified to long-term as at the statement of financial position date. In general, regarding classification of debt, IFRS requires that the statement of financial position show conditions existing at the statement of financial position date.

- The difference in standards between IFRS and ASPE for classification of debt between current and long-term can impact **key ratios** significantly.

- In accounting for product guarantees and customer programs (such as warranties, customer loyalty programs, and premiums and rebates), the **traditional expense approach**, for assurance-type warranties, has historically been used under ASPE. The full amount of sales revenue is recognized in the period of the sale, and in the same period, an estimated expense and liability for the product guarantees or customer programs related to the sale are recognized. In contrast, the **revenue approach**, used for service-type warranties and accepted under IFRS 15, focuses on the nature of the resulting asset and liability in the period of the sale, and therefore on the statement of financial position effect of the transaction. The revenue approach reflects that the original sale is for a **bundle** of goods and/or services and that part of the original sale amount should be recorded as unearned if goods and/or services are to be delivered in the future. For example, a $10,000 bundled sale, including a service-type warranty with a stand-alone value of $900, would be recorded as follows:

Cash/Accounts Receivable	10,000	
Sales Revenue		9,100
Unearned Warranty Revenue		900

If this was an assurance-type warranty, and the expense approach was used, the resulting liability would be a warranty liability, rather than an unearned warranty revenue. In subsequent periods, the unearned revenue is recorded as earned, perhaps on a straight-line basis over the service period, or as the goods and/or services are delivered.

- For service-type warranties, the unearned revenue recorded (such as unearned warranty revenue) is measured at **fair value**, whereas for assurance-type warranties, the liability recorded (such as estimated warranty liability) is measured at **cost**.

- Under ASPE, a contingent loss is accrued if both of the following conditions are met: (1) it is **likely** that a future event will confirm that an asset has been impaired or a liability has been incurred as at the date of the financial statements and (2) the loss amount can be **reasonably estimated (measured)**. If the loss is likely but not reasonably estimable, or if the likelihood of a confirming future event cannot be determined, the item should be disclosed in the notes to the financial statements (but not accrued). If it is only **unlikely** that a liability has been incurred, no accrual or note disclosure is required.

- Under current IFRS requirements, a loss is accrued if it is **probable** (or more likely than not) that a liability has been incurred as at the statement of financial position date. If the amount cannot be measured reliably, no accrual is required; however, IFRS indicates that only in very rare circumstances would the amount not be reliably measurable.

- Under current IFRS requirements, the criterion for accrual of a liability related to a contingency (probable, or more likely than not) is a somewhat lower hurdle than the ASPE criterion for accrual of a contingent loss (likely). This may mean that a particular contingency may result in an accrued liability for an entity under IFRS, but not for an entity under ASPE.

EXERCISE 13-1

PURPOSE: This exercise tests your ability to distinguish between current and non-current (long-term) liabilities.

Chalmers Corporation is a publicly accountable entity. Chalmers' 2017 financial statements are issued on February 15, 2018.

Instructions

For each of the following items, indicate whether the liability would be reported as current or non-current on Chalmers' statement of financial position as at December 31, 2017.

1. Obligation to supplier for merchandise purchased on credit (terms 2/10, n/30).
2. Note payable to bank maturing 90 days after statement of financial position date.
3. Bonds payable due January 1, 2020.
4. Property tax payable.
5. Interest payable on long-term bonds payable.
6. Income tax payable.
7. Portion of lessee's lease liabilities due in years 2019 through 2023.
8. Revenue received in advance, to be earned over the next six months.
9. Salaries and wages payable.
10. Rent payable.

11. Note payable to bank maturing six months after statement of financial position date. (Long-term refinancing of the note payable was completed under an agreement dated January 31, 2018.)

12. Instalment loan payment due three months after statement of financial position date.

13. Instalment loan payments due after one year.

14. Portion of lessee's lease obligations due within a year after the December 31, 2017 statement of financial position date.

15. Bank overdraft.

16. Accrued officer bonus.

17. Coupon offers outstanding.

18. Cash dividends declared but not paid.

19. Unearned rent revenue.

20. Stock dividends distributable.

21. Bonds payable due June 1, 2018.

22. Bonds payable due July 1, 2018; by contract, the bonds payable will be retired using a sinking fund that has been accumulated for this purpose. The sinking fund is classified as a long-term investment.

23. Discount to the bonds payable in item 3 above.

24. Current maturities of long-term debt.

25. Accrued interest on notes payable.

26. Customer deposits.

27. Sales tax payable.

28. Employee payroll withholdings.

29. Asset retirement obligation.

30. Lawsuit liability (more likely than not, and measurable).

31. Warranty liability.

32. Unearned warranty revenue.

33. Gift certificates outstanding.

34. Loan from shareholder.

35. Loan payable due on demand.

Solution to Exercise 13-1

Apply the criteria for classification of a liability as current. Recall that under IFRS, a liability is classified as current when one of the following conditions is met: (1) the liability is expected to be settled in the entity's normal operating cycle, (2) the liability is held primarily for trading, (3) the liability is due within 12 months from the end of the reporting period, or (4) the entity does not have an unconditional right to defer settlement of the liability for at least 12 months after the statement of financial position date. ASPE provides a similar definition; however, there are differences in application. ASPE suggests that current liabilities include amounts payable within one year from the balance sheet date or within the normal operating cycle, when that is longer than one year.

As a publicly accountable entity, Chalmers must follow IFRS.

1. Current liability (called Accounts Payable).
2. Current liability.
3. Non-current liability.
4. Current liability.
5. Current liability; interest on bonds is usually due semi-annually or annually.
6. Current liability.
7. Non-current liability.
8. Current liability.
9. Current liability.
10. Current liability.
11. Current liability; the refinancing agreement did not exist at December 31, 2017 (the reporting date). Under IFRS, the short-term debt expected to be refinanced is reported as a current liability.
12. Current liability.
13. Non-current liability.
14. Current liability.
15. Current liability (assuming no other bank accounts with positive balances in the same bank and with a legal right to offset).
16. Current liability.
17. Current liability; may also classify a portion as non-current liability, if applicable.
18. Current liability.
19. Current liability or non-current liability, depending on when the revenue is expected to be earned.
20. Does not meet the definition of a liability. Usually reported in shareholders' equity.
21. Current liability.
22. Non-current liability; even though it is coming due within a year, it will not require the use of current assets to be liquidated.
23. Contra non-current liability (deducted from the related bonds payable). Note that current practice also uses the net method of accounting for bonds payable (under which the initial bond payable is recorded at present value, rather than recording the maturity value of the bond in a bond payable account with a [contra] discount on bond payable account that together net to present value).
24. Current liability.
25. Current liability, generally; in rare cases may be non-current.
26. Current liability or non-current liability, depending on the time remaining before they are to be returned or earned.
27. Current liability.
28. Current liability.
29. Non-current liability, generally; current liability if it is coming due within a year.
30. Current liability or non-current liability, depending on the date that settlement is expected.

31. Current liability and/or non-current liability, depending on term of warranty. (This account title is used under the expense approach to accounting for warranties.)

32. Current liability and/or non-current liability, depending on term of warranty. (This account title is used under the revenue approach to accounting for warranties.)

33. Current liability, most likely; could have a portion as non-current liability.

34. Current liability or non-current liability, depending on the due date of the loan; loans with related parties are required to be separately disclosed; if this loan is due on demand, it must be classified as a current liability.

35. Current liability.

EXERCISE 13-2

PURPOSE: This exercise provides an example of accounting for an obligation to a provincial or federal government agency for unremitted sales tax.

During the month of September, Rachida's Boutique had cash sales of $702,000 and credit sales of $411,000, both of which include the 6% sales tax that must be remitted to the provincial government by October 15. Sales tax on September sales was lumped with the sales price and recorded as a credit to the Sales Revenue account.

Instructions

(a) Prepare the adjusting entry that should be recorded to fairly present the financial statements at September 30.

(b) Prepare the entry to record the remittance of the sales tax on October 5 if a 2% discount is allowed for payments received by the provincial government by October 10.

Solution to Exercise 13-2

(a) 9/30	Sales Revenue		63,000	
	Sales Tax Payable			63,000
	Calculation:			
	Sales plus sales tax ($702,000 + $411,000)	$1,113,000		
	Less sales exclusive of tax ($1,113,000 ÷ 1.06)	1,050,000		
	Sales tax	$ 63,000		

(b) 10/5	Sales Tax Payable	63,000	
	Cash (98% × $63,000)		61,740
	Other Income (2% × $63,000)		1,260

EXPLANATION: Sales tax on transfers of tangible personal property and on certain services must be collected from customers and remitted to the proper government authority. A liability account (Sales Tax Payable) is set up to provide for tax collected from customers but not yet remitted to the government. The Sales Tax Payable account should reflect the liability for sales tax due to the government.

EXERCISE 13-3

PURPOSE: This exercise will provide you with two examples of accounting for short-term debt expected to be refinanced.

Situation 1

On December 31, 2017, Mayor Frederick Specialty Foods Company had $1 million of short-term debt in the form of notes payable due February 4, 2018. On January 22, 2018, the company issued 20,000 common shares for $41 per share, receiving $800,000 proceeds after brokerage fees and other costs of issuance. On February 4, 2018, the proceeds from the share sale, supplemented by an additional $200,000 cash, were used to liquidate the $1 million of short-term debt. The December 31, 2017 statement of financial position was issued on February 20, 2018.

Situation 2

Included in Hubbard Corporation's liability account balances on December 31, 2017, were the following:

14% note payable issued October 1, 2014, maturing September 30, 2018	$500,000
16% note payable issued April 1, 2014, payable in six annual instalments of $200,000 beginning April 1, 2015	600,000

Hubbard's December 31, 2017 financial statements were issued on March 31, 2018. On January 13, 2018, the entire $600,000 balance of the 16% note was refinanced by issuance of a long-term obligation payable in a lump sum. In addition, on March 8, 2018, Hubbard consummated a non-cancellable agreement with the lender to refinance the 14%, $500,000 note on a long-term basis, with readily determinable terms that have not yet been implemented. Both parties are financially capable of honouring the agreement, and there have been no violations of the agreement's provisions.

Instructions

(a) For situation 1, show how the $1 million of short-term debt would be presented on the December 31, 2017 balance sheet, including note disclosure, under ASPE.

(b) For situation 1, show how the $1 million of short-term debt would be presented on the December 31, 2017 statement of financial position, including note disclosure, under IFRS.

(c) For situation 2, explain how the liabilities should be classified on the December 31, 2017 balance sheet, under ASPE. How much should be classified as a current liability? Would classification differ under IFRS? If so, how?

Solution to Exercise 13-3

(a)   **MAYOR FREDERICK SPECIALTY FOODS COMPANY**
                Partial Statement of Financial Position
                         December 31, 2017

Current liabilities:	
Notes payable (Note 1)	$200,000
Long-term debt:	
Notes payable refinanced in	
February 2018 (Note 1)	800,000

Note 1—Short-term debt refinanced

As at December 31, 2017, the Company had notes payable totalling $1 million due on February 4, 2018. On February 4, 2018, these notes were partially refinanced on a long-term basis using the $800,000 proceeds received from an issuance of common shares on January 22, 2018. The $200,000 notes payable balance was liquidated using current assets.

(b)   **MAYOR FREDERICK SPECIALTY FOODS COMPANY**
                Partial Statement of Financial Position
                         December 31, 2017

Current liabilities:	
Notes payable (Note 1)	$1,000,000

Note 1—Short-term debt refinanced

As at December 31, 2017, the Company had notes payable totalling $1 million due on February 4, 2018. On February 4, 2018, these notes were partially refinanced on a long-term basis using the $800,000 proceeds received from an issuance of common shares on January 22, 2018. The $200,000 notes payable balance was liquidated using current assets.

(c) Under ASPE, the entire $600,000 balance of the 16% note may be excluded from current liabilities as at the balance sheet date because it was refinanced on a long-term basis before financial statements were completed and issued. The $500,000 balance of the 14% note may also be excluded from current liabilities because as at the date financial statements were completed and issued, there was a non-cancellable agreement in place to refinance the note on a long-term basis with readily determinable terms, which both parties are capable of honouring.

Under IFRS, $200,000 of the $600,000 balance of the 16% note should be included in current liabilities, because long-term refinancing of this note was not firm as at the statement of financial position date. The $400,000 balance of the note would remain classified as a long-term liability. The $500,000 balance of the 14% note should be included in current liabilities as at the statement of financial position date, because the note did not have a firm long-term refinancing agreement in place as at the statement of financial position date.

APPROACH AND EXPLANATION: Review both ASPE and IFRS classification criteria for short-term debt expected to be refinanced, and apply the criteria to the situations at hand.

Under ASPE, an entity may exclude a short-term obligation from current liabilities if:

1. the liability has been refinanced on a long-term basis before the financial statements are completed, or if

2. before the financial statements are completed, there is a non-cancellable agreement in place to refinance the liability on a long-term basis, and nothing stands in the way of completing the refinancing.

Under IFRS, a short-term obligation must be included in current liabilities unless, as at the statement of financial position date, there is a firm and existing agreement in place to refinance, and the entity expects to refinance the liability under the agreement for at least 12 months, and the decision is solely at the entity's discretion. Under IFRS, even though the short-term liabilities in situation 2 were refinanced on a long-term basis before financial statements were issued, because the agreements were not entered into until after the statement of financial position date, the short-term liabilities should be classified as current.

Under both ASPE and IFRS, refinancing a short-term obligation on a long-term basis can be done by replacing the obligation with equity securities, as was done in situation 1. Whether refinanced by long-term debt or equity securities, the portion of the short-term obligation to be excluded from current liabilities may not exceed the proceeds from the new long-term debt or equity securities issued that are used to retire the short-term obligation. Similarly, if reclassification of a current liability to long-term is supported by the existence of a financing agreement, the amount of short-term debt that can be excluded from current liabilities cannot exceed the amount to be refinanced under the agreement.

IFRS criteria for long-term classification of short-term debt expected to be refinanced are more stringent than ASPE criteria. If the respective criteria are applied to the same case facts, there may be significantly different working capital and current ratio outcomes under IFRS versus ASPE.

EXERCISE 13-4

PURPOSE: This exercise will review accounting for compensated absences.

Milton Dobson Company began operations on January 2, 2017. It employs nine individuals who work eight-hour days and are paid hourly. Each employee earns 10 paid vacation days and five paid sick days annually. Vacation days may be taken after January 15 of the year following the year in which they are earned. Sick days may be taken as soon as they are earned; unused sick days accumulate but do not vest. Additional information is as follows:

Actual Hourly Wage		Vacation Days Used by Each Employee		Sick Days Used by Each Employee	
2017	**2018**	**2017**	**2018**	**2017**	**2018**
$12.00	$13.00	0	9	3	4

Milton Dobson Company has chosen not to accrue paid sick leave until used, and to accrue paid vacation time at expected future rates of pay without discounting. The company used the following projected rates to accrue vacation time:

Year in Which Vacation Time Was Earned	Projected Future Pay Rates Used to Accrue Vacation Pay
2017	$12.90
2018	$13.60

Instructions

(a) Prepare journal entries to record transactions related to compensated absences during 2017 and 2018.

(b) Calculate the amounts of any liability for compensated absences that should be reported on the statement of financial position at December 31, 2017 and 2018.

Solution to Exercise 13-4

(a) **2017**

Salaries and Wages Expense	9,288 (i)	
Vacation Wages Payable		9,288
(To accrue the expense and liability for vacations)		
Salaries and Wages Expense	2,592 (ii)	
Cash		2,592
(To record sick time paid)		
To record vacation time paid: No entry.		

2018

Salaries and Wages Expense	9,792 (iii)	
Vacation Wages Payable		9,792
(To accrue the expense and liability for vacations)		
Salaries and Wages Expense	3,744 (iv)	
Cash		3,744
(To record sick time paid)		
Salaries and Wages Expense	65	
Vacation Wages Payable	8,359 (v)	
Cash		8,424 (vi)
(To record vacation time paid)		

(i)   9 employees × \$12.90/hr. × 8 hrs./day × 10 days = \$9,288.

(ii) 9 employees × \$12.00/hr. × 8 hrs./day × 3 days = \$2,592.

(iii) 9 employees × \$13.60/hr. × 8 hrs./day × 10 days = \$9,792.

(iv) 9 employees × \$13.00/hr. × 8 hrs./day × 4 days = \$3,744.

(v) 9 employees × \$12.90/hr. × 8 hrs./day × 9 days = \$8,359.

(vi) 9 employees × \$13.00/hr. × 8 hrs./day × 9 days = \$8,424.

(b) Accrued liability at year end:

	2017 Vacation Wages Payable	2018 Vacation Wages Payable
Jan. 1 balance	\$ 0	\$ 9,288
+ accrued	9,288	9,792
− paid	(0)	(8,359)
Dec. 31 balance	\$ 9,288(a)	\$10,721(b)

(a) 9 employees × \$12.90/hr. × 8 hrs./day × 10 days =   \$ 9,288

(b) 9 employees × \$12.90/hr. × 8 hrs./day × 1 day   =   \$ 929

     9 employees × \$13.60/hr. × 8 hrs./day × 10 days =   9,792

                                     \$10,721

The expense and related liability for compensated absences should be recognized in the year in which the employees earn the rights to those absences. Vacation and holiday pay must be accrued if it vests or accumulates. Sick pay must be accrued only if it vests.

ILLUSTRATION 13-1

Accounting Treatment of Loss Contingencies

Loss Related to	ASPE	IFRS (current standards)	IFRS (proposed standards)
1. Risk of loss or damage of enterprise property by fire, explosion, or other hazards	Not accrued	Not accrued	Not accrued
2. General or unspecified business risks	Not accrued	Not accrued	Not accrued
3. Risk of loss from catastrophes assumed by property and casualty insurance companies, including reinsurance companies	Not accrued	Not accrued	Not accrued
4. Extended product warranty (beyond warranty expiration date)	Not accrued	Not accrued	Not accrued
5. Pending or threatened litigation	May be accrued*	May be accrued**	Accrued***
6. Actual or possible claims and assessments	May be accrued*	May be accrued**	Accrued***

*   Should be accrued if it is **likely** that a future event will confirm that an asset has been impaired or a liability has been incurred at the date of the financial statements, and the loss amount can be **reasonably estimated**. Liability would be measured at the **best estimate** in the range of possible outcomes; if none, the lowest point in the range is used, and the amount of the remaining exposure to loss is disclosed in the notes.

**   Should be accrued if it is **probable** (or **more likely than not**) that a future event will confirm that an asset has been impaired or a liability has been incurred at the date of the financial statements, and the loss amount can be **reliably measured** (although only in very rare circumstances would a loss not be reliably measurable). Liability would be measured at the **probability-weighted expected value** of the loss.

*** Should be accrued if the entity has an **unconditional** (or **non-contingent**) **obligation** at the statement of financial position date. Liability would be measured at the **probability-weighted expected value** of the loss.

EXERCISE 13-5

PURPOSE: This exercise will enable you to practise analyzing situations to determine whether a liability should be reported, and if so, at what amount.

Cleese Inc., a publishing company, is preparing its December 31, 2017 financial statements and must determine the proper accounting treatment for each of the following situations:

1. Cleese sells subscriptions to several magazines for a two- or three-year period. Cash receipts from subscribers are credited to Unearned Subscriptions Revenue. This account had a balance of $5.3 million at December 31, 2017, before adjustment. An analysis of outstanding subscriptions at December 31, 2017, shows that they expire as follows:

During 2018:	$ 800,000
During 2019:	900,000
During 2020:	1,200,000

2. On June 1, 2017, a suit for breach of contract against Cleese was filed by an author seeking damages of $1 million. The company's legal counsel believes that an unfavourable outcome is likely. A reasonable estimate of the court's award to the plaintiff is in the range between $200,000 and $800,000. The company's legal counsel believes the best estimate of potential damages is $350,000.

3. On January 2, 2017, Cleese discontinued collision, fire, and theft coverage on its delivery vehicles and became self-insured for these risks. Actual losses of $40,000 during 2017 were charged to Delivery Expense. The 2016 premium for the discontinued coverage amounted to $75,000, and the controller wants to set up a reserve for self-insurance by a debit to Delivery Expense of $35,000 and a credit to Liability for Self-Insurance of $35,000.

4. During December 2017, a competitor company filed suit against Cleese for copyright infringement, claiming $600,000 in damages. In the opinion of management and company counsel, it is possible that damages will be awarded to the plaintiff. The best estimate of potential damages is $175,000.

Instructions

For each of the situations above, prepare the journal entry that should be recorded as at December 31, 2017, under ASPE. Show supporting calculations in good form. Comment on how the liability would be accounted for under current IFRS standards, as well as proposed IFRS standards.

Solution to Exercise 13-5

1. Unearned Subscriptions Revenue   2,400,000*

        Revenue   2,400,000

            (To adjust the unearned revenue account)

    *Liability account:

Book balance at December 31, 2017	$5,300,000
Less adjusted balance ($800,000 + $900,000 + $1,200,000)	2,900,000
Adjustment required	$2,400,000

    The above liability would also be recorded under current IFRS standards, as well as proposed IFRS standards.

2. Litigation Expense   350,000

        Lawsuit Liability   350,000

            (To record estimated damages on breach-of-contract litigation)

    This situation involves a contingent loss. Because it is **likely** that a liability has been incurred and the loss is **reasonably estimable**, a loss should be accrued. Under ASPE, when the expected loss amount is in a range of possible amounts, the best estimate within the range is accrued. If no amount within the range is a better estimate than any other amount, the dollar amount at the low end is accrued and the amount of the remaining exposure to possible loss is disclosed in the notes.

    Under current IFRS standards, because an unfavourable outcome is probable (or more likely than not), and the amount is reliably measurable, a loss should also be accrued. However, under current IFRS standards, the accrual amount should be a probability-weighted expected value of the loss, or a sum of possible loss amounts, each multiplied by its probability of actually occurring. Thus, more information would be required to calculate the accrual amount under current IFRS standards.

    Under proposed IFRS standards, because Cleese has a present obligation as a result of past events (past transactions with the author), this is an unconditional obligation and a loss should be accrued in the amount of the probability-weighted expected value of the loss. Note that under proposed IFRS standards, this obligation would not be termed a contingent liability; it would be considered an unconditional liability. (Note that the term "contingent liability" is eliminated from proposed IFRS standards.)

3. Under ASPE, current IFRS standards, and proposed IFRS standards, no entry should be made to accrue for this expense because absence of insurance

coverage does not mean that an asset has been impaired or that a liability has been incurred as at the statement of financial position date. Cleese may, however, appropriate retained earnings for self-insurance as long as actual costs or losses are not charged against the appropriation of retained earnings, and no part of the appropriation is transferred to income. Appropriation of retained earnings and/or disclosure in notes to the financial statements is not required, but is recommended.

4. Under ASPE and current IFRS standards, because it is not likely or probable (respectively) that an asset has been impaired or that a liability has been incurred as at the statement of financial position date, no entry should be made for this loss contingency. Under ASPE, notes to the financial statements should include information about the nature of the contingency, the estimated amount of the contingent loss, and the extent of exposure to losses in excess of the estimated amount of loss. Under current IFRS standards, notes to the financial statements should also include an estimate of the loss, information about the uncertainties related to the amount or timing of any outflows, and whether any reimbursements are possible. Under proposed IFRS standards, because Cleese has a present obligation as a result of a past event (copyright infringement), it is an unconditional obligation as at the statement of financial position date, and an entry should be made to accrue the liability. Uncertainty about whether the plaintiff would be awarded any damages would be reflected in the measurement of the liability.

EXERCISE 13-6

PURPOSE: This exercise will provide an example of accounting for premium claims outstanding.

Bolton Corporation includes one coupon in each box of cereal that it packs and 15 coupons are redeemable for a premium (a toy). In 2017, Bolton purchased 10,000 premiums at 90 cents each and sold 120,000 boxes of cereal at $3.50 per box. Six percent of the amount received from customers relates to the premiums to be awarded. In 2017, 39,000 coupons were presented for redemption. It is estimated that 60% of the coupons will eventually be presented for redemption. This is the first year of this premium offering.

Instructions

(a) Prepare all entries that would be made to record cereal sales as well as the premium plan in 2017, applying the expense approach.

(b) Prepare all entries that would be made to record cereal sales as well as the premium plan in 2017, applying the revenue approach.

Solution to Exercise 13-6

(a) Expense approach:

Inventory of Premiums (10,000 × $0.90)	9,000	
Cash		9,000
Cash (120,000 × $3.50)	420,000	
Sales Revenue		420,000
Premium Expense [(39,000 ÷ 15) × $0.90]	2,340	
Inventory of Premiums		2,340
Premium Expense	1,980*	
Premium Liability		1,980

*[(120,000 × 60%) − 39,000] ÷ 15 × $0.90

EXPLANATION: The first entry records the purchase of 10,000 toys that will be used as premiums. The second entry records the sale of cereal (120,000 boxes). The third entry records the redemption of 39,000 coupons, with customers receiving one premium for every 15 coupons. The cost of the 2,600 toys distributed to these customers is recorded by a debit to premium expense. The fourth entry is an adjusting entry at the end of the accounting period to accrue the cost of additional premiums included in boxes of cereal sold this period that are likely to be redeemed in future periods. This is an application of the matching principle and the expense approach to recording estimated premium liability.

(b) Revenue approach:

Inventory of Premiums (10,000 × $0.90)	9,000	
Cash		9,000
Cash (120,000 × $3.50)	420,000	
Sales Revenue		394,800
Unearned Sales Revenue ($420,000 × 6%)		25,200
Premium Expense [(39,000 ÷ 15) × $0.90]	2,340	
Inventory of Premiums		2,340
Unearned Sales Revenue	13,650*	
Sales Revenue		13,650

*$25,200 × [39,000 ÷ (120,000 × 60%)]

EXPLANATION: The first entry records the purchase of 10,000 toys that will be used as premiums. The second entry records the sale of cereal (120,000 boxes), and allocation of the sales amount between sales revenue earned and unearned sales revenue related to premiums to be awarded. The third entry records redemption of 39,000 coupons, with customers receiving one premium for every 15 coupons. The cost of the 2,600 toys distributed to these customers is recorded by a debit to premium expense. The fourth entry is an adjusting entry at the end of the accounting period to record sales revenue related to premiums awarded in the period. This is an application of the revenue approach to recording sales revenue related to premiums.

EXERCISE 13-7

PURPOSE: This exercise will review the journal entries involved in accounting for a warranty that is included with the sale of a product (an assurance-type warranty). Two methods are examined—the expense approach, and the revenue approach.

Cynthia Mulder Corporation sells laptop computers under a three-year warranty contract that requires it to replace defective parts and provide necessary repair labour. During 2017, the corporation sold 600 computers for cash at a unit price of $2,000. Similar three-year warranty agreements are available separately and are estimated to have a stand-alone value of $270. On the basis of past experience, the per-unit, three-year warranty costs are estimated to be $100 for parts and $120 for labour. (For simplicity, assume that all sales occurred on December 31, 2017, rather than evenly throughout the year, and any warranty revenue is earned evenly over the three-year period.)

Instructions

(a) Assume the company follows ASPE, and record any necessary journal entries in 2017, applying the expense approach.

(b) Assume the company follows IFRS, and record any necessary journal entries in 2017, applying the revenue approach.

(c) Under each of the expense and revenue approaches, what liability relative to these transactions would appear on the December 31, 2017 statement of financial position and how would it be classified?

In 2018, actual warranty costs to Cynthia Mulder Corporation are $15,000 for parts and $18,000 for labour.

(d) Assume the company follows ASPE, and record any necessary journal entries in 2018, applying the expense approach.

(e) Assume the company follows IFRS, and record any necessary journal entries in 2018, applying the revenue approach.

Solution to Exercise 13-7

(a) Cash (600 × $2,000)   1,200,000
    Sales Revenue   1,200,000

   Warranty Expense [600 × ($100 + $120)]   132,000
    Warranty Liability   132,000

(b) Cash (600 × $2,000)   1,200,000
    Sales Revenue [600 × ($2,000 − $270)]   1,038,000
    Unearned Warranty Revenue (600 × $270)   162,000

(c) **Expense approach:**

Current Liabilities:

Warranty Liability	$44,000*

Long-Term Liabilities:

Warranty Liability	$88,000

*[600 × ($100 + $120)] ÷ 3

Revenue approach:

Current Liabilities:

Unearned Warranty Revenue	$ 54,000**

Long-Term Liabilities:

Unearned Warranty Revenue	$108,000

**(600 × $270) ÷ 3

(d)

Warranty Liability	33,000	
Inventory		15,000
Salaries and Wages Payable		18,000

(e)

Unearned Warranty Revenue	54,000	
Warranty Revenue		54,000
Warranty Expense	33,000	
Inventory		15,000
Salaries and Wages Payable		18,000

EXERCISE 13-8

PURPOSE: This exercise will review the journal entries involved in accounting for a warranty that is sold separately from the related product (service-type warranty).

Sterling Company sells scanners for $895 each and offers each customer a three-year warranty contract for $105 that requires the company to perform periodic services and to replace defective parts. During 2017, the company sold 600 scanners and 480 warranty contracts for cash. It estimates per-unit costs of the three-year warranty to be $25 for parts and $55 for labour. Assume all sales occurred on December 31, 2017, and that revenue from the sale of warranties is recognized on a straight-line basis over the life of the contract.

Instructions

(a) Record any necessary journal entries in 2017.

(b) With respect to these transactions, what liability would appear on the December 31, 2017 statement of financial position and how would it be classified?

In 2018, actual warranty costs related to 2017 scanner warranty sales are $3,000 for parts and $6,600 for labour.

(c) Record any necessary journal entries in 2018 related to 2017 scanner warranties.

(d) With respect to the 2017 scanner warranties, what liability would appear on the December 31, 2018 statement of financial position and how would it be classified?

Solution to Exercise 13-8

(a) Cash ($537,000 + $50,400)   587,400

    Sales Revenue (600 × $895)   537,000

    Unearned Warranty Revenue (480 × $105)   50,400

(b) Current Liabilities:

    Unearned Warranty Revenue $16,800

        (Note: Warranty costs are assumed to be
          incurred equally over the three-year period.)

    Long-Term Liabilities:

    Unearned Warranty Revenue $33,600

(c) Warranty Expense   9,600

    Inventory   3,000

    Salaries and Wages Payable   6,600

    Unearned Warranty Revenue   16,800

    Warranty Revenue   16,800

(d) Current Liabilities:

    Unearned Warranty Revenue $16,800

    Long-Term Liabilities:

    Unearned Warranty Revenue $16,800

EXERCISE 13-9

PURPOSE: This exercise will show how to calculate a bonus under two different agreements.

Merry Rawls, president of The Merry Music Company, has a bonus arrangement with the company under which she receives 15% of net income (after deducting tax and bonus) each year. For the current year, income before deducting either the provision for income tax or the bonus is $719,400. The bonus is deductible for tax purposes, and the effective income tax rate is 30%.

Instructions

(a) Calculate the amount of Merry's bonus.

(b) Calculate the appropriate provision for income tax for the year.

(c) Recalculate the amount of Merry's bonus if the bonus is to be 15% of income after bonus but before tax (round to the nearest dollar).

Solution to Exercise 13-9

(B = bonus; T = tax)

(a)
$$B = 15\% \times (\$719{,}400 - B - T)$$
$$B = 15\% \times [\$719{,}400 - B - 30\% \times (\$719{,}400 - B)]$$
$$B = 15\% \times [\$719{,}400 - B - \$215{,}820 + 30\% \times B)]$$
$$B = 15\% \times [\$503{,}580 - 70\% \times B)]$$
$$B = \$75{,}537 - 10.5\% \times B$$
$$1.105 \times B = \$75{,}537$$
$$B = \underline{\underline{\$68{,}359}}$$

(b)
$$T = 30\% \times (\$719{,}400 - B)$$
$$T = 30\% \times (\$719{,}400 - \$68{,}359)$$
$$T = 30\% \times (\$651{,}041)$$
$$T = \underline{\underline{\$195{,}312}}$$

(c)
$$B = 15\% \times (\$719{,}400 - B)$$
$$B = \$107{,}910 - 15\% \times B$$
$$1.15 \times B = \$107{,}910$$
$$\text{Bonus} = \underline{\underline{\$93{,}835}}$$

● Examine the equation to calculate the bonus. Make sure it is consistent with the wording of the agreement. For instance, if the bonus is based on net income **after** bonus and **after** tax, then income must be reduced by both bonus and tax in your formula (Net Income − B − T) (see part [a]). But if the bonus is based on income **after** bonus and **before** tax, then tax is not part of the formula (see part [c])

- Always "prove" the bonus figure calculated.

Proof—parts (a) and (b)

Income before bonus and before income tax	$719,400
Less bonus	(68,359)
Income before income tax	651,041
Less income tax (30% × $651,041) (agrees with [b])	(195,312)
Income after bonus and after income tax	455,729
Multiplied by bonus rate	15%
Bonus (agrees with [a])	$ 68,359

Proof—part (c)

Income before bonus and before income tax	$719,400
Less bonus	(93,835)
Income before income tax	625,565
Multiplied by bonus rate	15%
Bonus (agrees with [c])	$ 93,835

ANALYSIS OF MULTIPLE-CHOICE QUESTIONS

Question

1. A current liability is an obligation that:
    a. was paid during the current period.
    b. will be reported as an expense within the year or operating cycle that follows the statement of financial position date, whichever is longer.
    c. will be converted to a long-term liability within the next year.
    d. is due within 12 months from the end of the reporting period.

EXPLANATION: Before you read the answer selections, review the criteria for classification of a liability as a **current liability**, and compare each answer selection with the criteria. Under IFRS, a liability is classified as **current** when one of the following conditions is met: it is expected to be settled in the entity's normal operating cycle, it is held primarily for trading, it is due within 12 months from the end of the reporting period, or the entity does not have an unconditional right to defer its settlement for at least 12 months after the statement of financial position date. (Solution = d.)

Question

2. Robinson Company borrowed money from Amber Company for nine months by issuing a zero-interest-bearing note payable with a face value of $102,000. The proceeds amounted to $95,000. In recording the issuance of this note, what account should Robinson debit for $7,000?

    a. Interest Payable
    b. Interest Expense
    c. Prepaid Expenses
    d. Notes Payable

EXPLANATION: The excess of the face value of a zero-interest-bearing note payable and the proceeds collected upon its issuance is the cost of borrowing. This cost of borrowing (interest expense) should be recognized over the months the loan is outstanding. Therefore, the total interest ($7,000) is initially debited to the Notes Payable account. (In the initial entry to record the note, after a $102,000 credit and a $7,000 debit to the Notes Payable account, the Notes Payable account would have a net $95,000 credit balance.) The $7,000 debit included in the Notes Payable account is then amortized (allocated) to interest expense over the life of the note. (Solution = d.)

● A **zero-interest-bearing note** is often called a **non-interest-bearing-note.**

● Initially, the $7,000 amount may also be debited to a Notes Payable contra account called Discount on Notes Payable. However, current practice favours the **net approach** (described above).

Question

3. Madison's Boutique sells gift certificates. These gift certificates have no expiration date. Data for the current year are as follows:

Gift certificates outstanding, January 1	$250,000
Gift certificates sold	800,000
Gift certificates redeemed	640,000
Gross profit expressed as percentage of sales	35%

    At December 31, Madison should report unearned revenue of:
    a. $410,000.
    b. $306,000.
    c. $160,000.
    d. $143,500.

EXPLANATION: Draw a T account for the liability and enter the data given.

Gift Certificates Outstanding

Redeemed	640,000	Beginning Balance	250,000
		Sold	800,000
		Ending Balance	410,000
			(Solution = a.)

The gross profit percentage is not used in the calculation of unearned revenue. Revenue and unearned revenue are gross amounts, not net amounts.

Question

4. A local retailer is required to collect a 7% sales tax for the province's department of revenue, and to remit in the month that follows the sale. The retailer does not use a separate Sales Tax Payable account; rather, the sale prices of products sold and the related sales tax are all credited to Sales Revenue at the time of sale. During March 2017, credits totalling $26,215 were made to the Sales Revenue account. The amount to be remitted to the government in April for sales tax collected during the month of March:

   a. is $1,835.05.

   b. is $1,715.00.

   c. is $3,572.90.

   d. cannot be determined from the data given.

EXPLANATION: Set up a formula to relate the data given, and solve.

Sales + 7% × Sales = $26,215
$$1.07 \times Sales = \$26,215$$
$$Sales = \$26,215 \div 1.07$$
$$Sales = \$24,500$$
$26,215 Total − $24,500 Sales = $1,715 Sales Tax

(Solution = b.)

Question

5. Included in Arnold Howell Company's liability accounts at December 31, 2017, was the following:

   12% note payable issued in 2015 for cash, due in May 2018 $2,000,000

   On February 1, 2018, Arnold issued $5 million of five-year bonds with the intention of using part of the bond proceeds to liquidate the $2 million note payable maturing in May. On March 2, 2018, Arnold used $2 million of the bond proceeds to liquidate the note payable. Arnold's December 31, 2017 balance sheet is being issued on March 15, 2018. Under ASPE, how much of the $2 million note payable should be classified as a current liability on the December 31, 2017 balance sheet?

a. $0

b. $800,000

c. $1,000,000

d. $2,000,000

EXPLANATION: Review the definition of a current liability and the ASPE guidelines for classifying **short-term debt expected to be refinanced**. As at the date the balance sheet is being issued (March 15, 2018), the note payable was refinanced on a long-term basis (it was replaced with five-year bonds), and the proceeds from issuance of the five-year bonds exceeded the amount of the note. Therefore, the entire $2 million note payable should be classified as a long-term liability on the December 31, 2017 balance sheet. (Solution = a.)

Under IFRS, because there was no firm agreement in place to refinance the note on a long-term basis as at the statement of financial position date, the $2 million note would be classified as a current liability on the December 31, 2017 financial statements.

Question

6. An employee's net (or take-home) pay is determined by gross earnings minus amounts for income tax withholdings and the employee's:

a. portion of Employment Insurance premiums.

b. and employer's portions of Employment Insurance premiums.

c. portion of Employment Insurance premiums and Canada Pension Plan contributions.

d. portion of Canada Pension Plan contributions.

EXPLANATION: Before you read the answer selections, write down the model for the calculation of net (take-home) pay. Then find the answer selection that agrees with your model.

Employee's gross earnings for the current period

Less income tax withholdings

Less Canada Pension Plan contributions

Less Employment Insurance premiums

Net (or take-home) pay.   (Solution = c.)

The employer must also make Canada Pension Plan contributions and pay Employment Insurance premiums on behalf of each employee.

Question

7. An example of a contingent liability is:
   a. sales tax payable.
   b. accrued salaries.
   c. property tax payable.
   d. a pending lawsuit.

EXPLANATION: Review the definition of a contingent liability and think of some examples before you read the answer selections. Under current ASPE standards, the term "contingent liability" includes the whole population of existing or possible obligations that depend on the occurrence of one or more future events to confirm either their existence or the amount payable, or both. Under current IFRS standards, the term "contingent liability" is used only for those existing or possible obligations that are not recognized. Under proposed IFRS standards, the term "contingent liability" is eliminated. Sales tax payable, accrued salaries, and property tax payable are actual liabilities if they exist at the statement of financial position date. An example of a contingent liability is a pending or threatened lawsuit. (Solution = d.)

Question

8. Under current IFRS standards, a contingency with an outcome that cannot be determined should be:

	Accrued	**Disclosed**
a.	Yes	Yes
b.	Yes	No
c.	No	Yes
d.	No	No

EXPLANATION: Under current IFRS standards, a contingency that is probable (or more likely than not) and reasonably measurable should be accrued. If outcomes and/or related probabilities cannot be determined, the contingency should not be accrued but should be disclosed in the notes to the financial statements. Note that under ASPE, a contingency related to an outcome that cannot be determined would also not be accrued, and would be disclosed in the notes to the financial statements. (Solution = c.)

Question

9. Mayberry Co. prepares financial statements in accordance with ASPE and has a contingent loss to accrue. The loss amount is determined to be within a range of possible amounts. No single amount within the range is a better

estimate than any other amount within the range. The amount of loss to accrue should be:

a. zero.
b. the minimum of the range.
c. the mean of the range.
d. the maximum of the range.

EXPLANATION: Under ASPE, when the predicted loss amount is determined to be within a range of possible amounts, and a specific amount within the range is a better estimate than any other amount within the range, the specific amount (best estimate) is accrued. When no amount within the range is a better estimate than any other amount within the range, the minimum amount within the range is accrued. (Solution = b.)

Question

10. Stephens Corporation began operations at the beginning of 2017. It provides a two-year warranty with the sale of its product. The warranty is considered an assurance-type warranty. Stephens estimates that warranty costs will equal 5% of the selling price the first year after sale and 8% of the selling price the second year after the sale. The following data are available:

	2017	2018
Sales	$500,000	$600,000
Actual warranty expenditures	27,000	63,000

Stephens Corporation follows ASPE and uses the expense approach to account for assurance-type warranties. The balance of the Warranty Liability account at December 31, 2018, should be:

a. $15,000.
b. $51,000.
c. $53,000.
d. $78,000.

EXPLANATION: Draw a T account, enter the amounts that would be reflected in the account, and determine its balance.

Warranty Liability

(2) Expenditures in 2017	27,000	(1) Expense for 2017	65,000
(4) Expenditures in 2018	63,000	(3) Expense for 2018	78,000
		12/31/18 Balance	53,000

(Solution = c.)

(1) $500,000 × (5% + 8%) = $65,000 expense for 2017. Under the expense approach, the estimated total warranty cost related to the products sold during 2017 should be recognized in the period of sale (2017).

(2) Given (actual expenditures during 2017).

(3) $600,000 × (5% + 8%) = $78,000 expense for 2018.

(4) Given (actual expenditures during 2018).

> Because some items are sold near the end of the year and the warranty is for two years, a portion of the warranty liability should be classified as a current liability (the amount pertaining to the actual warranty expenditures estimated to occur in 2019), with the remainder classified as a long-term liability.

Question

11. Panda Corp. follows IFRS, and uses the revenue approach to account for service-type warranties. During 2017, the company sold $750,000 worth of products, all of which carried a two-year warranty (included in the price). It was estimated that 2% of the selling price represented the warranty portion, and that 60% of this related to 2017, and 40% to 2018. Assuming that Panda incurred costs of $3,900 to service the warranties in 2018, what is the net warranty revenue (revenue minus warranty costs) for 2018?

    a. $2,100
    b. $3,800
    c. $3,900
    d. $6,000

Explanation:

2018 Warranty revenue ($750,000 × 2% × 40%)	$6,000
2018 Warranty costs	(3,900)
2018 Net Warranty revenue	$2,100

(Solution = a.)

Question

12. Wild Wendy Theme Park is self-insured. Premiums for insurance used to cost $150,000 per year before Wild Wendy discontinued coverage. During 2017, Wild Wendy suffered losses of $47,000 that used to be (but are no longer) covered by insurance. Wild Wendy thinks this was a "light" year and that greater losses in future years will offset the lower amount paid in 2017. In order to avoid earnings volatility due to self-insurance, Wild Wendy wants to record a Liability for Self-Insurance. A reasonable estimate of losses to be incurred in

2018 is $160,000. The liability to be reported by Wild Wendy at December 31, 2017, is:

a. $0.

b. $103,000.

c. $150,000.

d. $160,000.

EXPLANATION: Even if the amount is estimable, future losses from self-insurance do not result in liabilities as at the statement of financial position date because the company does not have a present obligation as at the statement of financial position date (future losses will result from future events). It is not generally acceptable to accrue future losses from self-insurance. (Solution = a.)

Wild Wendy should report a loss of $47,000 on its 2017 income statement.

Question

13. Powercell, a manufacturer of batteries, offers a cash rebate to buyers of its size D batteries. The rebate offer is good until June 30, 2017. Under the expense approach, at December 31, 2016, the statement of financial position should include an estimated liability for unredeemed rebates in order to comply with the:

a. revenue recognition principle.

b. full disclosure principle.

c. matching principle.

d. time-period assumption.

EXPLANATION: Premium, coupon, and rebate offers are made to stimulate sales, and under the expense approach, their costs should be charged to expense in the period of the sale that benefits from the premium plan. At the end of the accounting period, many of these rebate offers may be outstanding and must be redeemed when presented by customers in subsequent periods. Under the expense approach, the number of outstanding rebate offers to be presented for redemption must be estimated in **order to reflect the existing current liability** and to match expenses with revenues. An adjusting entry is made with a debit to Premium Expense and a credit to Premium Liability. (Solution = c.)

Current IFRS standards support the **revenue approach** to accounting for premiums and rebates, under which some of the consideration received from the sale transaction is allocated to unearned revenue. The unearned revenue (representing the consideration from the sale transaction that relates to the premiums or rebates to be awarded) is recorded as earned in the period(s) in which the premiums or rebates are awarded or settled.

Question

14. The ratio of current assets to current liabilities is called the:
    a.   current ratio.
    b.   quick ratio.
    c.   current asset turnover ratio.
    d.   current liability turnover ratio.

EXPLANATION: Two major ratios used to measure an entity's liquidity are (1) the current ratio and (2) the quick (or acid-test) ratio. The current ratio is calculated by dividing current assets by current liabilities. The quick ratio is calculated by dividing quick assets (cash + marketable securities + net receivables) by current liabilities. Marketable securities in this context refer to short-term (trading) investments. The current ratio is sometimes called the working capital ratio; the quick ratio is often called the acid-test ratio. (Solution = a.)

Question

15. Gerry Holland, a manager of a local business, is to receive an annual bonus equal to 12% of the company's income in excess of $125,000 before income tax, but after deduction of the bonus. If income before income tax and bonus is $975,000 and the tax rate is 30%, the amount of the bonus would be:
    a. $20,100.
    b. $59,160.
    c. $91,071.
    d. $102,000.

EXPLANATION: Carefully write an equation that expresses the calculation. Notice what should be deducted from income before the bonus percentage is applied—$125,000 and the bonus (but not tax). Solve for the bonus (B). Prove your answer.

$B = 12\% \times (\$975,000 - \$125,000 - B)$
$B = \$117,000 - \$15,000 - 12\% \times B$
$1.12 \times B = \$102,000$
$B = \$102,000 \div 1.12$
$B = \$91,071$ (Solution = c.)

Proof:	Income before tax and bonus	$975,000
	Exclusion	(125,000)
	Bonus expense	(91,071)
	Income after exclusion and bonus and before tax	758,929
	Bonus rate	12%
	Bonus	$ 91,071

Question

16. The three essential characteristics of a liability include all but which of the following?
    a. They embody a duty or responsibility.
    b. The entity has little or no discretion to avoid the duty.
    c. The obligation is legally enforceable.
    d. The transaction or event that obliges the entity has occurred.

EXPLANATION: Under current IFRS and ASPE standards, items "a," "b," and "d" are included in the three essential characteristics of a liability. A transaction need not be legally enforceable to be a liability. (Solution = c.)

Question

17. It is important to present current liabilities separately from other liabilities for the following reason:
    a. When netted against current assets, it shows the working capital position of the company.
    b. It helps assess the company's liquidity since it shows the company's ability to realize its operating assets for payment of its operating liabilities.
    c. It helps users predict cash flow needs.
    d. All of the above.

EXPLANATION: Proper classification of current liabilities is very important for cash flow prediction, liquidity assessment, and assessment of working capital (defined as current assets minus current liabilities). (Solution = d.)

Question

18. Under ASPE, current debt that is expected to be refinanced through long-term debt may be classified as long-term as at the statement of financial position date, if which of the following sets of conditions holds?
    a. As at the financial statement issue date, there is a non-cancellable agreement in place with a financially solvent lender to refinance the current debt beyond one year, and the company is not in violation of any terms of the contract.
    b. The company fully intends to refinance the current debt and has contacted several interested parties, all of whom are financially solvent.
    c. There is a signed agreement to refinance the loan through a demand loan facility with a financially solvent lender, and the company is not in violation of any of the covenants under the agreement.

d. The company fully intends to refinance and has a verbal agreement with a financially solvent party, the company is not in violation of any terms of the agreement, and under the terms of the contract, the company may cancel the agreement at any time.

EXPLANATION: The key in selecting the best answer is the concept of a non-cancellable agreement. Answer "b" is based on intent and does not provide sufficient assurance; "c" is a demand loan, which is technically another current liability; and "d" allows the company to back out of the agreement. (Solution = a.)

Question

19. A company lacks fire insurance. Which of the following statements is true?
    a. This represents a contingent loss and should be accrued in the financial statements if estimable, and disclosed in the notes to the financial statements if not estimable.
    b. This results in uncertainty as to amounts and timing of losses; however, it should not be accrued since no asset has been impaired and no liability has been incurred prior to the event (the fire).
    c. This represents a contingent loss with an undeterminable outcome and therefore should be disclosed in the notes to the financial statements.
    d. This represents an uncertain situation that is unlikely to confirm that an asset has been impaired or that a liability has been incurred; however, disclosure in the notes to the financial statements is required.

EXPLANATION: Acts such as fires are random in occurrence and unpredictable. Since the event giving rise to a potential loss has not yet happened and may never happen, note disclosure is not required (although it may be desirable). Lack of insurance on key assets does represent a significant exposure that users may wish to be aware of (full disclosure principle). (Solution = b.)

Question

20. When analyzing a company's liquidity, which of the following statements is most true?
    a. The current ratio is the best measure and as long as it is greater than 2:1, the company is fine.
    b. The current ratio is a good measure of liquidity but it does not take into account the relative liquidity and illiquidity of the current assets.
    c. Ratios do not give useful information and users should focus on the cash flow statement instead.
    d. Ratios such as the current and quick ratios provide definitive quantitative information and therefore other information such as the nature of the business need not be considered.

EXPLANATION: The current ratio benchmark of 2:1 is often used; however, it is an incomplete benchmark when considered in isolation. Factors such as (1) the nature of the business, as well as (2) the company's stage of development (such as a start-up versus a mature company) should be considered, along with other factors. While the cash flow statement provides significant information, a better analysis would incorporate assessment of ratios as well as the factors noted above. The quick (or acid-test) ratio takes into account that some current assets are more liquid than others; it is therefore a more sensitive ratio. (Solution = b.)

Chapter 14

Long-Term Financial Liabilities

OVERVIEW

Long-term debt consists of present obligations that are not payable within a year or the operating cycle of the business, whichever is longer, but that require probable sacrifices of economic benefits in the future. Bonds payable, long-term notes payable, pension liabilities, and lease obligations are examples of long-term liabilities. Of these examples, this chapter focuses on bonds payable and long-term notes payable.

Accounting for long-term liabilities requires an understanding of the time value of money and its application in accounting procedures covered in this chapter. Accounting for long-term liabilities such as bonds payable and long-term notes payable also requires an understanding of the circumstances surrounding derecognition of such debt. For example, if derecognition involves repayment before maturity date, exchange of old debt for new debt, concessions granted by the creditor due to the debtor's financial difficulties (troubled debt restructuring), or funds specifically set aside to repay principal and interest directly to the creditor (defeasance), special accounting considerations and procedures are applied. The objective is to aid financial statement users in evaluating the business's solvency risk, and the amounts and timing of future cash flows.

STUDY STEPS

Understanding the Underlying Business Transactions

Bonds

Bonds are instruments used to raise long-term financing, usually when the amount of financing needed is too large for one lender to supply. Bonds are considered liabilities of the issuing company, as they generally require repayment of principal along with interest. Bonds usually have a face value (the value at which the bonds will be redeemed or repaid at maturity) and a stated interest rate (the interest rate written in the terms of the bond indenture and printed on the bond certificate). If the market interest rate (the current market interest rate for similar bonds with similar risk) is the same as the stated interest rate on the bond, the bond trades at face value. (For example, a bond with a face value of $100 and a stated interest rate of 10% will be bought and sold for $100 assuming that the current market interest rate for similar bonds with similar risk is 10%.)

If the market interest rate is lower than the stated interest rate, the bond becomes more valuable to investors, because the interest rate printed on the bond (stated interest rate) exceeds the interest rate that investors would be willing to accept (market interest rate). As a result, the bond would trade at a premium. (In the example above, the bond would sell at a price greater than $100.) Likewise, if the market interest rate is higher than the stated interest rate, the bond would trade at a discount. (In the example above, the bond would sell at a price lower than $100.)

Bond premium is the difference between the proceeds from the sale of the bonds and the face value (or maturity value) of the bonds, and arises if the bonds' stated interest rate exceeded the bonds' market interest rate at the time of issuance.

Bond discount is the difference between the face value of the bonds and proceeds from the sale of the bonds, and arises if the bonds' market interest rate exceeded the bonds' stated interest rate at the time of issuance.

The fair value of a bond varies with demand and market interest rate; it is therefore rare that a bond's fair value would be the same as either its face value or carrying value.

Derecognition of Debt

Repayment of debt is often called extinguishment of debt. When debt is repaid or extinguished, it is derecognized from the financial statements. From a financial reporting perspective, debt is considered to be extinguished when either of the following occurs:

1. The debtor discharges the liability by paying the creditor.
2. The debtor is legally released from primary responsibility for the liability by law or by the creditor (for example, due to cancellation or expiry).

If debt is **extinguished before its maturity date**, on the date of repayment, a loss (or gain) is calculated as the reacquisition price less the updated net carrying amount of the bonds redeemed. (A gain would result if the updated net carrying amount of the bonds redeemed is greater than the reacquisition price.) Often, early repayment (before maturity date) is not an allowable option under the terms of the debt agreement, or there may be penalties for early repayment. As an alternative, an entity may enter into a trust or business arrangement called **debt defeasance**. In a defeasance arrangement, the entity puts the funds it would otherwise have used to extinguish the debt in low-risk or risk-free investments that are set aside to repay the principal and interest directly to the creditor. In a defeasance arrangement, the investment and return on investment are only used to make scheduled repayments on the related debt as they come due (according to the original debt agreement).

Legal defeasance occurs when the original debt's creditors agree to the arrangement, look to the trust for repayment, give up their claim on the entity, and release the entity from further liability. In legal defeasance arrangements, the creditor usually wants to ensure that the investment funds will be used only for repayment of the related debt, often requiring that the investment funds be held in trust. Because the entity no longer has an obligation to the creditor, both ASPE and IFRS allow derecognition of debt under legal defeasance arrangements.

In-substance defeasance occurs when the original debt's creditors do not agree to release the entity from the primary obligation or liability to settle the debt, or when the entity does not inform the creditor of the defeasance arrangement. Because the debtor entity still has an obligation to the creditor (that is, the creditor has not released the entity from the debt obligation), both ASPE and IFRS do not allow derecognition of debt under in-substance defeasance arrangements.

Troubled Debt Restructurings

A troubled debt restructuring occurs when the creditor grants a concession to the debtor entity as a result of the debtor entity's financial difficulties. Troubled debt restructuring may result in **settlement** (early repayment or refunding and derecognition) of the original debt. Or it may result in **continuation** (revised terms and cash flows but no derecognition) of the original debt, but with a modification of its terms.

Settlement of debt may be done by a transfer of non-cash assets, share issue, or issue of new debt to another creditor, with the proceeds used to repay the original debt. Settlement of debt for less than its carrying amount results in derecognition of the related debt and usually recognition of a gain on restructuring of debt.

If the debtor **transfers non-cash assets** to settle debt, both the asset and debt are removed from the debtor's books at carrying amount. The asset's carrying amount less fair value is recorded as a loss on asset disposal (or gain on asset disposal if the asset's carrying amount is less than its fair value). Then the debt's carrying amount less the asset's fair value is recorded as a gain on restructuring of debt (or loss on restructuring of debt if the debt's carrying amount is less than the asset's fair value).

If the debtor **issues shares** to settle debt, the appropriate share capital account is credited for fair value of the shares, the debt is removed at carrying amount, and the debt's carrying amount less the fair value of the shares issued is recorded as a gain on restructuring of debt (or loss on restructuring of debt if the debt's carrying amount is less than the fair value of the shares issued).

Substantial modifications to a debt agreement exist when either:

1. the discounted cash flows of the debt under the new terms (discounted using the original effective interest rate) are at least 10% different from the discounted present value of the remaining cash flows under the original debt; or
2. there is a change in creditor and the original debt is legally discharged.

If there are substantial modifications to a debt agreement (that is, if either of the above two conditions is met), then the arrangement is accounted for as a settlement. This requires derecognition of the original debt, recognition of the new debt, and recognition of (usually) a gain on restructuring of debt.

If there are **non-substantial modifications** to a debt agreement (that is, if a debt agreement has been modified, but neither of the above two conditions is met), the original debt remains on the debtor's books as is, and a new effective interest rate is imputed by equating the carrying amount of the original debt with the present value of the revised cash flows. Going forward, at each interest payment date, interest expense is calculated as the carrying amount of the debt multiplied by the new effective interest rate, and the carrying amount of the debt is decreased by the difference between interest paid and interest expense.

Off–Balance Sheet Financing

Off–balance sheet financing occurs when a company borrows money in a way that does not result in recording of debt on the statement of financial position. For example, a company could sell inventory for cash up front and agree to repurchase it over time under certain conditions, transfer receivables while retaining the risks and rewards of ownership, or finance an equipment purchase through a lease. There are many examples of off–balance sheet financing, some of which serve valid business objectives. However, financial statement users should be aware that a company's management may inappropriately enter into off–balance sheet financing arrangements in order to disguise risks (including business risk and solvency risk). For this reason, complex business arrangements that are entered into for the purpose of raising funds should be analyzed carefully, and properly disclosed in notes, to provide users with a faithfully representative view of the economic substance of the transactions.

Becoming Proficient with Related Calculations

In this chapter, two main areas require fairly complex calculations:

- Measurement and valuation of bonds and notes
- Troubled debt restructuring

Working through the illustrations and exercises in this chapter will help you achieve proficiency with the related calculations.

Ratio Analysis

To properly analyze ratios, a detailed understanding of GAAP and classification of financial statement items is required.

There are two key ratios that help determine whether a company has undue liquidity or solvency risk associated with debt:

1. Debt to total assets: $\dfrac{\text{Total debt}}{\text{Total assets}}$

2. Times interest earned: $\dfrac{\text{Income before income taxes and interest expense}}{\text{Interest expense}}$

Debt to total assets measures the percentage of assets financed by debt, which is a riskier source of financing than equity. Note that many companies do not necessarily use "total debt" when calculating this ratio; long-term debt may be substituted for total debt if long-term debt to total assets is a more important measure. A high ratio of debt to total assets is associated with a high risk of default. Care should be taken when comparing ratios between companies.

It should also be noted that total debt reported on the statement of financial position might not include all debt. For example, the effects of off–balance sheet financing would not be included in total debt; good analysis by a financial statement user would include adjustments for off–balance sheet debt.

Times interest earned focuses on the company's ability to meet interest payments as they come due. In general, the higher this ratio is, the better.

TIPS ON CHAPTER TOPICS

- Bonds are typically issued in denominations (such as $100, $1,000, or $10,000). A bond's denomination is also called its **face value**. Other terms for face value are **par value**, **principal amount**, **maturity value**, and **face amount**.

- Bond prices are quoted in terms of percentage of par value. For example, a bond with a par value of $4,000 and a price quote of 102 is currently selling for $4,080 (102% of $4,000). A bond with a quote of 100 is selling for par value.

- A bond contract is called a bond **indenture**. This term is often confused with the term "debenture." A **debenture** bond is an unsecured bond.

- The interest rate written in the bond indenture, and often printed on the bond certificate, is the **stated rate**. Other terms for stated rate are **coupon rate**, **nominal rate**, and **contract (interest) rate**.

- The rate of interest actually earned by bondholders is called the **effective**, **yield**, or **market (interest) rate**.

- A bond's **issuance price** is the present value of all future cash flows (discounted using the effective interest rate at the date of issuance) promised by the bond, according to the terms stated in the bond indenture. Future cash flows include repayment of the bond's face value as well as interest payments. Excess of

(continued)

issuance price over face value is called a **premium**; excess of face value over issuance price is called a **discount**.

● To calculate the present value of a bond's future cash flows, its face value and interest payments are both discounted using the **same** interest rate (the effective interest rate stated on a per interest period basis). For example, if a 10-year bond has a stated interest rate of 10%, pays interest semi-annually, and is issued to yield 12%, a 6% rate (12% effective annual interest rate divided by two interest periods per year) is used in **all** present value calculations.

● Bond prices vary inversely with changes in the market interest rate. As the market interest rate goes down, bond prices go up; and as the market interest rate goes up, bond prices go down. At the date of issuance, if the market interest rate is below the bond's stated interest rate, the price of the bond will be above par; conversely, if the market interest rate is above the bond's stated interest rate, the price of the bond will be below par. Therefore, **a premium or discount is an adjustment to bond price required in order for the bond to yield the effective interest rate (or market interest rate) for the investor**. Over the period the bond is outstanding, the premium or discount is amortized to the carrying amount of the bond, causing the bond's carrying amount to equal the bond's face value at the time of maturity.

● Under ASPE, the **straight-line method** or the **effective interest method** is used for amortization of premium or discount. Under IFRS, the **effective interest method** is used for amortization of premium or discount. (The straight-line method is not permitted.)

● The **effective interest method** of amortization is sometimes called the **interest method** or the **present value method** or the **effective method**. When the effective interest method is used, the bond's carrying amount at the time of issuance equals its present value calculated using the market interest rate at the time of issuance.

● At initial recognition, the **discount or premium** on bonds payable is generally recorded as a reduction or addition, respectively, to the bonds payable account. Thus, for a discount on bonds payable, the initial credit to the bonds payable account is face value of the bonds payable less discount on the bonds payable. For a premium on bonds payable, the initial credit to the bonds payable account is face value of the bonds payable plus premium on the bonds payable. This is called the **net approach** to accounting for a discount or premium. In the past, discount or premium was recorded and amortized in a separate account called discount on bonds payable (a contra account to bonds payable) or premium on bonds payable (an adjunct account to bonds payable).

● At initial recognition, bond issue costs are recorded with a debit to the bonds payable account, and a new effective interest rate is determined using the revised beginning carrying amount and the future cash flows associated with the bond payable.

● Interest on notes payable is usually paid on a monthly or quarterly basis and interest on bonds payable is usually paid on a semi-annual basis. Despite these common practices, interest rates are usually expressed on an annual basis. Therefore, care must be taken to convert annual interest rates to "per period" interest rates before other calculations are performed.

● The amortization schedule for a bond or a note payable is not affected if the accounting period ends on a date other than an interest payment date. The

Illustration 14-1 43

amortization schedule is prepared according to the bond's periods, ignoring the end dates of accounting periods. Interest expense amounts shown in the amortization schedule are then apportioned to the appropriate accounting period(s). For example, if interest expense for the six months ended April 30, 2017, is $120,000, then $40,000 ($\frac{2}{6}$) of the amount would be included on the income statement for the 2016 calendar year, and $80,000 ($\frac{4}{6}$) of the amount would be included on the income statement for the 2017 calendar year.

- Generally, financial liabilities are initially recognized at **fair value**. For a **marketable security**, the imputed interest rate should equal the market interest rate, and therefore the fair value of the marketable security (based on the market interest rate) should be easily determinable. For a **non-marketable loan**, however, the imputed interest rate may not equal the market interest rate. In order to recognize the non-marketable loan at fair value, the loan should be recorded at the present value of its future cash flows discounted at the market interest rate (considering similar loans with similar terms). Any difference between the fair value of the loan and cash proceeds received should be accounted for separately and recognized in net income, unless it qualifies to be applied to a related asset or liability account.

- For notes issued in exchange for property, goods, and services, the note should also be recorded at its **fair value,** calculated as the present value of the note's future cash flows discounted at the market interest rate. If it is not possible to measure the fair value of the note, it may be measured and recorded at the fair value of the property, goods, or services received.

- In situations of troubled debt restructuring, **settlement** of debt (early repayment or refunding) or **continuation of debt with substantial modifications** results in derecognition of the original debt and recognition of a gain (or loss) on restructuring. **Continuation of debt with non-substantial modifications** does *not* result in derecognition of the original debt or recognition of a gain (or loss) on restructuring. For continuation of debt with non-substantial modifications, the original debt continues but with new terms and a new effective interest rate, which is imputed by equating the carrying amount of the original debt with the present value of the revised cash flows. The new effective interest rate is applied going forward, affecting income through revised interest expense, and affecting the carrying amount of the debt through revised amortization of the debt's carrying amount. This effectively brings the carrying amount of the debt to (revised) maturity value over the (revised) remaining life of the debt.

ILLUSTRATION 14-1

Calculation and Proof of Bond Issuance Price

On January 1, 2017, Gemple Company issued a five-year bond, with a January 1, 2022 maturity date and a stated interest rate of 6%. Market interest rate at the date of issuance is 5%, par value is $1,000, and interest is due annually on January 1.

The bond is a promise to pay $1,000 on January 1, 2022, and $60 (6% × $1,000) every January 1 beginning January 1, 2018, and ending January 1, 2022. The price of the bond is determined by calculating the present value of all future cash flows related to the bond, discounted at the market interest rate (5%):

PV	$259.77 ⟵—————————	$60
PV	783.53 ⟵—————————	$1,000
Total PV	$1,043.30	$n = 5; i = 5\%$

Present value of an ordinary annuity of $60 per period for five years at 5% interest ($60 × 4.32948)	$ 259.77
Present value of $1,000 due in five periods at 5% interest ($1,000 × 0.78353)	783.53
Total present value	$1,043.30

The factor of 0.78353 was read from the Present Value of 1 table and the factor of 4.32948 was read from the Present Value of an Ordinary Annuity of 1 table.

As discussed in Appendix 3B (Volume 1), present value calculations can be made using present value tables, financial calculators, or spreadsheets such as MS-Excel.

If a financial calculator or MS-Excel is used, the result may be slightly different than the result obtained using present value tables. The difference is due to rounding.

For example, if present value in the above Illustration is calculated using MS-Excel where

Rate = 5%

Nper = 5

Pmt = $60

FV = $1,000 (future value paid at maturity)

present value = $1,043.29.

Thus, the bond price would be $1,043.30. Theoretically, this is the sum that would be invested now at a 5% market interest rate compounded annually to allow for the periodic (in this case, annual) withdrawal of $60 (stated interest amount) at the end of each of five years and the withdrawal of $1,000 at the end of five years. The following is proof that $1,043.30 is the amount required.

Jan. 1, 2017	$1,043.30 ⟵———————		$1,043.30	
	+ 52.17 interest at 5% ⟵⎯		× .05	**market rate**
	1,095.47		⎯ 52.1650	effective interest
1st interest payment on 1/1/18	− 60.00			
	1,035.47 ⎯⎯⎯⎯⎯⎯⟶		1,035.47	
	+ 51.77 ⟵⎯		× .05	
	1,087.24		51.7735	

Illustration 14-2   4 5

2nd interest pay-ment on 1/1/19	− 60.00		
	1,027.24	⟶	1,027.24
	+ 51.36	⟵	× .05
	1,078.60		51.3620
3rd interest pay-ment on 1/1/20	− 60.00		
	1,018.60	⟶	1,018.60
	+ 50.93	⟵	× .05
	1,069.53		50.9300
4th interest pay-ment on 1/1/21	− 60.00		
	1,009.53	⟶	1,009.53
	+ 50.48	⟵	× .05
	1,060.01		50.4765
5th interest pay-ment on 1/1/22	− 60.00		
	1,000.01		
Principal payment	1,000.00		
	$ .01	Rounding difference	

An amortization schedule can be constructed using the calculations above. It would appear as follows:

Date	Stated Interest	Effective Interest	Premium Amortized	Carrying Amount
1/1/17				$1,043.30
1/1/18	$ 60.00	$ 52.17	$ 7.83	1,035.47
1/1/19	60.00	51.77	8.23	1,027.24
1/1/20	60.00	51.36	8.64	1,018.60
1/1/21	60.00	50.93	9.07	1,009.53
1/1/22	60.00	50.47[a]	9.53	1,000.00
	$300.00	$256.70	$43.30	

[a] The rounding difference of $0.01 is recorded in interest expense in the last interest period.

ILLUSTRATION 14-2

Common Calculations Involving Bonds Payable

1. Cash Interest per Period

   Par value
   × Stated rate of interest per period
   = Cash interest per period

   Cash interest is always a constant amount each period.

2. Interest Expense with Straight-Line Amortization of Discount or Premium

    Cash interest for the period
    + Discount amortization for the period
                OR
    − Premium amortization for the period
    = Interest expense for the period

    When discount or premium is amortized straight-line, interest expense is a constant amount each period.

3. Amortization per Period Using Straight-Line Amortization of Discount or Premium

     Issuance premium or discount
    ÷ Number of periods in bond's life
    = Amortization per period

4. Interest Expense with Effective Interest Amortization of Discount or Premium

    Carrying amount of bonds
    × Effective rate of interest per interest period
    = Interest expense for the interest period

5. Amortization Amount Using Effective Interest Amortization of Discount or Premium

    Interest expense for the interest period
    − Cash interest for the period
    = Amortization of discount for the interest period
                OR
    Cash interest for the period
    − Interest expense for the interest period
    = Amortization of premium for the interest period

6. Carrying Amount and Net Carrying Amount

    Par value
    − Unamortized discount
                OR
    + Unamortized premium
    = Carrying amount
    − Unamortized bond issue costs
    = Net carrying amount

    Amortization decreases the unamortized amount of discount or premium, and causes carrying amount to approach par value.

    Amortization decreases the unamortized amount of bond issue costs, and causes carrying amount to approach par value.

7. Gain or Loss on Derecognition

    Net carrying amount
    − Redemption price
    = Gain if positive; that is, if net carrying amount is greater
                OR
    = Loss if negative; that is, if redemption price is greater

- An **interest payment** promised by a bond is calculated by multiplying the bond's par value by the bond's stated interest rate. This interest payment amount is often referred to as **cash interest** or **stated interest**.

- Using the **straight-line method of amortizing** discount or premium, interest expense is determined by either adding the amount of discount amortization to the cash interest or deducting the amount of premium amortization from the cash interest. The periodic amount of amortization is determined by dividing the issuance discount or premium by the number of periods in the bond's life. **Straight-line amortization of discount or premium is allowed under ASPE, but not allowed under IFRS.**

- Interest expense using the effective interest method of amortizing discount or premium is determined by multiplying the bond's carrying amount at the beginning of the period by the bond's effective interest rate. The difference between cash interest and interest expense is the amount of premium or discount amortization for the period. The amount of premium or discount amortization for the period causes a reduction in the balance of the unamortized premium or unamortized discount, which in turn causes the carrying amount of the bond to change.

- A bond's **carrying amount (book value, carrying value)** is equal to (1) par value plus any unamortized premium, or (2) par value minus any unamortized discount. When the effective interest method of amortization is used and amortization is up to date, the bond's carrying amount is equal to its present value (all remaining interest payments and par value discounted at the bond's effective interest rate). A bond's **net carrying amount** is equal to its carrying amount minus any related unamortized bond issuance costs.

- The graph in **Illustration 14-3** compares the pattern of interest expense using the effective interest method with the pattern of interest expense using the straight-line method, for a bond issued at a discount and a bond issued at a premium. The relationship between interest expense and cash interest should also be noted. The difference between cash interest and interest expense for a period is the amount of amortization for the period.

EXERCISE 14-1

PURPOSE: This exercise will illustrate (1) the calculations and journal entries throughout a bond's life for a bond issued at a discount and (2) the journal entries required when bonds are called prior to their maturity date.

Howell Company issued bonds with the following details:

Face value	$150,000
Stated interest rate	5%
Market interest rate	9%
Maturity date	January 1, 2020
Date of issuance	January 1, 2017
Call price	103
Interest payments due	Annually on January 1
Method of amortization	Effective interest

Instructions

(a) Calculate the amount of issuance premium or discount.

(b) Prepare the journal entry for issuance of the bonds.

(c) Prepare the amortization schedule for the bonds.

(d) Prepare all of the journal entries that relate to these bonds (subsequent to the issuance date) for 2017 and 2018. Assume the accounting period coincides with the calendar year. Assume reversing entries are not used.

(e) Prepare the journal entry to record retirement of the bonds assuming they are called on January 1, 2019.

Solution to Exercise 14-1

(a) $150,000 par × 5% stated rate = $7,500 annual cash interest

Factor for present value of a single sum, $i = 9\%, n = 3$	0.77218
Factor for present value of an ordinary annuity, $i = 9\%, n = 3$	2.53130
$150,000 × 0.77218 =	$115,827.00
$7,500 × 2.53130 =	18,984.75
Issuance price	$134,811.75
Face value	$150,000.00
Issuance price	134,811.75
Discount on bonds payable	$ 15,188.25

(b) Cash   134,811.75

   Bonds Payable   134,811.75

EXPLANATION: The issuance of a bond is recorded with a credit to the Bonds Payable account for par value less discount or plus premium, less issuance costs (as long as the instrument is not subsequently measured using fair value). In this case, the credit amounts to $150,000.00 − $15,188.25 = $134,811.75.

(c)

Date	5% Stated Interest	9% Interest Expense	Discount Amortized	Carrying Amount
1/1/17				$134,811.75
1/1/18	$ 7,500.00	$12,133.06	$ 4,633.06	139,444.81
1/1/19	7,500.00	12,550.03	5,050.03	144,494.84
1/1/20	7,500.00	13,005.16[a]	5,505.16	150,000.00
	$22,500.00	$37,688.25	$15,188.25	

[a] Includes rounding difference of $0.62.

EXPLANATION: Stated interest is determined by multiplying the par value ($150,000) by the contract rate of interest (5%). Interest expense is calculated by multiplying the carrying amount at the beginning of the interest period by the bond's effective interest rate (9%). The amount of discount amortization for the period is the excess of interest expense over stated interest (cash interest) amount. The carrying amount at an interest payment date is the carrying amount at the beginning of the interest period plus the discount amortization for the period.

- The amount of interest expense of $12,550.03 appearing on the "1/1/19" payment line is the amount of interest expense for the interest period ending on that date. Thus, in this case, $12,550.03 is the interest expense for the 12 months preceding the date 1/1/19, which would be the 2018 calendar year.

- Any rounding difference should be included in the interest expense amount for the last interest period. Otherwise, there would be a small balance left in the Bonds Payable account after the bonds are extinguished.

- Notice that total interest expense ($37,688.25) over the three-year period equals total cash interest ($22,500.00) plus total issuance discount ($15,188.25). Thus, you can see that the issuance discount represents an additional amount of interest to be recognized over the life of the bonds.

(d) **December 31, 2017**

Interest Expense	12,133.06	
Interest Payable		7,500.00
Bonds Payable		4,633.06

January 1, 2018

Interest Payable	7,500.00	
Cash		7,500.00

December 31, 2018

Interest Expense	12,550.03	
Interest Payable		7,500.00
Bonds Payable		5,050.03

(e) **January 1, 2019**

Interest Payable	7,500.00	
Cash		7,500.00
Bonds Payable (1)	144,494.84	
Loss on Redemption of Bonds (2)	10,005.16	
Cash ($150,000 × 103%)		154,500.00

(1) See amortization table. The carrying amount updated to the date of retirement of the bonds is $144,494.84.

(2) The loss is equal to the excess of the payment to retire the bonds ($154,500) over the carrying amount of the bonds on the retirement date ($144,494.84).

There was a **call premium** (amount in excess of par required) of $4,500.00 in this situation, which is included in the loss calculation.

ILLUSTRATION 14-3

Graph to Depict Interest Patterns for Bonds

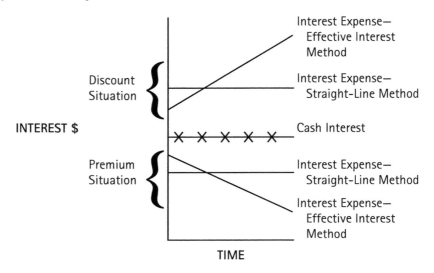

Regardless of whether the straight-line method of amortization or the effective interest method of amortization is used, the following applies:

1. The amount of cash interest (stated interest) is a constant amount each period.

2. If the bond is issued at a discount, its carrying amount increases over its life, due to amortization of the discount.

3. If the bond is issued at a premium, its carrying amount decreases over its life, due to amortization of the premium.

If the straight-line method of amortization is used, the following applies:

1. The amount of amortization is a constant amount each period.

2. The amount of interest expense is a constant amount each period.

If the effective interest method of amortization is used, the following applies:

1. The effective interest rate is constant each period.

2. If the bond is issued at a discount, interest expense is an increasing amount each period (because a constant effective interest rate is applied to an increasing carrying amount each period).

3. If the bond is issued at a premium, interest expense is a decreasing amount each period (because a constant effective interest rate is applied to a decreasing carrying amount each period).

4. The amount of amortization **increases** each period because the difference between effective interest expense and cash interest widens each period.

The effective interest method is required by IFRS. Under ASPE, either the straight-line method or the effective interest method may be used.

EXERCISE 14-2

PURPOSE: This exercise will provide an example of both issuance of bonds between interest payment dates and use of the straight-line method of amortization.

On May 1, 2017, Pan Tools Corporation issued bonds payable with a face value of $1.4 million at 104 plus accrued interest. They are registered bonds dated January 1, 2017, bearing interest at 9% payable semi-annually on January 1 and July 1, and maturing on January 1, 2027. The company uses the straight-line method of amortization.

Instructions

(a) Calculate the amount of bond interest expense to be reported on Pan's income statement for the year ended December 31, 2017. (Round calculations to the nearest dollar.)

(b) Calculate the amount of bond interest payable to be reported on Pan's balance sheet at December 31, 2017.

(c) Calculate the amount of bond interest expense to be reported on Pan's income statement for the year ended December 31, 2018.

Solution to Exercise 14-2

(a) Interest paid on July 1, 2017 ($1,400,000 $\times$ 9% $\times \frac{6}{12}$) $63,000

   Premium amortized on July 1, 2017 ($56,000 $\times \frac{2}{116}$)   (966)

   Accrued interest collected on May 1, 2017 ($1,400,000 $\times$ 9% $\times \frac{4}{12}$)   (42,000)

   Interest accrued on December 31, 2017 ($1,400,000 $\times$ 9% $\times \frac{6}{12}$)   63,000

   Premium amortized on December 31, 2017 ($56,000 $\times \frac{6}{116}$)   (2,897)

   Total bond interest expense for the year ended December 31, 2017 $80,137

APPROACH AND EXPLANATION: Prepare the journal entries to record issuance of the bonds, payment of interest, and amortization of premium on July 1, 2017, and year-end adjustment. Post the entries to the Interest Expense account and determine its balance at December 31, 2017.

May 1, 2017

Cash	1,498,000[c]	
Bonds Payable		1,456,000[a]
Interest Expense		42,000[b]

(To record sale of bonds at a premium plus accrued interest)

[a] $1,400,000 face value × 104% = $1,456,000 issuance price

[b] $1,400,000 × 9% × 4 months/12 months = $42,000 accrued interest (for January through April 2017)

[c] $1,456,000 issuance price + $42,000 accrued interest = $1,498,000 cash proceeds

July 1, 2017

Interest Expense ($63,000 − $966)	62,034	
Bonds Payable ($56,000 × $\frac{2}{116}$)	966	
Cash ($1,400,000 × 9% × $\frac{6}{12}$)		63,000

(To record semi-annual payment of interest and amortization of premium for two months)

Premium or discount is amortized over the period the bonds are outstanding (from date of issuance to date of maturity). In this case, May 1, 2017, to January 1, 2027, is four months short of 10 years, which amounts to 116 months.

December 31, 2017

Interest Expense ($63,000 − $2,897)	60,103	
Bond Payable ($56,000 × $\frac{6}{116}$)	2,897	
Interest Payable ($1,400,000 × 9% × $\frac{6}{12}$)		63,000

(To record accrual of interest since last payment date and amortization of premium for six months)

	Interest Expense				Interest Payable	
7/1/17	62,034	5/1/17	42,000	12/31/17	63,000	
12/31/17	60,103					
Balance				Balance		
12/31/17	80,137			12/31/17	63,000	

● Bonds are often issued between interest payment dates. When this occurs, the issuer requires the investor to pay market price for the bonds plus accrued interest since the last interest date. At the next interest payment date, the investor receives the full amount of interest due on the bonds as at that date. In this situation, on the issuance date, the issuer collects from the investor interest accrued between the bond registration date and the issuance date (between January 1, 2017, and May 1, 2017, or four months). At the next interest payment date (July 1, 2017), a full interest payment is made to the investor. Thus, at July 1, 2017, the investor receives the two months' interest earned from May 1, 2017, to June 30, 2017, plus the four months' accrued interest paid at the purchase date. Accrued interest at the date of bond issuance (and whenever bonds are purchased/sold between interest payment dates) is processed in this manner to expedite the issuer's interest payment procedures. At any interest payment date, interest for a full interest period is paid to each bondholder. There is no need to calculate the actual time a particular bondholder held the bond, or to prorate interest, because the investor has already paid any portion of the full interest payment it had not earned during that interest period.

● The journal entry to record the second interest payment on January 1, 2018, would be as follows (assuming reversing entries are not used):

Interest Payable	63,000	
Cash		63,000
(To record a full interest payment)		

● Refer to the journal entry on the date of issuance (May 1, 2017). Rather than credit Interest Expense for $42,000, Interest Payable could be credited for $42,000. However, crediting Interest Payable would require a modification to the July 1, 2017 entry. In the July 1, 2017 entry, instead of a debit to Interest Expense for $62,034, Interest Payable would be debited for $42,000 and Interest Expense would be debited for $20,034.

● Refer to the journal entry on December 31, 2017. Two separate entries may be recorded rather than the one compound entry. The equivalent separate entries would be as follows:

December 31, 2017

Interest Expense	63,000	
Interest Payable		63,000
(To record accrued interest for six months)		

($1,400,000 × 9% × $\frac{6}{12}$ = $63,000)

Bonds Payable	2,897	
Interest Expense		2,897
(To record premium amortization for six months)		

($56,000 × $\frac{6}{116}$ = $2,897)

(b) Accrued interest payable at December 31, 2017:

$1,400,000 × 9% × $\frac{6}{12}$ = $63,000

● Refer to the explanation of part (a) above and the balance of the T account for Interest Payable.

(c) Interest paid on July 1, 2018 ($1,400,000 × 9% × $\frac{6}{12}$) $ 63,000

    Premium amortized on July 1, 2018 ($56,000 × $\frac{6}{116}$)   (2,897)

    Interest accrued on December 31, 2018 ($1,400,000 × 9% × $\frac{6}{12}$)   63,000

    Premium amortized on December 31, 2018 ($56,000 × $\frac{6}{116}$)   (2,897)

    Total bond interest expense for the year ended December 31, 2018 $120,206

EXERCISE 14-3

PURPOSE: This exercise will illustrate the calculation of bond price when interest is due semi-annually, the effective interest method of amortization, and the journal entries required when the end of the accounting period does not coincide with the end of an interest period.

    Chilliwack Company sells $600,000 of 8% bonds on November 1, 2017. The bonds yield 10% and pay interest on May 1 and November 1. The bonds are due on May 1, 2021. Bond premium or discount is amortized at interest dates and at year end. The accounting period is the calendar year and no reversing entries are made.

Instructions

(a) Calculate the price of the bonds at the issuance date.

(b) Prepare the amortization schedule for the bonds.

(c) Prepare all relevant journal entries for this bond issue from the date of issuance through May 2019.

Solution to Exercise 14-3

(a) Time diagram:

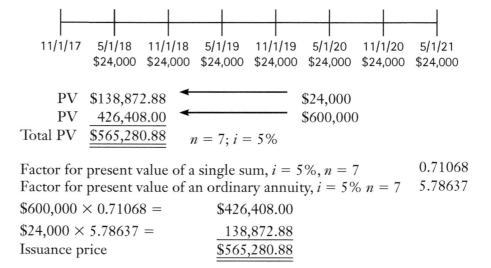

        PV $138,872.88 ←———————— $24,000
        PV   426,408.00 ←———————— $600,000
   Total PV $565,280.88 $n = 7; i = 5\%$

Factor for present value of a single sum, $i = 5\%, n = 7$ 0.71068
Factor for present value of an ordinary annuity, $i = 5\% \ n = 7$ 5.78637

$600,000 × 0.71068 = $426,408.00

$24,000 × 5.78637 =   138,872.88

Issuance price $565,280.88

(b)

Date	4% Stated Interest	5% Interest Expense	Discount Amortized	Carrying Amount
11/1/17				$565,280.88
5/1/18	$ 24,000.00	$ 28,264.04	$ 4,264.04	569,544.92
11/1/18	24,000.00	28,477.25	4,477.25	574,022.17
5/1/19	24,000.00	28,701.11	4,701.11	578,723.28
11/1/19	24,000.00	28,936.16	4,936.16	583,659.44
5/1/20	24,000.00	29,182.97	5,182.97	588,842.41
11/1/20	24,000.00	29,442.12	5,442.12	594,284.53
5/1/21	24,000.00	29,715.47[a]	5,715.47	600,000.00
	$168,000.00	$202,719.12	$34,719.12	

[a] Includes a rounding difference of $1.24

- There are two interest periods per year; therefore, the stated interest rate per interest period is the annual rate (8%) divided by 2, which is 4%.

- If calculations are rounded to the nearest cent, the rounding difference will be small. A small (less than $5.00) rounding difference provides some comfort that the amortization schedule is largely correct. A large rounding difference (more than $10.00) would indicate that there may be one or more calculation mistakes in the schedule or in the opening carrying amount (the issuance price of the bonds).

- The amortization schedule displays amounts according to the bond's interest periods. If one interest period overlaps two different accounting periods, to properly accrue expense and amortization for each interest period, expense and amortization for each period must be calculated and allocated to each accounting period.

- Instead of memorizing what goes in an amortization schedule, consider the content of each column. In the date column, the first date is the issuance date, followed by interest payment dates according to the terms of the bond. The stated interest amount is calculated by multiplying the bond's face value by the stated interest rate per interest period. Interest expense is calculated by multiplying the carrying amount at the beginning of the period (the carrying amount at the end of the previous period shown in the line above) by the market interest rate, or yield rate, per period. The difference between stated interest and interest expense for the period is amortization for the period. Discount amortized is added to the previous period's carrying amount (or premium amortized is deducted from the previous period's carrying amount) to arrive at the carrying amount at the end of the interest period.

(c)

November 1, 2017

Cash	565,280.88	
Bonds Payable		565,280.88

December 31, 2017

Interest Expense	9,421.35	
Bonds Payable		1,421.35
Interest Payable		8,000.00

($28,264.04 × $\frac{2}{6}$ = $9,421.35)

($4,264.04 × $\frac{2}{6}$ = $1,421.35)

($24,000 × $\frac{2}{6}$ = $8,000.00)

May 1, 2018

Interest Expense	18,842.69	
Interest Payable	8,000.00	
Bonds Payable		2,842.69
Cash		24,000.00

($28,264.04 − $9,421.35 = $18,842.69)

($4,264.04 − $1,421.35 = $2,842.69)

November 1, 2018

Interest Expense	28,477.25	
Bonds Payable		4,477.25
Cash		24,000.00

December 31, 2018

Interest Expense	9,567.04	
Bonds Payable		1,567.04
Interest Payable		8,000.00

($28,701.11 × $\frac{2}{6}$ = $9,567.04)

($4,701.11 × $\frac{2}{6}$ = $1,567.04)

($24,000.00 × $\frac{2}{6}$ = $8,000.00)

May 1, 2019

Interest Expense	19,134.07	
Interest Payable	8,000.00	
Bonds Payable		3,134.07
Cash		24,000.00

($28,701.11 − $9,567.04 = $19,134.07)

($4,701.11 − $1,567.04 = $3,134.07)

EXERCISE 14-4

PURPOSE: This exercise will help you identify data required to perform bonds payable calculations and apply terminology associated with bonds.

On January 1, 2017, Tuna Fishery sold $100,000 (face value) of bonds. The bonds are dated January 1, 2017, and will mature on January 1, 2022. Interest is to be paid annually on January 1. The following amortization schedule was prepared for the first two years of the bonds' life:

Date	Stated Interest	Effective Interest	Amortization	Carrying Amount
1/1/17				$104,212.37
1/1/18	$7,000.00	$6,252.74	$747.26	103,465.11
1/1/19	7,000.00	6,207.91	792.09	102,673.02

Instructions

Based on the information above, answer the following questions (round your answers to the nearest cent or percent) and explain your answers and calculations.

(a) What is the nominal or stated interest rate for this bond issue?

(b) What is the effective or market interest rate for this bond issue?

(c) Prepare the journal entry to record sale of the bond issue on January 1, 2017.

(d) Prepare the appropriate entry(ies) at December 31, 2019 (the end of the accounting year).

(e) Identify the amount of interest expense to be reported on the income statement for the year ended December 31, 2019.

(f) Show how the account balances related to the bond issue will be presented on the December 31, 2019 statement of financial position. Indicate the major classification(s) involved.

(g) What is the bonds' book value at December 31, 2019?

(h) If the bonds are retired for $100,500 (excluding interest) on January 1, 2020, will the bonds be extinguished at a gain or loss? What is the amount of that gain or loss?

Solution to Exercise 14-4

(a) Stated interest = Stated interest rate × Face value

$7,000 = Stated interest rate × $100,000

$7,000 ÷ $100,000 = Stated interest rate

7% = Stated interest rate

(b) Effective or market interest = Effective interest rate × Carrying amount at beginning of period

$6,252.74 = Effective interest rate × $104,212.37

$6,252.74 ÷ $104,212.37 = Effective interest rate

6% = Effective interest rate

(c) Cash ($100,000.00 + $4,212.37)   104,212.37
         Bonds Payable   104,212.37

(d) Interest Expense   6,160.38
         Bonds Payable   839.62
             Interest Payable   7,000.00
                  ($102,673.02 × 6% = $6,160.38)

(e) Bond interest expense $6,160.38
         ($102,673.02 × 6% = $6,160.38)

(f) **Current liabilities**
         Interest payable $7,000.00
     Long-term liabilities
         Bonds payable, 7%, due 1/1/22 $101,833.40[a]
     [a]$101,833.40 = $102,673.02 − $839.62

(g) $101,833.40 [See solution for part (f).]
     Book value is another name for "carrying amount" or "carrying value."
     Book value of $101,833.40 can also be calculated as follows:

     Carrying amount at 1/1/19 (per schedule) $102,673.02
     Amortization for 2019 [part (d)]   (839.62)
     Carrying amount at 12/31/19 $101,833.40

(h) The bonds will be extinguished at a gain because the $100,500.00 paid
     to retire the bonds is less than the bonds' carrying amount at the date of
     retirement:

     Net carrying value at 1/1/20 [part (g)] $101,833.40
     Retirement price   100,500.00
     Gain on extinguishment of debt $ 1,333.40

EXERCISE 14-5

Purpose: This exercise will illustrate how to account for redemption of bonds by
cash payment prior to maturity.

The balance sheet for Lake Corporation reports the following information on
December 31, 2017:

Long-term liabilities

8% Bonds payable, due December 31, 2022 $830,000

The bonds have a face value of $900,000 and were issued on January 1, 2017. Interest is payable annually on December 31. The straight-line method is used for amortization of bond discount or premium. In general, interest rates have declined since the bonds were issued. Lake Corporation decides to borrow money from another source at a lower interest rate to lower its overall annual interest expense. On July 1, 2018, Lake redeems all of the old outstanding bonds at 103. (Recall that bond prices vary inversely with changes in the market interest rate.)

Instructions

Prepare the journal entry(ies) to record redemption (extinguishment) of these bonds on July 1, 2018.

Solution to Exercise 14–5

Interest Expense	36,000	
Cash		36,000

   (To record payment of accrued interest at July 1, 2018)
     ($900,000 × 8% × $\frac{6}{12}$ = $36,000)

Interest Expense	7,000	
Bonds Payable		7,000

   (To record discount amortization for six months)
     [($70,000 ÷ 5 years) × $\frac{6}{12}$]

Bonds Payable	837,000[a]	
Loss on Redemption of Bonds	90,000[b]	
Cash		927,000[c]

   (To record the redemption of the bonds payable at 103)

[a] $830,000 carrying amount at December 31, 2017 + $7,000 discount for the period between January 1, 2018, and July 1, 2018 = $837,000 carrying amount at July 1, 2018
[b] $927,000 redemption price – $837,000 carrying amount = $90,000 loss on redemption of bonds
[c] $900,000 face value × 1.03 = $927,000 redemption price

EXPLANATION: Break the required entry into three simple parts: payment of accrued interest, discount amortization, and bond extinguishment. The bondholder is entitled to interest for the months between the last interest payment date (December 31, 2017) and the redemption date (July 1, 2018), which is six months in this case. Discount amortization must be updated to arrive at the carrying amount of the bonds as at the redemption date. In this case, six months of amortization must be recorded. The discount is amortized straight-line, so the total $70,000 discount is amortized evenly over the remaining five years of the bond's term. Discount amortization for six months would, therefore, be one half of the $14,000 annual amount.

    For the entry to record redemption, do the following. (1) Credit Cash to record payment of the redemption price, which is 103% of the bonds' face value. (2) Remove the bonds' carrying amount from the accounts by debiting Bonds Payable for their up-to-date carrying amount—the December 31, 2017 carrying amount ($830,000) plus the discount amortized from January 1, 2018, to July 1, 2018 ($7,000). (3) Record the difference between redemption (retirement) price and the bonds' carrying amount as a gain or loss on redemption of bonds. An excess of carrying amount over redemption price results in a gain. In this case, the redemption price ($927,000) exceeds the bonds' carrying amount ($837,000), resulting in a loss on redemption of $90,000.

EXERCISE 14-6

PURPOSE: This exercise will illustrate issuance of a note payable to acquire land when the note payable bears interest at a rate that is unreasonably low relative to the market interest rate.

On December 31, 2017, Weiss Inc. purchased land by paying $40,000 in cash plus a $500,000 face value note bearing interest at 3%. There was no established exchange price for the land, and no ready market for the note payable. The note is due on December 31, 2021. Interest is payable each December 31. Weiss's incremental borrowing rate is 10%.

Instructions

(a) Draw a timeline for the note and determine the amount to record as the cost of the land.

(b) Prepare the amortization schedule for the note payable.

(c) Determine the amount to report as interest expense on the income statement for the fiscal year ending March 31, 2019.

(d) Determine the amount to report as interest paid on the statement of cash flows for the fiscal year ending March 31, 2019.

(e) With respect to the above information, determine the amounts that should appear on the statement of financial position at March 31, 2019, and indicate the proper classification for each item.

Solution to Exercise 14-6

(a) Timeline:

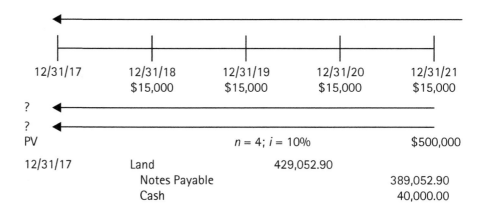

The market interest rate (Weiss's incremental borrowing rate) is used to calculate the present value of the note, which is used to establish the exchange price for the land. The $40,000.00 cash down payment plus the $389,052.90 present value of the note equals the $429,052.90 cost of the land. The market interest rate should be the rate the borrower would normally have to pay to borrow money for a similar loan.

Present value of $500,000 due in four years at 10% ($500,000 × 0.68301)	$341,505.00
Present value of $15,000 payable annually for four years at 10% ($15,000 × 3.16986)	47,547.90
Present value of the note and interest	389,052.90

(b)

Amortization Schedule

Date	3% Stated Interest	10% Effective Interest	Discount Amortized	Carrying Amount
12/31/17				$389,052.90
12/31/18	$15,000.00ª	$ 38,905.29ᵇ	$ 23,905.29ᶜ	412,958.19ᵈ
12/31/19	15,000.00	41,295.82	26,295.82	439,254.01
12/31/20	15,000.00	43,925.40	28,925.40	468,179.41
12/31/21	15,000.00	46,820.59ᶜ	31,820.59	500,000.00
Total	$60,000.00	$170,947.10	$110,947.10	

ª $500,000.00 face value × 3% stated interest rate = $15,000.00 stated interest.
ᵇ $389,052.90 present value × 10% effective interest rate = $38,905.29 effective interest.
ᶜ $38,905.29 effective interest − $15,000.00 stated interest = $23,905.29 discount amortization.
ᵈ $389,052.90 carrying amount at 12/31/17 + $23,905.29 discount amortization for 12 months = $412,958.19 carrying amount at 12/31/18.
ᵉ Includes rounding difference of $2.65.

EXPLANATION: When a debt instrument is issued in exchange for property, goods, or services in an arm's-length transaction, the cash flows from the debt instrument (in this case, the note payable) are discounted using the market interest rate. Fair value of the property received is measured by the cash down payment plus the present value of the debt instrument's future cash flows discounted at the market interest rate (an amount that reasonably approximates the debt's fair value). If fair value of the debt is not determinable, fair value of the property may be used to measure the transaction. Weiss Inc. issued a note in exchange for land. No information was given about fair value of the note or fair value of the land. Thus, Weiss's incremental borrowing rate of 10% was used to impute interest and determine the note's present value.

(c) Interest from April 1, 2018, through December 31, 2018:

$38,905.29 × $\frac{9}{12}$	$29,178.97
Interest from January 1, 2019, through March 31, 2019:	
$41,295.82 × $\frac{3}{12}$	10,323.96
Interest for the fiscal year ending March 31, 2019:	$39,502.93

- The amount of interest shown on the 12/31/18 line in the amortization schedule is the amount of interest that pertains to the interest period ending on that date (12/31/18). When interest is payable annually, each interest period is 12 months long. When interest is payable semi-annually, each interest period is 6 months long.

- When the end of an accounting period does not coincide with an interest payment date, interest must be apportioned to and accounted for in the proper periods. For example, referring to the amortization schedule above and assuming that the accounting period ends on March 31, 2018, effective interest of $38,905.29 for the calendar year ending December 31, 2018, must be apportioned between two fiscal years: the fiscal year ending March 31, 2018, and the fiscal year ending March 31, 2019. Interest expense of $\frac{3}{12} \times \$38,905.29 = \$9,726.32$ would be allocated to the fiscal year ending March 31, 2018, and $\frac{9}{12} \times \$38,905.29 = \$29,178.97$ interest expense would be allocated to the fiscal year ending March 31, 2019. The 12 months ending March 31, 2019, would include the $\frac{9}{12} \times \$38,905.29$ plus three months of the $41,295.82 interest amount shown on the 12/31/19 payment line.

- Entering interest amounts from the amortization schedule on a timeline may help clarify the calculations.

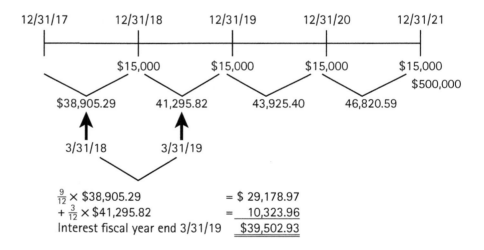

(d) Cash interest of $15,000 was paid on December 31, 2018. Thus, interest paid of $15,000 would be reported on the statement of cash flows for the fiscal year ending March 31, 2019.

(e)

Statement of Financial Position (Partial)
March 31, 2019

Property, Plant, and Equipment		Current Liabilities	
Land	$429,052.90	Interest Payable	$3,750.00[a]
		Long-Term Liabilities	
		Note Payable	$419,532.15[b]

[a] $\frac{3}{12} \times \$15,000 = \$3,750.00$

[b] $389,052.90	Carrying amount of Notes Payable on 12/31/17
23,905.29	Discount amortization for 1/1/18 to 12/31/18
6,573.96	Discount amortization for 1/1/19 to 3/31/19 ($\frac{3}{12} \times \$26,295.82 = 6,573.96$)
$419,532.15	Carrying amount of Notes Payable on 03/31/19

EXERCISE 14-7

PURPOSE: This exercise will illustrate the journal entries for a long-term note payable.

The Healthy Haven Clinic issued a $500,000, 9%, eight-year mortgage note on December 31, 2017. The terms require semi-annual instalment payments of $44,507.68 on June 30 and December 31. The note, along with $60,000 cash, was given in exchange for a new building. The accounting period is the calendar year.

Instructions

Prepare the journal entries to record:

(a) The mortgage payable and acquisition of the building.
(b) The first mortgage payment on June 30, 2018.
(c) The second mortgage payment on December 31, 2018.

Solution to Exercise 14-7

(a)   **December 31, 2017**

Buildings	560,000	
Cash		60,000.00
Mortgage Payable		500,000.00

(b)   **June 30, 2018**

Interest Expense	22,500.00[a]	
Mortgage Payable	22,007.68[b]	
Cash		44,507.68

[a] Principal balance at December 31, 2017	$500,000.00
Semi-annual interest rate	× 0.045
Interest expense for first six months	$ 22,500.00
[b] First payment	$ 44,507.68
Interest portion of first payment	(22,500.00)
Reduction in principal—first instalment payment	$ 22,007.68

(c)   **December 31, 2018**

Interest Expense	21,509.65[a]	
Mortgage Payable	22,998.03[b]	
Cash		44,507.68

[a]Principal balance at December 31, 2017	$500,000.00
Reduction in principal—first instalment payment	(22,007.68)
Principal balance at June 30, 2018	477,992.32
Semi-annual interest rate	× 0.045
Interest expense for second six months	$21,509.65
[b]Second payment	$44,507.68
Interest portion of second payment	(21,509.65)
Reduction in principal—second instalment payment	$22,998.03

EXPLANATION TO PART (A): The cost of the building is determined by the fair value of the consideration given, which was $60,000 cash plus the $500,000 present value of the mortgage payable.

EXPLANATION TO PARTS (B) AND (C): The mortgage payable is recorded initially at face value ($500,000), which is often referred to as the note's beginning principal. Each instalment payment reduces the outstanding principal amount. Instalment payments are in equal amounts; however, the portion of each instalment payment going toward interest and reduction in principal varies each period. In this exercise, instalment payments are due semi-annually; thus, the length of an interest period is six months and the annual interest rate (9%) must be expressed on a semi-annual basis (4.5%) in order to calculate interest each period. Interest is a function of outstanding balance, interest rate, and time. Thus, interest incurred in the first six months is determined by the mortgage payable's initial carrying amount (face value of $500,000), the annual interest rate of 9%, and the six-month time period. Interest incurred in the second six months is calculated based on the outstanding principal balance remaining after deduction of the principal portion of the first instalment payment. Although this exercise does not require a complete mortgage amortization schedule for this note, one is presented below for your observation and study. Notice that as subsequent instalment payments are made, a decreasing portion of each payment goes toward interest and an increasing portion of each payment goes toward reduction of the principal balance. This is because interest is calculated by multiplying a constant interest rate (4.5% each interest period) by a decreasing principal balance (carrying amount).

- The stated interest rate (9% in this case) is assumed to be equal to the market interest rate; therefore, the present value of the note at its inception is the same as the face value of the note ($500,000), and there is no discount or premium related to this mortgage payable.

- A mortgage note will usually require the borrower to make monthly payments; interest would then be compounded monthly. This exercise shows the borrower making semi-annual payments (interest compounded twice a year) in order to simplify the amortization schedule.

Mortgage Amortization Schedule

Semi-annual Interest Period	(A) Cash Payment	(B) Interest Expense (D) × 4.5%	(C) Reduction of Principal (A) – (B)	(D) Principal Balance (D) – (C)
12/31/2017				$500,000.00
6/30/2018	$ 44,507.68	$ 22,500.00	$ 22,007.68	477,992.32
12/31/2018	44,507.68	21,509.65	22,998.03	454,994.29
6/30/2019	44,507.68	20,474.74	24,032.94	430,961.35
12/31/2019	44,507.68	19,393.26	25,114.42	405,846.93
6/30/2020	44,507.68	18,263.11	26,244.57	379,602.36
12/31/2020	44,507.68	17,082.11	27,425.57	352,176.79
6/30/2021	44,507.68	15,847.96	28,659.72	323,517.07
12/31/2021	44,507.68	14,558.27	29,949.41	293,567.66
6/30/2022	44,507.68	13,210.54	31,297.14	262,270.52
12/31/2022	44,507.68	11,802.17	32,705.51	229,565.01
6/30/2023	44,507.68	10,330.43	34,177.25	195,387.76
12/31/2023	44,507.68	8,792.45	35,715.23	159,672.53
6/30/2024	44,507.68	7,185.26	37,322.42	122,350.11
12/31/2024	44,507.68	5,505.75	39,001.93	83,348.18
6/30/2025	44,507.68	3,750.67	40,757.01	42,591.17
12/31/2025	44,507.68	1,916.51	42,591.17	0.00
Total	$712,122.96[a]	$212,122.88	$500,000.00	

[a] Includes rounding difference of $0.09

- Notice that total interest incurred over the eight-year period on the loan of $500,000.00 is $212,122.88. Interest expense decreases each interest period because interest is a function of carrying amount, constant interest rate, and time.

EXERCISE 14-8

PURPOSE: This exercise will illustrate how an instalment note payable, such as a mortgage note, affects financial statements.

A mortgage note is a commonly used debt instrument to finance the acquisition of long-lived tangible assets. A mortgage note usually requires the borrower to repay the loan by equal periodic payments over the life of the loan. Each payment goes partly toward interest expense accrued during the period and partly toward reduction of the principal balance.

Instructions

Using the amortization schedule from **Exercise 14-7**, answer the following questions:

(a) How much interest expense would be reported on the income statement for the year ending December 31, 2018?

(b) How would the two payments during 2018 of $44,507.68 each be reflected in the statement of cash flows for the year ending December 31, 2018?

(c) How would the balance of $454,994.29 at December 31, 2018, be reported on a statement of financial position as at that date?

Solution to Exercise 14-8

(a) $22,500.00   Interest expense 1/1/18 – 6/30/18

    21,509.65   Interest expense 7/1/18 – 12/31/18

    $44,009.65   Total interest expense for the year ending 12/31/18

(b) The amounts paid during 2018 for principal reduction ($22,007.68 + 22,998.03 = **$45,005.71**) would be reported as repayments of debt, which are classified as cash outflows from financing activities on a statement of cash flows. The amounts paid during 2018 for interest ($22,500.00 + $21,509.65 = **$44,009.65**) would be classified as cash outflows from operating activities under ASPE, or classified as cash outflows from one of operating or financing activities under IFRS.

(c) The balance of the Mortgage Payable is reported as a liability on the statement of financial position. The principal portion of instalment payments due and scheduled to be paid within the next year (that is, within the year following the statement of financial position date) is reported in the current liability section of the statement of financial position. The remaining unpaid principal balance is reported in the long-term liability section of the statement of financial position.

  $ 24,032.94   Amount due June 30, 2019

    25,114.42   Amount due December 31, 2019

  $ 49,147.36   Current liability as at December 31, 2018

  $405,846.93   Long-term liability as at December 31, 2018

● **(Refer to Exercise 14-7)** If the Healthy Haven Clinic's accounting period ended on March 31, 2019, rather than December 31, 2018, the answers to parts (a), (b), and (c) of **Exercise 14-8** would be as follows:

(a) $11,250.00 $22,500.00 × $\frac{3}{6}$ interest expense 3/31/18 – 6/30/18

    21,509.65 $21,509.65 × $\frac{6}{6}$ interest expense 7/1/18 – 12/31/18

    10,237.37 $20,474.74 × $\frac{3}{6}$ interest expense 1/1/19 – 3/31/19

    $42,997.02   Total interest expense for the year ending 3/31/19

Illustration 14-4 67

- (b) The payments on 6/30/18 and 12/31/18 fall in the year ending March 31, 2019. Therefore, this answer would be the same as in **Exercise 14-8**: ($22,007.68 + 22,998.03 = **$45,005.71**) would be reported as repayments of debt and classified as cash outflows from financing activities; ($22,500.00 + $21,509.65 = **$44,009.65**) would be reported as interest paid and classified as cash outflows from operating activities under ASPE, or reported as cash outflows from one of operating or financing activities under IFRS.

- (c) On the statement of financial position:

    $ 10,237.37 Interest payable (3/6 × $20,474.74)

    24,032.94 Principal amount due June 30, 2019

    25,114.42 Principal amount due December 31, 2019

    $ 59,384.73 Current liability as at March 31, 2018

    $405,846.93 Long-term liability as at March 31, 2018

    Notice that the principal amounts in parts (b) and (c) above are the same as the answers to parts (b) and (c) in the **Solution to Exercise 14-8**. This is because cash payments are made at points in time, and principal reduction applies only at those points in time. Fractions (such as $\frac{3}{12}$ and $\frac{9}{12}$) are applied to interest amounts (which are calculated for periods of time) in order to appropriately apportion interest to accounting periods. Note that at December 31, 2018, Interest Payable is zero, because all interest would be paid up to date on the December 31, 2018 interest payment date.

ILLUSTRATION 14-4

Summary of Accounting for Troubled Debt Restructuring

Event	Accounting Procedure
1. Settlement of debt; debt may be settled by: (a) transfer of non-cash assets, (b) issuance of shares, or (c) issuance of new debt to another creditor in order to repay the original debt.	**Creditor:** Record assets or shares received (at fair value); derecognize loan receivable; record loss on loan impairment (or debit allowance for doubtful accounts if loss on loan impairment was previously recognized). **Debtor:** Derecognize assets given up (at carrying value) or record shares given up (at fair value); derecognize loan payable; record gain or loss on disposal of assets (if applicable); record gain on restructuring of debt.

Event	Accounting Procedure

2. Continuation of debt with substantial modification of terms; considered substantial if at least one of the following applies:
 	
  (a) discounted present value of cash flows under the new terms (discounted using the original effective interest rate) is at least 10% different from discounted present value of cash flows under the original debt, or
 	
  (b) there is a change in creditor and the original debt is legally discharged.
	Creditor: Reduce loan receivable to amount of net cash flows receivable (under modified terms) discounted at historical effective interest rate inherent in the loan; record loss based on reduction of loan receivable (similar to accounting for an impaired loan).
	
	Debtor: Derecognize original loan payable; record new loan payable at present value of new cash flows discounted at market interest rate at time of modification; record gain on restructuring of debt as the difference between these two amounts.

3. Continuation of debt with non-substantial modification of terms (if neither of the two conditions for substantial modification of terms applies).	**Creditor:** Reduce loan receivable to amount of net cash flows receivable (under modified terms) discounted at historical effective interest rate inherent in the loan; record loss based on reduction of loan receivable (similar to accounting for an impaired loan). **Debtor:** No entry at date of restructuring; impute new effective interest rate by equating carrying amount of original debt with present value of revised cash flows.

When a debt restructuring involves continuation of the debt with a modification of terms, it must be determined whether, in substance, the modification is considered a **settlement** of the original debt. Modifications are considered substantial (and therefore **settlement of the original debt**) if at least one of the following applies:

1. discounted present value of cash flows under the new terms (discounted using the original effective interest rate) is at least 10% different from discounted present value of the remaining cash flows under the original terms of the debt, or

2. there is a change in creditor and the original debt is legally discharged.

When a debt restructuring involves settlement of debt by transfer of non-cash assets, the debtor has the following gain-loss amounts to calculate:

1. the excess of carrying amount of debt over fair value of assets transferred is recorded as a gain on restructuring of debt, and

2. the difference between fair value of assets transferred and book value of assets transferred is recorded as a gain or loss on disposal of assets.

EXERCISE 14-9

PURPOSE: This exercise will illustrate the journal entries to record the transfer of non-cash assets to settle debt in a troubled debt restructuring.

Naples Co. owes $194,400 to Morgan Trust Co. The debt is a 10-year, 8% note. Because Naples Co. is in financial trouble, Morgan agrees to accept a piece of equipment in exchange for cancelling the entire debt. The equipment's original cost was $150,000. The equipment's accumulated depreciation to date is $80,000, and its fair value is $110,000.

Instructions

(a) Prepare the journal entry on Naples's books for the debt restructuring.

(b) Prepare the journal entry on Morgan's books for the debt restructuring.

Solution to Exercise 14-9

(a) **NAPLES'S ENTRY:**

Notes Payable	194,400	
Accumulated Depreciation—Equipment	80,000	
Equipment		150,000
Gain on Disposal of Equipment		40,000[a]
Gain on Restructuring of Debt		84,400[b]

[a]$110,000 − ($150,000 − $80,000) = $40,000
[b]$194,400 − $110,000 = $84,400

EXPLANATION: (1) Remove the original debt with a debit to Notes Payable for $194,400. (2) Remove the carrying value of the asset with a debit to Accumulated Depreciation—Equipment for $80,000 and a credit to Equipment for $150,000 (original cost). (3) Calculate and record the gain on restructuring of debt ($84,400 credit) and (4) calculate and record the gain on disposal of equipment ($40,000). (5) Double-check the entry to make sure it balances.

The debtor calculates the excess of the carrying amount of the debt ($194,400) over the fair value of the asset(s) transferred ($110,000) and reports the difference as a gain on restructuring of debt ($84,400). The difference between the fair value of the assets transferred and their carrying amounts is recognized as a gain or loss on disposal of assets. In this case, the fair value of $110,000 exceeds the carrying amount of $70,000; therefore, a gain on disposal of equipment of $40,000 is recognized. Both gain on restructuring of debt and gain on disposal of equipment are classified under other revenues and gains on the debtor's income statement.

(b) MORGAN'S ENTRY:

Equipment	110,000	
Loss on Impairment	84,400	
(or Allowance for Doubtful Accounts)		
Notes Receivable		194,400

EXPLANATION: (1) Remove the carrying amount of the receivable from the accounts with a credit to Notes Receivable for $194,400. (2) Record acquisition of the asset with a debit to Equipment for its fair value of $110,000. (3) Record loss on loan impairment or settlement of $84,400 with a debit to Loss on Impairment or Allowance for Doubtful Accounts (if a loss on loan impairment was previously recorded). (4) Double-check the entry to make sure it balances.

The creditor calculates the excess of the carrying amount of the receivable over the fair value of the assets received, and reports the difference as a loss on loan impairment or a decrease in allowance for doubtful accounts (if a loss on loan impairment was previously recorded). A loss on loan impairment is classified under other expenses and losses on the creditor's income statement.

ANALYSIS OF MULTIPLE-CHOICE QUESTIONS

Question

1. Bonds for which the owners' names are not registered with the issuing corporation are called:
    a. bearer bonds.
    b. term bonds.
    c. debenture bonds.
    d. secured bonds.

APPROACH AND EXPLANATION: Briefly define each answer selection. Bearer (or **coupon) bonds** are bonds that are not recorded or registered in the owner's name by the issuer. Bearer bondholders are required to send in coupons in order to receive interest payments, and the bonds may be transferred directly to another party. **Registered bonds** are bonds registered in the name of the owner. **Term bonds** are bonds that mature (become due for payment) on a single specified future date. **Debenture bonds** are unsecured bonds. **Secured bonds** are bonds backed by a pledge of some sort of collateral. (Solution = a.)

Question

2. Periodic amortization of a premium on bonds payable will:
    a. cause the carrying amount of the bonds to increase each period.
    b. cause the carrying amount of the bonds to decrease each period.

c. have no effect on the carrying amount of the bonds.

d. always cause the carrying amount to be less than the face value of the bonds.

EXPLANATION: Think about how a premium is recorded, how a premium is amortized, and how it affects the bonds' carrying amount. A premium is a bond price adjustment required in order for the bond to yield the effective interest rate, if the stated interest rate is higher than the effective interest rate at the time of issuance. A premium is credited to Bonds Payable initially. Therefore, the entry to amortize the premium involves a debit to Bonds Payable and a credit to Interest Expense. As a result, the carrying amount of bonds payable issued at a premium will decrease each period until the maturity date (at which time the carrying amount will equal the face value). (Solution = b.)

Question

3. A large department store issues bonds with a maturity date that is 20 years after the issuance date. If the bonds are issued at a discount, at the date of issuance, the:

a. nominal rate and the stated rate are equal.

b. nominal rate exceeds the yield rate.

c. effective yield rate exceeds the stated rate.

d. stated rate exceeds the effective rate.

EXPLANATION: Before reading the answer selections, write down the relationship that causes a bond to be issued at a discount: market interest rate exceeds stated interest rate. Then list the synonymous terms for (1) market interest rate and (2) stated interest rate, which are: (1) market rate, yield rate, effective yield rate, and effective rate; and (2) stated rate, nominal rate, coupon rate, and contract rate. Selection "a" is incorrect because the nominal rate and the stated rate are just different names for the same thing. Selections "b" and "d" are incorrect because an excess of nominal rate (stated rate) over yield rate (effective rate) will result in a premium, not a discount. Selection "c" is correct because when the effective yield rate (market rate) exceeds the coupon rate (stated rate), an issuance discount will result. (Solution = c.)

Question

4. Assume the face value of a bond is $1,500. If the bond's current price is quoted at $101\frac{3}{8}$, the bond price is:

a. $1,500.00.

b. $1,502.06.

c. $1,526.26.

d. $1,520.63.

EXPLANATION: Convert the fraction ($\frac{3}{8}$) to a decimal (0.375). Now take 101.375% of the bond's face value to determine its current price of $1,520.63. (Solution = d.)

Question

5. The amount of cash to be paid for interest on bonds payable for any given year is calculated by multiplying:
   a. face value by the stated interest rate.
   b. face value by the market interest rate at the date of issuance.
   c. carrying value at the beginning of the year by market interest rate at the date of issuance.
   d. carrying value at the beginning of the year by stated interest rate.

EXPLANATION: The amount of cash interest to be paid is the amount promised by the bond contract (indenture), which is the (contractual) stated interest rate multiplied by the face value of the bond. (Solution = a.)

Question

6. Amortization of a discount on bonds payable results in reporting an amount of interest expense for the period that:
   a. exceeds the amount of cash interest for the period.
   b. equals the amount of cash interest for the period.
   c. is less than the amount of cash interest for the period.
   d. has no relationship with the amount of cash interest for the period.

EXPLANATION: Think about the process of amortizing a discount on bonds payable and how it affects interest expense. A discount is a bond price adjustment required in order for the bond to yield the effective interest rate, if the effective interest rate is higher than the stated interest rate at the time of issuance. A discount is debited to Bonds Payable initially. Therefore, the entry to amortize the discount involves a credit to Bonds Payable and a debit to Interest Expense. Interest expense consists of the amount to be paid in cash for interest for the period plus the amount of discount amortization for the period. A discount is an additional amount of interest to be paid at maturity but is recognized (charged to expense) over the periods benefited (which would be the periods when the bonds are outstanding). (Solution = a.)

Question

7. If bonds are initially sold at a discount and the straight-line method of amortization is used, interest expense in the earlier years of the bond's life will:
   a. be less than the amount of interest actually paid.
   b. be less than the amount of interest expense in the later years of the bond's life.

c. be the same as what it would have been if the effective interest method of amortization was used.

d. exceed what it would have been if the effective interest method of amortization was used.

EXPLANATION: Quickly sketch the graph that shows the relationships between interest paid, interest expense using the straight-line method, and interest expense using the effective interest method. The graph appears in **Illustration 14-3**. Treat each of the possible answer selections as a true-false question.

Selection "a" is false because interest expense for a bond issued at a discount will be greater than interest actually paid throughout the bond's entire life, regardless of the amortization method used. Selection "b" is false because interest expense is a constant amount each period when the straight-line method is used; hence interest expense will be the same amount in the later years as it is in the earlier years. Selection "c" is false because for a bond issued at a discount, interest expense calculated using the straight-line method is greater than interest expense calculated using the effective interest method in the earlier years of life. Selection "d" is true. Interest expense will increase over a bond's life if the bond is issued at a discount and the effective interest method of amortization is used. In the earlier years of life, interest expense using the effective interest method is less than interest expense using the straight-line method; in the later years of life, interest expense using the effective interest method is more than interest expense using the straight-line method. (Solution = d.)

The straight-line method of amortization is not allowed under IFRS, but is permitted under ASPE.

Question

8. At the beginning of 2017, Lakeside Corporation issued 8% bonds with a face value of $600,000. The bonds mature in four years, and interest is paid semi-annually on June 30 and December 31. The bonds were sold for $561,221 to yield 10%. Lakeside uses a calendar-year reporting period. Using the effective interest method of amortization, what amount of interest expense should be reported for 2017? (Round your answer to the nearest dollar.)

    a. $44,898
    b. $56,122
    c. $56,325
    d. $56,666

APPROACH AND EXPLANATION: Write down the formula for calculating interest using the effective interest method of amortization. Use the data in the question to work through the formula.

Carrying amount at beginning of the period	$561,221.00
× Effective interest rate per interest period	5%
= Interest expense for the first interest period	28,061.05
− Cash interest for the interest period	24,000.00[a]
= Discount amortization for the first interest period	4,061.05
+ Carrying amount at beginning of the first period	561,221.00
= Carrying amount at beginning of the second period	565,282.05
× Effective interest rate per interest period	5%
= Interest expense for the second interest period	28,264.10
+ Interest expense for the first interest period	28,061.05
= Interest expense for fiscal year 2017	$ 56,325.15

[a] $600,000 × (8% ÷ 2) = $24,000 (Solution = c.)

Interest must be calculated on a per interest period basis. In this question, the interest period is six months. Interest for 2017 consists of interest for the bond's first two interest periods.

Question

9. As at December 31, 2017, Malloy Corporation has the following information regarding bonds payable:

Face value of bonds payable	$450,000
Discount on bonds payable	35,000
Interest payable	11,250
Unamortized bond issue costs	20,000

If the bonds are retired on January 1, 2018, at 101, what will Malloy report as a loss on extinguishment?
a. $70,750
b. $59,500
c. $48,250
d. $39,500

EXPLANATION: Write down the format for the calculation of gain or loss on repayment of debt and plug in the amounts from this question.

Face value	$450,000
− Unamortized discount	(35,000)
= Carrying amount	415,000
− Unamortized debt issue costs	(20,000)
= Net carrying amount	395,000
− Redemption price	(454,500)[a]
= Gain (loss) on extinguishment	$ (59,500)

[a] $450,000 × 101% = $454,500   (Solution = b.)

Question

10. "In-substance defeasance" refers to an arrangement whereby:
    a. a company gets a third party to cover its payments due on long-term debt.
    b. a government body issues debt instruments to corporations.
    c. a company provides for future repayment of a long-term debt by placing funds in an irrevocable trust.
    d. a company legally extinguishes debt before its due date.

EXPLANATION: **In-substance defeasance** is an arrangement whereby a company provides for future repayment of one or more of its long-term debt issues by placing funds in an irrevocable trust. Within the trust, the funds are invested in securities, the principal and interest of which are pledged to pay off the principal and interest of the company's own debt instruments as they mature. The company, however, is not legally released from being the primary obligor of the debt that is still outstanding. (Solution = c.)

Question

11. On December 31, 2017, Sugar Products Company borrows $100,000 from Candy Factory Company and gives Candy Factory a five-year, non-interest-bearing note with a face value of $100,000. The conditions of the note provide that Candy Factory can purchase $400,000 of products from Sugar Products at less than regular market price over the next five years. Sugar Products normally has to pay an interest rate of 10% when it borrows money from a bank to finance purchases of raw materials. Which of the following is **true?**
    a. Sugar Products should report the note payable at a carrying amount of $100,000 on its statement of financial position at December 31, 2017.
    b. Sugar Products should record no interest expense over the next five years in connection with this loan.
    c. At inception, Sugar Products should record a debit to Cash for the present value of the note using a 10% interest rate for discounting purposes.
    d. At inception, Sugar Products should record unearned revenue for the excess of the note's face value over its present value.

EXPLANATION: Record Sugar Products' journal entry at the inception of the note. The difference between present value of the note and cash received should be recorded both as a discount on the note and as unearned revenue. The journal entry would be as follows:

Cash	100,000	
Notes Payable		62,092[a]
Unearned Revenue		37,908[b]

[a] Present value of $100,000 due in five years discounted at 10% = $100,000 × 0.62092 = $62,092
[b] $100,000 face value − $62,092 present value = $37,908

The discount on the note will be amortized to interest expense over the five-year term using the effective interest method. The unearned revenue will be recognized as revenue as products are sold, based on each period's sales to the lender-customer relative to total sales to that customer for the term of the note. Thus, in this situation, amortization of the discount and recognition of revenue occur at different rates. (Solution = d.)

Question

12. Bandy Rentals borrowed money from a bank to build new mini-warehouses. Bandy gave a 25-year mortgage note in the amount of $150,000 with a stated rate of 8.75%. The lender charged $3,000 to close the financing. Based on this information:

    a. to record the $3,000 charge at the date the money is borrowed, Bandy should debit Interest Expense.

    b. Bandy's effective interest rate is now less than the 8.75% stated rate.

    c. Bandy should record the Mortgage Payable for only $147,000 since only $147,000 cash was received.

    d. Bandy should amortize the $3,000 to interest expense over the life of the loan.

EXPLANATION: Bandy will receive $147,000 cash but will have to repay $150,000 plus interest at 8.75%. Thus, the $3,000 charge raises the effective interest rate above the stated rate and should be accounted for as interest expense over the life of the loan. (Solution = d.)

Question

13. Kilinski Corporation borrowed money from a bank to build a building. The long-term note signed by the corporation is secured by a mortgage that pledges title to the building as security for the loan. Kilinski is to pay the bank $80,000 each year for 10 years to repay the loan. Which of the following statements applies to this situation?

a. The balance of mortgage payable at any given statement of financial position date will be reported as a long-term liability.

b. The balance of mortgage payable will remain a constant amount over the 10-year period.

c. The amount of interest expense will decrease each period the loan is outstanding, while the portion of the annual payment applied to the loan principal will increase each period.

d. The amount of interest expense will remain constant over the 10-year period.

EXPLANATION: Mortgages payable are initially recorded at face value, and entries are subsequently recorded for each instalment payment. Each payment is partially allocated to (1) interest on the unpaid principal balance of the loan, and (2) reduction of loan principal. Because a portion of each payment is applied to the principal, the principal balance decreases each period. Interest for a period is calculated by multiplying the stated (contract) interest rate by the principal balance outstanding at the beginning of the period. Thus, the amount of each payment allocated to interest decreases while the portion of each payment allocated to payment of loan principal increases each period. (Solution = c.)

Question

14. The debt to total assets ratio measures the:
    a. relationship between interest expense and income.
    b. percentage of total assets financed through creditor sources.
    c. portion of debt used to acquire assets.
    d. relationship between debt and interest expense.

EXPLANATION: Write down the ratio for debt to total assets and consider its components. The debt to total assets ratio is calculated by dividing total debt by total assets. This ratio measures the percentage of total assets provided by creditors. The higher the percentage of debt to total assets, the greater the risk that the company may be unable to meet its maturing obligations. (Solution = b.)

Question

15. The times interest earned ratio measures the:
    a. company's ability to meet interest payments as they become due.
    b. relationship between current liabilities and current assets.
    c. percentage of total assets financed by debt.
    d. relationship between debt and interest expense.

EXPLANATION: Write down the ratio for times interest earned and consider its components. The times interest earned ratio is calculated by dividing income before income taxes and interest expense by interest expense. This ratio measures the company's ability to meet interest payments as they come due. (Solution = a.)

Question

16. In a troubled debt restructuring, a debtor settles a debt by a transfer of land with a fair value that is less than the carrying amount of the debt but more than the book value of the land. Should a gain or loss on restructuring of debt be recognized? Should a gain or loss on the disposal of assets be recognized?

	Gain or Loss on Restructuring of Debt	Gain or Loss on Disposal of Assets
a.	Gain	Gain
b.	Gain	Loss
c.	Loss	Loss
d.	Loss	Gain

EXPLANATION: Assign amounts to (1) carrying amount of the debt, (2) book value of the land, and (3) fair value of the land. Be sure your assigned amounts maintain the relationships stated in the question. Then use a journal entry approach to solve. For instance, fair value of land, $100,000; book value of land, $65,000; and carrying amount of debt, $127,000 would maintain the relationships stated in the question. For the journal entry, debit the debt account(s) for $127,000; credit Land for $65,000; credit Gain on Disposal of Land for $35,000 (excess of fair value of land over book value of land). The rest of the entry is due to gain or loss on restructuring of debt. A $27,000 credit is needed for the entry to balance; hence, there is a gain on restructuring of debt. If a company is able to settle a debt by giving an asset with a fair value that is less than the carrying amount of the debt, the company's settlement of debt is advantageous; hence a gain on restructuring of debt is recognized.

Debt	127,000	
Land		65,000
Gain on Disposal of Land		35,000
Gain on Restructuring of Debt		27,000

(Solution = a.)

Question

17. Due to its serious cash flow problems, Unitech Company was able to negotiate a modification of the terms of an outstanding note payable with the creditor of the note. Unitech negotiated a reduction of the note's stated interest rate and reduction of the note's face value. Discounted present value of the note under the new terms (discounted using the original effective interest rate) is 8% different from discounted present value of the remaining cash flows under the original note. Which of the following statements applies to this situation?

a. Unitech should derecognize the original note and record issuance of the new note.

b. Unitech should record a loss on restructuring of debt.

    c.   Unitech should not record a journal entry as a result of this modification of terms.

    d.   None of the above.

EXPLANATION: In a troubled debt restructuring, a debtor may be able to negotiate one or more of the following modifications to the terms of an existing debt agreement: (1) reduction of the stated interest rate; (2) extension of the maturity date of the debt's face amount; (3) reduction of the debt's face amount; (4) reduction or deferral of any accrued interest; or (5) change in currency. However, modifications are only considered substantial if one of the following two criteria applies:

1.   discounted present value under the new terms (discounted using the original effective interest rate) is at least 10% different from the discounted present value of the remaining cash flows under the original debt, or

2.   there is a change in creditor and the original debt is legally discharged.

In a situation of substantial modification of terms, the original debt is derecognized and the new debt is recorded, along with a gain on restructuring of debt (measured as the difference between the current present value of the revised cash flows and the carrying amount of the original debt). In this case, however, neither of the two criteria for substantial modification of terms applies; therefore this is considered a non-substantial modification of terms. For a non-substantial modification of terms, the original debt remains on the books and no entry is recorded at the time of modification of terms. Instead, a new effective interest rate is imputed by equating the carrying amount of the original debt with the present value of the revised cash flows. (Solution = c.)

Chapter 15

Shareholders' Equity

OVERVIEW

Owners' equity of a corporation is called shareholders' equity because a corporation's owners hold shares as evidence of their ownership claims. Shareholders' equity typically consists of two major categories of corporate capital: contributed capital (share capital and contributed surplus) and earned capital (retained earnings and, under IFRS, accumulated other comprehensive income).

"Earnings" refers to net income for a period, whereas "retained earnings" refers to accumulated earnings retained for use in the business since inception of the corporation. Specifically, retained earnings is the total of all amounts reported as net income, less the total of all amounts reported as net loss and dividends declared, plus or minus the effects of any prior period adjustments (error corrections) through retained earnings, adjustments due to financial reorganization, and treasury share transactions, since inception of the corporation.

A dividend distribution may represent a distribution of income (return on capital) or a return of invested capital. A corporation may distribute dividends to its owners in the form of cash, non-cash assets, or additional shares. A dividend paid in the form of additional shares of the corporation results in capitalization of retained earnings or reclassification of earned capital to contributed capital (reclassification of retained earnings to share capital).

This chapter also discusses accounting for transactions related to share capital, including issuance, reacquisition, retirement, and cancellation of shares.

STUDY STEPS

Understanding the Nature and Purpose of Equity

Resources (assets) of a company are financed either by the company's internal operations or by debt or equity. Debt holders and shareholders each have different rights and claims on the company. Debt holders usually have more rights. For example, debt holders have preferential treatment with respect to return on their investment (interest) after a specified period of time, or on liquidation of the company.

All forms of debt and equity financing fit somewhere on a spectrum ranging from **lower risk of loss with no risks and rewards of ownership** (secured debt), to **highest risk of loss with risks and rewards of ownership** (common shares). Common shares are considered residual in nature because common shareholders get whatever is left after other claims on the company have been settled. (They are not guaranteed annual dividends or any return of capital if the corporation is dissolved.) However, common shareholders have voting rights (along with the ability to control management through these rights), and tend to profit most if the company is successful. Therefore, common shareholders have the highest risk of loss (of return on capital as well as return of capital), along with risks and rewards of ownership (voting rights and participation in the company's earnings/losses and appreciation/depreciation).

Preferred shares fit somewhere in between debt and equity, and have characteristics of both. Shares that have a fixed term or are retractable at the option of the preferred shareholder are considered more debt-like. Preferred shares that are convertible to common shares or are participating (in profit distributions that are higher than the prescribed rate of the preferred share) are considered more equity-like.

Shareholders' equity typically consists of two major categories of capital: **contributed capital** (share capital and contributed surplus), and **earned capital** (retained earnings and, under IFRS, accumulated other comprehensive income). Contributed capital consists of amounts invested by shareholders and amounts contributed to the company as a result of certain shareholder transactions. Earned capital is the cumulative amount earned by the company itself through net income and, under IFRS, other comprehensive income.

Understanding the Nature of Issuance and Reacquisition of Equity

Issuance of Shares

In a share issuance, the **net** amount that is received by the corporation (the net amount that is received, after payment of direct incremental costs and fees, such as underwriting costs, and accounting and legal fees) is credited to the appropriate share capital account. Thus, the **book value of share capital** includes the amounts invested by shareholders, net of the direct incremental costs and fees of issuing the related share capital.

When shares are sold on a **subscription basis**, the full price of the shares is not received immediately, and may result in defaulted subscription accounts. Resolution of defaulted subscription accounts is determined by the subscription contract, corporate policy, and any applicable law of the jurisdiction of the corporation.

Reacquisition of Shares

A corporation may buy back (reacquire or repurchase) some or all of its own outstanding shares. When this happens, it is likely that the repurchase price paid by the corporation will be different from the amount that was received by the corporation when the shares were originally issued. ASPE provides specific guidance for this scenario, and for accounting for the reacquisition of shares. Under IFRS, no explicit guidance is given for accounting for the reacquisition of shares, although the accounting may end up the same as it would under ASPE, using basic principles.

Understanding the Nature of Distributions of Equity

Contributed Capital versus Earned Capital

Contributed capital consists of share capital and contributed surplus, whereas earned capital consists of retained earnings and, under IFRS, accumulated other comprehensive income. **Retained earnings** is an earned surplus (of cumulative net income earned by the company but not yet distributed to shareholders). On the other hand, **contributed surplus** is not an earned surplus, because it is the result of certain shareholder transactions, such as par value share issues. As such, contributed surplus is not connected with the company's operations or earnings process.

Both retained earnings and contributed surplus are forms of surplus in the company. However, one is earned and the other is contributed. The distinction between retained earnings and contributed surplus may not always be clear, and may require professional judgement.

Dividends

Dividends are charged against retained earnings, and effectively represent distribution of the company's profits to its shareholders.

There are legal restrictions on dividend amounts. In general, a dividend should not be declared or paid if there are reasonable grounds for believing that the corporation is (or would be after payment of the dividend) unable to pay its liabilities as they become due, or if the realizable value of the corporation's assets would, as a result of the dividend, be less than its total liabilities and stated or legal capital for all classes of shares. Often there are other major reasons for restricting the dividend amount, including debt covenants and alternative uses for cash, such as financing of company growth or expansion.

Legal restrictions on dividend amounts need not be separately disclosed because it is presumed that legal restrictions are public knowledge. However, other restrictions on dividend amounts should be disclosed since this information is relevant to financial statement users.

Usually dividends are paid in cash; however, sometimes they are paid in the form of property or stock. A dividend paid in the form of property is called a **dividend in kind** and is generally valued at the fair value of the property given up, unless the transaction is considered a spinoff, restructuring, or liquidation, in which case the dividend is valued at the carrying value of the property given up. A dividend paid in the form of shares is called a **stock dividend** and is generally valued at the market value of the shares given up. A stock dividend usually results in capitalization of earnings (reclassification of retained earnings to share capital).

Liquidating dividends represent a return of contributed capital or return of capital to shareholders, and thus are usually charged against contributed surplus, rather than retained earnings.

Stock Dividends versus Stock Splits

A **stock dividend** is a dividend paid in the form of shares, and does not affect total assets, liabilities, or shareholders' equity. A stock dividend usually results in the reclassification of retained earnings to share capital and a lower book value per common share, due to the increased number of shares outstanding. A **stock split** also does not affect total assets, liabilities, or shareholders' equity, and results in a lower book value per common share (again, due to the increased number of shares outstanding). However, no journal entry is required for a stock split; it does not result in reclassification of retained earnings to share capital. A stock split is usually initiated in order to decrease the market price per share and to make the shares more accessible to a wide variety of investors. In general, a 2:1 stock split means that for each outstanding share before the split, there will be two outstanding shares after the split. Therefore, after the split, each (new) share will trade at approximately half of the previous price of one outstanding share.

When a **large stock dividend** is issued, in economic substance, the transaction may more closely resemble a stock split. For companies incorporated under the Canada Business Corporations Act (CBCA), stock dividends (whether small or large) are generally recorded as dividends and measured at market value of the shares given up. For companies incorporated under other legal jurisdictions, stock dividends that result in issuance of more than 20% to 25% of the number of shares previously outstanding may be accounted for as stock splits. Professional judgement should be exercised in accounting for large stock dividends.

Becoming Proficient in Related Calculations

There are a few complex calculations in this chapter. The par value method of accounting for shares is common in the United States; however, in Canada, most companies do not issue par value shares. (Under the CBCA and most provincial acts, par value shares are not permitted.) Under ASPE, the journal entries for reacquisition of shares and subsequent sale or cancellation may be tricky, and are the focus of a number of the multiple-choice questions and exercises that follow. Under IFRS, no explicit guidance is given regarding accounting for reacquisition of shares.

Understanding Financial Reorganizations

A **financial reorganization** occurs when a financially troubled company restructures its debt and equity through an agreement between existing creditors and shareholders. Often, existing creditors exchange their non-equity interests for equity in the company. In general, equity and non-equity interests are substantially realigned to place less of a financial burden on the company in order to allow the company to proceed with its plans for recovery and growth.

Under ASPE, if a financial reorganization involves a change in ownership or voting control (often it is the creditors who gain control), and new costs are reasonably determinable, the company should undergo a **comprehensive revaluation** of assets and liabilities. Comprehensive revaluation involves three steps: (1) bringing the deficit (negative retained earnings balance) to zero (by reclassifying it against accounts in shareholders' equity), (2) recording the changes in debt and equity, and (3) comprehensively revaluing assets and liabilities (and recording the revaluation adjustment against shareholders' equity). This gives the company a fresh start and allows retained earnings to start from zero.

Under IFRS, comprehensive revaluation is not discussed, and no specific guidance is given for accounting for financial reorganizations. However, note that IFRS does allow revaluation of property, plant, and equipment and intangibles (under the revaluation model), financial instruments (under the fair value option), and investment properties (under the fair value model).

TIPS ON CHAPTER TOPICS

- **Shareholders' equity** is often referred to as **capital**. In accounting for shareholders' equity, the emphasis is on the source of capital, which is classified into two categories: contributed capital and earned capital.

- **Contributed capital** consists of **share capital** and **contributed surplus**. **Earned capital** consists of **retained earnings** and, under IFRS, **accumulated other comprehensive income** (AOCI). (The concept of other comprehensive income does not apply under ASPE.) Earned capital is cumulative income that remains undistributed or is invested in the company. Contributed capital arises from amounts invested in the company by shareholders or contributed to the company as a result of certain shareholder transactions.

- **Share capital** accounts include Common Shares, Preferred Shares, Common Shares Subscribed, and Preferred Shares Subscribed.

- **Contributed surplus** can be affected by a variety of transactions, including par value share issue and/or retirement, treasury share transactions, liquidating dividends, share subscriptions forfeited, and donated assets by a shareholder.

- When a company sells or issues shares directly to new owners, the issuance is recorded on the company's books with an increase in assets and an increase in shareholders' equity. If a shareholder later sells his or her shares to another

(continued)

investor (in a **secondary market** or stock market), the company does **not** record a journal entry. The company only records the name of the new shareholder in its shareholder records. The assets, liabilities, and shareholders' equity of the company are **not** affected by secondary purchase (or sale) of shares by investors in the stock market.

● When a corporation issues more than one class of share capital, separate contributed surplus general ledger accounts should be maintained for each class of share capital. The balances of all contributed surplus accounts are usually summed and reported as a single amount on the statement of financial position under the caption Contributed Surplus.

● If shares from more than one class of share capital are issued in exchange for a lump-sum payment, the payment must be allocated between each class of share capital using either the **relative fair value method** or the **residual value method**. These methods are also applied in accounting for lump-sum purchases of property, plant, and equipment, and lump-sum revenue received for bundled sales.

● **Direct costs of share issuance** (including underwriting costs and accounting and legal fees) are debited to share capital because they represent a reduction of contributed capital (not operating expenses).

● Under IFRS, if shares are issued in a **nonmonetary exchange**, the fair value of the asset acquired should be used to measure the acquisition cost of the asset. (It is presumed that fair value of the asset acquired can be determined except in rare cases.) If the asset's fair value cannot be determined reliably, then the fair value and cost of the asset acquired are determined using the fair value of the shares given in exchange. Under ASPE, the acquisition cost of the asset may be measured by either the fair value of the asset acquired or fair value of the shares given up, whichever is more reliably determinable.

● Under ASPE, specific guidance is given for accounting for a reacquisition of shares. If the reacquisition cost is **greater than** the original issue amount, the reacquisition cost is allocated in this order. (1) First, it is allocated to **share capital**, in an amount equal to the par, stated, or assigned value of the shares. (2) Second, for any excess after the first allocation, it is allocated to **contributed surplus**, to the extent that contributed surplus was created by a net excess of proceeds over cost on a cancellation or resale of shares of the same class. (3) Third, for any excess after the second allocation, cost is allocated to **contributed surplus** in an amount equal to the pro rata share of the portion of contributed surplus that arose from transactions, other than those above, in the same class of shares. (4) Last, for any excess after the third allocation, cost is allocated to **retained earnings**. If the reacquisition cost is **less than** the original issue amount, the reacquisition cost is allocated (1) first, to **share capital**, in an amount equal to the par, stated, or assigned value of the shares; and (2) second, for the difference after the first allocation, to **contributed surplus**. Note that par value shares are not permitted under the CBCA; therefore, for most shares in Canada, the assigned value is equal to the average per share amount in the respective share capital account at the transaction date.

● Neither **par value** nor **treasury shares** are allowed under the CBCA. (Under the act, shares issued by corporations must be without par value, and reacquired shares are generally cancelled.) However, for companies incorporated in jurisdictions that allow par value and treasury shares, **par value** is a fixed per share amount printed on each share certificate. Par value usually has no direct relationship with the share's issuance price or fair value (the value at which it can be bought or sold) at any date subsequent to the issuance date. A **treasury share** is a corporation's own share that has been reacquired after having been issued and fully paid for, has not been cancelled, and is being held in the treasury for reissue.

- Treasury shares are not common in Canada; however, repurchase and cancellation of shares is common in Canada. Treasury shares are more common in the United States where reacquired shares are often not retired.

- The retained earnings account balance has **no** relationship with the amount of cash held by the company; retained earnings is simply a calculation of cumulative net income earned by the company not yet distributed to shareholders. Calculation of net income is affected by accounting accruals and other non-cash items, and cash is also generated and used in a variety of investing and financing transactions. It is possible for a company to have a large balance in its cash account with a small balance in its retained earnings account, or a small balance in its cash account with a large balance in its retained earnings account.

- There are three dates associated with declaration of any dividend: (1) **declaration date**, (2) **date of record**, and (3) **date of payment** (or distribution). A journal entry is required on the date of declaration and on the date of payment.

- Declaration of a cash dividend reduces working capital, but payment of a previously declared cash dividend has no effect on working capital. Unless otherwise indicated, a balance in dividends payable represents an obligation to be settled by cash.

- In recording the declaration of any dividend (except for a liquidating dividend), a temporary account called Dividends may be used, instead of debiting retained earnings directly. In the closing process at the end of the period, the balance of Dividends is closed to retained earnings.

- A dividend is usually considered a distribution of income, not a reduction of income (expense), unless the underlying security that generated the dividend is classified as debt (see Chapter 16).

- A **preferred** share's dividend preference is usually expressed either as a percentage of par or stated value, or in terms of dollars per share.

- **Dividends in arrears** are dividends on cumulative preferred shares that were not paid in the previous year(s). Until the board of directors formally declares that dividends in arrears are to be paid, they are **not** reported as a liability. However, dividends in arrears should be disclosed in the notes to the financial statements.

- A **dividend in kind** or **property dividend** (a dividend payable with assets of the corporation other than cash) is an example of a non-reciprocal transfer of nonmonetary assets. A dividend in kind is generally measured at the fair value of the assets given up unless the transaction is considered to

(continued)

represent a spinoff or other form of restructuring or liquidation, in which case the dividend should be recorded at the carrying value of the assets or liabilities transferred.

EXERCISE 15-1

PURPOSE: This exercise will highlight the relationships among authorized, issued, outstanding, and subscribed shares.

The following data are available regarding common shares of Daffy Corporation at December 31, 2017:

Authorized shares	200,000
Unissued shares	60,000
Subscribed shares	5,000
Treasury shares	12,000

Instructions

Calculate the number of outstanding shares. Assume treasury shares are allowed in Daffy's legal jurisdiction.

Solution to Exercise 15-1

Authorized shares	200,000
Unissued shares	(60,000)
Issued shares	140,000
Treasury shares	(12,000)
Outstanding shares	128,000

EXPLANATION: Write down the formula for the number of outstanding shares:

Number of issued shares − Number of treasury shares
= Number of outstanding shares

Determine the data required to calculate the number of outstanding shares according to the above formula. Authorized shares are either issued or unissued, and subscribed shares should be included in the number of unissued shares (because they are not issued until they are fully paid); therefore, the number of issued shares can be calculated from the facts given. Issued shares are either treasury shares or outstanding shares. Subtracting the number of treasury shares from the number of issued shares results in the number of outstanding shares.

ILLUSTRATION 15-1

Transactions That May Affect Contributed Surplus

Contributed surplus may be affected by a variety of transactions or events as noted below:

- Par value share issue and/or retirement
- Treasury share transactions including the resale and retirement of shares
- Liquidating dividends
- Financial reorganizations
- Stock options and warrants
- Issue of convertible debt
- Share subscriptions forfeited
- Donation of assets or capital by a shareholder
- Redemption or conversion of shares

EXERCISE 15-2

PURPOSE: This exercise will illustrate journal entries related to issuance of share capital.

Brighton Bay Corporation prepares financial statements under ASPE. On February 1, 2017, Brighton received authorization to issue 400,000 no par value common shares. The following transactions occurred during 2017:

Feb. 24   Issued 100,000 common shares for cash at a price of $16 per share.

Feb. 28   Issued 60,000 common shares in exchange for a group of modular warehouses.

Mar. 28   Received subscriptions for 25,000 common shares at $18 per share. Collected down payment of 25% of the subscription price from the subscribers.

Apr. 15   Collected 40% of the subscription price from the subscribers.

Apr. 30　　Collected the balance from the subscribers of 23,000 shares and issued the related shares. The remaining subscribers (of 2,000 shares) defaulted. The subscription agreement states that Brighton will refund only the amount collected in excess of 20% of the subscription price.

Nov. 4　　Issued 40,000 common shares at $22 per share.

Instructions

Prepare the journal entries to record the transactions listed above.

Solution to Exercise 15-2

February 24

Cash (100,000 × $16)	1,600,000	
Common Shares		1,600,000

February 28

Buildings (60,000 × $16)	960,000	
Common Shares		960,000

March 28

Share Subscriptions Receivable (25,000 × $18)	450,000	
Common Shares Subscribed		450,000

In accounting for share subscriptions, share capital increases (by crediting Common Shares Subscribed) on the date the subscriptions (contracts) are received, not when the related cash is received. However, if Share Subscriptions Receivable is classified as a contra shareholders' equity account (as it often is), total shareholders' equity is unaffected by the entry to record the receipt of subscriptions. Total shareholders' equity would increase only when cash is received, which would reduce Share Subscriptions Receivable, the contra shareholders' equity account.

Cash (25% × 25,000 × $18)	112,500	
Share Subscriptions Receivable		112,500

April 15

Cash (40% × 25,000 × $18)	180,000	
Share Subscriptions Receivable		180,000

April 30

Cash (35% × 23,000 × $18)	144,900	
Share Subscriptions Receivable		144,900

Common Shares Subscribed (23,000 × $18)	414,000	
Common Shares		414,000
Common Shares Subscribed (2,000 × $18)	36,000	
Cash (2,000 × 45% × $18)		16,200
Share Subscriptions Receivable (2,000 × 35% × $18)		12,600
Contributed Surplus - Forfeited Subscriptions (2,000 × 20% × $18)		7,200

November 4

Cash (40,000 × $22)	880,000	
Common Shares		880,000

EXPLANATION:

Feb. 24　**Issuance of shares in exchange for cash** is recorded by crediting Common Shares for the amount of the cash consideration received ($1.6 million).

Feb. 28　Under ASPE, **the issuance of shares in exchange for nonmonetary assets** requires the application of the following principle: acquisition cost of the assets (warehouses) may be measured by either the fair value of the assets (warehouses) or the fair value of the shares given up, whichever is more reliably determinable. Because some common shares were issued only four days earlier at $16 per share, there is good evidence of the fair value of the shares issued on February 28. There is no mention of the fair value of the warehouses; therefore, the transaction is recorded at a value of $960,000 (60,000 × $16).

Mar. 28　**Receipt of subscriptions** for shares is recorded with a debit to a receivable account (Share Subscriptions Receivable) for the total subscription (contract) price, and a credit to a share subscribed account (Common Shares Subscribed) for the same amount. Partial collection increases cash and reduces share subscriptions receivable. Common Shares Subscribed is classified as a share capital account, and only has a balance between the date of receipt of subscriptions and the date of final collection on the contract. Share Subscriptions Receivable is classified as a contra shareholders' equity account. Financial statement presentation of share subscriptions receivable is similar to that of treasury shares.

Apr. 15　**Collection of cash from subscribers** increases Cash and decreases Share Subscriptions Receivable, and since Share Subscriptions Receivable is a contra shareholders' equity account, total shareholders' equity increases.

Apr. 30   **Collection of additional cash from subscribers** increases Cash and decreases Share Subscriptions Receivable again. **Issuance of subscribed shares** reduces one share capital account (Common Shares Subscribed) and increases another share capital account (Common Shares) by the same amount. **Defaulted subscriptions** are recorded by the following steps. (1) Remove the subscription price of the related shares ($18 × 2,000 shares) from Common Shares Subscribed. (2) Credit Cash for the amount refunded (collection of 25% of subscription price on March 28 and 40% on April 15 totals 65%; however, according to the subscription agreement, Brighton is only required to refund the amount collected in excess of 20% of the subscription price, which amounts to 45% of $18 refunded to subscribers of 2,000 shares). (3) Credit share subscriptions receivable for the unpaid balance. (4) Credit contributed surplus for the 20% unrefunded portion of the subscription price paid by defaulting subscribers.

Nov. 4   **Issuance of shares in exchange for cash** is recorded by crediting Common Shares for the amount of the cash consideration received ($880,000).

EXERCISE 15-3

PURPOSE: This exercise will illustrate how the components of shareholders' equity are reported on the statement of financial position.

Assemble-All Corporation prepares financial statements under IFRS. Assemble-All's charter authorizes 400,000 common shares and 60,000 5% cumulative and non-participating preferred shares.

The corporation had the following share transactions between the date of incorporation and December 31, 2017:

1. Issued 50,000 common shares for $2,000,000.
2. Issued 15,000 preferred shares in exchange for machinery valued at $1,200,000.
3. Received subscriptions for 8,000 common shares and collected 30% of the subscription price of $45 per share.
4. Reacquired and cancelled 1,000 common shares at $37 per share.

At December 31, 2017, Assemble-All's retained earnings balance was $1.98 million.

Instructions

Prepare the shareholders' equity section of the statement of financial position in good form.

Solution to Exercise 15-3

ASSEMBLE-ALL CORPORATION
Partial Statement of Financial Position
December 31, 2017

Shareholders' equity

Preferred shares; 5% cumulative and non-participating; 60,000 shares authorized; 15,000 shares issued and outstanding	$1,200,000
Common shares; 400,000 shares authorized, 49,000 shares issued and outstanding	1,960,000
Common shares subscribed; 8,000 shares	360,000
Total share capital	3,520,000
Retained earnings	1,980,000
Total share capital and retained earnings	5,500,000
Contributed surplus	3,000
Less: Share subscriptions receivable	(252,000)
Total shareholders' equity	$5,251,000

APPROACH: Reconstruct journal entries to record the transactions. Use the resulting account balances to prepare the shareholders' equity section of the statement of financial position at December 31, 2017.

EXPLANATION:

1. Cash	2,000,000	
Common Shares		2,000,000
2. Machinery	1,200,000[a]	
Preferred Shares		1,200,000
3. Share Subscriptions Receivable (8,000 × $45)	360,000	
Common Shares Subscribed		360,000
Cash (30% × $360,000)	108,000	
Share Subscriptions Receivable		108,000
4. Common Shares (1,000 × $40)	40,000	
Contributed Surplus		3,000
Cash (1,000 × $37)		37,000

[a]Note that under IFRS, if shares are issued in a **nonmonetary exchange**, the fair value of the asset acquired (in this case, machinery) should be used to measure the transaction (unless the fair value of the asset acquired cannot be determined reliably, in which case the fair value of the shares given up should be used instead). In this case, the fair value of the machinery is provided; therefore, the value of the preferred shares given up is determined by the fair value of the machinery acquired.

EXERCISE 15-4

PURPOSE: This exercise will examine major classifications within the shareholders' equity section of the statement of financial position.

Shareholders' equity is an important element on a corporation's statement of financial position.

Instructions

Identify and discuss the general categories of shareholders' equity for a corporation. List specific sources of equity included in each general category.

Solution to Exercise 15-4

The general categories of shareholders' equity (or corporate capital) are as follows:

- Contributed capital (share capital plus contributed surplus)
- Earned capital (retained earnings plus, under IFRS, accumulated other comprehensive income)

Contributed capital usually consists of amounts **paid-in** for all classes of shares. Contributed capital also includes contributed surplus, which may be affected by a variety of transactions or events, including:

- par value share issue and/or retirement,
- treasury share transactions including the resale and retirement of shares,
- liquidating dividends,
- financial reorganizations,
- stock options and warrants,
- issue of convertible debt,
- share subscriptions forfeited,
- donations of assets or capital by a shareholder, and
- redemption or conversion of shares.

Earned capital is cumulative undistributed income that remains invested in the company. Earned capital includes retained earnings, which represents accumulated net earnings of a corporation in excess of net losses and dividends. A corporation may have appropriations (or restrictions) on retained earnings, which would make a portion of the retained earnings balance unavailable as a basis for dividends. Appropriations on retained earnings may arise as a result of restrictions per bond indentures or other formal agreements, or they may be initiated at the discretion of the board of directors.

Because other comprehensive income is not discussed under ASPE, accumulated other comprehensive income (AOCI) is a concept that applies only under IFRS. Therefore, for companies under IFRS, earned capital includes retained earnings as well as AOCI. AOCI is the cumulative change in equity due to revenues, expenses, gains, and losses that are excluded from the calculation of net income (and therefore bypass the income statement). Examples include unrealized gains on property revaluation, unrealized gains and losses on FV-OCI investments, and unrealized exchange differences on translation of foreign operations.

- A **liquidating dividend** is a distribution to shareholders from invested capital. Thus, a liquidating dividend results in a reduction of contributed capital and does not affect retained earnings. The shareholders' investment in the corporation is reduced, but not necessarily eliminated, by this type of dividend. If a dividend is only **partially liquidating** (it is partially a return of capital and partially a return on capital), both contributed capital and retained earnings are reduced.

- Although a stock dividend usually results in a reduction of retained earnings, contributed capital would increase by the same amount, resulting in **no change in total shareholders' equity**. The CBCA requires that any newly issued shares be measured at market value (including those issued as stock dividends).

- **Capitalization of retained earnings** refers to the transfer of retained earnings to contributed capital. Stock dividends result in capitalization of retained earnings (they are recorded with a debit to retained earnings and a credit to a contributed capital account), and they result in the retention of earned capital rather than the distribution of earned capital in the form of cash dividends.

- Stock Dividends Distributable is a share capital account and is therefore reported as an element of contributed capital. This account only has a balance during the short period between the date of stock dividend declaration and the date of stock dividend distribution.

- All changes in all shareholders' equity accounts for the period should be disclosed. Under IFRS, such changes (including changes in retained earnings, AOCI, and share capital) are required to be disclosed in a statement of changes in shareholders' equity. A popular format for presentation of the statement of changes in shareholders' equity is illustrated in the **Solution to Exercise 15-8**. Under ASPE, a statement of retained earnings is required, and any changes in share capital should be disclosed in the notes to the financial statements.

- If the return on common shareholders' equity is higher than the return on assets, the entity is (favourably) using borrowed money from bondholders and/or obtaining capital from preferred shareholders, and earning a return on those funds that is higher than the cost of using those funds. This is called **trading on the equity at a gain** or **favourably trading on the equity**. However, if cost of debt and/or cost of preferred dividends exceeds return on total assets, the entity is said to be **trading on the equity at a loss** or **unfavourably trading on the equity**, and the return on common shareholders' equity will be lower than return on assets.

ILLUSTRATION 15-2

Journal Entries for Recording Dividends and Stock Splits

Cash Dividend

Example	The board of directors declares a cash dividend of $100,000.		
Date of Declaration	Retained Earnings (or Dividends)	100,000	
	Dividends Payable		100,000
Date of Record	No entry.		
Date of Payment	Dividends Payable	100,000	
	Cash		100,000

Property Dividend (Dividend in Kind)

Example	On March 1, Jones Corporation declares a property dividend to be distributed to shareholders on April 15. The property is a fair value–net income investment in shares of Bonnie Corporation, which has a carrying value of $11,000. Fair value of the Bonnie shares is $14,000 on March 1, and $14,900 on April 15.		
Date of Declaration	FV-NI Investments	3,000	
	Gain		3,000
	Retained Earnings (or Dividends)	14,000	
	Property Dividends Payable		14,000
Date of Record	No entry.		
Date of Payment	Property Dividends Payable	14,000	
	FV-NI Investments		14,000

Any change in fair value of the property between the date of declaration and date of payment is ignored.

Liquidating Dividend

Example	Harness Corporation declares a liquidating dividend of $4,000.		
Date of Declaration	Contributed Surplus/Common Shares	4,000	
	Dividends Payable		4,000
Date of Record	No entry.		
Date of Payment	Dividends Payable	4,000	
	Cash		4,000

Illustration 15-2   9 7

Small Stock Dividend

Example	Henry Corporation (incorporated under the CBCA) has 100,000 common shares outstanding. On March 2, the board of directors declares a 10% stock dividend, distributable on April 4, to shareholders of record on March 16. Market value per common share is $24 on March 2, $23 on March 16, and $25 on April 4.		
Date of Declaration	Retained Earnings (or Dividends) 240,000		
	Stock Dividends Distributable		240,000
Date of Record	No entry.		
Date of Payment	Stock Dividends Distributable 240,000		
	Common Shares		240,000

Under ASPE and IFRS, there is no clear guidance on how to account for stock dividends; however, since Henry was incorporated under the CBCA, stock dividends should be treated as dividends and measured at the fair value of the shares given up.

Large Stock Dividend

Example	JJH Corporation (incorporated under the CBCA) has 100,000 common shares outstanding, with a book value of $10 per share (where book value per share is the total common shareholders' equity attributable to each common share). On March 2, the board of directors declares a 40% stock dividend distributable on April 3 to shareholders of record on March 15. Market value per common share is $4 on March 2, $5 on March 15, and $6 on April 3.		
Date of Declaration	Retained Earnings (or Dividends) 160,000		
	Stock Dividends Distributable		160,000
	(40% × 100,000 × $4 = $160,000)		
Date of Record	No entry.		
Date of Payment	Stock Dividends Distributable 160,000		
	Common Shares		160,000

Because JJH was incorporated under the CBCA, its stock dividends should be treated as dividends and measured at the market value of the shares given up. However, if the company was incorporated under another jurisdiction, given the significance of the stock dividend, it should be considered whether the economic substance of the transaction more resembles a stock split. Sometimes, a stock dividend of more than 20% to 25% of the number of shares previously outstanding is accounted for as a stock split. There is no specific guidance under ASPE or IFRS on this issue; in Canada, this is a matter of professional judgement. See **Exercise 15-5** for more detail on this topic.

The carrying value of Common Shares increases by $160,000, but the book value per share drops to $7.14 ($1,000,000 ÷ 140,000 shares).

Stock Split

Example	Howell Corporation has 100,000 common shares outstanding, with a book value per share of $10. On March 2, the board of directors declares a 4-for-1 stock split. The split is to be effective on April 2 for shareholders of record on March 13.
Date of Declaration	No entry.
Date of Record	No entry.
Date of Distribution	No entry. The number of shares outstanding is increased to 400,000.

The carrying value of Common Shares does not change, but the book value per share drops to $2.50 ($1,000,000 ÷ 400,000 shares).

EXERCISE 15-5

PURPOSE: This exercise will compare a large stock dividend with a small stock dividend.

Both stock splits and stock dividends change the number of shares outstanding.

Instructions

(a) Explain what is meant by a stock split carried out in the form of a dividend.

(b) From an accounting viewpoint, explain how a stock split carried out in the form of a dividend differs from an ordinary stock dividend.

(c) Explain how a stock dividend that has been declared but not yet issued should be classified on a statement of financial position.

Solution to Exercise 15-5

(a) A stock split carried out in the form of a dividend is a distribution of corporate shares to present shareholders, in proportion to each shareholder's current shareholdings, which is expected to cause a material decrease in market value per share. Usually a distribution in excess of 20% to 25% of the number of shares previously outstanding would cause a material decrease in market value per share, and may have the same effect on the market price of the share as a stock split.

(b) Because a distribution in excess of 20% to 25% of the number of shares previously outstanding would cause a material decrease in market value per share, it must be determined whether a large stock dividend is more like a stock split or a stock dividend. Under the CBCA, any newly issued shares must be measured at market value (including those issued as stock dividends). However, in jurisdictions where legal requirements for stated share capital values are not a constraint, a large stock dividend (such as a 40%, 50%, or 100% stock dividend) may be considered a stock split carried out in the form of a dividend, and may be treated for accounting purposes as a stock split. Accounting for a stock dividend as an ordinary stock dividend would require a debit to retained earnings and a credit to common shares for either the market value or par or stated value of the shares given up (and therefore capitalization of retained earnings). Accounting for a stock dividend as a stock split would not require any journal entries or capitalization of retained earnings. However, accounting for a stock dividend either as an ordinary stock dividend or as a stock split would decrease the book value per share in proportion to the increase in the number of shares outstanding.

(c) A declared but unissued stock dividend should be classified as part of contributed capital rather than as a liability. A stock dividend affects only shareholders' equity accounts (retained earnings decreases and contributed capital increases). Thus, there is no debt obligation, and no transfer of corporate assets when a stock dividend is distributed. Furthermore, at any time prior to issuance, a corporation's board of directors can revoke a stock dividend declared.

EXERCISE 15-6

Purpose: This exercise will allow you to practise recording various types of dividends.

Scot Corporation, incorporated under the CBCA, had the following shareholders' equity items at December 31, 2016:

Common shares; 200,000 shares authorized, 80,000 shares issued and outstanding	$ 800,000
Contributed surplus	2,400,000
Retained earnings	28,500,000
Total shareholders' equity	$31,700,000

Instructions

Record journal entries for each of the following transactions in 2017. Assume each transaction is **independent** of the others, unless otherwise indicated. Dividends are declared only on outstanding shares.

1. Declared a cash dividend of $0.50 per share.
2. Paid the dividend declared in item (1) above.
3. Declared a property dividend. Inventory with a cost of $160,000 and a fair value of $200,000 is to be distributed.

4. Distributed the property for the dividend declared in item (3) above.
5. Declared a 5% stock dividend when the market value was $14 per share.
6. Distributed shares for the stock dividend described in item (5) above.
7. Declared a liquidating dividend of $0.10 per share.
8. Distributed the dividend described in item (7) above.
9. Declared a 100% stock dividend when the market value was $14 per share.
10. Distributed the dividend declared in item (9) above.
11. Declared a 2:1 stock split.

Solution to Exercise 15-6

1.	Retained Earnings (or Dividends)	40,000	
	Dividends Payable		40,000
	(80,000 outstanding shares × $0.50 = $40,000)		
2.	Dividends Payable	40,000	
	Cash		40,000
3.	Inventory	40,000	
	Gain		40,000
	($200,000 fair value − $160,000 cost = $40,000)		
	Retained Earnings (or Dividends)	200,000	
	Property Dividends Payable		200,000
4.	Property Dividends Payable	200,000	
	Inventory		200,000
5.	Retained Earnings (or Dividends)	56,000	
	Stock Dividends Distributable		56,000
	(5% × 80,000 outstanding shares × $14 market value per share = $56,000)		
6.	Stock Dividends Distributable	56,000	
	Common Shares		56,000
7.	Contributed Surplus	8,000	
	Dividends Payable		8,000
	($0.10 × 80,000 outstanding shares = $8,000)		
8.	Dividends Payable	8,000	
	Cash		8,000
9.	Retained Earnings (or Dividends)	1,120,000	
	Stock Dividends Distributable		1,120,000
	(100% × 80,000 shares outstanding × $14 market value per share = $1,120,000)		
10.	Stock Dividends Distributable	1,120,000	
	Common Shares		1,120,000

Illustration 15-3 101

11. No journal entry required; memorandum-type entry noted for increase in number of shares issued and outstanding. Number of shares issued and outstanding is doubled (from 80,000 to 160,000), reducing carrying value per common share to one half of what it was previously (from $10 per share to $5 per share).

ILLUSTRATION 15-3

Steps in Allocating Dividends to Preferred and Common Shareholders

Step 1: Assign cumulative dividends in arrears, if any, to preferred shareholders.

If there are any cumulative dividends in arrears, allocate dividends to preferred shareholders first, in the amount of arrearage. Then, calculate the amount of dividends remaining to be allocated. (If the amount of dividends is not enough to cover the arrearage, no further steps in allocating dividends are performed, all dividends declared are allocated to preferred shareholders, and remaining arrearage is calculated and disclosed.)

Step 2: Assign current-period preference to preferred shareholders.

Calculate the amount of preferred shareholders' current-year preference, and allocate that amount to preferred shareholders. Then, calculate the amount of dividends remaining to be allocated. (If the amount of dividends is not enough to cover preferred shareholders' current-year preference, no further steps in allocating dividends are performed, and all dividends are allocated to preferred shareholders.)

Step 3: Assign common shareholders an equal percentage dividend.

Calculate the amount of dividends required to give common shareholders a "like" percentage dividend as was given to preferred shareholders (for current-year preference only), and allocate that amount to common shareholders. If the remaining amount of dividends is sufficient to cover this "like" percentage dividend, the remaining amount of dividends (after the "like" percentage dividend allocation to common shares) is the amount that both preferred and common shareholders will "participate" in. (If the amount of dividends is not enough to give common shareholders a "like" percentage dividend, whatever is remaining after preferred shareholders get their allocations as calculated in steps 1 and 2 is allocated to common shareholders.)

Step 4: Assign participation amounts to preferred and common shares.

If the preferred shares are non-participating, the remaining dividends are assigned to common shareholders. If the preferred shares are participating, the remaining dividends are allocated between preferred and common shareholders by prorating them based on their relative carrying amounts.

Step 5: Total amounts allocated and calculate per share amounts.

Assigned dividend amounts calculated from the steps above are added together, on a per class basis. The total amount of dividends assigned to preferred shareholders and to common shareholders is often expressed on a per share basis. To calculate dividend per share, the total dividend per class is divided by the number of shares outstanding in the class.

"Arrearage" refers to the amount of cumulative preferred dividends in arrears.

EXERCISE 15-7

PURPOSE: This exercise will illustrate the allocation of dividends when a corporation has both preferred and common shares outstanding.

Daly Corporation has the following shares outstanding, without any changes, for years 2016, 2017, and 2018.

100,000 preference shares, 5%	$ 600,000
300,000 common shares	1,200,000
	$1,800,000

Dividends are declared as follows:

2016	$ 25,000
2017	$ 45,000
2018	$105,000

Instructions

Calculate the amount of dividends (total and per share) to be allocated to preferred shareholders and to common shareholders for each of the three years under each of the independent assumptions below:

(a) The preferred shares are non-cumulative and non-participating.
(b) The preferred shares are cumulative and non-participating.
(c) The preferred shares are cumulative and fully participating.

Solution to Exercise 15-7

APPROACH: Calculate the preferred shares' current-year preference ($600,000 × 5% = $30,000) and the amount that would be required to give common shareholders a "like" percentage dividend ($1,200,000 × 5% = $60,000). Then refer to the steps listed in **Illustration 15-3** to solve.

(a)

		Preferred	Common	Total
2016:	Total to distribute			$ 25,000
	Step 1:			
	Step 2: Less than preference	$25,000		$ 25,000
	Step 3:			
	Step 4:			
	Step 5:	$25,000	$ -0-	$ 25,000
	÷ by number of shares outstanding	100,000	300,000	
	= Dividend per share	$ 0.25	$ 0.00	
2017:	Total to distribute			$ 45,000
	Step 1:			
	Step 2: 5% × $600,000	$30,000		$ 30,000
	Step 3: Remainder		$15,000	$ 15,000
	Step 4:			
	Step 5:	$30,000	$15,000	$ 45,000
	÷ by number of shares outstanding	100,000	300,000	
	= Dividend per share	$ 0.30	$ 0.05	
2018:	Total to distribute			$105,000
	Step 1:			
	Step 2: 5% × $600,000	$30,000		$ 30,000
	Step 3: 5% × $1,200,000		$60,000	$ 60,000
	Step 4: Remainder		$15,000	$ 15,000
	Step 5:	$30,000	$75,000	$105,000
	÷ by number of shares outstanding	100,000	300,000	
	= Dividend per share	$ 0.30	$ 0.25	

(b)

		Preferred	Common	Total
2016:	Total to distribute			$ 25,000
	Step 1:			
	Step 2: Less than preference	$25,000		$ 25,000
	Step 3:			
	Step 4:			
	Step 5:	$25,000	$ -0-	$ 25,000
	÷ by number of shares outstanding	100,000	300,000	
	= Dividend per share	$ 0.25	$ 0.00	

2017:	Total to distribute			$ 45,000
	Step 1: $30,000 − $25,000	$ 5,000		$ 5,000
	Step 2: 5% × $600,000	$30,000		$ 30,000
	Step 3: Remainder		$ 10,000	$ 10,000
	Step 4:			
	Step 5:	$35,000	$ 10,000	$ 45,000
	÷ by number of shares outstanding	100,000	300,000	
	= Dividend per share	$ 0.35	$ 0.033	

2018:	Total to distribute			$105,000
	Step 1:			
	Step 2: 5% × $600,000	$30,000		$ 30,000
	Step 3: 5% × $1,200,000		$ 60,000	$ 60,000
	Step 4: Remainder		$ 15,000	$ 15,000
	Step 5:	$30,000	$ 75,000	$105,000
	÷ by number of shares outstanding	100,000	300,000	
	= Dividend per share	$ 0.30	$ 0.25	

(c)		**Preferred**	**Common**	**Total**
2016:	Total to distribute			$25,000
	Step 1:			
	Step 2: Less than preference	$25,000		$25,000
	Step 3:			
	Step 4:			
	Step 5:	$25,000	$ -0-	$25,000
	÷ by number of shares outstanding	100,000	300,000	
	= Dividend per share	$ 0.25	$ 0.00	

2017:	Total to distribute			$45,000
	Step 1: $30,000 − $25,000	$ 5,000		$ 5,000
	Step 2: 5% × $600,000	$30,000		$30,000
	Step 3: Remainder		$10,000	$10,000
	Step 4:			
	Step 5:	$35,000	$10,000	$45,000
	÷ by number of shares outstanding	100,000	300,000	
	= Dividend per share	$ 0.35	$ 0.033	

Notice that in performing step 3, the amount of remaining dividends ($10,000) is not sufficient to give common shareholders a "like" percentage dividend (5% × $1,200,000 > $10,000), so the entire amount ($10,000) is allocated to common shareholders.

2018: Total to distribute			$105,000
Step 1:			
Step 2: 5% × $600,000	$30,000		$ 30,000
Step 3: 5% × $1,200,000		$60,000	$ 60,000
Step 4: To participate at 0.8%[a]	$ 5,000[b]	$10,000[c]	$ 15,000
Step 5:	$35,000	$70,000	$105,000
÷ by number of shares outstanding	100,000	300,000	
= Dividend per share	$ 0.35	$ 0.23	

[a]Amount to participate ÷ Total carrying value of participating shares = $15,000 ÷ $1,800,000 = 0.833%
[b]0.00833 × $600,000 = $5,000 allocated to preferred shareholders
[c]0.00833 × $1,200,000 = $10,000 allocated to common shareholders

EXERCISE 15-8

PURPOSE: This exercise will illustrate the preparation of a statement of changes in shareholders' equity and the related shareholders' equity section of the statement of financial position.

On January 1, 2017, Jenkins Corporation had the following shareholders' equity balances:

Common Shares (800,000 shares authorized, 400,000 issued)	$600,000
Contributed Surplus	575,000
Retained Earnings	410,000

During 2017, the following occurred in sequence:

- Issued 40,000 common shares for $160,000.
- Declared an $85,000 cash dividend.
- Reacquired and cancelled 15,000 shares at $4 per share.
- Declared and distributed a 4% stock dividend when the market value was $4 per share.
- Earned net income for the year of $280,000.

Of the contributed surplus of $575,000 as at January 1, 2017, $85,000 arose from net excess of proceeds over cost on a previous cancellation of common shares.

Instructions

(a) Prepare a statement of changes in shareholders' equity for the year ended December 31, 2017.

(b) Prepare the shareholders' equity section of the statement of financial position as at December 31, 2017.

Solution to Exercise 15-8

(a)

JENKINS CORPORATION
Statement of Changes in Shareholders' Equity
For the Year Ended December 31, 2017

	Total	Retained Earnings	Common Shares	Contributed Surplus
Balance, January 1	$1,585,000	$410,000	$600,000	$575,000
Shares reacquired and cancelled	(60,000)		(22,500)	(37,500)
Shares issued	160,000		160,000	
Cash dividends	(85,000)	(85,000)		
Stock dividends		(68,000)	68,000	
Net income	280,000	280,000		
Balance, December 31	$1,880,000	$537,000	$805,500	$537,500

Notice how the columns on this statement foot (add down) and crossfoot (add across).

EXPLANATION: Under IFRS, changes in all shareholders' equity accounts for the period are required to be disclosed in a statement of changes in shareholders' equity. Under ASPE, a statement of retained earnings is required, and any changes in share capital are usually disclosed in the notes to the financial statements. A statement of changes in shareholders' equity contains all of the information that a statement of retained earnings would contain plus information regarding changes in the other components of shareholders' equity.

Illustration 15-4 107

The journal entry for the reacquisition and cancellation of shares:

Common Shares (15,000 × $1.50)	22,500	
Contributed Surplus	37,500	
Cash (15,000 × $4)		60,000

Calculations for the stock dividend are as follows:

425,000 shares outstanding × 4% = 17,000 dividend shares.

17,000 shares × $4 market value per share = $68,000 decrease in Retained Earnings and increase in Common Shares.

(b)

JENKINS CORPORATION
Statement of Financial Position (Partial)
As at December 31, 2017

Shareholders' Equity	
Contributed capital	
Common shares, 800,000 shares authorized	
—442,000 shares issued and outstanding	$ 805,500
Contributed surplus	537,500
Total contributed capital	1,343,000
Retained earnings	537,000
Total shareholders' equity	1,880,000

ILLUSTRATION 15-4

Ratios for Analysis of Shareholders' Equity

The following four ratios use shareholders' equity amounts to evaluate a company's profitability and long-term solvency.

1. **Rate of return on common shareholders' equity.** This widely used ratio measures profitability from the common shareholders' viewpoint. This ratio shows how many dollars of net income were earned for each dollar invested by the owners, and is calculated as follows:

$$\text{Rate of return on common shareholders' equity} = \frac{\text{Net income} - \text{Preferred dividends}}{\text{Average common shareholders' equity}^a}$$

[a]The carrying value of preferred shares and any preferred dividends in arrears are deducted from total shareholders' equity to arrive at the amount of common shareholders' equity used in this ratio.

When rate of return on common shareholders' equity is greater than rate of return on total assets, the company is said to be "trading on the equity at a gain" or "favourably trading on the equity." **Trading on the equity** is the practice of using borrowed money at fixed interest rates, or proceeds from the issuance of preferred shares with constant dividend rates, to purchase assets in hopes of earning a rate of return on those assets that exceeds the rate of interest on the bonds and/or rate of constant dividends on the preferred shares. If this can be done, the capital obtained from bondholders and/or preferred shareholders will earn enough to pay interest on the bonds and/or dividends on the preferred shares, and still leave a margin for the common shareholders. When this occurs, trading on the equity is profitable.

2. **Payout ratio.** Payout ratio is the ratio of **cash** dividends to net income, and is calculated for common shareholders as follows:

$$\text{Payout ratio} = \frac{\text{Cash dividends (to common shareholders)}}{\text{Net income} - \text{Preferred dividends}}$$

Some investors prefer investing in shares that have a payout ratio sufficiently high to provide a good yield or rate of return on the shares. Other investors prefer investing in shares that have higher potential for share appreciation (increase in market value).

Another closely watched ratio is **dividend yield**, which is cash dividend per share divided by market price. This ratio gives investors some idea of the rate of return that will be received in the form of cash dividends.

3. **Price earnings (P/E) ratio.** Analysts often highlight this ratio when discussing the investment potential of a given company. It is calculated by dividing market price per share by earnings per share:

$$\text{Price earning ratio} = \frac{\text{Market price of share}}{\text{Earnings per share}}$$

● The P/E ratio is often referred to as a "multiple."

● When one company's P/E ratio is significantly different than another company's P/E ratio, the difference may be due to several factors; for example: relative business risk, stability of earnings, earnings trend, and market perception of growth potential and quality of earnings.

4. **Book value per share.** Book value or **equity value per share** is a much-used basis for evaluating the net worth of a corporation. Book value per share is the amount each share would receive if the company were liquidated, based on the

amounts reported on the statement of financial position. However, this ratio loses much of its relevance if the valuations on the statement of financial position do not approximate fair value. Assuming no preferred shares are outstanding, the ratio is calculated as follows:

$$\text{Book value per common share} = \frac{\text{Common shareholders' equity}}{\text{Number of common shares outstanding}}$$

To calculate book value per common share when there are also preferred shares outstanding, apply the following steps:

Step 1:

Allocate retained earnings between preferred shareholders and common shareholders, considering preferred dividends in arrears (if any), current-year preference dividends, and effect of participation (if the preferred shares are participating).

Step 2:

Calculate total shareholders' equity allocated between preferred shareholders and common shareholders, equal to contributed capital plus allocated retained earnings (from step 1), for each class.

Step 3:

Calculate book value per common share by dividing total shareholders' equity allocated to common shareholders (from step 2) by number of common shares outstanding.

EXERCISE 15-9

PURPOSE: This exercise will give you an example of how to calculate the rate of return on common shareholders' equity.

	Dec. 31, 2016	Dec. 31, 2017
Preferred shares; 8%, non-cumulative	$300,000	$ 300,000
Common shares	750,000	1,000,000
Retained earnings	180,000	415,000
Dividends paid on preferred shares for the year	30,000	30,000
Net income for the year	150,000	265,000

Instructions

Calculate the rate of return on common shareholders' equity (rounded to the nearest percentage) for 2017.

Solution to Exercise 15-9

Rate of return on common shareholders' equity

$$= \frac{\text{Net income} - \text{Preferred dividends}}{\text{Average common shareholders' equity}}$$

$$= \frac{\$265,000 - \$30,000}{1/2\ (\$930,000^a + \$1,415,000^b)}$$

$$= \frac{\$235,000}{\$1,172,500} = 20\%$$

[a]Beginning total shareholders' equity ($300,000 + $750,000 + $180,000) – carrying value of preferred shares ($300,000) = $930,000 beginning common shareholders' equity

[b]Ending total shareholders' equity ($300,000 + $1,000,000 + $415,000) – carrying value of preferred shares ($300,000) = $1,415,000 ending common shareholders' equity

EXPLANATION: **Return on common shareholders' equity** is a widely used ratio that measures profitability from the common shareholders' viewpoint. This ratio shows how many dollars of net income were earned for each dollar invested by the owners. It is calculated by dividing net income applicable to common shareholders (net income – preferred dividends) by average common shareholders' equity.

EXERCISE 15-10

PURPOSE: This exercise will illustrate the procedures applied in accounting for a financial reorganization.

The following facts pertain to Huang Corporation at December 31, 2017:

1. Retained earnings has a negative balance of $30,000.
2. Inventory cost exceeds fair value by $12,000.
3. Plant assets' total carrying value exceeds total fair value by $28,000.
4. There are 3,000 common shares with a carrying value of $300,000.
5. There is no contributed surplus.

Future prospects for successful operations are good. In order to eliminate the deficit (negative retained earnings balance), a financial reorganization is successfully negotiated with a change in control of the company. Huang prepares financial statements in accordance with ASPE.

Instructions

(a) Record all of the journal entries related to this financial reorganization.
(b) Explain what must be disclosed after the financial reorganization.

Solution to Exercise 15-10

APPROACH: Apply the three steps listed below.

Step 1: **Bring the deficit balance to zero.** Begin by recording any asset writedowns or impairments that existed prior to the reorganization. Then reclassify the deficit to Share Capital, Contributed Surplus, or a separately identified account within Shareholders' Equity.

Step 2: **Record the changes in debt and equity (as negotiated).** Often debt is exchanged for equity, causing a change in control.

Step 3: **Comprehensively revalue assets and liabilities.** Assign appropriate going concern values to all assets and liabilities based on the negotiations. The total difference between carrying values prior to the reorganization and new values is called the "revaluation adjustment." The revaluation adjustment and any costs incurred to carry out the financial reorganization are accounted for as capital transactions and are closed to Share Capital, Contributed Surplus, or a separately identified account within Shareholders' Equity. Note that the total of the new values of the identifiable assets and liabilities must not exceed the entity's fair value (if known).

(a) Journal entries:

Step 1:	Common Shares	70,000	
	Retained Earnings		30,000
	Inventory		12,000
	Plant Assets		28,000
Step 2:	No additional entry required.		
Step 3:	No additional entry required.		

(b) After a financial reorganization, the following must be disclosed: the date of the reorganization, a description of the reorganization, and the amount of change in each major class of assets, liabilities, and shareholders' equity resulting from the reorganization. In the following fiscal period, in subsequent reports, the following must be disclosed: the date of the reorganization, the revaluation adjustment amount and the shareholders' equity account in which it was recorded, and the amount of the deficit that was reclassified and the account to which it was reclassified.

A financial reorganization is often called a **fresh start**.

ANALYSIS OF MULTIPLE-CHOICE QUESTIONS

Question

1. Which of the following rights does a preferred shareholder normally possess?
   a. Right to vote
   b. Right to receive a dividend before common shareholders
   c. Pre-emptive right
   d. Right to participate in management

EXPLANATION: A preferred shareholder usually has dividend preference and priority claim on assets (upon dissolution of the company) over common shareholders. In exchange for these special preferences and claims, a preferred shareholder normally has to sacrifice other rights, including the right to vote on operational and financial decisions, and the pre-emptive right. A common shareholder normally has the right to vote (and, along with other common shareholders, can exercise control over corporation management by electing the board of directors to make major decisions for them), and the pre-emptive right (the right to maintain the same percentage ownership when additional common shares are issued). (Solution = b.)

Question

2. Wabasca Corporation has 20,000 common shares authorized. The following transactions took place during 2017, the first year of the corporation's existence:

   - Sold 1,500 common shares for $20 per share.
   - Issued 2,000 common shares in exchange for a patent valued at $25,000.
   - Reported net income of $8,000.

   At the end of Wabasca's first year, total contributed capital amounts to:
   a. $30,000.
   b. $25,000.
   c. $55,000.
   d. $63,000.

EXPLANATION: (1) Write down the components of contributed (paid-in) capital: (a) share capital, and (b) contributed surplus. (2) Reconstruct the journal entries for the transactions listed. (3) Calculate the balances of the relevant accounts. (4) Sum the relevant account balances.

Cash	30,000	
Common Shares		30,000
Patent	25,000	
Common Shares		25,000
Income Summary	8,000	
Retained Earnings		8,000
Common shares	$55,000	
Contributed surplus	0	
Total contributed capital	$55,000	(Solution = c.)

Retained earnings is considered **earned capital**.

Question

3. Which of the following represents the total number of shares that a corporation may issue under the terms of its charter?
   a. Authorized shares
   b. Unissued shares
   c. Outstanding shares
   d. Treasury shares

EXPLANATION: Explain each of the terms listed as possible answers. Issued shares (shares the corporation has issued to date) **plus** unissued shares (shares that have not been issued yet but may be issued in future under the terms of the charter) **equals** total authorized (approved) shares. Outstanding shares are issued shares that are now in the hands of shareholders. Treasury shares are shares that have been reacquired after having been issued and fully paid, have not been cancelled, and are not outstanding at the present time. (Solution = a.)

Question

4. Under IFRS, if common shares are issued for non-cash assets, the common shares should be recorded at:
   a. fair value of the non-cash assets received.
   b. par value of the shares issued.
   c. legal value of the shares issued.
   d. book value of the non-cash assets on the seller's books.

EXPLANATION: Under IFRS, if shares are issued in a nonmonetary exchange, the fair value of the assets acquired should be used to measure the transaction; if the fair value of the assets acquired cannot be determined reliably, then the transaction should be measured at the fair value of the shares given up. Assuming equipment with a fair value of $70,000 is received in exchange for common shares, the journal entry to record the transaction would be as follows:

Equipment	70,000	
Common Shares		70,000

(Solution = a.)

Under ASPE, shares issued in a nonmonetary exchange may be measured either by the fair value of the assets received or the fair value of the shares given up, whichever is more reliably determinable.

Question

5. The balance of Share Subscriptions Receivable should be classified as:
   a. a current asset.
   b. contra to the sum of share capital and retained earnings.
   c. contra to retained earnings.
   d. contra to common shares.

EXPLANATION: Under ASPE, whether the Share Subscriptions Receivable account should be presented as an asset or a contra to equity is a matter of judgement. Conceptually, it makes sense to present the balance of Share Subscriptions Receivable as a reduction of equity. (Solution = b.)

Question

6. Treasury shares are:
   a. shares held as an investment by the treasurer of the corporation.
   b. shares held as an investment of the corporation.
   c. shares that are issued but not outstanding.
   d. unissued shares.

EXPLANATION: Treasury shares are a corporation's own shares that were issued and fully paid for, and subsequently reacquired by the corporation but **not** retired (cancelled). Treasury shares refer to a company's own shares so they cannot be an investment of the corporation; acquisition of treasury shares represents a contraction of capital (shareholders' equity), not acquisition of an asset. Treasury shares are considered issued but not outstanding (as the corporation has reacquired them). (Solution = c.)

For companies incorporated under the CBCA, repurchased shares are usually cancelled, and if the company's articles limit the number of authorized shares, the cancelled shares revert to authorized but unissued status.

Question

7. Wheeler Company incorporated in 2017 and issued 15,000 common shares for $22 each. On April 15, 2017, 12,000 common shares were issued in exchange for a piece of land adjacent to property currently owned by Wheeler. An independent valuator determined that the land had an appraised value of $400,000. Wheeler's shares are actively traded and had a market price of $37 per share on April 15, 2017. Under IFRS, the total amount of contributed capital resulting from the above transactions would be:
   a. $774,000.
   b. $330,000.
   c. $444,000.
   d. $730,000.

EXPLANATION: Under IFRS, if shares are issued in a nonmonetary exchange, the fair value of the asset acquired should be used to measure the acquisition cost of the asset; if the asset's fair value cannot be determined reliably, then the fair value of the shares given up should be used instead. In this case, the common shares given up in the nonmonetary exchange should be measured at $400,000. The common shares given up in the nonmonetary exchange of $400,000 plus the initial common share issuance of $330,000 equals total contributed capital of $730,000. (Solution = d.)

Question

8. Preferred shares that can be returned to the corporation and exchanged for common shares at the option of the shareholder are referred to as:
   a. cumulative preferred shares.
   b. convertible preferred shares.
   c. participating preferred shares.
   d. callable preferred shares.

EXPLANATION: Holders of **convertible preferred shares** have an option to exchange their preferred shares for common shares at a predetermined ratio. Holders of **cumulative preferred shares** are entitled to receive dividends in arrears and the current-period dividend preference, before any dividends can be paid to common shareholders. Holders of **participating preferred shares** share (at the same rate as common shareholders) in any dividend distributions beyond the preferred shares' annual dividend preference. **Callable preferred shares** give the issuing corporation the option to call or redeem the outstanding preferred shares at specified future dates and at stipulated prices. (Solution = b.)

Question

9. Which of the following transactions will cause a net increase in total contributed surplus?
   a. Sale of no par value common shares
   b. Sale of no par value preferred shares
   c. Sale of bonds at a price higher than face value
   d. Share subscriptions forfeited, with partial payment collected

EXPLANATION: Recall what affects contributed surplus. Proceeds received from issuance of no par value common and preferred shares are included in their respective share capital accounts. Premium on bonds payable is accounted for in the liability section, not the shareholders' equity section. Contributed surplus increases if partially paid share subscriptions are forfeited. (Solution = d.)

Question

10. The date that determines who is considered a shareholder for purposes of dividend distribution is the:
    a. declaration date.
    b. record date.
    c. payment date.
    d. distribution date.

EXPLANATION: The date the board of directors formally declares (authorizes) a dividend and announces it to shareholders is called the **declaration date.** On the **record date**, ownership of outstanding shares is determined for dividend distribution purposes, according to records maintained by the corporation. On the **payment date**, dividend cheques are mailed to shareholders. (Solution = b.)

Question

11. Declaration and payment of cash dividends by a corporation will result in a(n):
    a. increase in Cash and an increase in Retained Earnings.
    b. increase in Cash and a decrease in Retained Earnings.
    c. decrease in Cash and an increase in Retained Earnings.
    d. decrease in Cash and a decrease in Retained Earnings.

EXPLANATION: Prepare the journal entries required to record declaration and payment of a cash dividend. Analyze each debit and credit to determine how Cash and Retained Earnings are affected. Assuming cash dividends of $10,000 are declared, the entries and analysis are as follows:

At the date of declaration:		Effect
Retained Earnings	10,000	Decrease in Retained Earnings
Dividends Payable	10,000	Increase in current liabilities

At the date of payment:		Effect
Dividends Payable	10,000	Decrease in current liabilities
Cash	10,000	Decrease in Cash

The net effect of declaration and payment of a cash dividend is a decrease in retained earnings (and, thus, total shareholders' equity) and a decrease in Cash (and, thus, total assets). (Solution = d.)

Question

12. Barney's Corporation has a fair value–net income investment in DePaulo Corporation of 2,000 common shares at a carrying value of $60,000. These shares are used in a dividend in kind (property dividend) to shareholders of Barney's. The dividend in kind is declared on March 23 and distributed on April 30 to shareholders of record on April 15. Market value per share of DePaulo's stock is $40 on March 23, $42 on April 15, and $46 on April 30. The net effect of this dividend in kind is a reduction in retained earnings of:

   a. $60,000.
   b. $80,000.
   c. $84,000.
   d. $92,000.

EXPLANATION: Write down the journal entries involved in accounting for this dividend and summarize the results. The entries and their effects on retained earnings (RE) are as follows:

				Effect on RE
3/23	FV-NI Investments	20,000		-0-
	Gain		20,000	$20,000
	[($40 × 2,000) – $60,000 = $20,000]			
	Retained Earnings	80,000		(80,000)
	Property Dividends Payable		80,000	-0-
4/30	Property Dividends Payable	80,000		-0-
	FV-NI Investments		80,000	-0-
	Net effect on retained earnings =			$(60,000)

(Solution = a.)

Although a property dividend is recorded at the **fair value** of the asset to be distributed, retained earnings decreases by the **carrying value** of the asset because the increase or decrease in the asset's fair value is also recorded (which goes through net income, and is closed to retained earnings).

Question

13. The net effect of the declaration and payment of a liquidating dividend is a decrease in:
    a. retained earnings and a decrease in total assets.
    b. total contributed capital and a decrease in total assets.
    c. total contributed capital and an increase in retained earnings.
    d. total shareholders' equity and an increase in liabilities.

EXPLANATION: A **liquidating dividend** represents return of contributed capital to shareholders, and is therefore based on contributed capital (rather than retained earnings). (Solution = b.)

Question

14. What effect does declaration and distribution of a 30% stock split carried out in the form of a dividend have on the following? (Assume that the company is incorporated under the CBCA.)

	Retained Earnings	Total Contributed Capital	Total Shareholders' Equity
a.	Decrease	Increase	No Effect
b.	Decrease	No Effect	No Effect
c.	Decrease	No Effect	Decrease
d.	No Effect	No Effect	No Effect

EXPLANATION: Write down the journal entries for declaration and distribution of a large stock dividend. Analyze each entry to determine how the above three amounts are affected.

Under the CBCA, the journal entry to record the declaration of a stock dividend will reduce Retained Earnings (or increase Dividends) and increase Stock Dividends Distributable (a component of share capital and, therefore, a component of total contributed capital). That entry will **decrease Retained Earnings** and **increase total contributed capital** by identical amounts, and thus have **no effect on total shareholders' equity.** The entry to record distribution will reduce Stock Dividends Distributable (contributed capital) and increase Common Shares. Therefore, the entry to record distribution will have **no effect** on any major total (or category) within shareholders' equity. (Solution = a.)

Question

15. A 300% stock dividend will have the same impact on the number of shares outstanding as a:

    a. 2-for-1 stock split.

    b. 3-for-1 stock split.

    c. 4-for-1 stock split.

    d. 5-for-1 stock split.

EXPLANATION: Set up an example with numbers. For instance, assume we begin with 10,000 shares outstanding. A 300% stock dividend would cause 30,000 new shares to be distributed, for a total of 40,000 total shares outstanding. A 2-for-1 stock split would cause 10,000 shares to be replaced with 20,000 shares. A 3-for-1 stock split would cause 10,000 shares to be replaced with 30,000 shares. A 4-for-1 stock split would cause 10,000 shares to be replaced with 40,000 shares. The example proves that a 300% stock dividend (a 300% increase in shares) has the same effect on the number of shares outstanding as a 4-for-1 stock split (each share is replaced with four shares). (Solution = c.)

Question

16. Trim Corporation declared a stock dividend of 15,000 shares when market value was $6 per share and the number of shares outstanding was 150,000. If Trim Corporation was incorporated under the CBCA, how does the entry to record this transaction affect retained earnings?

    a. No effect

    b. $15,000 decrease

    c. $60,000 decrease

    d. $90,000 decrease

EXPLANATION: Under the CBCA, all stock dividends are recorded as dividends (debit to Retained Earnings and credit to Common Shares) and measured at the market value of the shares issued. A stock dividend of 15,000 shares multiplied by the $6 market price per share means retained earnings decreases by $90,000. (Solution = d.)

Question

17. A 4-for-1 stock split will cause a decrease in:

    a. total assets.

    b. total shareholders' equity.

    c. book value per share.

    d. retained earnings.

EXPLANATION: A stock split involves the issuance of additional shares to existing shareholders based on the number of shares currently outstanding. A stock split does **not** result in capitalization of retained earnings; however, book value per share decreases in proportion to the increase in the number of shares outstanding. Thus, in a 2-for-1 stock split, the number of shares is doubled and book value per share is cut in half. In a 4-for-1 stock split, there are four times as many shares outstanding after the split, and book value per share decreases to one quarter of book value per share before the split. Assets are not affected. (Solution = c.)

Question

18. The balance in Retained Earnings represents:
    a. cash set aside for specific purposes.
    b. earnings for the most recent accounting period.
    c. unrestricted cash on hand.
    d. total of all amounts reported as net income minus the total of all amounts reported as net loss and dividends declared since inception of the corporation.

EXPLANATION: Define retained earnings and select the answer that most closely matches the definition. Retained earnings is cumulative net income retained in a corporation. Net income (earnings for a period) increases retained earnings, and dividends (distributions of earnings to shareholders (owners)) decrease retained earnings. (Solution = d.)

Question

19. Assume common shares is the only class of shares outstanding in Min-Kyu Corporation. Total shareholders' equity divided by number of common shares outstanding is called:
    a. book value per share.
    b. par value per share.
    c. stated value per share.
    d. market value per share.

EXPLANATION: Briefly define each of the answer selections. **Book value** per share represents the equity a common shareholder has in the net assets of the corporation. When only one class of shares is outstanding, book value per share is determined by dividing total shareholders' equity by the number of shares outstanding. **Par value** is an arbitrary value that does not have much significance except in establishing legal capital and in determining the increase in the Common Shares account for each share issued. **Stated value** refers to an arbitrary value that may be placed on shares by the board of directors, and has about the same significance as par value. **Market value** refers to the price at which shares are currently being bought and sold in the open market. (Solution = a.)

Question

20. If a corporation has two classes of shares outstanding, rate of return on common shareholders' equity is calculated by dividing net income:
    a. minus preferred dividends by the number of common shares outstanding at the statement of financial position date.
    b. plus interest expense by the average amount of total assets.
    c. by the number of common shares outstanding at the statement of financial position date.
    d. minus preferred dividends by the average amount of common shareholders' equity during the period.

EXPLANATION: Rate of return on common shareholders' equity is calculated by dividing the amount of earnings available to common shareholders by the average amount of common shareholders' equity during the period. The amount of earnings available to common shareholders is net income for the period less the preferred dividend entitlement for the period. (Solution = d.)

Question

21. A corporation with a $3 million deficit undergoes a financial reorganization as at August 1, 2017. Certain assets will be written down by $600,000 to fair value. Liabilities will remain unchanged. Common shares have a carrying value of $5 million and contributed surplus of $4 million before the reorganization. How will the entries to record the financial reorganization on August 1, 2017, affect the following?

	Contributed Surplus	Retained Earnings	Total Shareholders' Equity
a.	Increase	Decrease	No Effect
b.	Decrease	Increase	Decrease
c.	Decrease	Increase	No Effect
d.	No Effect	Increase	Increase

EXPLANATION: Write down the journal entry to record this reorganization. Analyze it to determine how the above three amounts will be affected.

The entry would be as follows:

Contributed Surplus	3,600,000	
Assets		600,000
Retained Earnings		3,000,000

(Solution = b.)

Question

22. Which of the following items is **not** included in accumulated other comprehensive income (AOCI)?
    a. Gains on property revaluation
    b. Unrealized gains and losses on FV-NI investments
    c. Unrealized gains and losses on FV-OCI investments
    d. Exchange differences on translation of foreign operations

EXPLANATION: Recall the definition and components of accumulated other comprehensive income. Gains on property revaluation and exchange differences on translation of foreign operations are included in AOCI. Adjustments to mark FV-NI investments to fair value are included in net income, and therefore retained earnings. Unrealized gains and losses on FV-OCI investments are included in other comprehensive income, and therefore AOCI. (Solution = b.)

It is important to reconcile the components of AOCI because they may be transferred to net income when realized (depending on the accounting treatment of the item related to each component).

Chapter 16

Complex Financial Instruments

OVERVIEW

Complex financial instruments are used by companies to manage risk, raise capital, and minimize cost of capital and taxes. Complex financial instruments include derivatives (such as options and warrants, forwards, and futures) and hybrid/compound instruments (such as convertible debt, debt with detachable warrants, and perpetual debt). The value of a derivative is derived from the value of its underlying primary financial instrument, index, or non-financial item. Some companies use derivatives or other instruments to offset risks. This is called hedging. Hybrid/compound instruments have both debt and equity characteristics, and may have a debt component as well as an equity component. Stock options are often included in employee share-based compensation plans, which are also discussed in this chapter.

STUDY STEPS

Understanding the Underlying Business Arrangements related to Complex Financial Instruments and Share-Based Compensation Plans

Derivatives

Primary financial instruments include most basic financial assets and financial liabilities such as accounts receivable, accounts payable, and long-term debt. In contrast, derivative financial instruments "derive" their value from an underlying primary financial instrument, index, or non-financial item. Derivatives are defined as **financial instruments that create rights and obligations that have the effect of transferring, between parties to the instrument, one or more of the financial risks that are inherent in an underlying primary financial instrument. They transfer risks that are inherent in the underlying primary instrument without either party having to hold any investment in the underlying** (per *CPA Canada Handbook*, Part II S. 3856.05 and IAS 32.AG16). Derivatives have three characteristics:

1. Their value changes in response to the **underlying** instrument.
2. They require **little or no initial** investment.
3. They are settled at a **future** date.

Derivatives include options and warrants, forwards, and futures.

Businesses face many financial risks, including **credit** risk, **liquidity** risk, and **market** risk, which are defined in IFRS as follows:

1. "**Credit risk** is the risk that one party to a financial instrument will cause a financial loss for the other party by failing to discharge (respect) an obligation."
2. "**Liquidity risk** is the risk that an entity will have difficulty meeting obligations that are associated with financial liabilities ..."
3. "**Market risk** is the risk that the fair value or future cash flows of a financial instrument will fluctuate because of changes in market prices." There are three types of market risk: currency risk, interest rate risk, and other price risk.

Derivatives help companies in many different industries manage risk. For example, a company that has market risk related to its inventory faces the risk that the value of its inventory may change while the company is holding the inventory. To help manage this market risk, the company may enter into a forward contract to sell and deliver a quantity of inventory units on an agreed-upon date at an agreed-upon price, as specified in the forward contract.

Options may be **purchased** options (purchased by the company or option holder) or **written** options (sold by the company to an option holder). An option gives the option holder the right to buy (**call**) or sell (**put**) an underlying instrument (called "the underlying") at a certain price (exercise price) over a certain period (exercise period), regardless of changes in market value of the underlying over the exercise period. An option or right to do something in the future is valuable; as a result, an option holder usually pays an upfront fee or premium to purchase an option. For example, an investor may pay a $1 fee for a call option to buy a share of a company (the underlying) for $10 (exercise price) at some time in the exercise period. If the share's market price increases to above $10 (exercise price) at some time in the exercise period, the option is considered "in-the-money" at that time. For example, if market price of the share goes up to $20, the investor need only pay $10 (exercise price) to acquire the share, and total cost to the investor would be $11 ($10 exercise price plus $1 option fee), for a share with market value of $20. If the share's market price decreases to below $10 (exercise price), the option is considered worthless and "out-of-the-money." However, the investor is not obligated to exercise his or her option to purchase the share for $10 (exercise price) and would only lose $1 (the option fee). Therefore, options allow the option holder to benefit from changes in market value of the underlying instruments, while limiting exposure to loss.

Warrants are similar to options, but are often attached to debt, and may be detachable (sold separately). A company may attach warrants to debt to increase the investor's potential yield on the instrument and "sweeten" the deal, thus allowing the company to pay lower interest on the debt portion of the instrument and manage its liquidity risk.

Forwards are contracts under which both parties commit to perform or do something in the future. Parties in a forward contract may not opt out of their commitment. For example, if one party agrees to buy U.S. $100 in 30 days for $120 cash, and the other party agrees to sell U.S. $100 under those terms, the price and time period are locked in under the forward contract and both parties must honour their commitment regardless of changes in exchange rate. In this example, both parties are managing currency risk. Forward contracts are usually unique to the parties involved, and are therefore not actively traded.

Futures are standardized forward contracts that are actively traded. Futures contracts also require a deposit of collateral (usually a percentage of the contract's value) to a margin account (similar to a bank account) with the exchange or broker.

Recall that the value of a derivative is derived from the value of its underlying primary instrument, index, or non-financial item. Referring to the examples above, the call option derives its value from the underlying company shares, and the forward contract derives its value from the market price of a U.S. dollar (versus the contract price). Because the value of a derivative is derived from the value of its underlying, a derivative can be used to offset, or **hedge**, risks associated with an underlying. For example, if a company purchases an investment and would like to offset the risk that fair value of the investment (the underlying) will decrease, the company may enter into a **fair value hedge** by, for example, purchasing a put option to sell the investment at a certain price. If fair value of the investment does in fact decrease, fair value of the put option would increase. A derivative can also be used to offset risks associated with an underlying series of payments. For example, if a company agrees to make a series of payments to a debt holder at a variable interest rate, and would like to offset the risk that the interest rate will increase, the company may enter into a **cash flow hedge** by, for example, swapping payments in an interest rate swap. In an interest rate swap, the company would pay a fixed interest rate to a counterparty and receive the variable interest rate from the counterparty, which would be used to pay the variable interest rate payments to its debt holder.

Special **hedge** accounting is optional, and may or may not be necessary. There are five steps that can be used to help determine if hedge accounting is necessary:

1. Identify the hedged item.
2. Identify the hedging item.
3. Identify how the hedged item is being accounted for without hedge accounting.
4. The hedging item, which is normally a derivative, will be accounted for using FV-NI unless hedge accounting is applied. Therefore, if the hedged item is accounted for in any other way, we may need to consider using hedge accounting if IFRS and/or ASPE allow it.
5. Locate where the recognized gains and losses for the hedged and hedging item are recognized. If they do not offset, then we may need to consider hedge accounting if IFRS and/or ASPE allow it.

Hybrid/Compound Instruments

Hybrid/compound instruments have both debt and equity characteristics, and may have a debt component as well as an equity component. Contractual terms and economic substance of hybrid/compound instruments and the conceptual framework definitions of liability and equity must be analyzed to determine proper classification of these instruments as debt, equity, or part debt/part equity. Examples of hybrid/compound instruments include perpetual debt, convertible debt, and debt with detachable warrants.

Perpetual debt is debt with no maturity date, but with a steady stream of interest payments. Because perpetual debt represents an obligation to pay interest (a debt-like feature), but has no maturity date (an equity-like feature), it is considered to have both debt and equity characteristics. However, perpetual debt is classified as debt (a liability) because it represents a contractual obligation to pay cash (interest), and is measured at present value of interest to be paid (in perpetuity).

Convertible debt is debt that carries with it an option for the holder to convert the debt to common shares of the company. Convertible debt allows the holder to limit his or her risk and still participate in the rewards of common share ownership, by receiving stable interest payments that rank in payout priority (over dividends on preferred shares) and having the option to convert to common shares if the value of common shares increases significantly. Convertible debt holders have added security if the convertible debt they hold is secured by company assets. Because convertible debt offers holders greater choice, it is generally more valuable, and allows the issuing company to obtain the related convertible debt financing at a lower interest rate. Because convertible debt has a debt component as well as an equity component (conversion option), it is classified as part debt/part equity.

Share-Based Compensation

The intent of employee share-based compensation plans is generally to motivate senior employees to improve the company's performance in the long term. Share-based compensation plans also help companies conserve cash because they do not require any cash payment. In fact, if options in a share-based compensation plan are exercised, employees will pay cash into the company upon exercise.

It is important to note that not all employee stock option plans are **compensatory** (in payment for employee services provided). For example, **employee stock option or purchase plans (ESOPs)** are usually made available to a wide variety of employees to give them an opportunity to invest in the company. Employees in ESOPs usually pay for their options, either fully or partially, and the company records these options as increases in assets (cash) and shareholders' equity (contributed surplus). In contrast, **compensatory stock option plans (CSOPs)** are usually made available to senior executives or restricted groups of employees, and are considered part of their remuneration package. Therefore, fair value of options in CSOPs are recorded as compensation expense, allocated to the periods that the company expects to benefit from the related (employees') services. Determining whether an employee stock option plan is compensatory or not may require professional judgement and analysis of various factors, including option terms (compensatory options tend to have more flexible terms), amount of discount from market price (compensatory options tend to have a larger discount from market price), and eligibility (compensatory options are usually offered only to certain restricted groups of employees).

Stock appreciation rights plans (SARs), sometimes called "phantom" stock plans, award employees for increases in share price by giving them the right to receive compensation equal to share appreciation (excess of market price per share at exercise date over a pre-established price) multiplied by a notional number of shares or SARs held. Therefore, SARs plans are always compensatory. Share appreciation may be paid in cash, shares, or a combination of both. SARs plans allow employees to benefit from share appreciation without having to pay cash on the exercise date and without requiring the company to issue the related shares to the employee. It is expected that if the executive (employee) is more productive and effective, the company will perform better and its share price will increase, causing the value of the executive's SARs plan to increase. SARs plans are often in effect for a limited time, and employees under SARs plans may exercise their SARs at any time during the pre-established SARs period. The notional number of shares or SARs held may reflect the executive's status in the company. For example, a more senior executive would generally have more notional shares or SARs.

Understanding the Presentation and Measurement Issues related to Complex Financial Instruments and Share-Based Compensation Plans

Derivatives

In general, derivatives are recognized in financial statements at cost when the company becomes party to the contract, and are subsequently remeasured to fair value with gains and losses through net income. (At subsequent remeasurements, fair value of the derivative is affected by fair value changes in the underlying.) However, there are some significant exceptions to this general rule, including purchase commitments, derivatives involving the entity's own shares, and hedges accounted for under special optional hedge accounting. See **Illustration 16-1** for further discussion.

Hybrid/Compound Instruments

Consistent with the conceptual framework definition of a liability, a hybrid/compound instrument is classified as debt or part debt/part equity if the instrument represents or includes a contractual obligation that the company is required to satisfy. Under IFRS, if the instrument includes a settlement provision that is contingent on a future event and if the event is outside the company's control, the instrument is classified as a liability. Under ASPE, the instrument would be classified as a liability only if the contingency is highly likely to result in a liability.

Under IFRS, the value of a hybrid/compound instrument that is part debt/part equity is allocated to each component based on the **residual value method**, with the debt component being valued first (at fair value or present value of future cash flows discounted at the market rate for similar straight debt), and the residual being allocated to the equity component. Under ASPE, the equity component of a hybrid/compound instrument that is part debt/part equity may be measured at $0; or, the component that is more easily measurable may be measured first, with the residual being allocated to the other component.

Sometimes the issuer wants to encourage the conversion of its convertible debt to reduce interest costs or to improve its debt to equity ratio. If a financial incentive is offered, this is referred to as **induced conversion**. The additional premium is allocated between the debt and equity components in an approach consistent with the method used at the time the debt was originally recorded.

Share-Based Compensation Plans

Because share-based compensation plans are compensatory (in payment for employee services provided), they result in recording of compensation expense or salaries and wages expense, which must be recognized and measured in the periods in which the employee performs the related services.

Compensatory stock option plans (CSOPs) are recorded at fair value of the options that are expected to vest (that employees are expected to earn the right to). Fair value is measured at the date the options are granted to employees (grant date), using market prices or an options pricing model. The grant date is therefore the measurement date. No adjustments are made after the grant date in response to increases or decreases in share price. The options pricing model incorporates several input measures as follows:

- The exercise price
- The expected life of the option
- The current market price of the underlying stock
- The volatility of the underlying stock
- The expected dividend during the option life
- The risk-free rate of interest during the option life

Fair value of the options that are expected to vest is allocated over the periods in which the employee performs the related services (service period), which is usually also the vesting period. The vesting period is the time between grant date and vesting date.

Stock appreciation rights (SARs) plans give rise to different measurement issues. Under a stock option plan, the employee receives a fixed number of shares upon option exercise. However, under a SARs plan, the employee receives an amount of cash, shares, or a combination of both cash and shares, based on excess of market share price at exercise date over a pre-established price. As a result, total compensation cost is not known until exercise date. However, for faithfully representative financial reporting, total compensation expense must still be estimated and allocated over the service period. Under IFRS, total compensation expense is estimated using an options pricing model. Under ASPE, total compensation expense is estimated as the difference between current market share price and pre-established price (intrinsic value), multiplied by the number of SARs outstanding. Estimated total compensation expense is recalculated, based on current information, at the end of each interim period that the SARs are outstanding. Compensation expense for each interim period is recorded based on percentage of total service period that has elapsed, multiplied by updated estimated total compensation expense, minus compensation expense that has already been recognized in previous years.

Accounting standards require certain fair value disclosure for financial instruments. Some of this has been discussed in previous chapters. One requirement is that both the cost and the fair value of all financial instruments be reported in the notes to the financial statements. Additionally, the IASB requires that companies disclose information that enables users to determine the extent of usage of fair value and the inputs used to implement fair value measurement.

TIPS ON CHAPTER TOPICS

- **Financial liability** is defined as any liability that is a contractual obligation (a) to deliver cash or other financial assets to another entity, or (b) to exchange financial assets or financial liabilities with another entity under conditions that are potentially unfavourable to the entity.

- An **equity instrument** is a contract that represents a residual interest in the assets of an entity after deducting all of its liabilities.

- A **primary financial instrument** is an instrument whose value is not derived from the value of another instrument, index, or non-financial item. Most basic financial instruments are primary financial instruments, including accounts receivable, accounts payable, and long-term debt.

- A **derivative financial instrument** is an instrument whose value is derived from the value of an underlying primary instrument, index, or non-financial item (for example, underlying company shares, market price of the U.S. dollar, market interest rates, or gold). Derivative financial instruments include options and warrants, forwards, and futures.

(continued)

- **Derivative financial instruments** are used mainly to help companies hedge against and manage various financial risks, including **credit** risk, **liquidity** risk, and **market** risk (which includes **currency** risk, **interest rate** risk, and **other price** risk). Examples of **derivative financial instruments** include forward contracts and interest rate swap contracts.

- In general, derivatives are recognized in financial statements at cost when the company becomes party to the contract, and are subsequently remeasured to fair value with gains and losses through net income. However, some significant exceptions to this general rule include purchase commitments, derivatives involving the entity's own shares, and hedges accounted for under special optional hedge accounting. All derivatives are subject to extensive disclosure requirements.

- **Purchase commitments** are generally considered **executory contracts** (where neither party has performed or fulfilled its part of the contract). A company with a purchase commitment agrees to take delivery of inventory at an agreed-upon price on an agreed-upon date, as specified in the purchase commitment contract. Purchase commitments technically meet the definition of derivatives. (For example, the value of a purchase commitment changes with the value of the underlying inventory.) However, under ASPE, purchase commitments are not accounted for as derivatives because they are not exchange traded and are therefore difficult to measure. Under IFRS, in general, if the company intends to take delivery of the underlying inventory according to the purchase commitment contract, the purchase commitment is not accounted for as a derivative. A purchase commitment that is not accounted for as a derivative does not affect the company's statement of financial position until the company takes delivery of the underlying inventory.

- An example of a **derivative involving the entity's own shares** is a purchased call option, which gives the entity the right to buy an amount of the entity's own shares at the exercise price. IFRS states that the cost of the option in this example should be recorded as contra-equity, and not as an investment. If the derivative involving the entity's own shares is a written call option, the entity agrees to issue a fixed number of shares for a fixed amount of cash consideration; these contracts are also generally presented as equity. However, there are some exceptions to this "fixed for fixed" rule. See **Illustration 16-1** for further discussion.

- Under IFRS, **special optional hedge accounting** is discussed in two basic categories: fair value hedges and cash flow hedges. Under ASPE, special optional hedge accounting may only be applied to certain specific types of hedging transactions that also qualify as effective and properly documented hedges. In all, the objective of hedge accounting is to achieve symmetry in, or match, recording of gains and losses due to changes in fair value of the derivative, with recording of gains and losses due to changes in fair value of the derivative's underlying instrument or future transactions. For example, in a fair value hedge, hedge accounting results in recognition of gains and losses (resulting from remeasurement to fair value) of both the hedge and its underlying instrument through net income, even if the underlying instrument is normally accounted for as fair value through other comprehensive income.

- **Hybrid/compound instruments** have both debt and equity characteristics, and may have a debt component as well as an equity component. The most

Illustration 16-1 131

common example of a hybrid/compound instrument is convertible debt. **Convertible debt** is considered part debt/part equity and must be bifurcated (split into its component debt and equity parts).

- **Preferred shares that are redeemable at the option of the holder** is another common example of a hybrid/compound financial instrument. These instruments are usually classified as a liability, but may be classified as equity if certain criteria are met, including, for example, if the instruments are "in-substance" equity instruments and have the same characteristics as equity, but for legal purposes are not called equity.

ILLUSTRATION 16-1

Accounting for Derivatives

In general, derivatives (including options and warrants, forwards, and futures) are recognized in financial statements at cost when the company becomes party to the contract, and are subsequently remeasured to fair value with gains and losses through net income. (At subsequent remeasurements, fair value of the derivative is affected by fair value changes in the underlying.) However, there are some significant exceptions to this general rule:

1. **Purchase commitments.** Purchase commitments are executory contracts (contracts to do something in the future, with no cash or goods exchanged upfront). Most purchase commitments are not accounted for as derivatives, and therefore most purchase commitments do not affect the statement of financial position until the related goods are received. However, under IFRS, if the purchase commitment can be **settled on a net cash basis** or by transferring other assets (instead of taking delivery of the underlying goods) *and* if the goods are not **expected use** (the company does not expect to take delivery of the underlying goods), then the purchase commitment is accounted for as a derivative.

2. **Derivatives involving the entity's own shares**. If the derivative's underlying is the company's own shares, the derivative may not be recorded as either a financial asset or financial liability, as a normal derivative would be. Under IFRS, if the derivative will be settled by issuing a fixed amount of cash for a fixed number of shares (**fixed for fixed**), then the derivative should be recorded as either contra-equity or equity. However, IFRS identifies some exceptions to this general "fixed for fixed" rule: (1) if the derivative represents an obligation to pay cash or other assets, it should be recorded as a financial liability, and (2) if the derivative can be settled on a net cash basis or by exchanging shares, unless all possible settlement options result in the instrument being equity, the derivative should be recorded as either a financial asset or financial liability. ASPE does not give explicit guidelines regarding derivatives involving the entity's own shares; however, if the derivative meets the definition of an asset or liability, it should be recorded as such.

3. **Hedges accounted for under special optional hedge accounting.** Under IFRS, if the derivative is a fair value hedge or a cash flow hedge, it may be accounted for under special optional hedge accounting. Under hedge accounting for **fair value hedges**, the underlying or hedged item is recognized and measured at fair value with gains and losses through net income, in order to match or offset its fair value hedge (the derivative), which is also recorded at fair value with gains and losses through net income. Under hedge accounting for **cash flow hedges**, the cash flow hedge (the derivative) is recorded at fair value with gains and losses through other comprehensive income, because changes in value (and resulting gains and losses) related to the cash flow hedge's underlying future variable cash flows are not captured in financial statements. The gains and losses on the derivative that are booked through other comprehensive income may be recycled to net income when the hedged item is booked to net income. Under ASPE, special optional hedge accounting may only be applied to certain specific types of hedging transactions that also qualify as effective and properly documented hedges. In all, the objective of hedge accounting is to achieve symmetry in, or match, recording of gains and losses due to changes in fair value of the derivative, with recording of gains and losses due to changes in fair value of the derivative's underlying instrument or future transactions.

EXERCISE 16-1

PURPOSE: This exercise will illustrate how to account for purchased call options.

On July 1, 2017, Dalton Corporation paid $150 for a call option to buy 1,500 shares of Burlington Corporation at an exercise price of $32 per share any time during the next six months. The market price of Burlington's shares was $26 per share on July 1, 2017. On November 30, 2017, the market price of Burlington's shares was $40 per share, and the fair value of the option was $13,000.

Instructions

(a) Prepare the journal entry to record the purchase of the call option on July 1, 2017.

(b) Prepare the journal entry(ies) to recognize the change in the call option's fair value as at November 30, 2017.

(c) Prepare the journal entry that would be required if Dalton exercised the call option and took delivery of the shares as soon as the market opened on December 1, 2017.

Solution to Exercise 16-1

(a) Derivatives—Financial Assets/Liabilities   150
    　　Cash   150

(b) Derivatives—Financial Assets/Liabilities   12,850

     Gain   12,850[a]

[a]$13,000 – $150

(c) Fair Value—Net Income Investments   60,000[b]

     Loss   1,000

       Cash   48,000[c]

       Derivatives—Financial Assets/Liabilities   13,000

[b]1,500 × $40 market price per share

[c]1,500 × $32 exercise price per share

EXPLANATION: A call option gives the holder the contractual right to purchase an underlying instrument at a fixed price (the exercise price) within a defined term (the exercise period). In this exercise, Dalton purchased a call option and has the contractual right to purchase 1,500 shares of Burlington at $32 per share within the exercise period, which ends on December 31, 2017. In general, derivatives (including options and warrants, forwards, and futures) are recognized in financial statements at cost when the company becomes party to the contract, and are subsequently remeasured to fair value with gains and losses through net income.

- The **fair value of a call option** is based on intrinsic value and time value. **Intrinsic value** is the difference between the market price of the underlying and the exercise price at any point in time. **Time value** refers to the option's value over and above its intrinsic value.

- In this exercise, the option is a six-month option and it was exercised at the five-month point. At November 30, 2017, with one month remaining in the exercise period, Dalton may exercise the call option on any date in December 2017. The $13,000 fair value of the option on November 30, 2017, includes $12,000 intrinsic value [1,500 × ($40 – $32)] and $1,000 time value, where the $1,000 time value reflects the possibility that the price of Burlington shares will continue to increase during the remaining month of the exercise period. Therefore, the loss recorded on December 1, 2017, is a result of the lost time value for the one month that is remaining in the exercise period. Note that the loss recorded on December 1, 2017, may be considered net against the gain recognized the day before, and that the $11,850 net gain on the transaction ($12,850 – $1,000) is equal to the increase in intrinsic value from the date of purchase of the call option to the exercise date, less the cost of the call option itself [1,500 × ($40 – $32) – $150 = $11,850].

EXERCISE 16-2

PURPOSE: This exercise will illustrate how to record issuance of convertible debt and subsequent conversion to common shares.

Wagagoostui Corporation has 300,000 common shares outstanding on January 1, 2017, when it issues convertible bonds. The debt issue is composed of 1,000 bonds at $1,000 face value with a 20-year term and a 10% coupon rate. Each bond is sold at 101 and is convertible into 20 common shares. Wagagoostui incurs costs of $80,000 related to the issue. An underwriter advises Wagagoostui that the bonds would likely have sold for 99 without the conversion feature. The straight-line method is used to amortize any premium or discount, as well as bond issue costs. Wagagoostui prepares financial statements in accordance with ASPE.

Instructions

(a) Record issuance of the convertible bonds on January 1, 2017.

(b) Record conversion of 50% of the bonds on January 1, 2019, assuming the book value method is used.

Solution to Exercise 16-2

(a) Cash (1,000 × $1,000 × 101% − $80,000)   930,000

    Bonds Payable   910,000[a]

    Contributed Surplus—Stock Options   20,000

[a]1,000 × $1,000 × 99% − $80,000 issue costs

- Under ASPE, to record issuance of an instrument with a debt component as well as an equity component, the **residual value method** may be used, with the more easily measurable component being measured first. In this exercise, similar straight bonds would have sold for 99, which is an estimate of fair value of the bonds without the conversion feature. Therefore, the debt component (bond payable) is measured first, and the equity component is assigned the residual value. Issue costs are also deducted from initial carrying amount of the bonds, and are amortized (in this example, using the straight-line method) to an expense account over the life of the bond.

- Under ASPE, to record issuance of an instrument with a debt component as well as an equity component, the equity component may instead be measured at $0, in which case, the entire net proceeds of the bond issue would be allocated to debt (or in this case, bonds payable).

- A bond discount of $10,000 is included in the above calculation of initial carrying amount of bonds payable, equal to $1,000,000 (1,000 × $1,000) maturity value less $990,000 (1,000 × $1,000 × 99%) fair value of the bonds.

(b) Bonds Payable   459,500[b]

    Contributed Surplus—Stock Options   10,000

    Common Shares   469,500

[b](50% × $1,000,000) − (50% × $10,000 × 18/20) − (50% × $80,000 × 18/20)

EXPLANATION: Net book value of bonds payable is removed from the accounts and recorded in appropriate shareholders' equity accounts. A proportionate share of contributed surplus is reclassified to common shares. No gain or loss is recorded.

- This method of recording bond conversion is referred to as the **book value method** and simply removes net book value of the bonds and **transfers the amount to appropriate shareholders' equity accounts. No gain or loss is recorded** when the book value method is used.

- Recall that **book value** is synonymous with **carrying value** and **carrying amount.**

- Interest, dividends, gains, and losses related to a hybrid/compound instrument are accounted for consistently. For example, if a preferred share is classified as debt because it represents an obligation to pay cash, the preferred share's dividends are recorded as interest or dividend expense (and not directly debited against retained earnings).

EXERCISE 16-3

PURPOSE: This exercise will illustrate how to account for convertible preferred shares.

Regal Corporation has 2,000 shares of $60 par, 5% convertible preferred shares outstanding at December 31, 2017. Each share was issued in a prior year at $63. The preferred shares are convertible into common shares.

Instructions

(a) Record conversion of 100 preferred shares if one preferred share is convertible into three common shares.

(b) Record conversion of 100 preferred shares if the conversion ratio is 5:1.

Solution to Exercise 16-3

(a) Convertible Preferred Shares (100 × $63)   6,300

    Common Shares   6,300

If a contributed surplus account was used to record the difference between the $60 par value and the $63 issue price, a proportion of the contributed surplus account would also be closed to common shares.

(b) Convertible Preferred Shares (100 × $63)   6,300

    Common Shares   6,300

Note that the journal entry would be the same in both situations. However, financial statements would be updated and show different numbers of convertible preferred shares and common shares issued under each situation.

EXERCISE 16-4

PURPOSE: This exercise will review the accounting procedures for issuance of debt with detachable warrants.

A new issue of 1,000 bonds was sold at 102.5 on January 1, 2017. Each bond had a face amount of $1,000 and one detachable warrant attached. One warrant allowed the holder to purchase 10 common shares at $43 per share. Market price per common share was $46 on January 1, 2017. Shortly after issuance of the bonds and warrants, quotes were 98.5 for a bond ex-warrant and $48 for a common share warrant. A few months later, 800 warrants were exercised. Two years later, the remaining 200 warrants expired. The company prepares its financial statements in accordance with IFRS.

Instructions

(a) Record issuance of the 1,000 bonds with detachable warrants.

(b) Record the exercise of 800 warrants.

(c) Record the expiration of 200 warrants.

(d) Indicate the effect of each of the entries [in parts (a), (b), and (c)] above on (1) assets, (2) contributed surplus (paid-in capital), and (3) number of common shares outstanding. State the direction and amount of each effect.

(e) Explain how the journal entry for part (a) would differ if market value of a bond ex-warrant were unknown.

Solution to Exercise 16-4

(a) Cash (1,000 × $1,000 × 102.5%)   1,025,000
        Bonds Payable (1,000 × $1,000 × 98.5%)   985,000
        Contributed Surplus—Stock Warrants
        ($1,025,000 − $985,000)   40,000

EXPLANATION: Under IFRS, for bifurcation of a hybrid/compound instrument that has a debt component as well as an equity component, the **residual value method** (incremental method) must be used and the debt component measured first (at fair value or present value of future cash flows discounted at the market rate for similar straight debt), with the remainder of proceeds allocated to the equity component. In this exercise, market price for a bond ex-warrant was 98.5, which is an estimate of fair value of the bonds without the conversion feature, and is used to measure initial carrying amount of bonds payable. The residual (the difference between total proceeds and initial carrying amount of bonds payable) is allocated to equity.

Illustration 16-2   137

- A bond discount of $15,000 is included in the initial carrying amount of bonds payable, equal to $1,000,000 (1,000 × $1,000) maturity value less $985,000 (1,000 × $1,000 × 98.5%) fair value of the bonds.

- Recall from your study of bonds payable that a bond's price is quoted in terms of a percentage of its par value. Carefully calculate the bond's price; in this exercise, a very common error would be to use $98.50 for the price of one bond rather than the **correct** price of $985.00 (98.5% of $1,000 par).

(b) Cash (800 × 10 × $43)   344,000
    Contributed Surplus—Stock Warrants
    (800 ÷ 1,000 × $40,000)   32,000
        Common Shares   376,000

The number of shares obtainable upon exercise of one warrant does **not** affect the calculations in part (a) (at time of issuance of bonds plus warrants) but it does affect the calculations in part (b) (at time of exercise of the warrants).

(c) Contributed Surplus—Stock Warrants
    ($40,000 − $32,000)   8,000
    Contributed Surplus—from Expired
    Stock Warrants   8,000

(d) Effect on:

	(1) Assets	(2) Total Contributed Surplus	(3) Number of Common Shares Outstanding
Entry (a)	Increase $1,025,000	Increase $40,000	No effect
Entry (b)	Increase $344,000	Increase $344,000	Increase 8,000
Entry (c)	No effect	No effect	No effect

(e) If market value of a bond ex-warrant was unknown, the bond payable would be measured at present value of interest payments (if any) plus present value of the bond itself ($1 million) discounted using an effective interest rate applicable to similar straight bonds. The remainder of the proceeds would then be allocated to the warrants.

ILLUSTRATION 16-2

Accounting for Stock Option Plans Issued to Employees

Before accounting for stock options issued to employees, it is necessary to determine whether the stock options are compensatory (used to compensate employees for their services provided) or non-compensatory (used to give employees an opportunity to invest in the company or to raise capital). **Employee stock option plans (ESOPs)** are usually fully or partially paid for by employees and considered non-compensatory. Therefore, stock options under ESOPs increase assets (cash) and increase shareholders' equity (contributed surplus and, if options are exercised, common shares). In contrast, **compensatory stock option plans (CSOPs)** are considered compensatory and in payment for the employee's services provided. Therefore, fair value of options granted under CSOPs is recognized as an expense (compensation expense) and allocated to the periods that the company benefits from the employee's services.

Some factors to consider in determining whether or not a stock option plan is compensatory are as follows:

- **Option terms**—Non-standard terms giving employees a longer time to enrol and the ability to cancel the option would imply that the options are compensatory.

- **Discount from market price**—A larger discount would imply that the options are compensatory. Note that non-compensatory plans might also offer options at less than fair value, but the discount would be small and represent savings on issue costs.

- **Eligibility**—Availability only to certain restricted groups of employees (such as executives) would imply that the options are compensatory.

In accounting for stock option plans that are compensatory, the issues usually revolve around recognition and measurement of compensation expense.

The steps in determining compensation expense are as follows:

1. Total compensation expense is measured by the **fair value method.** Using the fair value method, total compensation expense is measured at fair value of the options that are expected to vest (that employees are expected to earn the right to), at the date the options are granted to employees (or grant date), using market prices or an options pricing model.

2. Allocate total compensation expense to one or more periods in which the employees are required to provide services to the company in exchange for the options (often called the **service period**). The grant or award may specify the service periods, or the service periods may be inferred from grant terms or from patterns of past grants or awards. Unless otherwise specified, the service period is the vesting period (the time between grant date and vesting date). The vesting date is the date that the employees' right to receive or retain shares or cash under the grant is no longer contingent upon remaining employed by the company.

- The consideration that a corporation receives for shares issued through a CSOP consists of cash or other assets received from the employees, if any, plus the employees' services provided during the service period.

- Although the measurement date for a stock option plan may be the grant date, it is sometimes later. For example, assume a stock option plan provides for the company's president to obtain 1,000 common shares between January 1, 2017, and January 1, 2019, at a price equal to 20% of the market price at the date of exercise. The measurement date for this plan is the exercise date; the option price is unknown until the exercise date. If the measurement date is later than the grant date, the company should record compensation expense each period from the grant date to the measurement date based on an estimate of the final number of shares and the option price. This estimate may need to be adjusted in a later period.

EXERCISE 16-5

PURPOSE: This exercise will illustrate application of the fair value method in accounting for a compensatory stock option plan.

Worldwise Corporation granted options for 10,000 common shares to certain executives on January 1, 2017, when the market price was $52 per share. The option price is $44 per share and the options must be exercised between January 1, 2019, and December 31, 2021, after which time they expire. The options state that the related service period is January 1, 2017, to December 31, 2018. An options pricing model determined that, at the date of grant, estimated fair value of these options was $500,000.

Instructions

(a) Calculate total compensation expense.

(b) Explain when compensation expense should be recognized.

(c) Prepare the journal entries for the following (items 3 and 4 are independent assumptions):

1. To record issuance of the options (grant of options) on January 1, 2017

2. To record compensation expense, if any. Date the entry(s). Assume all employees remain employed by Worldwise.

3. To record exercise of the options, assuming all of the options were exercised on the earliest possible date, January 1, 2019

4. To record expiration of the options, assuming all of the options were **not** exercised because market price fell below exercise price before January 1, 2019, and stayed below exercise price for the balance of the option period

Solution to Exercise 16-5

(a) Using the fair value method, total compensation expense is $500,000 (fair value of the options measured at grant date).

The **option price** is often called the **exercise price**.

(b) Compensation expense should be recognized in the periods the executives perform services for which the options are granted. The service period is either stated or inferred. In this case, the stated service period is from January 1, 2017 (grant date), to December 31, 2018. Thus, compensation expense should be recognized evenly over the two-year service period, equal to $250,000 per year.

When answering exam questions on this subject, use the stated service period if it is clearly indicated. If it is not stated, indicate the period you assume to be the service period. (Choose from grant date to vesting date, from grant date to date the options first become exercisable, or from grant date to date the options expire.) If the question is multiple-choice and you cannot state your assumption, use the amount of time from grant date to date the options first become exercisable as the service period. If your resulting solution does not match one of the answer selections, redo your calculations using the amount of time from grant date to date the options expire as the service period. Your new solution should now match one of the answer selections given.

(c)

(1)   **January 1, 2017**
                 No entry

(2)   **December 31, 2017**

Compensation Expense	250,000	
Contributed Surplus—Stock Options		250,000

December 31, 2018

Compensation Expense	250,000	
Contributed Surplus—Stock Options		250,000

(3)   **January 1, 2019**

Cash	440,000	
Contributed Surplus—Stock Options	500,000	
Common Shares		940,000

The entry to record exercise of these options is not affected by the exercise date. Thus, this same entry would record exercise if it took place on December 31, 2018. If there is a situation in which the options are exercised prior to the end of the service period (**prior** to the date that total compensation expense is charged to expense), an unearned compensation cost account is charged. The balance of this Unearned Compensation Cost account is classified as contra shareholders' equity.

(4) **December 31, 2021**
Contributed Surplus—Stock Options   500,000
    Contributed Surplus—Expired Stock Options   500,000

The fact that a stock option is not exercised does not mean that compensation expense attributable to the stock option plan should not have been recorded. Therefore, compensation expense is not adjusted upon expiration of options. However, if a stock option is forfeited because an employee fails to satisfy a service requirement (by leaving the company, for example), compensation expense recorded in the current period should be adjusted (as a change in estimate). This change in estimate would be recorded by debiting Contributed Surplus—Stock Options and crediting Compensation Expense, thereby decreasing compensation expense in the period of forfeiture.

EXERCISE 16-6

PURPOSE: This exercise will illustrate application of hedge accounting for a cash flow hedge.

Waddington Corp. issued a $150,000, five-year note at prime plus 1% variable interest, on January 2, 2017, with interest payable semi-annually. On the same date, Waddington entered into an interest rate swap where it agreed to pay 5% fixed and receive prime plus 1% for the first six months on $150,000. At each six-month period, the variable rate will be reset. The prime interest rate is 4.7% on January 2, 2017, and is reset to 5.7% on June 30, 2017. On December 31, 2017, the fair value of the swap has increased by $30,000. Waddington follows ASPE and uses hedge accounting. Assume that the swap qualifies for hedge accounting under ASPE.

Instructions

(a) For this transaction:
1. identify the hedged item.
2. identify the hedging item.
3. identify how the hedged item is being accounted for without hedge accounting.
4. identify how the hedging item is being accounted for.
5. indicate how the gains and losses for the hedged and hedging items are recognized.

(b) Calculate the net interest expense to be reported for this note and the related swap transaction as at June 30 and December 31, 2017.

(c) Prepare the journal entries relating to the interest for the year ended December 31, 2017.

(d) Explain why this is a cash flow hedge.

(e) Assume instead that Waddington follows IFRS. Prepare the journal entries for this cash flow hedge.

Solution to Exercise 16-6

(a) Steps to help determine if hedge accounting is necessary:

1. The hedged item is the variable interest note. It has the risk of cash flow uncertainty.
2. The hedging item is the interest rate swap. It is designed to offset the risk of the note.
3. Under ASPE, the note is recognized at amortized cost, with interest payments accrued as interest expense.
4. The swap is not recognized under ASPE; any interest received from the swap is accrued as a credit to interest expense.
5. The changes in the fair value of the swap are not recognized under ASPE.

(b) Calculation of net interest expense

June 30, 2017	Note	Rate	Amount
Interest paid	$150,000	2.85%[a]	$4,275
Cash received on swap	$150,000		(525)[b]
Interest expense		2.5%	$3,750

[a](4.7% + 1%) × 6/12
[b](4.7% + 1% − 5%) × $150,000 × 6/12

December 31, 2017	Note	Rate	Amount
Interest paid	$150,000	3.35%[c]	$5,025
Cash received on swap	$150,000		(1,275)[d]
Interest expense		2.5%	$3,750

[c](5.7% + 1%) × 6/12
[d](5.7% + 1% − 5%) × $150,000 × 6/12

(c)

June 30, 2017

Interest Expense	4,275	
Cash		4,275
Cash	525	
Interest Expense		525

December 31, 2017

Interest Expense	5,025	
Cash		5,025
Cash	1,275	
Interest Expense		1,275

(d) The interest rate swap is a cash flow hedge because the hedge is entered into to protect Waddington against variations in future cash flows caused by the changes in the prime interest rate. At the time of entering into the contract, Waddington had not yet incurred the interest charges for the note. The cash flows are therefore related to future interest payments. Consequently, the hedge cannot be a fair value hedge.

(e) Under IFRS, the journal entries related to interest would be identical to those under ASPE as recorded in part (c). In addition, the gain in the swap must be recorded in Other Comprehensive Income.

December 31, 2017

Derivatives—Financial Assets/Liabilities	30,000	
Unrealized Gain or Loss		30,000

ANALYSIS OF MULTIPLE-CHOICE QUESTIONS

Question

1. Market risk is the risk that fair value or future cash flows of a financial instrument will fluctuate due to:
   a. one of the parties to the financial instrument contract failing to fulfill its obligation.
   b. the company itself not being able to fulfill its obligation under the financial instrument contract.
   c. change in foreign exchange rates, market interest rates, or other market factors.
   d. none of the above.

EXPLANATION: Market risk is the risk that fair value or future cash flows of a financial instrument will fluctuate due to change in foreign exchange rates (**currency risk**), market interest rates (**interest rate risk**), and/or other market factors (**other price risk**). **Credit risk** is the risk that one of the parties to the contract will fail to fulfill its obligation. **Liquidity risk** is the risk that the company itself will not be able to fulfill its obligation under the contract. (Solution = c.)

Question

2. An example of a derivative financial instrument is:
   a. a bond payable.
   b. a forward contract to buy U.S. currency at a fixed rate in the future.
   c. an account receivable.
   d. redeemable/retractable preference shares.

EXPLANATION: Bonds payable, accounts receivable, and redeemable/retractable preference shares are examples of primary financial instruments because their value is not derived from an underlying instrument, index, or non-financial item. A forward contract is a derivative financial instrument because its value is derived from an underlying primary instrument, index, or non-financial item; in this case, market price of the U.S. dollar (versus the contract price). (Solution = b.)

Question

3. Alicia Company has forward contracts to buy U.S. $200,000 at a rate of $1.10 in 180 days. The U.S. exchange rate is currently $1.15 (at the statement of financial position date). Alicia Company would show the following on its statement of financial position:

    a.   an asset of U.S. $10,000 (in equivalent Canadian dollars).

    b.   a liability of U.S. $10,000 (in equivalent Canadian dollars).

    c.   a liability of $220,000 (Canadian).

    d.   an asset equal to fair value of the contract at the statement of financial position date, with an offsetting credit to income.

EXPLANATION: In general, derivatives are recognized in financial statements when the entity becomes party to the contract, and are measured at fair value with gains and losses booked through net income. In this case, as of the statement of financial position date, the forward contract may potentially be settled with favourable terms. Therefore, the forward contract is a financial asset as of the statement of financial position date, and should be measured at fair value, resulting in recognition of a gain on the income statement. (Solution = d.)

There are some significant exceptions to the above-stated general principles in accounting for certain derivatives, including purchase commitments, derivatives involving the entity's own shares, and hedges accounted for under special optional hedge accounting. See **Illustration 16-1** for further discussion.

Question

4. On December 1, 2017, Puree Company enters into a purchase commitment to buy apples in two months at an agreed-upon price. Puree intends to use the apples in production of Delicious Apple Puree, its best-selling product. No cash or product was exchanged when Puree became party to the purchase commitment. However, the terms of the commitment contract state that the contract can be settled on a net basis by paying cash instead of taking delivery of the apples. Puree prepares financial statements in accordance with IFRS. The purchase commitment should be presented on the December 31, 2017 financial statements as:

    a.   a derivative measured at fair value with gains and losses booked through net income.

b. a derivative measured at fair value with gains and losses booked through other comprehensive income.

c. an executory contract, and therefore not recognized until the apples are delivered.

d. a liability measured at fair value.

EXPLANATION: Under IFRS, a purchase commitment contract that has **net settlement features** (and can be settled on a net basis by paying cash or other assets instead of taking delivery of the underlying product) is not accounted for as a derivative as long as the purchase commitment is **expected use** (and the company intends to take delivery of the underlying product). In this example, Puree intends to take delivery of and use the apples in its production process; therefore, the purchase commitment should be accounted for as an executory contract and Puree's statement of financial position should not be affected until the apples are delivered (even though the contract has net settlement features). Note that because this purchase commitment contract has net settlement features, if the purchase commitment was not "expected use," it would generally be accounted for as a derivative and measured at fair value with gains and losses booked through net income. (Solution = c.)

Under ASPE, purchase commitments are generally accounted for as executory contracts (not recognized until the underlying non-financial item is delivered) because they are not exchange traded, and are therefore difficult to measure.

Question

5. Barrie Company has issued written call options, which entitle option holders to buy a fixed number of Barrie shares for a fixed amount of cash. Barrie has no contractual obligation to pay cash or other assets as a result of these call options. Barrie prepares financial statements in accordance with IFRS. The written call options should be presented in Barrie's financial statements as:

a. an increase in shareholders' equity.

b. a reduction from shareholders' equity.

c. a financial asset.

d. a financial liability.

EXPLANATION: Under IFRS, a **written call option** that is settleable using the entity's own shares is presented as an increase in shareholders' equity if the holder has the right to buy a fixed number of the company's shares for a fixed amount of consideration (called the **fixed for fixed** principle), and there is no contractual obligation to pay cash or other assets. The terms of Barrie's written call options are consistent with the conditions for application of the fixed for fixed principle; therefore, the written call options should be presented in Barrie's financial statements as an increase in shareholders' equity. (Solution = a.)

- In general, if a derivative that is settleable using the entity's own shares also gives rise to a **contractual obligation** to pay cash or other assets (even if fixed for fixed conditions exist), the fixed for fixed principle is overridden, and the derivative is generally accounted for as a financial liability.

- Under IFRS, a **purchased call or put option** that is settleable using the entity's own shares is presented as a reduction in shareholders' equity (contra-equity) if the company has the right to buy or sell a fixed number of its own shares for a fixed amount of cash, and there is no contractual obligation to pay cash or other assets.

- Under ASPE, rules surrounding derivatives that are settleable using the entity's own shares are not as specific. In classifying such derivatives, professional judgement is required in applying conceptual framework definitions of "financial asset," "financial liability," and "equity."

Question

6. Which of the following are not considered to be dilutive securities?
   a. Debt that is convertible into preferred shares
   b. Convertible preferred shares
   c. Stock options
   d. Stock warrants

EXPLANATION: Dilution is the act of diluting common shareholders' interest in the company, as well as their share of the earnings. As such, warrants, options, and convertible preferred shares are dilutive since, if they are issued or converted, there would be more common shares outstanding, and therefore a smaller amount of earnings for each of the remaining groups of common shareholders. (Solution = a.)

Question

7. A corporation issues bonds with detachable warrants. Under IFRS, the amount to be recorded as Contributed Surplus—Stock Warrants is:
   a. zero.
   b. calculated as excess of total proceeds over present value of future cash flows or fair value of the bonds.
   c. equal to the market value of the warrants.
   d. based on the relative market values of the bonds and detachable warrants.

EXPLANATION: Under IFRS, instruments that have both debt and equity components are required to be bifurcated (split into their debt and equity parts and presented separately in the financial statements) using the residual method with the debt component being measured first (at fair value or present value of future cash flows discounted at the market rate for similar straight debt). Under

ASPE, the residual method may be used (with the more easily measurable component being measured first); or, the equity component may be measured at $0. (Solution = b.)

Question

8. Guildwood Corporation issued 2,000 6% convertible bonds with a face value of $1,000 each at a price of 103. An underwriter advised the corporation that without the conversion feature, the bonds could not have been issued at a price above 99. Guildwood prepares its financial statements in accordance with IFRS. At date of issuance, the amount to be recorded as contributed surplus attributable to the conversion feature is:

   a. $0.   c. $60,000.

   b. $20,000.   d. $80,000.

EXPLANATION: Recall that under IFRS, instruments that have both debt and equity components are required to be bifurcated (split into their debt and equity parts and presented separately in the financial statements) using the residual method with the debt component being measured first, at fair value or present value of future cash flows discounted at the market rate for similar straight debt. Since the above bonds would have been issued at a discount (99) without the conversion feature, 99 is an estimate of fair value of the bonds without the conversion feature, and the conversion feature is the reason the bonds were issued at a premium. The journal entry to record issuance would be as follows:

Cash	2,060,000	
Bonds Payable		1,980,000
Contributed Surplus—Conversion Rights		80,000

(Solution = d.)

Question

9. To induce conversion, a corporation offers its convertible bondholders a $15,000 cash premium to convert to common shares. Upon conversion, the $15,000 cash premium should be reported as:

   a. an expense of the current period.

   b. an unusual loss.

   c. a direct reduction of shareholders' equity.

   d. a split between expense (debt retirement cost) and issue cost.

EXPLANATION: When an issuer offers some form of additional consideration (called a "sweetener") to induce conversion of convertible debt, the consideration is allocated between debt and equity components using the method originally used at time of issuance (to bifurcate the convertible debt). In most cases, this will be the residual (book value) method, which would require a portion of the consideration to be expensed as a debt retirement cost, with the remainder treated as a capital transaction similar to a redemption cost. (Solution = d.)

Question

10. A corporation issued convertible bonds with a face value of $1,000,000 at a discount. At a date when the unamortized discount was $90,000, and the Contributed Surplus—Conversion Rights balance was $25,000 (related to these bonds), the bonds were converted to common shares having a market value of $1,130,000. Using the book value method, the amount of gain or loss to record on conversion is:
    a. $0.
    b. $130,000.
    c. $195,000.
    d. $885,000.

EXPLANATION: Reconstruct the journal entry to record conversion. Book value of the bonds is removed from the accounts and recorded in the appropriate shareholders' equity accounts. There is **never** a gain or loss recognized when the book value method is used to record conversion of bonds to shares. The journal entry is as follows:

Bonds Payable	910,000	
Contributed Surplus—Conversion Rights	25,000	
Common Shares		935,000

(Solution = a.)

Question

11. Which of the following is **not** a factor in determining whether an employee stock option plan is compensatory or non-compensatory?
    a. Discount from market price of the shares
    b. Time frame for exercising the option
    c. Eligibility
    d. Option terms

EXPLANATION: Referring to the factors listed in **Illustration 16-2**, it is evident that size of the discount from market price of the shares is a factor (the higher the discount, the more likely it is that the plan is compensatory); eligibility is a factor (if the plan is restricted to a group of employees, such as executives, it is likely compensatory); and finally, the option terms are a factor (non-standard terms indicate that the plan is likely compensatory). (Solution = b.)

Question

12. The cost of a compensatory employee stock option plan (CSOP) is accounted for as follows:

   a. a capital transaction that is measured at grant date.

   b. an expense that is measured at grant date.

   c. an expense that is measured at exercise date.

   d. none of the above.

EXPLANATION: The cost of a CSOP is measured at grant date at fair value (which is estimated using market prices or a valuation technique such as an options pricing model), and expensed over the service period. The cost should be expensed over the service period since it is the period that the employee is motivated to work harder as a result of the plan. The service period is normally the period between grant date and vesting date. Any fluctuations in value of the options during the service period are not accounted for by the company; the employee is considered to be the bearer of this risk. (Solution = b.)

Question

13. Stock options allowing selected executives to acquire 10,000 common shares are granted on January 1, 2017. Market price per share on January 1, 2017, is $22, and the option price is $10. The options are for services to be performed. The options become exercisable on January 1, 2019, and expire on December 31, 2021. Fair value of the options is determined to be $120,000 at grant date. The amount of compensation expense related to these options for 2017 is:

   a. $24,000.

   b. $30,000.

   c. $60,000.

   d. $120,000.

EXPLANATION: (1) Calculate total compensation expense. Total compensation expense is $120,000, or fair value of the options determined at grant date. (2) Determine the service period, or the span of time over which employees are required to provide services to the company in exchange for the options. In this example, the service period is the vesting period of 2 years: 2017 and 2018. (3) Divide total compensation expense ($120,000) by number of years in the service period (two years) to arrive at $60,000 per year. (Solution = c.)

Question

14. On January 1, 2017, Chandler Inc. granted stock options to officers and key employees for the purchase of 1,000 common shares at $20 per share as additional compensation for their services to be provided over the next two years. The options are exercisable during a four-year period beginning January 1, 2019, by grantees still employed by Chandler. Fair value of the options determined at grant date is $6,000. Market price per common share was $26 at grant date. The journal entry to record compensation expense related to these options for 2017 would include a credit to Contributed Surplus—Stock Options for:
   a. $20,000.
   b. $6,000.
   c. $3,000.
   d. $1,000.

EXPLANATION: Reconstruct the journal entry to record compensation expense for 2017:

Compensation Expense	3,000	
Contributed Surplus—Stock Options		3,000

Total compensation expense is fair value of the options determined at grant date, $6,000 in this case. Total compensation expense is allocated to the periods included in the two-year service period ($6,000 ÷ 2 = $3,000 per year). (Solution = c.)

Question

15. A phantom stock option plan (stock appreciation rights plan) may best be described as:
   a. an employee compensation plan whereby the employee is entitled to the increase in value of the company's shares without having to actually hold the shares.
   b. an employee compensation plan whereby the employee is entitled to the increase in value of the company's shares and must also hold the shares.
   c. an employee compensation plan whereby the employer sets aside shares for employees who are allowed to buy the shares at a fixed price within a pre-specified time period.
   d. an employee compensation plan whereby the employer sets aside shares in a separate trust for later issue to employees upon exercise of options.

EXPLANATION: The main feature of a stock appreciation rights (SARs) plan or phantom stock option plan is that the employee is entitled to participate in the increases in value of the company's shares without actually having to buy the shares. (Solution = a.)

Question

16. Thériault-Morin Corporation has $500,000 in long-term debt in Canadian funds at a fixed rate of 7%, with no other long-term debt outstanding. It believes that market interest rates will drop in the next few years. The best way to "manage" or "hedge" this exposure is to:

    a. lend money at a floating rate.

    b. pay off the debt immediately.

    c. enter into a forward contract to buy sufficient U.S. dollars at the maturity date to pay off the debt and perhaps gain on the exchange.

    d. enter into an interest rate swap contract with a party that has floating rate debt and believes that interest rates will go up.

EXPLANATION: While it is usually best to pay off debt, it is presumed that the company is unable to do this. This presumption would also exclude the possibility of lending money at a floating interest rate. The most common method of managing interest rate risk is to enter into an interest rate swap contract. Recall that any company that has long-term debt will be exposed to interest rate risk. Those with fixed rate debt face the risk that market interest rates will go down, and those with floating rate debt face the risk that market interest rates will go up. (Solution = d.)

Question

17. Using the facts above, assume that Thériault-Morin enters into an interest rate swap contract to pay the equivalent floating (market) rate to another party based on a notional principal of $100,000 for the next three years. Assume that the market interest rate averaged 8% in the first year. The interest expense that Thériault-Morin will record in the first year is:

    a. zero (all interest will be recorded when the contract is up and the rates are definite).

    b. $40,000.

    c. $35,000.

    d. $36,000.

EXPLANATION: In an interest rate swap contract, no principal amount is exchanged between the parties. Rather, each party pays the other party's interest rate based on the agreed notional principal. Therefore, Thériault-Morin Corporation pays the market interest rate (instead of its own fixed rate) on $100,000 of its long-term debt, and pays its own fixed rate (7%) on the remainder of its long-term debt. Interest expense totals $36,000: $400,000 × 7% plus $100,000 × 8%. (Solution = d.)

The interest rate swap contract is a derivative because it derives its value from the market interest rate (versus its fixed rate of 7%). Therefore, the contract should be disclosed in financial statements and measured at fair value (which, at the end of the first year, would be approximated by the present value of paying 1% more than it otherwise would have paid, multiplied by the notional principal, over two years).

Question

18. Continuing with the above example, how would the contract be presented on the statement of financial position at the end of the first year?

    a. The contract would not be presented on the statement of financial position since market interest rates will change frequently over the contract.

    b. An asset would be presented at fair value.

    c. A liability would be presented at fair value.

    d. None of the above.

EXPLANATION: The interest rate swap contract is a derivative and would be recorded on the statement of financial position (in this case, as a liability) at fair value. (Solution = c.)

Chapter 17

Earnings per Share

OVERVIEW

Earnings per share (EPS) is a widely quoted financial ratio used by shareholders and potential investors in evaluating a company's profitability and value. Calculation of earnings per share is more complicated if the entity has potential common shares such as convertible securities, options, warrants, or other dilutive securities that could dilute earnings per share if they are converted or exercised. This chapter examines how basic and diluted earnings per share are calculated, and discusses their usefulness in financial analysis.

STUDY STEPS

Understanding the Calculations Required in Preparing Earnings per Share Information

Basic EPS

EPS is residual income available to common shareholders stated on a per-common-share basis, and is an indication of the amount of income that each common share earned during the year. Therefore, EPS allows common shareholders to determine how much of the company's available income can be attributed to the shares that they own. EPS is not necessarily related to the amount of dividends paid out. Rather, it represents the amount of net income attributed to each common share after paying operating costs (including interest) and paying or allocating a return to shareholders who rank higher in preference (for example, preferred shareholders).

Calculation of **basic EPS** is as follows:

$$\frac{\text{Net income} - \text{Preferred dividends}}{\text{Weighted average number of common shares outstanding}}$$

Preferred dividends in the above formula include current year dividends on **cumulative preferred shares**, whether declared or not. This is because dividends on cumulative preferred shares are cumulative and will eventually have to be paid. However, dividends on **non-cumulative preferred shares** are only included in preferred dividends (and deducted from net income) if they were declared. This is because the rights to dividends on non-cumulative preferred shares do not accumulate if not declared in the year, and the company never has to make up a lost dividend on these shares.

Weighted average number of common shares outstanding is a calculation of the number of shares outstanding during the period, weighted by the fraction of the period that each number of shares was outstanding. Stock dividends and stock splits are treated as though they took place at the beginning of the year, even if they took place partway through the year or after year end (before issuing the financial statements). Calculation of the weighted average number of shares outstanding requires restatement of the number of shares outstanding before the stock dividend or stock split, so that earnings per share calculated before the stock dividend or stock split may be compared with earnings per share calculated after the stock dividend or stock split.

There are two types of EPS calculations:

- Basic EPS (discussed above)—an "actual" calculation, based on actual earnings and actual number of common shares outstanding
- Diluted EPS—a "what if" calculation, based on potential conversion of dilutive securities that might have a negative impact on EPS

Diluted EPS

Diluted EPS is what EPS would look like if dilutive potential common shares were actually converted to common shares, or exercised to purchase common shares, at the beginning of the period (or at the time of issuance if dilutive potential common shares were issued during the period). Dilutive potential common shares are securities or other contracts that may give holders the right to obtain common shares during or after the end of the reporting period, including convertible securities, options, and warrants that were outstanding during the period. In calculating diluted EPS, the numerator of basic EPS is adjusted to exclude the effect of preferred dividends and after-tax interest that would have been avoided if the dilutive potential common shares were converted or exercised at the beginning of the year (that is, if the extra common shares were outstanding for the whole year). The denominator of basic EPS is adjusted to include the increase in the number of common shares outstanding if the dilutive potential common shares were converted or exercised at the beginning of the year (that is, if the extra common shares were outstanding for the whole year).

In general, the effect of dilutive potential common shares (potential common shares that would decrease EPS) is included in diluted EPS; the effect of antidilutive securities (potential common shares that would increase EPS) is *not* included in diluted EPS.

TIPS ON CHAPTER TOPICS

- An entity with a **simple capital structure** (with only common shares and preferred shares and/or debt without conversion rights) must report **basic EPS** amounts for income from continuing operations and for net income on the face of the income statement. An entity with a **complex capital structure** (with one or more securities outstanding that could have a dilutive effect) must report **basic and diluted EPS** for income from continuing operations and for net income on the face of the income statement with equal prominence. EPS related to discontinued operations (net of tax) may be reported either on the face of the income statement or in the notes to the financial statements.

- A **dilutive security** is a security that would reduce EPS (or increase net loss per share) if it was converted to common shares or exercised to purchase common shares. An **antidilutive security** is a security that would increase EPS (or decrease net loss per share).

- **Antidilutive securities** are excluded from the calculation of diluted EPS. This means that in calculating diluted EPS, a convertible bond is assumed to be converted to common shares **only if** the effect of that assumption is dilutive. If conversion of a convertible bond would be antidilutive, calculation of diluted EPS would assume that the bond would not be converted to common shares.

(continued)

Inclusion of antidilutive securities would increase diluted EPS, which would contradict the purpose of diluted EPS: to present the effects of what will likely occur and the worst-case dilutive situation.

- Securities such as convertible bonds, convertible preferred shares, options, warrants, mandatorily convertible instruments, and contingently issuable shares are referred to as "potential common shares," "potential ordinary shares," or "potentially dilutive securities."

- Common shares are sometimes referred to as **ordinary shares**.

- **Mandatorily convertible instruments** are assumed to be converted for purposes of calculating basic EPS, because the issuance of common shares related to these securities will be required in future.

- **Contingently issuable shares** are potential common shares that are issuable in exchange for little or no consideration once a condition involving uncertainty has been resolved. For example, in an acquisition of another company, as part of the payment for the acquisition, the acquirer may promise to issue additional shares at a later date, if the acquired company earns profit above a certain amount in the year after acquisition. Contingently issuable shares that are issuable simply based on the passage of time are not considered contingently issuable since it is certain that time will pass; these shares are considered outstanding in the calculation of basic EPS. Contingently issuable shares that are issuable depending on the outcome of a condition (for example, future profit levels or performance targets) are considered outstanding in the calculation of basic EPS when the conditions are satisfied. See **Illustration 17-1** for further discussion.

- ASPE does not prescribe standards for calculating EPS, or require EPS disclosure in financial statements, whereas IFRS does. Therefore, EPS standards apply only to those entities in Canada that present EPS and apply IFRS.

ILLUSTRATION 17-1

Calculation of Earnings per Share

Step 1: Calculate weighted average number of common shares outstanding.

(a) If common shares were issued during the period, weight them according to the length of time in the period the shares were outstanding, relative to the total time in the period.

(b) If common shares were issued in connection with a stock dividend or a stock split declared during the period, treat these shares retroactively (assume they have been outstanding since the beginning of the year), even if the stock dividend or stock split is declared partway through the year or after the end of the period (but before financial statements are published). Also adjust prior periods' comparative EPS presented for the effects of the stock dividend or stock split.

Illustration 17-1   1 5 7

See **Illustration 17-2** for a shortcut method of calculating weighted average number of common shares outstanding.

Step 2: Calculate basic EPS (EPS before any assumptions or adjustments).

Basic formula: $\dfrac{\text{Net income} - \text{Preferred dividends}}{\text{Weighted average number of common shares outstanding}}$

The numerator represents income available to common shareholders, or net income minus **dividends on preferred shares**, where dividends on preferred shares include dividends declared on non-cumulative preferred shares and current year dividends on cumulative preferred shares (whether declared or not). Dividends in arrears on cumulative preferred shares have no effect on current year basic EPS.

- Dividends declared and/or paid during the year on common shares have no effect on basic EPS.

- If there is a net loss rather than net income, preferred dividends are added to the net loss in the numerator of basic EPS.

- **Mandatorily convertible instruments** are assumed to be converted for purposes of calculating basic EPS, because the issuance of common shares related to these securities will be required in future.

Step 3: Calculate diluted EPS.

(a) *Adjust the formula for basic EPS*:

$$\frac{\text{Net income} - \text{Preferred dividends} \pm \text{Adjustments}}{\substack{\text{Weighted average number of common shares outstanding} + \\ \text{Weighted average number of potential common shares}}}$$

(b) *Convertible securities*

1. Apply the **if-converted** method. For each convertible security, assume conversion to common shares if conversion to common shares would be dilutive.

- Conversion to common shares would be **dilutive** if it would result in a lower EPS. Conversion to common shares would be **antidilutive** if it would result in a higher EPS or a decrease in net loss per share.

- A quick test to determine if a **convertible debt** instrument is antidilutive is as follows: If the amount of interest (net of tax) that would have been avoided (if converted) per additional common share exceeds basic EPS, the convertible debt is antidilutive.

- A quick test to determine if a **convertible preferred share** is antidilutive is as follows: If the amount of preferred dividends that would have been avoided (if converted) per additional common share exceeds basic EPS, the effect is antidilutive.

2. Assume that **convertible debt** was converted at the beginning of the period for which EPS is being calculated (or at the time of issuance, if convertible debt was issued during the period). Add back interest (net of tax savings on interest expense) that would have been avoided as a result of the conversion, which should increase the EPS numerator. Add the appropriate weighted average number of common shares outstanding to the EPS denominator, to reflect the additional common shares that are assumed to be issued.

3. Assume that **convertible preferred shares** were converted at the beginning of the period for which EPS is being calculated (or at the time of issuance, if convertible preferred shares were issued during the period). Add back preferred dividends that were deducted in the calculation of basic EPS, thereby increasing the EPS numerator. Add the appropriate weighted average number of common shares outstanding, to reflect the additional common shares that are assumed to be issued.

In using the "if-converted" method for convertible debt, interest expense is added back to the EPS numerator and the related tax savings are deducted. In using the "if-converted" method for a convertible preferred share, preferred dividends are added back to the EPS numerator (because they were deducted in the calculation of basic EPS); however, there is **no** related tax effect to adjust for because preferred dividends are not tax deductible.

4. If there is a scale of conversion rates, use the rate that is most advantageous from the security holder's standpoint.

(c) *Options and warrants*

1. If exercising options or warrants would decrease EPS, include the effect of exercising the dilutive options or warrants in the calculation of EPS.

A written call option or warrant is dilutive if the average market price per common share during the period is greater than the exercise price of the option or warrant. A written put option or warrant is dilutive if the exercise price of the option or warrant is greater than the average market price per common share during the period.

2. For dilutive written call options and warrants, apply the treasury stock method. If **written call options and warrants** are exercised, the option holder normally pays cash into the company to purchase the company's shares. The dilutive effect of written call options and warrants is calculated using the **treasury stock method**. This method assumes that (1) the options and warrants are exercised at the beginning of the period (or at the time of issuance, if options and warrants were issued during the period) resulting in issuance of the agreed-upon number of common shares (per option terms) and (2) the proceeds from the exercise would be used to purchase common shares in the open market at the average market price per share during the period, to return some shares to the treasury. Note that no adjustment to the EPS numerator is required to include the dilutive

Illustration 17-1   1 5 9

effect of written call options and warrants—only the EPS denominator is affected. In summary, the EPS denominator is adjusted to reflect the increase in the number of shares issued upon the exercise of options and warrants, less the number of shares purchasable in the open market (at average market price per share during the period) with the proceeds from the exercise.

3. For dilutive written put options and forward purchase contracts, apply the reverse treasury stock method. If **written put options and forward purchase contracts** are exercised or settled, the holder would sell the company's shares to the company, normally requiring the company to pay cash to the holder. The dilutive effect of written put options and forward purchase contracts is calculated using the **reverse treasury stock method**. This method assumes that (1) the company would issue enough common shares in the open market at the beginning of the period (or at the time of issuance, if options and warrants were issued during the period) to generate enough cash to buy the agreed-upon number of common shares (per option or forward terms), with issuance calculated at the average market price per share during the period and (2) the number of shares received from the holder (per option or forward terms) would be returned to the treasury. In summary, the EPS denominator is adjusted to reflect the increase in the number of shares issued in the open market (at average market price per share during the period) to obtain enough proceeds to purchase the common shares from the holders (per option or forward terms), less the number of common shares received from the holders (per option or forward terms).

4. Purchased options and warrants will always be antidilutive, because it is assumed that the company will exercise the options or warrants only when they are in the money. Therefore, purchased options and warrants are not included in the calculation of diluted EPS.

(d) *Contingently issuable shares*

1. Common shares that are issuable only after passage of a certain amount of time (in the future) are considered outstanding when calculating both basic and diluted EPS because it is certain that time will pass. They are not considered contingently issuable shares.

2. Contingently issuable common shares that are issuable if a certain condition is met (for example, if a certain profit or market share price level is met) are considered outstanding from the beginning of the current period, if all conditions have been met as required. If the condition has **not** yet been met, but may be in the future, the contingently issuable common shares are included in diluted EPS only if the required condition to be met in the future (such as the share's market price or level of earnings) has reached the required level by the end of the current reporting period.

● **Calculation of diluted EPS should not assume the conversion, exercise, or issuance of securities that would have an antidilutive effect on EPS.** However, the *actual* conversion, exercise, or issuance of securities that had an antidilutive effect on EPS is included in the calculation of EPS, with an increase in the number of common shares outstanding weighted according to date of conversion, exercise, or satisfaction of conditions.

(continued)

- In determining whether potential common shares are dilutive or antidilutive, each issue or series of issues of potential common shares should be considered separately rather than in aggregate.

- Convertible securities may be dilutive on their own but antidilutive if included with other potential common shares in the calculation of diluted EPS. To determine **maximum potential dilution**, each issue or series of issues of potential common shares is considered in sequence from most dilutive to least dilutive. That is, dilutive potential common shares with the lowest incremental effect per share are included in diluted EPS before those with a higher incremental effect per share. (Generally, options and warrants are included first because the treasury stock method does not affect the EPS numerator.)

- An entity that reports discontinued operations should use income before discontinued operations or income from continuing operations (adjusted for preferred dividends) as the "control number" in determining whether potential common shares are dilutive or antidilutive. That is, the same number of potential common shares used in calculating diluted EPS for income before discontinued operations should be used in calculating all other diluted EPS amounts even if those amounts will be antidilutive relative to their respective basic per-share amounts. For example, assume that Corporation A has income before discontinued operations of $2,400, loss from discontinued operations of $(3,600), net loss of $(1,200), and 1,000 common shares and 200 potential common shares outstanding. Corporation A's basic per-share amounts would be $2.40 for income before discontinued operations, $(3.60) for discontinued operations, and $(1.20) for net loss. Corporation A would include the 200 potential common shares in the denominator of its diluted per-share amount before discontinued operations because the resulting $2.00 per share is dilutive. (For illustrative purposes, assume no numerator effect on those 200 potential common shares.) Because income before discontinued operations is the control number, Corporation A must also include those 200 potential common shares in the calculation of the other diluted per-share amounts, even though the resulting per-share amounts [$(3.00) per share from discontinued operations and $(1.00) per share for net loss] are antidilutive relative to (resulting in a smaller loss per share compared with) their respective basic per-share amounts.

- If an entity has a **loss from continuing operations** or a loss from continuing operations available to common shareholders (after subtraction of preferred share dividends), including potential common shares in the diluted per-share calculation will always be antidilutive, and will result in a smaller per-share loss from continuing operations. Therefore, if an entity has a loss from continuing operations or a loss from continuing operations available to common shareholders (after subtraction of preferred share dividends), no potential common shares should be included in the calculation of any diluted per-share amounts. However, as noted above, if an entity has income from continuing operations, but a loss from discontinued operations and a net loss, calculation of all diluted per-share amounts should include potential common shares.

- If an entity has a complex capital structure, requiring presentation of both basic and diluted EPS, it must also disclose a reconciliation of the numerators and denominators of both basic and diluted EPS for income before discontinued operations, including individual income and share amounts for each class of securities that affects EPS.

Illustration 17-2   1 6 1

ILLUSTRATION 17-2

Shortcut Method for Calculating Weighted Average Number of Common Shares Outstanding

Step 1: Begin with the number of common shares outstanding at the beginning of the period and assume they were outstanding for the entire year. (Multiply or weight the number by $\frac{12}{12}$.) Enter the amount in the Weighted Shares column.

Step 2: Find the first transaction that occurred during the year that changed the number of common shares outstanding, and adjust the balance in the Weighted Shares column accordingly.

  (a) **If shares were issued for cash or other assets, weight the number of new shares** by multiplying the number of new shares by a fraction, where the numerator of the fraction is the number of months in the period the shares were outstanding and the denominator is the number of months in the period. Add the resulting amount to the Weighted Shares column to arrive at a new balance.

  (b) **If shares were issued in a stock dividend or a stock split, adjust for these shares retroactively** by taking an appropriate multiple of the balance in the Weighted Shares column to arrive at a new balance. Ignore the date of the stock dividend or stock split; the multiple is determined by the size of the stock dividend or stock split.

  (c) **If shares were acquired as treasury shares or retired by the corporation,** weight the shares to account for the time they were not outstanding, and deduct the amount from the Weighted Shares balance to arrive at a new balance.

Step 3: In chronological order, analyze each of the other transactions that occurred during the year that changed the number of common shares outstanding. Adjust the balance in the Weighted Shares column accordingly (as discussed in Step 2 above).

EXAMPLE

Data:

January 1, 2017	100,000 common shares were outstanding.
April 1, 2017	Issued 40,000 common shares for cash.
June 1, 2017	Declared a 40% stock dividend.
October 1, 2017	Declared a 2-for-1 stock split.
December 1, 2017	Issued 60,000 common shares for cash.

Calculations:

Date		Weighted Shares
1/1/17	$100{,}000 \times \frac{12}{12} =$	100,000
4/1/17	$40{,}000 \times \frac{9}{12} =$	30,000
	New balance	130,000
6/1/17	40% stock dividend	$\times\ 140\%$[a]
	New balance	182,000
10/1/17	2-for-1 stock split	$\times\ 2$[b]
	New balance	364,000
12/1/17	$60{,}000 \times \frac{1}{12}$	5,000
	New balance	369,000

[a]The appropriate multiple for a stock dividend is 100% plus the percentage of the stock dividend. In this example, 100% + 40% stock dividend = 140% or 1.4 multiple.

[b]The appropriate multiple for a stock split is the size of the split. Thus, for a 2-for-1 stock split, multiply by 2.

● Notice how the calculation of the weighted average number of common shares outstanding for the period differs from the calculation of the actual number of common shares outstanding at the end of the period. Actual number of common shares outstanding at December 31, 2017, is calculated as follows:

Date		Actual Shares
1/1/17	Balance	100,000
4/1/17	Issued for cash	40,000
	New balance	140,000
6/1/17	40% stock dividend	56,000
	New balance	196,000
10/1/17	2:1 split	196,000
	New balance	392,000
12/1/17	Issued for cash	60,000
	Actual number of outstanding shares, 12/31/17	452,000

● Assume that in addition to the transactions listed above, a 10% stock dividend was declared on January 7, 2018, before the 2017 financial statements were issued. Weighted average number of common shares outstanding for purposes of calculating EPS for 2017 would be 405,900 (369,000 × 110% = 405,900). The actual number of common shares outstanding to be reported on the statement of financial position at December 31, 2017, however, would remain unchanged at 452,000.

EXERCISE 17-1

PURPOSE: This exercise will apply the guidelines for calculating the weighted average number of common shares outstanding.

When the number of common shares outstanding varies during the year, the weighted average number of common shares outstanding must be calculated before EPS can be calculated.

Listed below are details regarding common shares outstanding for four different companies:

1. Johnson Corporation had 120,000 common shares outstanding on January 1, 2017. On April 1, 10,000 common shares were issued for cash.
2. Barrett Corporation had 120,000 common shares outstanding on January 1, 2017. On April 1, 10,000 common shares were issued for cash. On August 1, a 3-for-1 stock split was declared.
3. Hartford Corporation had 120,000 common shares outstanding on January 1, 2017. On April 1, 10,000 common shares were reacquired by Hartford.
4. Vickers Corporation had 120,000 common shares outstanding on January 1, 2017. On April 1, 10,000 common shares were issued for cash. On June 1, a 12% stock dividend was declared. On November 1, 15,000 common shares were issued for cash.

Instructions

(a) Calculate the weighted average number of common shares outstanding for 2017 (for the purposes of calculating EPS) for **each** of the **independent** situations above.

(b) Calculate the number of common shares outstanding to be reported on the statement of financial position at December 31, 2017, for Vickers Corporation (situation 4).

Solution to Exercise 17-1

(a) **EXPLANATION:** Use the shortcut method explained in **Illustration 17-2**.

Date		Weighted Shares
1. 1/1/17	$120,000 \times \frac{12}{12} =$	120,000
4/1/17	$10,000 \times \frac{9}{12} =$	7,500
	New balance	127,500

Calculation of the weighted average number of common shares outstanding uses the same concept that is applied in the calculation of equivalent units of production for a manufacturing firm. In the situation above, the calculation indicates that having 10,000 shares outstanding for 9 months of the year is equivalent to having 7,500 shares outstanding for 12 months. Weighted average number of shares outstanding is sometimes referred to as "equivalent shares."

	Date		Weighted Shares
2.	1/1/17	$120{,}000 \times \frac{12}{12} =$	120,000
	4/1/17	$10{,}000 \times \frac{9}{12} =$	7,500
		New balance	127,500
	8/1/17	3-for-1 stock split	× 3
		New balance	382,500
3.	1/1/17	$120{,}000 \times \frac{12}{12} =$	120,000
	4/1/17	$(10{,}000) \times \frac{9}{12} =$	(7,500)
		New balance	112,500
4.	1/1/17	$120{,}000 \times \frac{12}{12} =$	120,000
	4/1/17	$10{,}000 \times \frac{9}{12} =$	7,500
		New balance	127,500
	6/1/17	12% stock dividend	× 112%
		New balance	142,800
	11/1/17	$15{,}000 \times \frac{2}{12} =$	2,500
		New balance	145,300

Weighted average number of common shares outstanding for Vickers Corporation can also be calculated as follows:

Dates Outstanding	Actual Shares[a]	Restatement	Fraction	Weighted Shares
1/1/17 to 3/31/17	120,000	1.12	$\frac{3}{12}$	33,600
4/1/17 to 5/31/17	130,000	1.12	$\frac{2}{12}$	24,267
6/1/17 to 10/31/17	145,600		$\frac{5}{12}$	60,667
11/1/17 to 12/31/17	160,600		$\frac{2}{12}$	26,766
				145,300

[a]See solution to part (b) for calculations.

For calculation of EPS, a stock dividend or a stock split requires retroactive adjustment of the number of shares outstanding. A 12% stock dividend causes a 12% increase in the number of shares outstanding. Therefore, to retroactively adjust the number of shares outstanding, previous amounts of actual shares outstanding are multiplied by 112% (which is 1.12 in decimal form).

When shares are issued for cash or other assets, the shares are weighted by the number of months they are outstanding in the period relative to the number of months in the period for which EPS is being calculated. When shares are issued in a stock dividend or a stock split, they are not weighted; rather, the number of shares outstanding is retroactively adjusted. The reason for the difference in treatment is that when cash or other assets are received, the entity has more resources, and therefore, it has an opportunity to increase net income by earning a return on those new assets for the months that the new assets are available. When shares are issued in connection with a stock dividend or a stock split, the entity does not receive any new resources, and in order for the entity's EPS calculations in successive periods to be meaningful, all EPS calculations must be based on the entity's rearranged capital structure. As a result, stock dividends and stock splits must be treated retroactively. This **retroactive treatment** causes an adjustment to the weighted average number of common shares outstanding **for any other comparative years presented**. When comparative financial statements for a prior period are presented, EPS amounts for the prior period are also restated to reflect all stock dividends and stock splits that occurred in subsequent periods. Thus, a stock dividend declared in 2017 requires retroactive restatement of 2016 EPS amounts when the 2016 income statement is republished in 2017 for comparative purposes.

(b)

Date		Actual Shares
1/1/17	Balance	120,000
4/1/17	Issued for cash	10,000
	New balance	130,000
6/1/17	12% stock dividend	15,600
	New balance	145,600
11/1/17	Issued for cash	15,000
	New balance	160,600

EXERCISE 17-2

PURPOSE: This exercise will illustrate the application of the treasury stock method.

Stanley Corporation had 250,000 common shares outstanding during 2017. On January 1, 2017, 60,000 stock options were granted. Each option entitles the holder to purchase one common share at $44. The options become exercisable in 2019.

Net income for 2017 was $425,000. For 2017, the average market price per share during the year was $55; the closing market price per share at the end of the year was $58.

Instructions

(a) Calculate the amount(s) that Stanley Corporation should report for EPS for 2017.

(b) Explain how your answer(s) to part (a) would change if the options were issued on April 1, 2017, rather than January 1, 2017.

Solution to Exercise 17-2

(a) **APPROACH:** Follow the steps for calculating EPS as outlined in **Illustration 17-1**.

Step 1: Calculate weighted average number of common shares outstanding.

There were no changes in the 250,000 common shares outstanding during 2017. Therefore, the weighted average number of common shares outstanding is 250,000.

Step 2: Calculate basic EPS (EPS before any assumptions or adjustments).

$$\frac{\$425,000 - \$0}{250,000} = \$1.70$$

Step 3: Calculate diluted EPS.

- For the written call options, apply the treasury stock method.
- Use the quick test to determine if the options are dilutive. Compare average market price per share with exercise price of the option. The exercise price ($44) is less than average market price per share ($55), so the options are dilutive.
- Adjust the basic formula:

$$\frac{(\$425,000 - \$0)}{(250,000 + (60,000^a - 48,000^b))} = \$1.62$$

[a]Number of shares to be issued upon exercise of the options.
[b]Number of shares that could be purchased in the open market at average market price per share during the period ($55), using the proceeds from assumed exercise of the options:

   $60,000 \times \$44 = \$2,640,000$ proceeds

   $\$2,640,000 \div \$55 = 48,000$ shares assumed returned to the treasury

● Notice that the incremental number of shares calculated using the treasury stock method is 12,000 in this example (60,000 − 48,000). If average market price per share was less than the exercise price, the number of shares

assumed to be returned to the treasury would exceed the number of shares issued upon exercise of the options, resulting in a decrease in the EPS denominator, which would have an antidilutive effect on EPS. Therefore, if the average market price per share was less than the exercise price, exercise of the options would **not** be assumed. **In calculating diluted EPS, never make assumptions that are antidilutive.**

● Notice why the treasury stock method is so named; proceeds from the assumed exercise of options are assumed to be used for purchase of treasury shares.

For 2017, Stanley Corporation should report dual presentation of EPS as follows:

$1.70 basic earnings per share, and
$1.62 diluted earnings per share.

(b) If the options were issued on April 1, 2017, exercise of the options would be assumed to take place on April 1 rather than on January 1. Therefore, adjustment to the EPS denominator would be weighted as follows: $\frac{9}{12} \times (60,000 - 48,000) = 9,000$.

Diluted EPS would be calculated as follows:

$$\frac{\$425,000}{(250,000 + 9,000)} = \$1.64 \text{ diluted EPS}$$

EXERCISE 17-3

PURPOSE: This exercise will illustrate the proper treatment of convertible securities in calculating EPS.

The following data pertain to Lakeside Corporation at December 31, 2017:

Net income for the year	$1,800,000
5% convertible bonds issued at par in a prior year, convertible into 250,000 common shares	$3,600,000
6% convertible, cumulative, preferred shares, $100 stated value, issued in a prior year (each share is convertible into 8 common shares)	$2,700,000
Common shares, issued in prior years (800,000 outstanding)	$8,000,000
Contributed capital	$3,000,000
Retained earnings	$4,500,000
Tax rate for 2017	25%

During 2017, there were no changes in the number of common shares, preferred shares, or convertible bonds outstanding. There are no treasury shares held.

Instructions

(a) Calculate basic EPS for 2017.
(b) Calculate diluted EPS for 2017.
(c) Explain whether dual presentation of EPS (presentation of both basic and diluted EPS) is required for 2017.

Solution to Exercise 17-3

(a) $2.05. (See Step 2 below.)
(b) $1.53. (See Step 3 below.)
(c) Yes, dual presentation of EPS is required for 2017, because Lakeside has some dilutive securities outstanding.

For the calculation of EPS, follow the steps (in order) listed in **Illustration 17-1**. By following an organized approach to the calculation of EPS, you are less likely to overlook guidelines that may affect your solution.

EXPLANATION:

Step 1: Calculate weighted average number of common shares outstanding.

There was no change in the number of common shares outstanding during 2017. There are no treasury shares; thus, the weighted average number of common shares outstanding equals the number of shares issued, which is 800,000 (given).

Step 2: Calculate basic EPS (EPS before any assumptions or adjustments).

$$\frac{(\$1,800,000 - \$162,000^a)}{800,000} = \$2.05$$

^{a}6% × $2,700,000 par = $162,000 preferred dividends.

Recall that for cumulative preferred shares, the current year dividend is deducted from the EPS numerator, whether it was declared or not.

Step 3: Calculate diluted EPS.

$$\frac{(\$1,800,000 - \$162,000 + (\$180,000^b - \$45,000^c) + \$162,000)}{(800,000 + 250,000 + (8 \times 27,000^d))} = \$1.53$$

[b]5% × $3,600,000 par = $180,000 interest expense.
[c]$180,000 interest × 25% tax rate = $45,000 tax effect of interest.
[d]$2,700,000 par ÷ $100 stated value per share = 27,000 preferred shares issued.

Notice why the "if-converted" method is so named; diluted EPS is calculated assuming the conversion of dilutive convertible securities.

When there is more than one potentially dilutive security outstanding, the steps for calculating diluted EPS are as follows:

1. For each dilutive security, determine the incremental effect per additional share assuming exercise or conversion.

2. Using the results from step 1, rank the dilutive securities from smallest to largest in terms of incremental effect per share; that is, rank the dilutive securities from most dilutive to least dilutive.

3. Beginning with basic EPS (i.e., using the weighted average number of common shares outstanding, or $2.05 in this problem), recalculate EPS by adding the effect of the most dilutive security (the security with the smallest incremental effect per share, according to the calculations in step 2). If the result from the recalculation of EPS is less than $2.05, add the effect of the next most dilutive security and recalculate EPS again. Continue this process until recalculated EPS is no longer smaller than the previous recalculation of EPS, or there are no more dilutive securities to test.

This means that the most dilutive potential common shares are included in diluted EPS calculations before those that are less dilutive.

These three steps are now applied to Lakeside Corporation. Lakeside has two securities (5% convertible bonds and 6% convertible, cumulative, preferred shares) that could reduce EPS.

The first step in calculating diluted EPS is to determine the incremental effect per additional share of each potentially dilutive security.

Step 1: For each dilutive security, determine the incremental per-share effect on EPS assuming exercise or conversion.

Convertible bonds:

Interest expense for the year (5% × $3,600,000)	$180,000
Income tax reduction due to interest expense (25% × $180,000)	45,000
Interest expense avoided (net of tax)	$135,000
Number of additional common shares issued assuming conversion of bonds	250,000
Incremental per-share effect:	
Incremental numerator effect: $135,000	$0.54
Incremental denominator: 250,000	

Convertible preferred shares:

Current year dividend requirement on cumulative preferred (27,000 × $100 stated value × 6%)	$162,000
Income tax effect (dividends are not tax deductible)	none
Preferred dividend avoided	$162,000
Number of additional common shares issued assuming conversion of preferred shares (8 × 27,000 shares)	216,000
Incremental per-share effect:	
Incremental numerator effect: $162,000	
Incremental denominator: 216,000	$0.75

Step 2: Rank the results from Step 1.

Ranking of the two potentially dilutive securities (from lowest to highest incremental effect per share) is as follows:

	Effect per Incremental Share
1. 5% convertible bonds	$0.54
2. 6% convertible preferred shares	0.75

Step 3: Calculate diluted EPS.

The next step is to calculate diluted EPS based on the ranking above. Starting with basic EPS of $2.05 calculated previously, add the incremental effect of converting the bonds, as follows:

5% Convertible Bonds

Numerator from previous calculation (basic EPS)	$1,638,000
Add: Interest expense avoided (net of tax)	135,000
Total	$1,773,000
Denominator from previous calculation (basic EPS)	800,000
Add: Number of additional common shares issued assuming conversion of bonds	250,000
Total	1,050,000
Recalculated EPS ($1,773,000 ÷ 1,050,000 shares)	$1.69

Since recalculated EPS is smaller compared with the previous calculation of EPS (EPS decreased from basic EPS of $2.05 to recalculated EPS of $1.69), the effect of converting the bonds is dilutive.

Because the incremental per-share effect of the convertible preferred shares (of $0.75) is lower than the recalculated $1.69, the next step is to recalculate EPS again, this time adding the incremental effect of converting the preferred shares:

6% Convertible Preferred Shares

Numerator from previous calculation	$1,773,000
Add: Preferred dividend avoided	162,000
Total	$1,935,000
Denominator from previous calculation	1,050,000
Add: Number of additional common shares issued assuming conversion of preferred shares	216,000
Total	1,266,000
Recalculated EPS ($1,935,000 ÷ 1,266,000 shares)	$1.53

Since the recalculated EPS amount is smaller than the previous recalculation of EPS (EPS decreased from $1.69 to $1.53), the effect of converting the preferred shares is dilutive. Therefore, diluted EPS is $1.53.

EXERCISE 17-4

PURPOSE: This exercise will illustrate more complex EPS calculations.

EPS Limited (EL) has the following capital structure at December 31, 2017:

8% convertible bonds, issued June 30, 2017, convertible into 2 pre–stock split common shares for every $100 bond	$1,000,000
10% bonds, due in annual instalments of $500,000 on January 1 of each year, beginning January 1, 2017	$5,000,000
4% cumulative preferred shares (125,000 outstanding)	$3,000,000
Common shares—400,000 outstanding	$4,000,000

The following additional information is available:

- During the year, the entire $1 million of previously issued 6% convertible bonds were converted into 20,000 common shares on June 30, 2017. The 8% convertible bonds were issued at the same time.
- On March 31, 2016, 25,000 warrants were issued for $2 each, allowing holders to purchase one pre-split common share per warrant for $50. All warrants are still outstanding at December 31, 2017.
- On September 30, 2017, there was a 2-for-1 stock split.
- At year end, EL common shares were trading at $28 per share, a $4 increase over market price per share at the beginning of the year (including the effect of retroactive adjustment due to the stock split).
- The income tax rate for 2017 is 30%.
- Net income after tax for the year ended December 31, 2017, was $1.1 million.

- It is EL's company policy to update all agreements after a stock split such that arrangements made prior to the stock split are adjusted to reflect the split. For instance, if a bond was convertible into two pre-split shares, after the stock split, the bond would be convertible into four post-split shares.

Instructions

(a) Calculate basic EPS for the year ended December 31, 2017.
(b) Calculate diluted EPS.

Solution to Exercise 17-4

(a) Net income − Preferred dividends = $1,100,000 − ($3,000,000 × 0.04) = $980,000

Weighted average number of common shares outstanding:

$$180,000^a \times \frac{12}{12} \quad = \quad 180,000$$

$$20,000 \times \frac{6}{12} \quad = \quad \underline{10,000}$$

$$190,000$$

$$\underline{\times 2}$$

$$\underline{380,000}$$

$^a(400,000 ÷ 2) − 20,000$

Basic EPS = $980,000 ÷ 380,000 = $2.58

(b) Diluted EPS should be calculated since there are dilutive securities outstanding. First, identify the dilutive securities, and determine the incremental per-share effect on EPS assuming the exercise or conversion of each:

- 8% convertible bonds
- 6% convertible bonds
- Warrants

Second, rank the dilutive securities from lowest to highest incremental effect per share.

Third, calculate diluted EPS.

8% Bonds

Impact on EPS numerator

$$\$1,000,000 \times 8\% \times (1 - 30\%) \times \frac{6}{12} = \$28,000$$

Had the bonds been converted, $28,000 in interest expense would have been avoided. This is an after-tax amount since basic EPS is based on net income after tax. This is also a half-year amount since the bonds were issued on June 30.

Impact on EPS denominator

$$20,000 \times \frac{6}{12} \times 2 = 20,000$$

$1,000,000 ÷ 100 × 2 = 20,000 common shares would have been issued; however, this amount is weighted since the bonds were issued on June 30. (If the bonds had been outstanding since the beginning of the year, there would have been no need to weight the number of shares.) This amount also takes the 2-for-1 stock split into account (2 pre-split common shares for every $100 bond).

Incremental effect per additional share

$$\$28,000 \div 20,000 = \$1.40$$

Since the incremental effect per additional share is less than basic EPS, the 8% bonds are dilutive.

6% Bonds

Impact on EPS numerator

$$\$1,000,000 \times 6\% \times (1 - 30\%) \times \frac{6}{12} = \$21,000$$

We must consider the effect of these bonds even though they were already converted during the year. The objective is to consider all actual and potential dilutive conversions as though they took place at the beginning of the year (unless the dilutive securities were issued during the year).

Impact on EPS denominator

$$20,000 \times 2 \times \frac{6}{12} = 20,000$$

This amount is adjusted for the stock split, and weighted because conversion took place on June 30.

Incremental effect per additional share

$$\$21,000 \div 20,000 = \$1.05$$

Since the incremental effect per additional share is less than basic EPS, the 6% bonds are considered dilutive.

Warrants

Impact on EPS denominator

Average market price per common share during the year is calculated as follows:

Calculate X, which is market price at January 1, 2017

$X + 4 = \$28$, so $X = \$24$

Average market price per common share during the year $= \dfrac{\$28 + \$24}{2} = \$26$

If the 25,000 warrants were exercised, the company would receive 25,000 × $50 = $1,250,000, which would be used to purchase shares in the open market (with purchase calculated at average market price per common share during the year).

$\$1,250,000 \div \$26 = 48,077$ shares

Therefore, EL would have a net increase of 1,923 in common shares outstanding (50,000 − 48,077), and the warrants are considered dilutive.

The final step is to calculate diluted EPS, starting with the instrument that has the most dilutive effect first.

	EPS Numerator	EPS Denominator	EPS
Basic	$ 980,000	380,000	$2.58
Warrants	0	1,923	
	980,000	381,923	2.57
6% bonds	21,000	20,000	
	1,001,000	401,923	2.49
8% bonds	28,000	20,000	
	1,029,000	421,923	2.44

EPS information would be presented at the bottom of the income statement. If comparative financial statements are reported, basic and diluted EPS would be shown for the current year and the comparative year(s). Remember that comparative year(s') EPS calculations would be adjusted to reflect the stock split.

ANALYSIS OF MULTIPLE-CHOICE QUESTIONS

Question

1. When calculating basic EPS, the numerator should be adjusted for:
   a. all dividends declared in the year.
   b. dividends declared in the year for preferred shares only.

c. dividends declared in the year for the current year only.

d. dividends declared in the year for all preferred shares and current year undeclared dividends on cumulative preferred shares.

EXPLANATION: Care should be taken to deduct current year undeclared dividends on cumulative preferred shares, as well as any other preferred share dividends declared in the year. (Solution = d.)

Question

2. Wong Corporation reported net income of $780,000 for 2017. During 2017, a dividend of $150,000 was declared on preferred shares and another dividend of $120,000 was declared on common shares. There were no changes in shares outstanding during 2017 (120,000 common shares were outstanding and 60,000 preferred shares were outstanding). There were no potentially dilutive securities outstanding. EPS to be reported for 2017 is:

a. $6.50.

b. $5.25.

c. $4.33.

d. $4.25.

e. none of the above.

EXPLANATION: Write down the formula for basic EPS. Solve using the data provided.

$$\frac{\text{Net income} - \text{Preferred dividends}}{\text{Weighted average number of common shares outstanding}}$$

$$= \frac{(\$780,000 - \$150,000)}{120,000} = \$5.25$$

(Solution = b.)

Question

3. Which of the following does not require retroactive adjustment when calculating the weighted average number of common shares outstanding for basic EPS?

a. A stock split

b. A reverse split

c. A stock dividend

d. A share conversion

EXPLANATION: If a transaction does not change each shareholder's relative interest in the company's earnings and net assets, retroactive adjustment is required when calculating the weighted average number of common shares outstanding for basic EPS. A share conversion would be accounted for prospectively since it would affect each shareholder's interest in earnings and net assets. (Solution = d.)

Question

4. Compton Corporation has the following data for 2017:

January 1, 2017	Common shares outstanding	600,000
May 1, 2017	Common shares issued	90,000
July 1, 2017	Treasury shares purchased	50,000
October 1, 2017	Common shares issued as a result of a 60% stock dividend	384,000

The number of shares to be used in calculating EPS for 2017 is:
   a. 1,074,000.
   b. 614,400.
   c. 1,016,000.
   d. 524,000.

EXPLANATION: Follow the steps listed in **Illustration 17-2** to calculate the weighted average number of common shares outstanding for 2017.

Date		**Weighted Shares**
1/1/17	$600,000 \times \frac{12}{12} =$	600,000
5/1/17	$90,000 \times \frac{8}{12} =$	60,000
	New balance	660,000
7/1/17	$50,000 \times \frac{6}{12} =$	(25,000)
	New balance	635,000
10/1/17	60% stock dividend	$\times 160\%$ [a]
	New balance	1,016,000
		(Solution = c.)

[a]The appropriate multiple for a stock dividend is 100% plus the percentage used in the dividend. Thus, 100% + 60% stock dividend = 160% multiple.

Question

5. Refer to Question 4 above. The number of common shares actually outstanding at the end of 2017 is:

a. 1,124,000.

b. 1,074,000.

c. 1,024,000.

d. 384,000.

EXPLANATION:

Date		Actual Shares
1/1/17	Balance	600,000
5/1/17	Issued for assets	90,000
	New balance	690,000
7/1/17	Acquired for treasury	(50,000)
	New balance	640,000
10/1/17	60% stock dividend	384,000
	New balance	1,024,000

(Solution = c.)

Question

6. At December 31, 2016, Pearl Company had 250,000 common shares and 10,000 6%, $100 stated value cumulative preferred shares outstanding. No dividends were declared on either preferred or common shares in 2016 or 2017. On February 10, 2018, prior to the issuance of financial statements for the year ended December 31, 2017, Pearl declared a 100% stock split on its common shares. Net income for 2017 was $500,000. In its 2017 financial statements, Pearl's 2017 EPS should read:

a. $2.00.

b. $1.76.

c. $1.00.

d. $0.88.

EXPLANATION:

$$\frac{(\$500,000 - (10,000 \times 6\% \times \$100))}{(250,000 \times 2)} = \$0.88$$

Current year dividend on **cumulative** preferred shares is deducted in the EPS numerator, whether declared or not. However, dividends in arrears (prior years' dividends) do not affect calculation of EPS. Stock dividends and stock splits are treated retroactively for all periods presented, even if they occur partway through the year or after the end of the current year (but before the financial statements are issued). (Solution = d.)

Question

7. Tamworth Inc. had 225,000 common shares issued and outstanding at December 31, 2016. On July 1, 2017, an additional 225,000 common shares were issued for cash. Tamworth also had stock options outstanding at the beginning and end of 2017, which allow the holders to purchase 80,000 common shares at $18 per share. Tamworth's average market price per share was $16 during 2017. Tamworth's market price per share was $20 at December 31, 2017. What is the number of shares that should be used in the denominator of EPS for the year ended December 31, 2017?

    a. 337,500

    b. 417,500

    c. 450,000

    d. 470,000

EXPLANATION: Use the treasury stock method to determine the number of shares to be used in calculating diluted EPS. **However,** only make assumptions about the exercising of options when the effects are dilutive. A quick test to determine whether these options are dilutive or antidilutive is to compare average market price per share ($16) with exercise price ($18). Average market price per share is not higher; so in applying the treasury stock method, assumed exercise of the options would have an antidilutive effect. Therefore, the exercise of options should not be assumed. Only the weighted average number of common shares actually outstanding should be used in calculating EPS:

Jan. 1	Shares outstanding: $225,000 \times \frac{12}{12}$	=	225,000
July 1	Issued for assets: $225,000 \times \frac{6}{12}$	=	112,500
	Weighted average number of common shares outstanding	=	337,500

(Solution = a.)

You could calculate basic EPS, and calculate diluted EPS assuming exercise of the options and application of the treasury stock method. The $1.44 million in exercise proceeds would be assumed to be used to buy shares in the open market (at $16 average market price per share) for return to the treasury. This would result in the following adjustments to the EPS denominator:

● Add 80,000 shares due to the assumed exercise of options.

● Deduct 90,000 ($1.44 million ÷ $16 per share) shares due to the assumed purchase of shares in the open market for return to the treasury.

● The net result of these assumptions is a **decrease** in the number of shares used to calculate diluted EPS, which has an antidilutive effect on EPS. Thus, in this example, the exercise of options should not be assumed in calculating diluted EPS.

Question

8. Refer to the facts of Question 7 above. If Tamworth's average market price per share was $20 rather than $16 during 2017, what is the number of shares that should be used in calculating diluted EPS for the year ended December 31, 2017?

   a. 522,000
   b. 409,500
   c. 377,500
   d. 345,500

EXPLANATION: Use the treasury stock method to determine the number of shares to be used in calculating diluted EPS. The weighted average number of common shares actually outstanding is 337,500 (see the explanation to Question 7 above for this calculation). If the average market price per share was $20, the average market price per share ($20) would exceed the exercise price of the options ($18), and the assumed exercise of the options would have a dilutive effect on EPS. The number of shares to be used in calculating diluted EPS would be as follows:

Weighted average number of common shares outstanding for basic EPS	337,500
Shares assumed issued upon exercise of options	80,000
Shares assumed purchased for the treasury ($1.44 million ÷ $20 per share)	(72,000)
Number of shares to be used in calculating diluted EPS	345,500
	(Solution = d.)

A comparison of 345,500 shares (the number of shares to be used in calculating diluted EPS determined using the treasury stock method) with the weighted average number of common shares outstanding for basic EPS (337,500) also indicates a dilutive effect on EPS.

Question

9. A convertible bond issue should be included in calculating diluted EPS if the effect of its inclusion is:

	Dilutive	**Antidilutive**
a.	Yes	Yes
b.	Yes	No
c.	No	Yes
d.	No	No

EXPLANATION: A convertible security is a potentially dilutive security. All potentially dilutive securities that have a dilutive effect on EPS should be included in calculating diluted EPS. No potentially dilutive securities that have an antidilutive effect on EPS should be included in calculating diluted EPS. (Solution = b.)

Question

10. Which of the following are never considered dilutive securities?
    a. Debt that is convertible into preferred shares
    b. Convertible preferred shares
    c. Stock options
    d. Stock warrants

EXPLANATION: Dilution pertains to the effect on the number of potential common shares and the act of diluting individual common shareholders' proportionate interests in the entity, as well as in their share of the earnings. Therefore, convertible preferred shares, stock options, and stock warrants are potentially dilutive because if converted or exercised, they result in more common shares outstanding and (usually) lower earnings per common share. (Solution = a.)

Chapter 18

Income Taxes

OVERVIEW

Most revenue transactions are taxable (and therefore increase taxable income) in the current period or in a future period. As well, most expense transactions are deductible for tax purposes (and therefore decrease taxable income) in the current period or in a future period. Under IFRS's temporary difference approach, and ASPE's future income taxes method, interperiod tax allocation is applied when a revenue or expense item is reported on the income statement for financial reporting purposes in one period, but included in taxable income for tax purposes in a different period. Interperiod tax allocation refers to recognition of tax effects in the accounting period when the related transactions or events are recognized for financial reporting purposes, usually resulting in recognition of a deferred (or future income) tax liability and/or a deferred (or future income) tax asset on the statement of financial position. After proper interperiod tax allocation, the income tax consequences of revenues and expenses are reflected on the income statement in the same year that the related revenues and expenses are reported on the income statement, regardless of whether or not those revenues and expenses affect the same year's current income tax payable.

STUDY STEPS

Understanding the Nature of Income Taxes

Accounting Income versus Taxable Income

Income tax payable is calculated based on income as defined by the Income Tax Act, or **taxable income**. Accounting for income taxes is complicated because income as defined by GAAP (ASPE or IFRS), or **accounting income**, usually does not equal taxable income. Accounting income is calculated according to ASPE or IFRS accounting principles or standards to provide information that is useful for decision-making, whereas taxable income is calculated according to rules and regulations stated in the Income Tax Act. The Income Tax Act is specific and rules-based regarding the calculation of taxable income. The federal government does this for various reasons, such as to stimulate spending in certain areas by allowing certain expenditures to be deductible immediately, to discourage certain expenditures (such as club dues) by disallowing their deduction in the calculation of taxable income, or to increase government tax revenues.

Because income tax actually paid to the government per the tax return is based on current year taxable income, which often does not include all the tax effects of every revenue or expense amount included in the current year income statement, a deferred or future income tax expense or benefit is often recognized on the income statement to reflect the income tax consequences of revenues and expenses that were not included in current year taxable income. Recognition of a deferred or future income tax expense or benefit (and recognition of a deferred or future income tax liability, or a deferred or future income tax asset) is called the **temporary difference approach** under IFRS, and the **future income taxes method** under ASPE. Under ASPE, an entity is not required to apply the future income taxes method; instead, it may choose to apply the simpler taxes payable method. However, under IFRS, an entity is required to apply the temporary difference approach.

Interperiod versus Intraperiod Tax Allocation

Interperiod tax allocation refers to recognition of tax effects in the accounting period when the related transactions or events are recognized for financial reporting purposes, usually resulting in recognition of a deferred or future income tax liability and/or a deferred or future income tax asset on the statement of financial position. In contrast, **intraperiod tax allocation** refers to allocation of income tax expense or benefit between different areas or lines on the income or other financial statement. On the income statement, this allocation includes such things as presenting income tax expense on income from continuing operations separately, reporting items in discontinued operations on a net-of-tax basis, and reporting items in other comprehensive income on a net-of-tax basis. On the statement of changes in equity or the statement of retained earnings, this allocation includes such things as reporting a prior period adjustment on a net-of-tax basis. This chapter focuses on interperiod tax allocation since it is more complex than intraperiod tax allocation.

Special Tax Rules Relating to Loss Years

If a company's deductible expenses and losses exceed its taxable revenues and gains in a year, the company reports a **loss for income tax purposes**, or a **tax loss**, and does not pay income tax in the year. Furthermore, the company may refile the tax returns of one or more previous years in which it earned taxable income, and deduct the tax loss from those years' taxable income. The company can then recover some or all of the income tax paid in those years (the difference between income tax paid in those years and income tax payable based on revised taxable income as a result of the tax loss carryback). The tax loss may also be carried forward to offset and reduce future taxable income, thereby reducing income tax payable in a future period (or periods).

The company has a benefit to the extent that it can recover income tax paid in a previous year or reduce income tax payable in a future year. According to the Income Tax Act, a company may carry the tax loss back three years (called the **loss carryback period**) and/or forward 20 years (called the **loss carryforward period**).

If taxable income was earned in one or more of the three previous years, the tax loss is often carried back in order to recover taxes already paid (and obtain the cash refund sooner). However, the company may choose to carry the tax loss forward (for example, if the tax loss is small, or if future income tax rates are expected to be higher than previous years' income tax rates).

Becoming Proficient in Related Calculations

Accounting for income taxes is theoretically and technically complex. In addition, the terminology can be difficult to grasp.

Therefore, you should devote a significant amount of time to studying the exercises and illustrations in this chapter, which are structured to take you through the learning process gradually. As with most accounting topics, a solid understanding of the fundamental concepts will make it easier to understand the complex concepts.

TIPS ON CHAPTER TOPICS

- The term **accounting income (loss)** refers to the difference between revenues earned and expenses incurred (other than income tax expense) on an accrual basis income statement in a given year. The term **taxable income (loss)** refers to the difference between taxable revenues and deductible expenses on a tax return in a given year. **Accounting income** appears on the income statement with the caption "Income before income taxes." Accounting income is often referred to as **income for book purposes, pre-tax financial income**, or **income for financial reporting purposes**.

- An excess of deductible expenses over taxable revenues on an entity's tax return is called a **tax loss**. The Income Tax Act provides that a tax loss may be carried back three years or forward 20 years. Although loss carryback is

(continued)

optional, most textbook questions will assume or require full loss carryback to the extent possible.

- **Income tax payable for a period** is the amount of **current income tax expense** and is determined by applying the provisions of the Income Tax Act to taxable income (or loss) for the period. If a current year tax loss is carried back, the entity will have an **income tax receivable** (rather than an income tax payable), which results in a **current tax benefit** (or a recovery of income tax) on the income statement.

- Under ASPE, an entity can choose to apply either the **taxes payable method** (and calculate only current income tax expense) or the **future income taxes method** (and calculate current income tax expense as well as future income tax expense). The future income taxes method under ASPE is also known as the **asset and liability approach** and the **temporary difference approach**. Under IFRS, this method is known as the **temporary difference approach**, and it is required. Note that it and the future income taxes method under ASPE are almost identical.

- A revenue or expense amount that appears on an income statement for financial reporting purposes or a tax return in one year but **never** appears on the other report is called a **permanent difference**. Future income tax expense is **never** recorded for permanent differences because these differences will never reverse (that is, they will never cause a future taxable amount or a future deductible amount). Examples of permanent differences appear below in **Illustration 18-1**.

- A **temporary difference** is a difference between the reported amount (book value or carrying amount) of an asset or liability for financial reporting purposes, and the tax base of the asset or liability, which will result in taxable or deductible amounts in future years when the reported amount of the asset or liability is recovered or settled. Temporary differences that will result in taxable amounts when the related assets are recovered are often called **taxable temporary differences**. Temporary differences that will result in deductible amounts when the related assets or liabilities are settled are often called **deductible temporary differences**.

- Under IFRS, a taxable temporary difference gives rise to a **deferred tax liability**, a deductible temporary difference gives rise to a **deferred tax asset**, and the related expense is referred to as a **deferred tax expense (benefit)**. Under ASPE, a taxable temporary difference gives rise to a **future income tax liability**, a deductible temporary difference gives rise to a **future income tax asset**, and the related expense is referred to as a **future income tax expense (benefit)**.

- Most temporary differences are caused by reporting the same revenues or expenses in different periods for financial reporting purposes and for income tax purposes. Examples of temporary differences appear below in **Illustration 18-2**.

- **Deferred tax expense (or benefit) for a period results from changes in the deferred tax asset account or deferred tax liability account.** A **deferred tax expense** results from an increase in a deferred tax liability or a decrease in a deferred tax asset. A **deferred tax benefit** results from an increase in a deferred tax asset or a decrease in a deferred tax liability. This is true because the other half of a journal entry dealing with a deferred tax asset or a deferred tax liability (both statement of financial position accounts) is a deferred tax expense or deferred tax benefit (both income statement accounts). Deferred tax expense **increases** total income tax expense for the period. Deferred tax benefit **reduces** total income tax expense for the period.

- **Deferred tax benefit** is an income statement account to which credits to (or decreases in) deferred tax expense are recorded. Deferred tax benefit is considered a tax income account.

- **Total income tax expense (or benefit)** is the sum of **current income tax expense (or benefit)** and **deferred tax expense (or benefit)**. Income tax expense is often referred to as "provision for income tax." Hence, provision for income tax usually includes both a current portion and a future portion. The meaning of the word "current" used in the context of provision for income taxes bears **no relationship** to the meaning of the word "current" used in the context of the statement of financial position classification of deferred taxes.

- A reversible (or reversing or timing) difference in the current period that causes an increase in a deferred tax liability, or a decrease in a deferred tax asset, will also cause a debit (charge) to deferred tax expense on the income statement. A reversing difference in the current period that causes a decrease in a deferred tax liability, or an increase in a deferred tax asset, will also cause a credit to a deferred tax benefit on the income statement.

- Pay close attention to terminology in this chapter and be careful not to confuse the many terms introduced. When describing deferred taxes from a statement of financial position perspective, the reference is to deferred tax asset and/or deferred tax liability. When discussing the effects of deferred taxes on the income statement, the reference is to deferred tax expense and/or deferred tax benefit. There is a correlation, however, because changes in a deferred tax asset and/or a deferred tax liability on the statement of financial position result in changes in deferred tax expense and/or deferred tax benefit on the income statement.

- To be recognized as assets and liabilities, a deferred tax asset and a deferred tax liability must meet the definition of an asset and a liability, respectively, as set out in the **conceptual framework**. A deferred tax asset should only be recognized if it is an economic resource that is capable of producing cash flows. A **deferred tax asset** is only capable of producing future cash inflows or reducing future cash outflows to the extent that the entity will earn enough taxable income in the future against which the related temporary difference can be applied.

- Under ASPE, a future tax asset may be recognized for the future tax effects of all deductible temporary differences, unused tax losses, and income tax reductions. Under ASPE, companies can choose to use a separate **valuation allowance** to bring the future tax asset to an amount that is more likely than not to be realized in future. However, under IFRS, a valuation allowance is not used; rather, the deferred tax asset is only **recognized at an amount at which realization of the deferred tax asset will be probable**.

- Under ASPE, future tax asset and future tax liability amounts are broken down between **current and non-current** assets and liabilities according to the classification of the asset or liability that gave rise to each future tax asset or future tax liability. (If no particular asset or liability gave rise to the future tax asset or future tax liability, classification is based on when the temporary difference is

(continued)

expected to reverse.) One net current and one net non-current amount are then determined. The current portion of the net future tax asset or net future tax liability is reported as current on the statement of financial position, and the non-current portion of the net future tax asset or net future tax liability is reported as non-current on the statement of financial position. However, under IFRS, all deferred tax asset and deferred tax liability amounts are classified as **non-current**.

● A corporation often pays estimated tax payments (instalments) during the year and may charge the payments to an account called Income Tax Receivable. The balance of this account is used to offset the balance of Income Tax Payable for financial reporting purposes. The net amount is classified as a current asset if the receivable account has the larger balance. The net amount is classified as a current liability if the payable account has the larger balance.

● The **effective tax rate** for a period is calculated by dividing total income tax expense on the income statement by income before income taxes on the income statement. The effective tax rate for a period may differ from the statutory tax rate (the rate set by government legislation) for the same period because of (a) permanent differences, and/or (b) changes in deferred tax assets and/or deferred tax liabilities as a result of differences between the current statutory tax rate and future statutory tax rates. A reconciliation of the effective tax rate to the statutory tax rate is required to be disclosed under IFRS.

● The deferred tax asset and deferred tax liability are **not** discounted amounts.

● **Future deductible amounts** are often called **future tax deductible amounts**.

ILLUSTRATION 18-1

Examples of Permanent Differences

1. **Revenues or gains that are recognized for financial reporting purposes but are never included in taxable income:**
   - Dividends received from other taxable Canadian corporations
   - Proceeds from life insurance policies carried by the company on key officers or employees

2. **Expenses or losses that are recognized for financial reporting purposes but are never deductible for tax purposes:**
   - Golf and social club dues
   - Premiums paid on life insurance policies carried by the company on key officers or employees (where the company is the beneficiary)
   - Certain fines and penalties

3. **Revenues or gains that are included in taxable income but are never recognized for financial reporting purposes:**
   - No examples exist at the current time.

4. **Expenses or losses or other deductions that are deductible for tax purposes but are never recognized for financial reporting purposes:**
   - Depletion allowance of natural resources in excess of their cost

Illustration 18-2 187

ILLUSTRATION 18-2

Examples of Reversing (or Timing) Differences

1. **Revenues or gains that are included in taxable income in a period after they are included in accounting income (or recognized for financial reporting purposes):**

    *   An example is use of the accrual method in accounting for instalment sales for financial reporting purposes, and use of the cash instalment method in calculating taxable income for tax purposes. (Note also that this situation causes the reported amount of the account receivable asset on the statement of financial position to be higher than its tax basis, which will result in taxable amounts in future year(s) when the asset is recovered—in the years when cash is collected.)

    *   Other examples include:

        o   use of the percentage-of-completion method in accounting for revenue recognition of long-term contracts for financial reporting purposes, and use of the zero-profit method (under IFRS) or the completed-contract method (under ASPE) in calculating taxable income for tax purposes;

        o   accrual of revenues in the period earned for financial reporting purposes, and inclusion of revenues in taxable income as cash is collected; and

        o   recognition of unrealized holding gains for financial reporting purposes, and inclusion of gains in taxable income in the year they are realized.

2. **Expenses or losses that are deductible for tax purposes in a period after they are included in accounting income (or recognized for financial reporting purposes):**

    *   An example is accrual of an expense or loss (such as litigation accrual) for financial reporting purposes, which is only deductible for tax purposes when it is settled. (Note also that this situation causes the reported amount of the liability on the statement of financial position to exceed its tax basis of zero. This will result in deductible amounts in future year(s) when the litigation liability is settled.)

    *   Other examples include:

        o   product warranty expenses and liabilities;

        o   estimated losses and liabilities related to discontinued operations or restructurings;

        o   accrued pension expenses and the pension liability; and

        o   holding or impairment losses on investments or other assets and the carrying amount of such assets.

3. **Revenues or gains that are included in taxable income in a period before they are included in accounting income (or recognized for financial reporting purposes):**

    *   An example is revenue received in advance for rent or subscriptions. For tax purposes, the revenue may have to be included in taxable income in the

period when the cash is received; however, the revenue is not included in accounting income until it is earned. (Note also that this situation causes the reported amount of the liability, such as unearned revenue, to exceed its tax basis of zero. This will result in deductible amounts in future year(s) when the liability is settled.)

- Other examples include:
  - o sale and leaseback gains, including a deferral of profit for financial reporting purposes that would be reported as realized for tax purposes; and
  - o royalties received in advance.

4. **Expenses or losses that are deductible for tax purposes in a period before they are included in accounting income (or recognized for financial reporting purposes):**

- An example is depreciating an asset faster for tax purposes (according to the capital cost allowance, or CCA rules) than for accounting purposes. (Note also that this causes the PP&E asset's reported value on the statement of financial position to exceed its tax basis or UCC. This will result in taxable amounts in future years when depreciation expense exceeds the CCA or when the asset is sold.)

- Other examples include:
  - o property and depletable resources that are depreciated/depleted faster for tax purposes than for financial reporting purposes;
  - o deductible pension funding that exceeds the pension expense that is recognized; and
  - o prepaid expenses that are deducted in calculating taxable income in the period when they are paid, but are expensed in the income statement when the benefits are received.

ILLUSTRATION 18-3

Reconciliation of Accounting Income to Taxable Income

Accounting Income

+/− **Permanent Differences:**
− Revenues recognized in accounting income this period, but never included in taxable income
+ Expenses recognized in accounting income this period, but never deductible for tax purposes
+ Revenues included in taxable income this period, but never recognized in accounting income
− Expenses deducted for tax purposes this period, but never recognized in accounting income

Illustration 18-3 189

+/− Originating Reversible (Timing) Differences:

− Revenues recognized in accounting income this period, but to be included in taxable income in a later period

+ Expenses recognized in accounting income this period, but to be deducted for tax purposes in a later period

+ Revenues included in taxable income this period, but to be recognized in accounting income in a later period

− Expenses deducted for tax purposes this period, but to be deducted from accounting income in a later period

+/− Reversing Reversible (Timing) Differences:

− Revenues recognized in accounting income this period, but included in taxable income in an earlier period

+ Expenses recognized in accounting income this period, but deducted for tax purposes in an earlier period

+ Revenues included in taxable income this period, but recognized in accounting income in an earlier period

− Expenses deducted for tax purposes this period, but recognized as an expense in accounting income in an earlier period

= *Taxable Income*

- **No** deferred tax expense or deferred tax benefit is recognized for permanent differences because they will not have any future tax consequences.

- Timing differences that **originate** in the current period and give rise to **future taxable amounts** are **deducted** from accounting income in the reconciliation of accounting income to taxable income. These differences will also cause a **deferred tax liability** account to be recognized on the statement of financial position in the current period, representing the deferred tax expense on those future taxable amounts.

- Timing differences that **originate** in the current period and give rise to **future deductible amounts** are **added** to accounting income in the reconciliation of accounting income to taxable income. These differences will also cause a **deferred tax asset** account to be recognized on the statement of financial position in the current period, representing the deferred tax benefit of those future deductible amounts.

- Refer to **Illustration 18-1** for examples of permanent differences; refer to **Illustration 18-2** for examples of reversible or timing differences. The four types of examples addressed in **Illustration 18-1** and **Illustration 18-2** appear in the same order as they are referenced in this illustration. Thus, the first type of permanent difference listed in **Illustration 18-3** corresponds to the first type of permanent difference described in **Illustration 18-1**. Also, the first type of reversible/timing difference listed in **Illustration 18-3** corresponds to the first type of reversible/timing difference described in **Illustration 18-2**.

- This reconciliation will help you in solving some homework assignments and exam questions, but it is not relevant in all situations. The timing differences included in this reconciliation are **only** the ones that originated in or are reversed in the current year. This reconciliation can be used to solve for taxable income, accounting income, and changes in the related temporary differences on the statement of financial position in the current year. This reconciliation does **not** identify the temporary differences that exist at year end.

CASE 18-1

PURPOSE: This case provides practice in distinguishing between reversible or timing differences and permanent differences. It also provides practice in distinguishing between differences that will be taxable or deductible in the future.

In reviewing a client's records, you find the items listed below pertaining to the current year.

Instructions

Indicate whether each item involves,

(a) a reversing difference that will result in future deductible amounts,
(b) a reversing difference that will result in future taxable amounts, or
(c) a permanent difference.

_____   1. For some depreciable assets, a 20% declining-balance method was used for depreciation for tax purposes, and a 10-year straight-line method was used for depreciation for accounting purposes.

_____   2. The client is a landlord and collected some rents in advance.

_____   3. An instalment sale of an investment was accrued for accounting purposes, but is taxable on an instalment (cash) basis for tax purposes.

_____   4. Dividends were received from taxable Canadian corporations.

_____   5. Costs of guarantees and warranties were estimated and accrued for accounting purposes.

_____   6. Fines and penalties for nonpayment of income tax were deducted from accounting income.

_____   7. Proceeds were received from a life insurance company due to the death of a key officer. (The company carries a life insurance policy on key officers.)

_____   8. For some assets, straight-line depreciation was used for both accounting purposes and tax purposes, but the assets' lives are shorter for tax purposes.

_____   9. Expenses incurred for golf and social club dues were expensed in accounting income.

_____   10. Estimated losses on pending lawsuits and claims were accrued for accounting purposes. These losses will be deductible for tax purposes in the year(s) they are settled.

_____   11. An intangible asset is amortized over 20 years for accounting purposes and over 15 years for tax purposes.

_____   12. The company recognized a loss on its income statement due to a decline in the fair value of its investments in marketable equity securities.

_____ 13. The company has a construction division that uses the percentage-of-completion method for accounting purposes and the zero-profit method for tax purposes.

_____ 14. The company has made a formal plan to discontinue a segment of its business. A loss of $500,000 is expected on disposal of the segment's assets.

_____ 15. Prepaid advertising is deferred and amortized for accounting purposes and deducted as an expense when paid for tax purposes.

_____ 16. The company owns a patent and allows another company to use the rights embodied in the patent in exchange for royalty payments, which are collected in advance.

_____ 17. A gain on a sale and leaseback transaction during the year was treated as realized for tax purposes. The gain is required to be deferred and amortized over the term of the lease for accounting purposes.

_____ 18. The amount contributed to the company pension plan this year was less than the amount expensed for accounting purposes. Only the amount contributed is deductible on this year's tax return.

_____ 19. The company collected subscriptions in advance for a magazine it publishes.

_____ 20. An accrual for post-retirement benefits other than pensions was recorded for accounting purposes. This amount will be deducted for tax purposes in the year(s) these benefits are paid.

_____ 21. Capital assets were acquired in the current year. Depreciation expense reported for accounting purposes exceeded the capital cost allowance reported for tax purposes in the current year.

_____ 22. An accrued revenue was reported on the income statement in the current year; the revenue will be taxable when it is collected.

Solution to Case 18-1

1. (b)

2. (a)

3. (b) Use of the accrual method for accounting purposes causes the entire profit from the instalment sale to be reflected in the income statement in the period of sale. Use of the instalment (cash) method for tax purposes causes the profit to be allocated or taxed over the collection period (as cash is collected). The amount of profit taxed in a period is proportionate to the amount of revenue collected in the period.

4. (c) Dividends between taxable Canadian corporations flow tax-free.

5. (a)

6. (c)

7. (c)

8. (b)

9. (c)

10. (a)

11. (b) When an asset is amortized or depreciated faster for tax purposes than it is amortized or depreciated for accounting purposes, more amortization or CCA is deducted in determining taxable income in the current period. This means that the excess CCA, for example, deducted in the current year will have to be added to taxable incomes in the future. That is, this results in net future taxable amounts.

12. (a) This unrealized holding loss is not deductible for tax purposes until it is realized (in the future period in which the securities are sold).

13. (b)

14. (a) This loss is not deductible for tax purposes until it is realized.

15. (b)

16. (a) The royalty receipts are included in taxable income in the period they are received.

17. (a) The gain is generally deferred for accounting purposes but included in current taxable income for tax purposes. (Under IFRS, the gain is recognized over the lease term. Under ASPE, the gain is amortized on the same basis as the depreciation of the leased asset.)

18. (a)

19. (a) Subscriptions collected in advance are included in taxable income in the period received. The related revenue is deferred for accounting purposes until it is earned.

20. (a)

21. (a)

22. (b)

ILLUSTRATION 18-4

Journal Entry to Record Income Taxes

To record income taxes, the best approach is to perform the following steps in order.

1. **Calculate income tax payable for the current period.** This is always based on the amount of taxable income and the tax rate in the current year. This amount is recorded with a debit to current income tax expense and a credit to income tax payable. If there is a tax loss in the current year, the benefit of a loss carryback is recorded with a debit to income tax receivable and a credit to current income tax benefit.

Illustration 18-4   193

2. **Calculate the change required in the deferred tax asset and/or deferred tax liability.** The balance of the deferred tax asset and/or deferred tax liability account at the statement of financial position date must be determined. This may require the preparation of a schedule. The appropriate balance of the deferred tax asset and/or deferred tax liability represents the future tax consequences of the (cumulative) temporary differences and tax loss carryforwards existing at the statement of financial position date. The difference between the correct ending balance at year end and the unadjusted beginning balance of a deferred tax account is equal to the deferred tax expense or benefit, depending on whether a debit or a credit is required. The adjustment brings the deferred tax asset or liability account to the correct balance, with the same amount recognized as the deferred tax expense or benefit.

3. **Record income tax expense.** Total income tax expense is the total of the current income tax expense (or benefit) and the deferred tax expense (or benefit). The current expense (benefit) is offset by a credit (debit) to income tax payable (receivable).

- A temporary difference is equal to the cumulative amount of timing differences that still exist at year end between an asset or liability's carrying amount in the accounts and its tax value or tax base.

- In calculating deferred taxes at a statement of financial position date, the amount of temporary differences must be determined. Information on when each temporary difference originated is **not** required; some or all of the differences could have originated in years prior to the current period. Information about the individual future years when each temporary difference is expected to reverse is generally **not** needed if the statutory tax rate is the same flat rate year after year going forward. However, if the future statutory tax rates have been enacted and will differ from the current rate, information about the individual future years when each temporary difference is expected to reverse **is** needed. Thus, if a single statutory tax rate applies to all future years, an aggregate calculation of the deferred tax asset/liability is appropriate. However, if different statutory tax rates apply to individual future years, a schedule of when the temporary differences will become taxable or deductible amounts is required, including a separate calculation for each future year affected.

- In determining the future income tax consequences of temporary differences (Step 2), a phased-in change in statutory tax rates requires a schedule to be prepared showing each future year in which existing temporary differences will reverse, resulting in taxable or deductible amounts. In determining the applicable statutory tax rate, you must make assumptions about whether the entity will report taxable income or a tax loss in each future year affected by the reversal of existing temporary differences. When calculating income tax payable or receivable in the future due to existing temporary differences, the provisions of the tax law and enacted statutory tax rates for the relevant future years must be applied. The following guidelines are used to determine the applicable statutory tax rate:

  1. If taxable income is expected in a year when a future taxable or deductible amount is scheduled to reverse, use the enacted statutory tax rate for the future year to calculate the related deferred tax liability or deferred tax asset.

  (continued)

2. If a tax loss is expected in a year when a future taxable or deductible amount is scheduled to reverse, use the enacted statutory tax rate of the prior year to which the tax loss would be carried back or the enacted statutory tax rate of a future year to which the tax loss carryforward would be applied, whichever is appropriate, in order to calculate the related deferred tax liability or deferred tax asset.

● It is more straightforward to prepare separate journal entries to record current income taxes and deferred income taxes. With separate journal entries, you could perform Step 1 above and record the results with either a credit to income tax payable (if there is taxable income in the current period) or a debit to income tax receivable (if there is a tax loss in the current period and a loss carryback is applied). The other half of this first journal entry would be a debit or credit (whichever is needed to make the entry balance) to current income tax expense or current income tax benefit. A second journal entry would be recorded for the results of Step 2 above. In this journal entry, a debit or credit would be recorded to the deferred tax asset or deferred tax liability account to bring it to its correct year-end balance on the statement of financial position. The other half of this second journal entry would be either a debit or credit to deferred tax expense or deferred tax benefit, as appropriate, to make the entry balance. Step 2 can be repeated (and another journal entry recorded) if there is more than one reason for having temporary differences and separate entries are preferred. Thus, if the entity has three types of temporary differences, Step 2 might be performed three times, making a total of four single journal entries to record income taxes for the period. This approach to recording separate entries for income taxes is illustrated in parts (a) and (b) of the Solution to **Exercise 18-1**.

CASE 18-2

PURPOSE: This case examines the temporary difference approach and the steps in the calculation of the deferred tax assets and deferred tax liabilities at the reporting date.

The objectives of accounting for income taxes are to recognize (a) the amount of income tax payable or receivable for the current year, and (b) the amount of deferred tax liabilities and/or deferred tax assets that arise due to the future tax consequences of transactions and events that have been recognized in an entity's financial statements and tax returns.

Instructions

(a) If a revenue item is reported on the income statement in 2017, but is included on the tax return in 2018, explain whether the related income tax effect should be reflected on the income statement in 2017 or 2018, and explain why.

(b) Explain whether the temporary difference approach to accounting for deferred taxes focuses on proper valuation of assets and liabilities (and therefore the statement of financial position) or on income determination (and therefore the income statement).

(c) List the steps required in the calculation of deferred tax liabilities and deferred tax assets.

Solution to Case 18-2

(a) The income tax consequences of a transaction or event are recognized in the same period that the transaction or event is recognized in the financial statements. This is the essence of the temporary difference approach. Thus, the income tax effect of revenue recognized in 2017 should also be recognized on the income statement in 2017, even if payment of the related income tax is deferred to a later year.

(b) At any reporting date, the correct balance of the deferred tax account is calculated by multiplying the future taxable and deductible amounts stemming from temporary differences existing at the statement of financial position date by the applicable statutory tax rate(s). As such, a deferred tax liability (or a deferred tax asset) is recognized representing the likely income tax effect of existing temporary differences in future years. The amount of deferred tax expense (or benefit) recognized on the income statement is determined by the change in the deferred tax liability and/or deferred tax asset balance from the previous statement of financial position date to the current reporting date. Therefore, deferred tax expense (or benefit) is a residual figure, often called a "plug" figure. Under IFRS, a deferred tax asset is recognized only to the extent that it is probable that the tax benefit will be realized in the future. Under ASPE, if a future income tax asset is recognized, it may be offset by a valuation allowance to bring the future income tax asset to an amount that is more likely than not to be realized in the future. Therefore, both the temporary difference approach and the future income taxes method focus on proper valuation of assets and liabilities (and therefore the statement of financial position).

(c) The steps required in the calculation of deferred tax liabilities and deferred tax assets are as follows:

1. Identify (a) the types and amounts of existing temporary differences, and (b) the nature and amount of any tax loss available for carryforward and the remaining length of the carryforward period.

2. Measure the total deferred tax liability resulting from taxable temporary differences, using the applicable statutory tax rates.

3. Measure the total deferred tax asset resulting from deductible temporary differences and tax loss carryforwards, using the applicable statutory tax rates.

4. Ensure the proper valuation of deferred tax assets or future income tax assets. Under IFRS, recognize a deferred tax asset only to the extent that it is probable that the benefits will be realized in the future. Under ASPE, apply the **"more likely than not"** rule by offsetting the total future income tax asset by a valuation allowance to bring the future income tax asset to an amount that is more likely than not to be realized in the future. ASPE permits a choice between using a valuation allowance and determining only the net amount as under IFRS.

EXERCISE 18-1

PURPOSE: This exercise illustrates how to record current income tax expense and deferred tax expense when one taxable temporary difference exists. It will also demonstrate the effect of reversal of the same temporary difference on income tax expense.

Gary Winarski Inc. has accounting income of $500,000 for 2017. There are no permanent differences in calculating taxable income, and there were no deferred taxes at the beginning of 2017. At the end of 2017, there are temporary differences of $95,000, which are expected to result in taxable amounts in 2019. The statutory tax rates enacted in 2017 are as follows:

Year	Tax Rate
2016	34%
2017–2018	32%
2019 and later	30%

Instructions

(a) Calculate taxable income for 2017 and record income tax payable.

(b) Calculate the deferred tax liability at December 31, 2017, and record the change in the deferred tax liability, assuming that taxable income is expected in all future years.

(c) Draft the income tax expense section of the income statement for 2017 (beginning with "Income before income taxes").

(d) Draft the income tax expense section of the income statement for 2019 assuming taxable income for 2019 is $350,000 (beginning with "Income before income taxes").

Solution to Exercise 18-1

(a) Accounting income $500,000

   Originating reversible difference resulting in
      future taxable amounts   (95,000)
   Taxable income $405,000

   Current Tax Expense   129,600
      Income Tax Payable ($405,000 × 32%)   129,600
(To record current income tax expense)

EXPLANATION: Use the reconciliation format in **Illustration 18-3** to calculate taxable income. Since there were no deferred taxes (and, thus, no temporary differences) existing at the beginning of 2017, all $95,000 of temporary differences existing at the end of 2017 must have originated (come about) in 2017. Because these originating reversible or timing differences will result in future taxable amounts, they cause taxable income to be lower than accounting income in 2017.

(b) Taxable temporary differences at December 31, 2017 $95,000

Statutory tax rate for applicable future year	30%
Correct balance of deferred tax liability at December 31, 2017	28,500
Balance of deferred tax liability at January 1, 2017	0
Increase in deferred tax liability in 2017	$28,500

Deferred Tax Expense	28,500	
Deferred Tax Liability		28,500[a]

(To record the change in the deferred tax liability)

[a]See calculation above.

EXPLANATION: The deferred tax liability at December 31, 2017, is measured using the statutory tax rate of the future year (2019) in which the underlying temporary difference is expected to reverse and result in a taxable amount in that year.

(c)

Income before income taxes		$500,000
Income tax expense		
Current tax expense	$129,600	
Deferred tax expense	28,500	158,100
Net income		$341,900

> Notice that the effective tax rate for 2017 is 31.62% ($158,100 ÷ $500,000 = 0.3162), which is lower than the 32% statutory tax rate for 2017. This is because $405,000 of the $500,000 is taxed at 32% and $95,000 of the $500,000 is expected to be taxed at 30%.

(d)

Income before income taxes		$255,000[b]
Income tax expense		
Current income tax expense	$105,000[c]	
Deferred tax benefit	(28,500)[d]	76,500
Net income		$178,500

[b]Accounting income	$	X
Reversing taxable difference	+	95,000
Taxable income	$	350,000

Solving for X: X + $95,000 = $350,000
$$X = \$350,000 - \$95,000$$
$$X = \$255,000 = \text{Accounting income}$$

^{c}Taxable income for 2019	$350,000
Statutory tax rate	30%
Current tax expense and income tax payable for 2019	$105,000

^{d}There are no temporary differences remaining at the end of 2019 so the balance in the deferred tax liability account would be eliminated. A decrease (debit) in the deferred tax liability account results in a deferred tax benefit (credit) to the income tax expense on the income statement.

● Notice that the effective tax rate for 2019 is 30% ($76,500 ÷ $255,000 = 0.30), which equals the statutory tax rate for 2019.

● Think about the journal entry(s) that would be required in 2019 to record income taxes. They would appear as follows:

Current Tax Expense	105,000	
Income Tax Payable ($350,000 × 30%)		105,000
(To record current tax expense)		
Deferred Tax Liability	28,500	
Deferred Tax Benefit		28,500
(To record deferred tax expense/benefit)		

EXERCISE 18-2

PURPOSE: This exercise illustrates how to account for income taxes when there are both permanent and reversing differences involved and the same statutory tax rate is enacted for all periods affected.

Monte Corporation has accounting income of $200,000 for 2017 (its first year of operations). The accounts where there were differences between the revenues and expenses reported on the 2017 tax return and the 2017 income statement are as follows:

	Tax Return	Income Statement
CCA/Depreciation expense	$80,000	$62,000
Insurance expense		8,000
Warranty expense	10,000	19,000
Dividends from taxable		
Canadian corporations	-0-	2,000
Rent revenue	6,200	5,000

The insurance expense was for life insurance policies carried by Monte on key officers, for which Monte is the beneficiary.

The tax rate for 2017 is 25%, and no new rate has been enacted for future years.

Instructions

(a) Calculate taxable income for 2017.

(b) Prepare the journal entries to record income taxes for 2017.

(c) Prepare the bottom of the 2017 income statement beginning with the caption "Income before income taxes."

Solution to Exercise 18-2

(a)

Accounting income for 2017	$200,000
Nondeductible expense—life insurance on officers	8,000
Nontaxable revenue—dividends	(2,000)
Excess of CCA over depreciation expense	(18,000)
Additional warranty expense per books	9,000
Additional rent revenue per tax return	1,200
Taxable income for 2017	$198,200

(b)

Current Tax Expense ($198,200 × 25%)	49,550	
Income Tax Payable		49,550
Deferred Tax Expense	1,950	
Deferred Tax Asset (re: warranties)	2,250ᵃ	
Deferred Tax Asset (re: rents)	300ᵇ	
Deferred Tax Liability (re: CCA/depreciation)		4,500ᶜ
Alternatively, one deferred entry could have been recorded as follows:		
Deferred Tax Expense	1,950	
Deferred Tax Liability		1,950ᵈ

ᵃ$9,000 × 25% = $2,250 − $0 = $2,250
ᵇ$1,200 × 25% = $300 − $0 = $300
ᶜ$18,000 × 25% = $4,500 − $0 = $4,500
ᵈAnalysis: Deductible (taxable) temporary differences at December 31, 2017:

UCC and book value of PP&E	$62,000 − $80,000 =	$(18,000)
Warranty liability	$19,000 − $10,000 =	9,000
Unearned rent	$6,200 − $5,000 =	1,200
		$ (7,800)

Correct balance, net deferred tax liability $7,800 × 25% =		$ 1,950 cr.
Balance before adjustment		0
Adjustment needed to Deferred Tax Liability		$ 1,950 cr.

While only one deferred tax asset or deferred tax liability account may be used as shown above, the use of separate deferred tax accounts for each type of temporary difference (as illustrated above) may be helpful if deferred tax assets and liabilities are later classified between current and non-current on the balance sheet (as required under ASPE).

(c) Income before income taxes $200,000
     Provision for income taxes
       Current income tax expense $49,550
       Deferred tax expense   1,950   51,500
     Net income $148,500

EXERCISE 18-3

PURPOSE: This exercise illustrates the steps involved in calculating and recording income taxes when two types of temporary differences exist and there is a phased-in change in tax rates.

Benyon Corporation has the following facts available:

1. Accounting income for Year 1 is $120,000.
2. Year 1 is the first year of operations.
3. One temporary difference exists at the end of Year 1 that will result in deductible amounts of:
       $25,000 in Year 2.
       $30,000 in Year 3.
4. Another temporary difference exists at the end of Year 1 that will result in taxable amounts of:
       $12,000 in Year 2.
       $15,000 in Year 3.
5. Statutory tax rates enacted by the end of Year 1 are:
       36% for Year 1.
       32% for Year 2.
       28% for Year 3.
6. Taxable income is expected in all future years.
7. Benyon Corporation prepares financial statements in accordance with IFRS.

Instructions

(a) Calculate taxable income for Year 1, assuming there are no permanent differences.

(b) Calculate deferred taxes to be reported on the statement of financial position at the end of Year 1.

(c) Prepare the journal entries to record income taxes for Year 1.

(d) Draft the income tax expense section of the income statement for Year 1.

Solution to Exercise 18-3

(a)

Accounting income for Year 1	$120,000
Originating reversing differences	
Difference #1	55,000
Difference #2	(27,000)
Taxable income for Year 1	$148,000

(b) At December 31, Year 1, a net deferred tax asset of $8,360 should be reflected on the statement of financial position and classified as non-current, because under IFRS, all deferred tax assets and deferred tax liabilities are classified as non-current. Deferred taxes are calculated using a schedule as follows:

	Future Years		
	Year 2	Year 3	Total
Future deductible amounts	$ 25,000	$ 30,000	$ 55,000
Future taxable amounts	(12,000)	(15,000)	(27,000)
Statutory tax rates	32%	28%	
Deferred tax asset	$ 8,000	$ 8,400	$ 16,400
Deferred tax liability	(3,840)	(4,200)	(8,040)
Net deferred tax asset, Dec. 31, Year 1			$ 8,360

(c)

Current Tax Expense	53,280	
Income Tax Payable ($148,000 × 36%)		53,280
Deferred Tax Asset	8,360[a]	
Deferred Tax Benefit		8,360

[a]See the schedule in part (b) for calculation of the Dec. 31, Year 1 $8,360 deferred tax asset. $8,360 minus the balance of the deferred tax asset account before adjustment of $0 = $8,360 adjustment needed.

(d) The relevant section of the income statement for Year 1 would appear as follows:

Income before income taxes		$120,000
Income tax expense		
Current tax expense	$53,280	
Deferred tax benefit	(8,360)	44,920
Net income		$ 75,080

EXERCISE 18-4

PURPOSE: This exercise reviews a situation that involves both a deferred tax asset and a deferred tax liability at the beginning and at the end of the year. It also reviews a reconciliation of accounting income to taxable income.

The following facts relate to Tasty Bits Corporation:

1. Deferred tax liability, January 1, 2017, $80,000.
2. Deferred tax asset, January 1, 2017, $0.
3. Taxable income for 2017, $164,000.
4. There are no permanent differences in 2017.
5. Temporary difference at December 31, 2017, giving rise to future taxable amounts, $440,000.
6. Temporary difference at December 31, 2017, giving rise to future deductible amounts, $70,000.
7. Tax rate for all years, 25%.
8. The company is expected to operate profitably in all future years.
9. The company prepares financial statements in accordance with IFRS.

Instructions

(a) Prepare the journal entries to record current and deferred taxes for 2017.
(b) Draft the income tax expense section of the income statement for 2017, beginning with the line "Income before income tax."

Solution to Exercise 18-4

(a) Journal entries:

Current Tax Expense	41,000	
Income Tax Payable ($164,000 × 25%)		41,000

Deferred Tax Expense	12,500	
Deferred Tax Liability		12,500

Supporting calculations:

Temporary Difference	Future Taxable (Deductible) Amounts	Tax Rate	Deferred Tax Liability (Asset)
Taxable	$440,000	25%	$110,000
Deductible	(70,000)	25%	(17,500)
Net deferred tax liability, 12/31/17			$ 92,500
Correct balance, deferred tax liability, 12/31/17			$ 92,500
Balance, deferred tax liability, before adjustment			80,000
Increase in net deferred tax liability and deferred tax expense, 2017			$ 12,500

(b) Income before income taxes		$214,000ᵃ
Income tax expense		
Current income tax expense	$41,000	
Deferred tax expense	12,500	53,500
Net income		$160,500

ᵃBecause the statutory tax rate is the same for all years, the amount of taxable temporary difference at the beginning of the year can be calculated by dividing the $80,000 beginning balance in Deferred Tax Liability by 25%, which amounts to $320,000. There were no deductible temporary differences at the first of the year. This information may be combined with the other facts given in the exercise to solve for accounting income for 2017 as follows:

Accounting income, 2017	$ X
Originating timing difference in 2017 giving rise to future taxable amounts ($320,000 − $440,000)	(120,000)
Originating timing difference in 2017 giving rise to future deductible amounts	70,000
Taxable income, 2017	$164,000

Solving for X: X − $120,000 + $70,000 = $164,000
              X = $214,000

EXERCISE 18-5

PURPOSE: This exercise will illustrate the application of guidelines for classification of future tax assets and future tax liabilities.

The following information relates to The Chip Corporation, which has several temporary differences existing at December 31, 2017:

1. The carrying value of capital assets exceeds the tax basis (the UCC) of those assets by $500,000.
2. A long-term pension liability of $700,000 appears on the statement of financial position as a result of accrual of pension costs. Only funds contributed have been deducted from taxable income over the years.
3. For tax purposes, $400,000 of gross profit on contracts has been deferred until 2018. This profit is included in the year-end balance of inventory and in 2017 accounting income.
4. Disposal of an operating segment is scheduled for 2018; an accrued liability of $80,000 for related plant closing costs is classified as a current liability.
5. An allowance for doubtful accounts of $220,000 appears on the statement of financial position. Uncollectible accounts are deductible for tax purposes only when individual accounts are written off. All accounts receivable are classified as current assets.
6. An estimated liability for litigation settlements of $130,000 appears in the long-term liability section of the statement of financial position. The liability has a tax basis of zero.

The statutory tax rate is 25% for all years.

Chip Corporation prepares financial statements in accordance with ASPE.

Instructions

Calculate current and non-current future tax assets and/or future tax liabilities to appear on the statement of financial position at December 31, 2017. Indicate how they are to be classified.

Under ASPE, future income tax assets and future income tax liabilities are reported on the statement of financial position in a **net** current and a **net** non-current amount. A future income tax asset or future income tax liability is classified as current or non-current based on the classification of the related asset or liability for financial reporting purposes. A future income tax asset or future income tax liability that is **not** related to an asset or liability for financial reporting purposes, including a future income tax asset related to loss carryforwards, is classified as current or non-current based on the expected reversal date of the temporary difference.

Solution to Exercise 18-5

Temporary Difference	Resulting Future Income Tax (Temporary Difference × 25%)		Related Balance Sheet Account	Future Income Tax Classification
	Asset	(Liability)		
1. Net book value in excess of UCC for capital assets		$(125,000)	Capital Assets (PP&E)	Non-current
2. Pension liability in excess of tax basis of $0	$175,000		Net Defined Benefit Liability	Non-current
3. Contract inventory in excess of its tax value		(100,000)	Inventory	Current
4. Accrual of plant closing costs in excess of tax value of $0	20,000		Accrued Liability for Plant Closing Costs	Current
5. Tax basis of net account receivable in excess of book value	55,000		Allowance for Doubtful Accounts	Current
6. Litigation accrual in excess of its tax basis of $0	32,500		Litigation Liability	Non-current
	$282,500	$(225,000)		

SUMMARY: The net current amount to be reported on the balance sheet is a future income tax liability of $25,000 ($100,000 − $20,000 − $55,000 = $25,000). The net non-current amount to be reported on the balance sheet is a future income tax asset of $82,500 ($175,000 + $32,500 − $125,000 = $82,500).

EXPLANATION:

1. $500,000 future taxable amount × 25% = $125,000 future income tax liability. The related assets, capital assets (PP&E), are classified as non-current on the balance sheet. Therefore, the resulting future income tax liability is classified as non-current.

2. $700,000 future deductible amount × 25% = $175,000 future income tax asset. The related liability, Net Defined Benefit Liability, is a non-current liability on the balance sheet. Therefore, the resulting future income tax asset is classified as non-current.

3. $400,000 future taxable amount × 25% = $100,000 future income tax liability. The related asset would likely be an inventory account. Therefore, the future income tax liability is classified as current.

4. $80,000 future deductible amount × 25% = $20,000 future income tax asset. The related liability, Accrued Liability for Plant Closing Costs, is classified as current on the balance sheet. Therefore, the resulting future income tax asset is classified as current.

5. $220,000 future deductible amount × 25% = $55,000 future income tax asset. The related contra asset account, Allowance for Doubtful Accounts, is classified as current on the balance sheet. Therefore, the resulting future income tax asset is classified as current.

6. $130,000 future deductible amount × 25% = $32,500 future income tax asset. The related accrued liability account, Litigation Liability, is classified as non-current on the balance sheet. Therefore, the resulting future income tax asset is classified as non-current.

- Under ASPE, the term "current" is used in the description of **two totally unrelated amounts** in accounting for income taxes. These two amounts are **current income tax expense on the income statement** and **future income tax asset or future income tax liability classified as current on the balance sheet**. Both current and future income tax expense are presented in the income tax expense section of the income statement. Current income tax expense on the income statement refers to the amount of income tax expense for the current period based on the current period tax return. Having taxable income in the current period results in a current income tax expense reported on the income statement. A tax loss in the current period, if carried back to a prior year, results in a current income tax benefit reported on the income statement. Under ASPE, future income tax assets and liabilities are classified as current or non-current on the balance sheet based on the classification of the underlying asset or liability that resulted in the future income tax asset or future income tax liability. The total change during the period in both current and non-current future income taxes on the balance sheet determines the amount of future income tax expense or benefit on the income statement.

- Under IFRS, all deferred tax assets and deferred tax liabilities are **classified as non-current**.

EXERCISE 18-6

PURPOSE: This exercise reviews the accounting procedures for a tax loss (or loss for income tax purposes).

Evans Corporation has had no permanent or reversible differences since it began operations. Information regarding taxable income and taxes paid is as follows:

Year	Taxable Income (Loss)	Tax Rate	Taxes Paid
1	$ 75,000	36%	$27,000
2	90,000	36%	32,400
3	95,000	32%	30,400
4	150,000	32%	48,000
5	(380,000)	28%	

The statutory tax rate for Year 6 and subsequent years is 25%.

Evans Corporation prepares financial statements in accordance with IFRS.

Instructions

(a) Assuming the tax loss in Year 5 is carried back to the extent possible, prepare the journal entries to record the loss carryback and to record the expected benefits of any related loss carryforward. Assume it is probable that the benefits of any loss carryforward will be fully realized.

(b) Explain how all of the accounts in the journal entries from part (a) are to be reported in the financial statements for Year 5. Draft the income tax expense section of the income statement for Year 5, beginning with the line "Operating loss before income taxes."

(c) Assuming taxable income is $125,000 (before considering the loss carryforward) in Year 6, prepare the journal entries to record income taxes. Also, draft the income tax expense section of the income statement for Year 6, beginning with the line "Income before income taxes."

Solution to Exercise 18-6

(a) Income Tax Refund Receivable   110,800

  Current Tax Benefit   110,800

  ($32,400 + $30,400 + $48,000 = $110,800)

Deferred Tax Asset   11,250

  Deferred Tax Benefit   11,250

  ($380,000 − $90,000 − $95,000 − $150,000 = $45,000)

  ($45,000 × 25% = $11,250; and $11,250 − previous
  balance of $0 = $11,250)

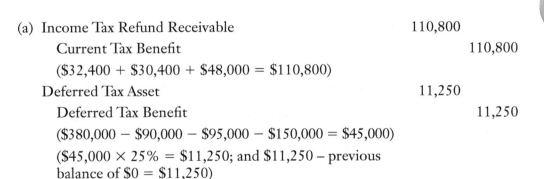

● The benefit of a tax loss carryforward is recognized in the year of the loss that gives rise to the loss carryforward if it is probable that the benefit will be realized. The statutory tax rate for the future year in which the benefits are expected to be realized is used to calculate the related deferred tax asset.

(continued)

- Current Tax Benefit and Deferred Tax Benefit are both negative components of income tax expense; therefore, they are credits to the income statement.

- In this exercise, we are asked to assume that it is probable that the benefits of any loss carryforward will be fully realized. However, if realization of the full $11,250 deferred tax asset was not probable, under IFRS, the above journal entry would be for an amount less than $11,250 (an amount at which realization in future would be probable).

- If Evans Corporation prepared financial statements in accordance with ASPE, the $11,250 future income tax asset could be set up, and could be offset by a valuation allowance if the full $11,250 was not **more likely than not** to be realized in the future. A valuation allowance would be established with a debit to Future Income Tax Expense and a credit to Allowance to Reduce Future Income Tax Asset to Expected Realizable Value. For example, in this exercise, if one half of the benefit of the loss carryforward was not expected to be realized within the loss carryforward period, an adjusting entry for $5,625 would be recorded with a debit to Future Income Tax Expense (re: Loss Carryforward) and a credit to Allowance to Reduce Future Income Tax Asset to Expected Realizable Value. For simplicity, Evans might choose not to set up the future income tax asset only to effectively draw it down again. If the future income tax asset is not set up and the benefit is realized in a later year, the benefit of the reduction in future taxes would be accounted for in that future year.

(b) Income Taxes Receivable would be classified as a current asset on the statement of financial position, and Deferred Tax Asset would be classified as a non-current asset on the statement of financial position.

The other two accounts are negative components of income tax expense. The income tax expense section of the income statement would appear as follows:

Operating loss before income taxes		$(380,000)
Income tax benefit		
Current benefit due to loss carryback	$110,800	
Deferred benefit due to loss carryforward	11,250	122,050
Net loss		$(257,950)

Under IFRS, all deferred tax assets and deferred tax liabilities are classified as non-current. However, if Evans Corporation prepared financial statements in accordance with ASPE, the future income tax asset would be classified as a current asset if the benefit of the loss carryforward was expected to be realized in the year that immediately followed the balance sheet date.

(c) Current Income Tax Expense	20,000	
Income Tax Payable		20,000[a]
Deferred Tax Expense	11,250	
Deferred Tax Asset ($45,000 × 25%)		11,250

[a]$125,000 − $45,000 loss carryforward = $80,000 revised taxable income for Year 6.
$80,000 × 25% = $20,000 income tax payable.

Income before income taxes		$125,000
Income tax expense		
Current tax expense	$ 20,000	
Deferred tax expense	11,250	31,250
Net income		$ 93,750

EXERCISE 18-7

PURPOSE: This comprehensive exercise illustrates how interperiod allocation of income taxes affects financial statements.

The following facts pertain to Hampton Corporation:

• There were no future income taxes on the December 31, 2016 balance sheet.
• Accounting income for 2017 is $125,000.
• $40,000 of revenue reported on the 2017 income statement will be included on the 2018 income tax return.
• $13,000 of expense reported on the 2017 income statement will be reported on the 2019 income tax return.
• There are no differences between accounting income and taxable income for 2017, other than the two items mentioned above.
• Statutory tax rates as at December 31, 2017, are as follows:

Year	Rate
2017	35%
2018	31%
2019	27%

• Taxable income is expected in all future years.
• Hampton Corporation prepares financial statements in accordance with ASPE.

Instructions

(a) Calculate taxable income for the year ended December 31, 2017.
(b) Calculate income tax payable for the year ended December 31, 2017.
(c) Describe how each of the two reversible differences will affect future income tax returns.
(d) Calculate the future income taxes to be reported on the balance sheet at December 31, 2017. Describe how they will affect the income statement for the year ended December 31, 2017.
(e) Prepare the journal entries to record income taxes for 2017.

(f) Describe how the future income tax account(s) will be reported on the balance sheet at December 31, 2017.

(g) Prepare the income tax expense section of the income statement for 2017, beginning with "Income before income taxes."

Solution to Exercise 18-7

(a)
Accounting income for 2017	$125,000
Originating reversible differences	
Revenue – taxable in the future	(40,000)
Expense – deductible in the future	13,000
Taxable income for 2017	$ 98,000

(b)
Taxable income for 2017	$ 98,000
Statutory tax rate for 2017	35%
Income tax payable for 2017	$ 34,300

(c) The $40,000 of revenue that will be included on the 2018 tax return will result in a **taxable amount** (an amount that increases taxable income) on the 2018 income tax return. The $13,000 of expense that will be included on the 2019 tax return will result in a **tax deductible amount** (an amount that reduces taxable income) on the 2019 income tax return.

(d)

	Future Years		
	2018	**2019**	**Total**
Future (taxable) deductible amounts			
Revenue deferred for tax purposes	$(40,000)		$(40,000)
Expense deferred for tax purposes		$13,000	13,000
Statutory tax rate	31%	27%	
Future income tax (liability)	$(12,400)		$(12,400)
Future income tax asset		$ 3,510	3,510
Net future income tax (liability)			$ (8,890)

There were no future income taxes on the December 31, 2016 balance sheet. Therefore, the journal entry to record income taxes for 2017 will include an increase in Future Income Tax Liability (credit) of $8,890. This will cause a corresponding increase in Future Income Tax Expense (debit) of $8,890.

- Notice that the $12,400 increase in future income taxes, as a result of the deferral of the $40,000 of revenue, is recognized on the income statement in 2017 (which is the year in which the revenue appears on the income statement). Also, notice that the $3,510 decrease in future income taxes, as a result of the deferral of the $13,000 of expense, is recognized on the income statement in 2017 (which is the year in which the expense appears on the income statement).

- Analyze the definitions of "taxable temporary difference," "future income tax liability," and "future income tax expense" and how they apply to this situation. The definitions and analysis are as follows:

    Taxable temporary difference: *Definition*—a temporary difference that will result in taxable amounts in a future year(s) when the related asset or liability is recovered or settled, respectively. *Analysis*—$40,000 of revenue is being recognized for accounting purposes in 2017, but deferred for tax purposes to 2018. The revenue may be an accrued revenue that results in recording of an account receivable or accrued receivable for accounting purposes in 2017. In 2018, this asset (receivable) is expected to be recovered (collected), which will result in reporting of the $40,000 of revenue on the 2018 tax return. That is, a taxable amount of $40,000 will appear on the 2018 tax return. Thus, at December 31, 2017, there is a $40,000 taxable temporary difference, which will be taxable in 2018.

    Future income tax liability: *Definition*—the future tax consequence of a taxable temporary difference. *Analysis*—the $40,000 taxable temporary difference existing at December 31, 2017, will cause an increase of $12,400 in income tax payable in the future when the $40,000 amount is included in taxable income on the 2018 tax return.

    Future income tax expense: *Definition*—the change in the balance sheet future income tax asset or future income tax liability account from the beginning to the end of the accounting period. *Analysis*—the $12,400 increase in future income tax liability in 2017 combined with the $3,510 increase in future income tax asset in 2017 results in a net future income tax expense of $8,890 on the income statement for 2017.

- Analyze the definitions of "deductible temporary difference" and "future income tax asset" and how they apply to this situation. The definitions and analysis are as follows:

    Deductible temporary difference: *Definition*—a temporary difference that will result in deductible amounts in a future year(s) when the related asset or liability is recovered or settled, respectively. *Analysis*—$13,000 of expense is being recognized for accounting purposes in 2017, but is deferred for tax purposes to 2019. The expense may be an accrued expense that results in recording of an account payable or accrued payable for accounting purposes in 2017. In 2019, this liability (payable) is expected to be settled (paid), which will result in reporting of the $13,000 of expense on the 2019 tax return. That is, a deductible amount of $13,000 will appear on the 2019 tax return. Thus, at December 31, 2017, there is a $13,000 deductible temporary difference, which will be deductible for tax purposes in 2019.

    Future tax asset: *Definition*—the future tax consequence of a deductible temporary difference or loss carryforward. *Analysis*—the $13,000 deductible temporary difference existing at December 31, 2017, will cause a decrease of $3,510 in income tax payable in the future when the $13,000 amount is deducted on the 2019 tax return.

(e) The journal entries to record income taxes for 2017 are as follows:

Current Tax Expense	34,300	
Income Tax Payable ($98,000 × 35%)		34,300
Future Income Tax Expense	8,890	
Future Income Tax Liability		8,890[a]

[a]See the schedule in part (d) for calculation of the $8,890 future income tax liability.

(f) Because Hampton prepares financial statements in accordance with ASPE, each temporary difference and related future income tax asset or future income tax liability must be classified as current or non-current based on the classification of the asset or liability underlying each specific temporary difference. Assuming the $40,000 revenue has a related receivable on the books classified as a current asset, the resulting $12,400 future income tax liability is classified as a current liability on the balance sheet. Assuming the $13,000 expense has a related payable on the books classified as a non-current liability, the resulting $3,510 future income tax asset will be classified as a non-current asset on the balance sheet. Under ASPE, future income tax assets and future income tax liabilities are netted for reporting purposes, by netting future income tax asset and future income tax liability amounts that are classified as current (net current) and by netting future income tax asset and future income tax liability amounts that are classified as non-current (net non-current).

(g)

Income before income taxes		$125,000
Income tax expense		
Current tax expense	$34,300	
Future tax expense	8,890	43,190
Net income		$ 81,810

- Notice that the effective tax rate for 2017 ($43,190 ÷ $125,000) is not equal to the statutory tax rate for 2017 (35%). This is because the future statutory tax rates of 31% and 27% will apply to the $40,000 revenue and the $13,000 expense, respectively, that are included in 2017's $125,000 income before income taxes.

- Recall the objectives of the future income taxes method of accounting for income taxes and review the solution above to see how these objectives are met. These objectives are:

  1. to recognize income tax payable (or receivable) for the current year, and

  2. to recognize future income tax liabilities and/or future income tax assets representing the **future tax consequences** of transactions and events that have been recognized in the current year's financial statements or tax returns.

- Think about what will happen in 2018 when the $40,000 taxable temporary difference reverses. The $40,000 amount will be included as a revenue item on the tax return but not on the income statement for that year. There will be no remaining future income tax liability on the December 31, 2018 balance sheet related to the $40,000 amount. The reduction in the future income tax liability (debit) in 2018 will result in a future income tax benefit (credit) of $12,400 as part of the total income tax expense on the 2018 income statement.

● Think about what will happen in 2019 when the $13,000 deductible temporary difference reverses. The $13,000 amount will be deducted on the tax return but not on the income statement for that year. There will be no remaining future income tax asset related to the $13,000 amount on the December 31, 2019 balance sheet. The reduction in the future income tax asset (credit) in 2019 will result in a future income tax expense (debit) of $3,510 on the 2019 income statement.

ANALYSIS OF MULTIPLE-CHOICE QUESTIONS

Question

1. A temporary difference arises when a revenue item is reported for tax purposes in a period:

	After It Is Reported in Accounting Income	**Before It Is Reported in Accounting Income**
a.	Yes	Yes
b.	Yes	No
c.	No	Yes
d.	No	No

EXPLANATION: Revenue that is taxable in a period **after** the period when it is recognized in accounting income creates a temporary difference between the tax basis of an asset (zero) and its reported amount on the statement of financial position. This temporary difference will result in a taxable amount in a future period(s) when the asset is recovered (payment is collected). For example, if revenue is earned and accrued in a period in advance of the period in which the related cash is collected and taxed, cash collection is the taxable event, and a receivable is reported on the statement of financial position for accounting purposes until cash collection occurs.

Revenue that is taxable in a period **before** the period when it is recognized in accounting income creates a temporary difference between the tax basis of a liability (zero) and its reported amount on the statement of financial position. This temporary difference will result in a deductible amount in a future period(s) when the liability is settled (goods or services are delivered). For example, if revenue is collected in a period in advance of the period in which it is earned, cash collection is the taxable event, and an unearned revenue is reported on the statement of financial position for accounting purposes until the revenue is earned. (Solution = a.)

Question

2. Which of the following should be recorded to recognize future tax consequences attributable to temporary differences that will result in deductible amounts in future years?

	Deferred Tax Asset	**Deferred Tax Liability**
a.	Yes	Yes
b.	Yes	No
c.	No	Yes
d.	No	No

EXPLANATION: A temporary difference giving rise to future deductible amounts requires recognition of a deferred tax asset for the amount of the future tax consequences related to the temporary difference. A temporary difference giving rise to future taxable amounts requires recognition of a deferred tax liability for the amount of the future tax consequences related to the temporary difference. (Solution = b.)

Question

3. Assuming a 25% tax rate applies to all years involved, which of the following situations will give rise to a deferred tax liability on the statement of financial position?

  I. A revenue is deferred for financial reporting purposes but not for tax purposes.

  II. A revenue is deferred for tax purposes but not for financial reporting purposes.

  III. An expense is deferred for financial reporting purposes but not for tax purposes.

  IV. An expense is deferred for tax purposes but not for financial reporting purposes.

      a. Item II only

      b. Items I and II only

      c. Items II and III only

      d. Items I and IV only

EXPLANATION: Notice that each situation describes a difference in timing of revenue or expense recognition for financial reporting purposes (accounting purposes or book purposes) and tax purposes (tax reporting purposes). Thus, each situation also results in a temporary difference. For each situation, determine if future taxable or deductible amounts will occur. Since a constant tax rate applies to all periods involved, a temporary difference resulting in net future taxable amounts will give rise to a deferred tax liability, and a temporary difference resulting in net future deductible amounts will give rise to a deferred tax asset. Items II and III will give rise to future taxable amounts; items I and IV will give rise to future deductible amounts. (Solution = c.)

Question

4. At the December 31, 2017 statement of financial position date, Brooks Corporation reports an accrued receivable for financial reporting purposes but not for tax purposes. When this asset is recovered in 2018, a future taxable amount will occur and:

    a. accounting income will exceed taxable income in 2018.

    b. Brooks will record a decrease in deferred tax liability in 2018.

    c. total income tax expense for 2018 will exceed current income tax expense for 2018.

    d. Brooks will record an increase in deferred tax asset in 2018.

EXPLANATION: The accrued receivable is likely the result of revenue earned but not collected; the revenue has been recorded for accounting purposes but not for tax purposes. When this asset (accrued receivable) is recovered (collected) in 2018, it will result in a taxable revenue amount being included in taxable income on the 2018 income tax return. Thus, in 2018, taxable income will be higher than accounting income because of the reversal of the temporary difference. Also in 2018, Brooks will record a decrease in the deferred tax liability account, resulting in a deferred tax benefit on the 2018 income statement. This will cause total income tax expense to be lower than current tax expense for 2018. (Solution = b.)

Question

5. Kanak Corporation collects rent revenue in advance from tenants. Collection of $50,000 in 2017 is reported as revenue for tax purposes, but will be reported as revenue for accounting purposes in 2018 when it is earned. This situation will:

    a. result in future deductible amounts.

    b. result in a deferred tax liability on the statement of financial position at the end of 2017.

    c. cause total income tax expense to be less than income tax payable in 2018.

    d. cause accounting income to exceed taxable income in 2017.

EXPLANATION: Collecting and reporting of revenue for tax purposes in a period before it is earned and recognized for accounting purposes will result in future deductible amounts. A deferred tax asset is recognized to represent the future tax consequences of the revenue already reported for tax purposes. In a later period, the unearned revenue on the statement of financial position (a liability) will be settled by delivery of goods or services to customers, resulting in recognition of revenue, or perhaps by refunding customers' money. In that later period, taxable income will be lower than accounting income. Also in that later period, total income tax expense will exceed current income tax expense by the amount of the decrease in Deferred Tax Asset due to the reversal of the related temporary difference. (Solution = a.)

Question

6. Kaminsky Company reported deferred tax expense of $70,000 on its income statement for the year ended December 31, 2017. This could be the result of an increase in:

	Deferred Tax Asset	Deferred Tax Liability
a.	Yes	Yes
b.	No	No
c.	Yes	No
d.	No	Yes

EXPLANATION: Think about the journal entry to record deferred tax expense. The journal entry involves a debit to Deferred Tax Expense and a credit to a statement of financial position account for deferred taxes. This credit is therefore either an increase in Deferred Tax Liability or a decrease in Deferred Tax Asset. (Solution = d.)

Question

7. Milton Corporation reported $60,000 in revenues on its 2017 income statement, of which $24,000 will not be included in taxable income on its tax return until 2018. The statutory tax rate is 32% for 2017 and 28% for 2018. Assuming there are no other temporary differences related to similar situations, what amount should Milton report for the deferred tax liability on its statement of financial position at December 31, 2017?

a. $6,720

b. $7,680

c. $10,080

d. $11,520

EXPLANATION: At the statement of financial position date, December 31, 2017, there is a temporary difference of $24,000, which will be taxable in 2018. The income tax payable on that amount will be $6,720 ($24,000 × 28%) in 2018; however, future tax consequences related to transactions and events recorded in 2017 should be reflected on the financial statements for 2017. The journal entry to record these future tax consequences (assuming no balance of deferred taxes at the beginning of the period) would be a credit to Deferred Tax Liability and a debit to Deferred Tax Expense for $6,720. Therefore: (1) revenues of $60,000, and (2) current income tax expense of $11,520 ($36,000 × 32%), and (3) deferred tax expense of $6,720 ($24,000 × 28%) will be reflected on the 2017 income statement. Thus, both the $60,000 in revenues and the current and future tax consequences of the $60,000 in revenues appear on the same income statement in the same year, regardless of when the taxes are paid. (Solution = a.)

Question

8. Bradley Inc. uses the accrual method of accounting for financial reporting purposes and uses the cash instalment method of accounting for income tax purposes. Profits of $600,000 recognized for accounting purposes in 2017 will be collected in the following years:

	Collection of Profits
2018	$ 75,000
2019	125,000
2020	180,000
2021	220,000

The statutory tax rates are 30% for 2017 and 2018, 25% for 2019, and 20% for 2020 and 2021. Taxable income is expected in all future years. What amount should be included on the December 31, 2017 statement of financial position for the deferred tax liability related to the above temporary difference?

a. $22,500
b. $120,000
c. $133,750
d. $180,000

EXPLANATION: This temporary difference will cause future taxable amounts, taxable at the statutory tax rates enacted for each applicable future period. Calculation of the deferred tax liability is as follows:

2018	$ 75,000 × 30%	=	$ 22,500
2019	125,000 × 25%	=	31,250
2020	180,000 × 20%	=	36,000
2021	220,000 × 20%	=	44,000
Balance of deferred tax liability, Dec. 31, 2017			$133,750

(Solution = c.)

Question

9. CMP Corporation prepared the following reconciliation for its first year of operations:

Accounting income for 2017	$800,000
Tax-free dividends	(100,000)
Originating reversible difference	(180,000)
Taxable income	$520,000

The originating difference will reverse evenly over the next three years at a statutory tax rate of 28%. The statutory tax rate for 2017 is 32%. What amount should be reported on the 2017 income statement for total income tax expense?

a. $50,400

b. $166,400

c. $216,800

d. $256,000

EXPLANATION:

Current income tax expense ($520,000 × 32%)	$166,400
Deferred tax expense ($180,000 × 28%) − $0	50,400
Total income tax expense for 2017	$216,800

The originating reversible difference causes taxable income to be lower than accounting income in 2017; therefore, it will result in future taxable amounts. An increase in the deferred tax liability causes a deferred tax expense to be reported on the income statement. No deferred taxes are recorded for the tax-free dividends (a permanent difference). (Solution = c.)

Question

10. Refer to the facts of Question 9 above. In CMP's 2017 income statement, what amount should be reported for the deferred portion of its provision for income taxes?

a. $216,800 debit

b. $166,400 debit

c. $50,400 credit

d. $50,400 debit

EXPLANATION: The temporary difference existing at December 31, 2017, will result in future taxable amounts, and therefore gives rise to a deferred tax liability of $50,400 ($180,000 temporary difference × 28%) to be reported on the statement of financial position at that date. There was no beginning deferred tax liability since 2017 is CMP's first year of operations. Therefore, the $50,400 increase in deferred tax liability results in a deferred tax expense (debit) of $50,400 on the 2017 income statement. No deferred taxes are recorded for permanent differences, such as tax-free dividends, because they will never reverse. (Solution = d.)

Recall that "provision for income taxes" is another term for "income tax expense."

Question

11. Refer to the facts of Question 9 above. In CMP's 2017 income statement, what amount should be reported as the current portion of its provision for income taxes?

    a. $256,000
    b. $216,800
    c. $166,400
    d. $224,000

EXPLANATION: The taxable income of $520,000 multiplied by the statutory tax rate of 32% for 2017 amounts to current tax expense of $166,400. (Solution = c.)

Question

12. Seong Company has the following taxable temporary differences:

12/31/2017	12/31/2016
$450,000	$320,000

    The statutory tax rate for 2017 is 30%, and the statutory tax rate enacted for future years is 25%. Taxable income for 2017 is $800,000 and there are no permanent differences. Seong's accounting income for 2017 is:

    a. $350,000.
    b. $670,000.
    c. $930,000.
    d. $1,250,000.

EXPLANATION: Use the format for the reconciliation of accounting income to taxable income (see **Illustration 18-3** and its accompanying **tips**). Enter the data given. Solve for the unknown. (Solution = c.)

Accounting income	$ X
Net originating reversible differences that will result in future taxable amounts ($450,000 − $320,000)	(130,000)
Taxable income	$800,000

Solving for X: $X - \$130,000 = \$800,000$

$X = \$930,000$

The statutory tax rates were not required in this solution.

Question

13. At December 31, 2017, Norman Corporation has a future income tax asset of $60,000, which is based on the recognition of 100% of the potential tax benefits of a tax loss carryforward. The statutory tax rates are as follows: 30% for 2017 to 2019; 28% for 2020; and 26% for 2021 and thereafter. Norman Corporation prepares financial statements in accordance with ASPE. Assuming that management expects that only 40% of the related benefits will actually be realized, a valuation account should be established in the amount of:

   a. $24,000.
   b. $9,000.
   c. $8,400.
   d. $7,800.

EXPLANATION: Prepare the journal entry to record the necessary valuation account for the future income tax asset. The journal entry is as follows:

Future Income Tax Benefit/Expense		
(Due to Loss Carryforward)	24,000	
Allowance to Reduce Future Income Tax		
Asset to Expected Realizable Value		24,000

Since only 40% of the potential tax benefits are expected to be realized, a contra asset valuation account is required for the 40% of the future income tax asset (40% × $60,000 = $24,000) that is not expected to be realized. The tax rates are not relevant in this question, because applicable future income tax rates were already applied in calculating the $60,000 future income tax asset. (Solution = a.)

- For simplicity, Norman might choose not to record the full future income tax asset only to effectively reduce it through the allowance. If the full future income tax asset is **not** recorded and the tax benefit of the total loss carryforward is realized in a later year, the tax benefit of the portion not previously recognized would be recognized in the year it is realized.

- Under IFRS, a valuation account is not used for deferred tax assets. A deferred tax asset is only permitted to be recognized at an amount at which realization in future periods is probable.

Question

14. At December 31, 2016, Malcolm Corporation reported a deferred tax liability of $60,000, which was attributable to a taxable temporary difference of $240,000. The temporary difference is scheduled to reverse in 2019. During 2017, a new tax law increased the corporate tax rate from 25% to 35%. Which

of the following entries would correctly account for the effect of this change in future taxes?

a.	Retained Earnings	24,000	
	Deferred Tax Liability		24,000
b.	Retained Earnings	6,000	
	Deferred Tax Liability		6,000
c.	Deferred Tax Expense	6,000	
	Deferred Tax Liability		6,000
d.	Deferred Tax Expense	24,000	
	Deferred Tax Liability		24,000

EXPLANATION: When a change in the tax rate is enacted (or substantively enacted) into law, deferred tax liabilities and deferred tax assets are adjusted accordingly in the period of the change. The effect is included in income from continuing operations as a component of deferred tax expense [($240,000 × 35%) − $60,000 = $24,000]. (Solution = d.)

Question

15. Freeman Corporation began operations in 2013. There have been no permanent differences or temporary differences to account for since inception of the business. The following data are available:

Year	Tax Rate	Taxable Income	Taxes Paid
2013	50%	$100,000	$ 50,000
2014	40%	200,000	80,000
2015	40%	250,000	100,000
2016	30%	300,000	90,000
2017	25%		
2018	20%		

In 2017, Freeman has a loss for tax purposes of $510,000. What amount of income tax benefits should be reported on the 2017 income statement as a result of this tax loss?

a. $198,000
b. $127,500
c. $153,000
d. $102,000

EXPLANATION: A tax loss can be carried back three years and/or forward 20 years. Freeman's tax loss should be carried back three years and applied to the earliest year first as higher tax rates were applied in those years (resulting in higher benefit of the loss carryback). The $510,000 loss should be applied as follows:

2014	$200,000 × 40%	=	$ 80,000
2015	250,000 × 40%	=	100,000
2016	60,000 × 30%	=	18,000
Benefit of loss carryback			$198,000

The future income tax rate (2018 and beyond) would only be used to calculate the benefit of a tax loss carryforward. A loss carryforward would result if the tax loss was larger than the combined taxable income for the three preceding years in the loss carryback period, or if the company elected to forego the loss carryback and carry the loss forward instead. The income tax rate for the current period (2017) is not used in calculating the benefits of a tax loss carryback or carryforward. (Solution = a.)

Chapter 19

Pensions and Other Post-Employment Benefits

OVERVIEW

Post-employment benefits discussed in this chapter include (a) post-retirement plans, such as pensions, that provide benefits after an employee's retirement; (b) post-employment plans that provide benefits after an employee's employment but before retirement; and (c) plans covering accumulating and vested compensated absences. Post-employment benefit plans are generally either defined contribution plans or defined benefit plans. Under a defined contribution plan, the employer's obligation is limited to amounts to be contributed according to the plan. Under a defined benefit plan, the benefits to be received by the employee in the future or the method of determining those benefits is specified in the benefit plan, and the benefits often vest after the employee has worked a specified number of years. As such, the employer's obligation to pay benefits in the future on account of services provided by its employees up to the statement of financial position date must be estimated (by an actuary). Recognition and measurement of the employer's defined benefit obligation and the plan assets under a defined benefit plan are complex. As such, the specific requirements under IFRS and ASPE are explained. In this chapter, accounting for defined benefit plans is discussed extensively, with a focus on defined benefit pension plans.

STUDY STEPS

Understanding the Nature of Post-Employment Benefit Plans

What Is a Benefit Plan?

A **benefit plan** is any arrangement between an entity and its employees whereby, as part of the compensation to its employees, the entity is obligated to provide benefits after an employee's retirement (a post-retirement benefit plan), after an employee's employment but before retirement (a post-employment benefit plan), or during an employee's absence from work (a plan covering accumulating and vested compensated absences).

The employer contributes funds to the benefit plan each year based on one of two options. In the case of a **defined contribution plan**, the required payments are stated in the benefit plan. In the case of a **defined benefit plan**, contributions are based on an established funding pattern calculated by an actuary to ensure that enough funds will be available to provide the benefits that have been promised. The benefit plan is often a separate legal entity administered by an independent third party or trustee that is also responsible for investment of the benefit plan assets and distribution of those assets (for example, to retirees in the case of a pension plan).

In summary, in the case of a pension plan, the employee earns future benefits during his or her period of employment with the employer, and is paid these benefits during his or her period of retirement. The employer contributes funds to the benefit plan during the employee's period of employment, and the benefit plan pays the employee benefits during his or her period of retirement.

The Parties Involved in a Benefit Plan

Often, a benefit plan has a **trustee** (such as a trust company) that administers the plan, invests the plan assets, and distributes the plan assets to the participating employees. The trustee retains the plan assets, which include securities held as the plan's investments and amounts in the plan's bank account, to which employer contributions are paid.

An **actuary** calculates an appropriate funding (contribution) pattern to ensure that enough funds will be available to provide the future benefits that have been promised. The actuary also calculates various amounts used in accounting for the plan, including the defined benefit obligation, annual cost of servicing the plan, and cost of amendments to the plan. The actuary incorporates many assumptions in his or her calculations, including discount rates, rates of return on assets, and mortality rates. The actuary may use conservative assumptions since the employer is relying on the actuary's calculations to determine its funding (contribution) pattern, and the employer is ultimately responsible for providing the future benefits that have been promised.

Most pension plans require a specific minimum number of years of service to the **employer** before the employee's future benefits vest. That is, most future benefits vest after an **employee** has worked for the employer for a certain pre-specified amount of time. **Vesting** occurs when an employee becomes legally entitled to future benefits even if the employee leaves and no longer works for the employer. If the employee leaves the employer prior to the vesting date, he or she forfeits the right to any future benefits. As long as the employee remains with the employer until the vesting date, he or she is entitled to receive the full amount of accumulated benefits in future.

Defined Contribution Plans versus Defined Benefit Plans

There are two types of benefit plans: defined contribution and defined benefit. Under **defined contribution plans**, the employer only promises to contribute a certain amount to the benefit plan each year; the employer does not agree to pay a certain amount of benefits in the future. In contrast, under **defined benefit plans**, the employer promises to pay a certain amount of benefits in the future, and therefore assumes the economic risks involved in meeting the obligation, including changes in plan costs and fluctuations in investment returns on plan assets.

An example of a defined benefit pension plan benefit formula is as follows: 2% of the employee's best year of salary (of the years that the employee worked for the employer) multiplied by the number of years worked for the employer. Therefore, if the best year of salary is estimated to be $40,000 and the employee has worked 10 years to date, he or she will be entitled to a payout on retirement of:

$$\$40,000 \times 2\% \times 10 \text{ years} = \$8,000 \text{ per year}$$

This chapter focuses mainly on accounting for defined benefit plans since accounting for defined contribution plans is relatively straightforward.

The benefit plan itself has assets and a defined benefit obligation. The **plan assets** are accumulated contributions from the employer and investment returns on plan assets up to the statement of financial position date minus benefits paid to retirees. The **defined benefit obligation (DBO)** is estimated future benefits earned by employees up to the statement of financial position date. The benefit plan's assets and defined benefit obligation are *not* recognized in the employer's financial statements, but are tracked by the employer in off–balance sheet or memo accounts.

Recognition and Measurement Differences: IFRS and ASPE

The employer (or benefit plan sponsor) records an **annual pension expense** and a **net defined benefit liability/asset**. The amount of annual pension expense and the amount of net defined benefit liability/asset are affected by (1) the accounting approach used; (2) application of optional recognition and measurement rules available under ASPE such as use of a current settlement rate for interest cost; (3) changes in the benefit plan's plan assets and defined benefit obligation; and (4) estimated inputs such as discount rate.

Both IFRS and ASPE follow what used to be referred to under ASPE as the **immediate recognition approach** in determining pension expense (since the deferral and amortization approach was eliminated there is only one approach used now, so ASPE no longer refers to a separate immediate recognition approach). There are, however, a few differences in the application of the approach between IFRS and ASPE. A comparison follows:

1. **Current service cost:** the cost of benefits earned by employees during the current period; is included in pension expense for the same period under both IFRS and ASPE

2. **Net interest (finance) cost:**

   Under both IFRS and ASPE, the same discount rate is used for interest cost on the DBO and for interest assumed to be earned on the plan assets.

   (a) Under IFRS, the net interest on the net defined benefit liability/asset is recognized in net income. Any remeasurement of plan assets resulting from actual returns and returns calculated using the discount rate to determine the DBO are reported in other comprehensive income (OCI).

   (b) Under ASPE, all interest costs are included in net income, and any remeasurement gain or loss resulting in differences in actual returns and returns calculated using the discount rate to determine the DBO are also included in net income (but remeasurement gains and losses are required to be disclosed separately).

3. **Past service costs, curtailments, and settlements:** are included in pension expense for the period under both IFRS and ASPE

4. **Actuarial gains and losses:** gains and losses resulting from such items as changes in actuarial assumptions and experience adjustments

   (a) Under IFRS, are reported in OCI

   (b) Under ASPE, are reported in net income as part of the remeasurement gain or loss that is required to be separately disclosed (see also 2 (b) above)

Other Post-Employment Benefit Plans

Other post-employment benefit plans include plans that provide health care or life insurance benefits, service-related long-term disability benefits, and unrestricted sabbaticals. In general, employers do not contribute to post-employment benefit plans other than pensions in advance of benefit payments, and benefits related to these plans are more difficult to measure. Under IFRS, the same accounting standards that apply to defined benefit pension plans apply only to other long-term benefit plans. Under ASPE, the same accounting standards that apply to defined benefit pension plans also apply to other post-employment benefit plans that vest or accumulate.

Under both IFRS and ASPE, if a benefit plan does not vest or accumulate, no accrued cost or liability is recorded; instead, costs and liabilities are recorded when incurred, or when an obligating event occurs.

Becoming Proficient in Related Calculations: The Work Sheet/Spreadsheet

Accounting for pensions and other post-employment benefits is theoretically and technically complex. Therefore, a significant amount of time should be devoted to studying the exercises and illustrations in this chapter and understanding the related calculations.

The work sheet approach (shown in the text) is an excellent tool for analysis of a defined benefit pension plan in a given year and for calculation of the annual journal entry amounts. Therefore, you should familiarize yourself with it as soon as possible.

Remember that an objective of the work sheet is to calculate the costs associated with the post-employment benefits plan. This is in order to accrue pension expense in the periods in which the employees provide services to earn the future benefits, and thus match pension expense with revenues generated by the employees in those periods. The end result of the work sheet is the following:

1. calculation of pension expense for the year (recorded with a debit to Pension Expense, and a credit to Net Defined Benefit Liability/Asset);

2. calculation of the remeasurement gain or loss and actuarial gain or loss reported in OCI under IFRS (recorded with a debit to Remeasurement Loss (OCI) or credit to Remeasurement Gain (OCI), and a credit or debit to Net Defined Benefit Liability/Asset); and

3. recording of contributions to the plan (with a debit to Net Defined Benefit Liability/Asset and a credit to Cash).

Thus, under IFRS the net defined benefit liability/asset changes by the difference between the amount of pension expense and remeasurement gain or loss included in OCI for the year, and the cash contributions paid into the plan in the year.

The work sheet is needed only for defined benefit plans. It is not necessary for defined contribution plans because they do not have similar complications.

TIPS ON CHAPTER TOPICS

- The **defined benefit obligation (DBO)** is a measure of the pension obligation at the statement of financial position date. The DBO is based on the projected benefit method, or present value of vested and non-vested benefits earned up to the statement of financial position date, with the benefits measured using employees' future salary levels. Under **ASPE**, the DBO is based on actuarial valuation for funding purposes, or a separate actuarial valuation prepared for accounting purposes, and represents the present obligation at the balance

(continued)

sheet date. Notice whether the beginning-of-period or end-of-period balance of DBO is required for a particular calculation; for example:

1. The **beginning** balance of DBO is used to calculate the interest cost included in pension expense for the period, assuming that all other transactions that affect DBO take place at the end of the year.

2. The **ending** balance of DBO is used to reconcile the funded status of the plan with the net defined benefit liability/asset reported on the employer's statement of financial position.

-   Under IFRS, **interest cost** on the DBO must be calculated using a current market rate (for example, the current yield on high-quality debt instruments such as high-quality corporate bonds). Under ASPE, interest cost on the DBO can be calculated using a current market rate (for example, the current yield on high-quality debt instruments such as high-quality corporate bonds) or a current settlement rate (for example, the rate implied in an insurance contract that could be purchased to effectively settle the pension obligation).

-   Under both IFRS and ASPE, the same discount rate is used to calculate **interest cost** on the DBO and the **expected return on plan assets**.

-   **Actual return on plan assets** is the income generated on plan assets, from interest, dividends, and realized and unrealized changes in fair value of the plan assets. Actual return on plan assets can be calculated by (1) calculating the change in fair value of plan assets, (2) deducting contributions, and (3) adding benefits paid. Under IFRS, **remeasurement gain or loss on plan assets** (the difference between expected return on plan assets and actual return on plan assets) is included in the remeasurement gain or loss in OCI. Under ASPE, remeasurement gain or loss is included in pension expense for the current period (and is disclosed separately).

-   Under IFRS, **actuarial gains and losses** (differences between the actuary's assumptions and actual experience, and resulting from changes in the assumptions that are used by the actuary in calculating the defined benefit obligation) are included in the remeasurement gain or loss reported in OCI. Under ASPE, **actuarial gains and losses** are included in pension expense for the current period (and are considered part of the remeasurement gain or loss that is required to be disclosed separately).

-   Plan adoptions or amendments often include provisions to increase future benefits based on employee services provided in prior years. Both IFRS and ASPE require that these **past service costs** be included in pension expense immediately (in the year of plan initiation or amendment).

-   The balances of DBO and plan assets do not appear on the employer's statement of financial position. However, they have an impact on the calculation of amounts that appear on the employer's statement of comprehensive income (or income statement), statement of financial position, and notes to financial statements.

-   A pension work sheet calculates amounts for both formal journal entries and memo journal entries. The journal entry to record pension expense is a debit to Pension Expense for the amount calculated on the pension work sheet, a debit to Remeasurement Loss (OCI) or a credit to Remeasurement Gain (OCI) for the amount calculated on the pension work sheet under IFRS, and a debit or a credit to Net Defined Benefit Liability/Asset for the difference. The entry to record the contributions to the fund include a credit to Cash for the amount contributed for the period, and a debit to Net Defined Benefit Liability/Asset.

Illustration 19-1   229

ILLUSTRATION 19-1

Components of Pension Expense

Calculation of Pension Expense—IFRS Approach

	Current service cost
+	Interest cost on defined benefit obligation
−	Expected return on plan assets (using same discount rate as for interest cost)
+	Past service cost due to plan adoption or amendments in the current period
=	Pension expense

Calculation of Pension Expense—ASPE Approach

	Current service cost
+	Interest cost on defined benefit obligation
+/−	Actual return on plan assets
+	Past service cost due to plan adoption or amendments in the current period
+/−	Liability actuarial gain/loss (due to experience gain or loss, or change in actuarial assumptions in the current period)
=	Pension expense

Description of Components:

Current service cost: This is the cost of the benefits that are to be provided in the future in exchange for the services that the employees provided in the current period. The actuary calculates current service cost as present value of the additional benefits earned by employees in the current year.

Interest cost on defined benefit obligation: Because a pension is a deferred compensation arrangement, the time value of money is a factor. Defined benefit obligation is recorded at present value, and interest accrues each year on the defined benefit obligation, just as it would on any other discounted debt.

Actual return on plan assets: This is income generated on plan assets (from interest, dividends, and realized and unrealized changes in fair value of the plan assets).

Expected return on plan assets: For both ASPE and IFRS, the expected rate is the same rate as the discount rate used to determine interest costs for the period. The asset actuarial gain or loss (the difference between expected return on plan assets and actual return on plan assets) is included in the remeasurement gain or loss reported in OCI. Under ASPE, any asset actuarial gain or loss is included in the net income and is disclosed separately as a part of any remeasurement gain or loss.

Past service cost: This is the cost of additional future benefits (or in rare cases, the decrease in future benefits) based on employee services provided in prior years, as a result of pension plan adoption or amendments. Both IFRS and ASPE require that past service costs be included in pension expense immediately in the period of plan initiation or amendment.

Actuarial gain/loss: This is what arises from differences between the actuary's assumptions and actual experience, and from changes in the assumptions that are used by the actuary in calculating the defined benefit obligation. Under IFRS, the actuarial gain/loss is included in the remeasurement gain or loss recognized in OCI. Under ASPE, the actuarial gain/loss is included in pension expense and is disclosed separately as a part of any remeasurement gain or loss.

EXERCISE 19-1

PURPOSE: This exercise will enable you to practise calculating pension expense based on the IFRS and ASPE approaches.

The following data relate to Tower Company's pension plan for the year 2017:

Net defined benefit liability at January 1, 2017	$ 23,000
Actual return on plan assets	44,000
Benefits paid	55,000
Contributions to plan	97,000
Actuarial loss in the current period	32,000
Past service cost due to plan amendment effective January 1, 2017	68,000
Fair value of plan assets at January 1, 2017	722,000
Defined benefit obligation at January 1, 2017	757,000
Current service cost	75,000
Interest (discount) rate	8%

Illustration 19-2   2 3 1

Instructions

(a) Calculate pension expense to be included in net income for 2017 based on the IFRS approach.

(b) Calculate pension expense to be included in net income for 2017 based on the ASPE approach.

Solution to Exercise 19-1

(a) IFRS approach

Current service cost	$ 75,000
Interest cost on defined benefit obligation (($757,000 + $68,000) × 8%)	66,000
Expected return on plan assets ($722,000 × 8%)	(57,760)
Past service cost	68,000
Pension expense for 2017 included in net income	$151,240

(b) ASPE approach

Current service cost	$ 75,000
Interest cost on accrued benefit obligation (($757,000 + $68,000) × 8%)	66,000
Actual return on plan assets	(44,000)
Past service cost	68,000
Actuarial loss	32,000
Pension expense for 2017 included in net income	$197,000

APPROACH: When calculating pension expense, refer to **Illustration 19-1**.

ILLUSTRATION 19-2

Components of Defined Benefit Obligation and Plan Assets

Calculation of Defined Benefit Obligation

	Defined benefit obligation, beginning balance
+	Current service cost
+	Interest cost on defined benefit obligation

−	Benefits paid to employees and retirees during the period
+/−	<u>Liability actuarial (experience) gain (−) or loss (+) for the period</u>
=	<u>Defined benefit obligation, ending balance</u>

Calculation of Plan Assets

	Plan assets, beginning balance
+	Contributions to plan (from employer and employees) during the period
−	Benefits paid to employees and retirees during the period
+/−	<u>Actual return on plan assets during the period[a]</u>
=	<u>Plan assets, ending balance</u>

[a] Includes **realized** earnings such as dividends, interest, and gains and losses due to sales of plan assets, and **unrealized** asset gains and losses due to changes in fair value of plan assets.

- Calculation of the defined benefit obligation and plan assets is the same under both IFRS and ASPE.

- It is helpful to know the various components of the defined benefit obligation and plan assets. If you are given the amounts contributed by the employer during the year, the benefits paid to employees and retirees from the pension fund during the year, and the net increase in the fair value of plan assets for the year, you can solve for the actual return on plan assets for the year.

- Although the balance of the defined benefit obligation and the balance of plan assets are **not** reported on the employer's statement of financial position, they have an impact on the calculation of amounts that appear on the employer's statement of comprehensive income (or income statement), statement of financial position, and notes to financial statements.

- One of the components of the defined benefit obligation is the actuarial (experience) gain or loss for the period, which may be due to differences between the actuary's assumptions and actual experience, or changes in the assumptions that are used by the actuary in calculating the defined benefit obligation. Actuarial gains **reduce** the defined benefit obligation, whereas actuarial losses **increase** the defined benefit obligation.

EXERCISE 19-2

PURPOSE: This exercise will illustrate the mechanics of the pension work sheet.

The following data relate to Omega Company's pension plan for the year 2017:

Actual return on plan assets	$ 70,000
Benefits paid	45,000
Contributions to plan	87,000
Fair value of plan assets at January 1, 2017	600,000
Cost of past service benefits granted effective December 31, 2017	34,000
Defined benefit obligation at January 1, 2017	627,000
Current service cost	82,000
Actuarial loss	39,000
Interest (discount) rate	8%

Instructions

(a) Prepare a pension work sheet for 2017 based on the IFRS approach. Show the journal entries for pension expense and contribution for 2017.

(b) Prepare a pension work sheet for 2017 based on the ASPE approach. Show the journal entries for pension expense and contribution for 2017.

Solution to Exercise 19-2

(a) IFRS approach

	Pension Work Sheet – 2017[a]					
	General Journal Entries				Memo Record	
	Remeasurement (Gain) Loss OCI	Annual Pension Expense	Cash	Net Defined Benefit Liability/ Asset	Defined Benefit Obligation	Plan Assets
Balance, Jan. 1, 2017				27,000 Cr.	627,000 Cr.	600,000 Dr.
(1) Service cost		82,000 Dr.			82,000 Cr.	
(2) Net interest/finance cost		2,160 Dr.			50,160 Cr.	48,000 Dr.
(3) Remeasurement gain	22,000[b] Cr.					22,000[b] Dr.
(4) Contributions			87,000 Cr.			87,000 Dr.
(5) Benefits paid					45,000 Dr.	45,000 Cr.
(6) Past service cost		34,000 Dr.			34,000 Cr.	
(7) Actuarial loss	39,000 Dr.				39,000 Cr.	
Expense entry, 2017	17,000 Dr.	118,160 Dr.		135,160 Cr.		
Contribution entry, 2017			87,000 Cr.	87,000 Dr.		
Balance, Dec. 31, 2017				75,160 Cr.	787,160 Cr.	712,000 Dr.

[a] The use of this pension entry work sheet is recommended. It was illustrated by Paul B.W. Miller, "The New Pension Accounting (Part 2)," *Journal of Accountancy* (February 1987), pp. 86–94.
[b] Actual return on plan assets – expected return on plan assets = 70,000 – 48,000

(b) ASPE approach

	Pension Work Sheet – 2017[a]				
	General Journal Entries			Memo Record	
	Annual Pension Expense	Cash	Net Defined Benefit Liability/Asset	Defined Benefit Obligation	Plan Assets
Balance, Jan. 1, 2017			27,000 Cr.	627,000 Cr.	600,000 Dr.
(1) Service cost	82,000 Dr.			82,000 Cr.	
(2) Net interest/finance cost	2,160 Dr.			50,160 Cr.	48,000 Dr.
(3) Remeasurement gain	22,000 Cr.				22,000 Dr.
(4) Contributions		87,000 Cr.			87,000 Dr.
(5) Benefits paid				45,000 Dr.	45,000 Cr.
(6) Past service cost	34,000 Dr.			34,000 Cr.	
(7) Actuarial loss	39,000 Dr.			39,000 Cr.	
Expense entry, 2017	135,160 Dr.		135,160 Cr.		
Contribution entry, 2017		87,000 Cr.	87,000 Dr.		
Balance, Dec. 31, 2017			75,160 Cr.	787,160 Cr.	712,000 Dr.

[a] The use of this pension entry work sheet is recommended. It was illustrated by Paul B.W. Miller, "The New Pension Accounting (Part 2)," *Journal of Accountancy* (February 1987), pp. 86–94.

● In the pension work sheet, the balance of **net defined benefit liability/asset** equals the net of the balances in the (off–balance sheet) memo accounts. If the memo accounts net to a **credit** balance, a net defined benefit liability is reported on the statement of financial position. If the memo accounts net to a **debit** balance, a net defined benefit asset is reported on the statement of financial position.

EXERCISE 19-3

PURPOSE: This exercise will illustrate the calculation of the actual return on plan assets.

Milette Company reports the following pension plan data:

Fair value of plan assets, January 1, 2017	$3,200,000
Fair value of plan assets, December 31, 2017	3,600,000
Benefits paid during 2017	460,000
Contributions to the plan during 2017	640,000

Instructions

Calculate actual return on plan assets during 2017.

Solution to Exercise 19-3

Fair value of plan assets, January 1, 2017	$3,200,000
Contributions to the plan during 2017	640,000
Benefits paid during 2017	(460,000)
Actual return on plan assets during 2017	X
Fair value of plan assets, December 31, 2017	$3,600,000
Solving for X: X =	$ 220,000

APPROACH: Write down the formula for reconciling the beginning and ending balance of plan assets at fair value (see **Illustration 19-2**). Enter the data given. Solve for the unknown.

EXERCISE 19-4

PURPOSE: This exercise will illustrate the calculation of the expected return on plan assets and discuss the effect of the expected return on plan assets in calculation of pension expense.

Assume that Milette Company (from **Exercise 19-3**) also reports:

Expected return on plan assets   8%

Instructions

(a) Calculate the expected return on plan assets during 2017 and the remeasurement gain or loss under the IFRS approach.

(b) Explain how the expected return on plan assets and remeasurement gain or loss enter into the calculation of pension expense under the IFRS approach.

(c) Explain how the expected return on plan assets and remeasurement gain or loss enter into the calculation of pension expense under the ASPE approach.

Solution to Exercise 19-4

(a) 8% × $3,200,000 fair value of plan assets at January 1, 2017 = $256,000 expected return on plan assets.

Expected return on plan assets	$256,000
Actual return on plan assets (**Exercise 19-3**)	220,000
Remeasurement loss	$ 36,000

(b) Under the IFRS approach, the expected return on plan assets of $256,000 is included in the calculation of current pension expense, reducing the expense by this amount. The difference between the expected and actual return on assets is included in OCI as a remeasurement loss.

(c) Under the ASPE approach, pension expense is reduced directly by the actual return of $220,000. The expected return on plan assets of $256,000 and remeasurement loss of $36,000 net to the actual return on plan assets of $220,000, but are not calculated separately.

EXPLANATION: In parts (a) and (b) of this exercise, the expected return on plan assets is calculated by multiplying the fair value of the plan assets (beginning balance) by the same discount rate used to calculate the interest cost. It is assumed that contributions to the plan and benefits paid from the plan took place at the end of the year. However, if a contribution to the plan was made at the beginning of the year, the calculation shown in this exercise would not reflect the economic reality that more assets were available for investing than were used in the calculation of expected return. Therefore, if there were contributions to the plan and benefits paid from the plan throughout the year, the expected return on plan assets is calculated using a weighted average balance of fair value of plan assets.

EXERCISE 19-5

PURPOSE: This exercise will illustrate accounting for post-retirement benefits other than pensions.

Handy Company reports the following data related to post-retirement benefits for 2017:

Defined benefit obligation at January 1, 2017	$540,000
Actual return on plan assets in 2017	27,000
Expected return on plan assets in 2017	30,000
Current service cost	52,000
Discount rate	10%
Benefits paid	43,000
Contributions to the plan	60,000

Handy follows IFRS.

Instructions

(a) Calculate post-retirement benefit expense for 2017.

(b) Prepare the journal entries to record post-retirement benefit expense and Handy's contribution for 2017.

(c) Calculate the defined benefit obligation at December 31, 2017.

Solution to Exercise 19-5

(a)

Current service cost	$52,000
Interest cost (10% × $540,000)	54,000
Expected return on plan assets	(30,000)
Post-retirement benefit expense—2017	$76,000

EXPLANATION: The components used to calculate post-retirement benefit expense are the same as the components used to calculate pension expense.

- Current service cost is the cost of the benefits that are to be provided in the future in exchange for the services that the employees provided in the current period.
- Interest cost is the discount rate multiplied by the defined benefit obligation at the beginning of the year. However, interest cost may also be calculated using a weighted average amount of defined benefit obligation. See discussions above regarding calculation of interest cost and expected return on plan assets for pensions.

(b)

Post-retirement Expense	76,000	
Post-retirement Asset/Liability		76,000
Post-retirement Asset/Liability	60,000	
Cash		60,000

EXPLANATION: The journal entries to record post-retirement benefit expense are similar to the entries to record pension expense.

(c)

Defined benefit obligation at January 1, 2017	$540,000
Current service cost	52,000
Interest cost	54,000
Benefits paid during the period	(43,000)
Defined benefit obligation at December 31, 2017	$603,000

EXPLANATION: Similar to the defined benefit obligation for pension benefits, the defined benefit obligation for post-retirement benefits increases by current service cost and interest cost, and decreases by the amount of benefits paid during the period. A liability actuarial (experience) gain or loss for the period would also affect the balance of the defined benefit obligation for post-retirement benefits.

ANALYSIS OF MULTIPLE-CHOICE QUESTIONS

Question

1. Salmon Corp. has a defined benefit pension plan. Information for the plan for 2017 is as follows:

Current service cost	$325,000
Actual return on plan assets	72,000
Expected return on plan assets	55,000
Interest on defined benefit obligation	110,000

Based on the IFRS approach, what amount should Salmon report as pension expense on its statement of comprehensive income for 2017?
a. $270,000
b. $363,000
c. $380,000
d. $435,000

EXPLANATION: Pension expense is calculated as follows:

Current service cost	$325,000
Interest on defined benefit obligation	110,000
Expected return on plan assets	(55,000)
Pension expense for 2017	$380,000

(Solution = c.)

Question

2. Which of the following items should be included in the calculation of net pension expense under the ASPE approach to accounting for defined benefit plans?

	Fair Value of Plan Assets	**Past Service Cost**
a.	Yes	Yes
b.	Yes	No
c.	No	Yes
d.	No	No

EXPLANATION: Review the components of pension expense (refer to **Illustration 19-1**). Under both IFRS and ASPE, the approach requires that past service costs be included in pension expense immediately (in the year of plan initiation or amendment). While actual return on plan assets is a component of pension expense under the ASPE approach, fair value of the plan assets is not. (Solution = c.)

Question

3. The following information relates to the pension plan of Sunbridge Company, which is accounted for based on the IFRS approach:

	1/1/16	12/31/16	12/31/17
Plan assets (at fair value)	$2,500,000	$3,200,000	$3,600,000
Defined benefit obligation	2,900,000	2,900,000	3,800,000
Liability actuarial loss	-0-	475,000	450,000
Interest (discount) rate for the year		7%	6%

In 2017, Sunbridge's contribution was $400,000, and benefits paid totalled $360,000. Actual return on plan assets for 2017 is:
   a. $360,000.
   b. $400,000.
   c. $160,000.
   d. $960,000.

EXPLANATION: Recall that actual return on plan assets can be determined by (1) calculating the change in plan assets (at fair value), (2) deducting contributions during the year, and (3) adding benefits paid during the year:

Plan assets (at fair value), 12/31/17	$3,600,000
Plan assets (at fair value), 12/31/16	3,200,000
Increase in fair value of plan assets in 2017	400,000
Contributions during the year	(400,000)
Benefits paid during the year	360,000
Actual return on plan assets, 2017	$ 360,000

(Solution = a.)

Question

4. Refer to the data for Sunbridge Company in Question 3. Knowing that the actual return on plan assets is $360,000 in 2017, the asset remeasurement gain or loss recognized in OCI for 2017 is:
   a. $144,000 gain.
   b. $168,000 gain.
   c. $157,000 gain.
   d. $186,000 gain.

EXPLANATION: Expected return on plan assets is calculated as expected rate of return multiplied by plan assets (at fair value) at the beginning of the year. For 2017, expected return on plan assets is $192,000 (6% × $3.2 million). Since the actual return on plan assets is $360,000, there is an asset remeasurement gain of $168,000 ($360,000 − $192,000) for 2017. (Solution = b.)

Question

5. Refer to the data for Sunbridge Company in Question 3. The net remeasurement gain or loss reported in OCI for 2017 is:
   a. $450,000 gain.
   b. $450,000 loss.
   c. $282,000 gain.
   d. $282,000 loss.

EXPLANATION: The net remeasurement gain or loss reported in OCI in 2017 includes both the remeasurement gain or loss on plan assets (the difference between expected return on plan assets and actual return on plan assets), and the actuarial gain or loss. Therefore, Sunbridge's net remeasurement gain or loss reported in OCI in 2017 is a $282,000 loss ($168,000 remeasurement gain on plan assets − $450,000 actuarial loss). (Solution = d.)

Question

6. Refer to the data for Sunbridge Company in Question 3. The service cost for 2017 is:
   a. $636,000.
   b. $726,000.
   c. $900,000.
   d. $1,086,000.

EXPLANATION: Service cost can be determined by (1) calculating change in defined benefit obligation (at fair value), (2) deducting interest cost, (3) adding benefits paid during the year, and (4) deducting actuarial loss:

Defined benefit obligation (at fair value), 12/31/17	$3,800,000
Defined benefit obligation (at fair value), 12/31/16	2,900,000
Increase in defined benefit obligation in 2017	900,000
Interest cost for 2017 ($2,900,000 × 6%)	(174,000)
Benefits paid during the year	360,000
Actuarial loss for 2017	(450,000)
Service cost for 2017	$ 636,000

(Solution = a.)

Question

7. Greenberg Corporation has a defined benefit plan. Under IFRS, a net defined benefit liability will result at the end of the first year of the plan if:

    a. the defined benefit obligation exceeds the fair value of the plan assets.
    b. the fair value of the plan assets exceeds the defined benefit obligation.
    c. the amount of employer contributions exceeds the net periodic pension expense.
    d. none of the above.

EXPLANATION: Under IFRS, a net defined benefit liability will result at the end of the first year of the plan if the defined benefit obligation exceeds the fair value of the plan assets. (Solution = a.)

Question

8. Kent Company has the following information related to its pension plan as at December 31, 2017:

Defined benefit obligation	$5,600,000
Plan assets (at fair value)	4,100,000
Pension expense for 2017	400,000
Contributions for 2017	360,000

    Under the ASPE approach, the amount to be reported as net defined benefit liability on the December 31, 2017 balance sheet is:

    a. $1,860,000.
    b. $1,500,000.
    c. $1,460,000.
    d. $1,100,000.

EXPLANATION:

Defined benefit obligation	$5,600,000 Cr.
Plan assets (at fair value)	4,100,000 Dr.
Underfunded, and net defined benefit liability	1,500,000 Cr.
	(Solution = b.)

Question

9. Sampat Corp. has a defined benefit plan for its employees, and prepares financial statements in accordance with IFRS. All of the following must

be disclosed, either in the body of the financial statements or in the notes, **except:**

a. the characteristics of the defined benefit plans and risks associated with them.

b. a schedule showing changes in employees covered by the plan.

c. the amounts in the financial statements arising from the plans.

d. reconciliations of the opening to closing balances of the net defined benefit liability/asset, plan assets, and the defined benefit obligation.

EXPLANATION: The disclosure requirements for pensions are extensive. Under IFRS, information is disclosed, either in the body of the financial statements, or in the notes to the financial statements, that:

1. explain the characteristics of the defined benefit plans and risks associated with them.

2. identify and explain the amounts in the financial statements arising from the plans.

3. explain how the defined benefit plans may affect the amounts, timing, and likelihood of the cash flows that are associated with future benefits.

4. reconcile the opening to closing balances of the net defined benefit liability/asset, plan assets, and the defined benefit obligation.

5. show the amounts included in periodic net income, including the amounts included in expense, such as current service cost, interest cost, and expected return on plan assets, along with amounts recognized in OCI.

6. show the sensitivity information for each significant actuarial assumption, including the impact on the defined benefit obligation.

(Solution = b.)

Question

10. The following information relates to Black Company's post-retirement benefit plan for 2017:

Defined benefit obligation at January 1, 2017	$330,000
Current service cost	80,000
Discount rate	10%
Actual return on plan assets in 2017	15,000
Expected return on plan assets in 2017	19,000

Under the ASPE approach, the amount of post-retirement benefit expense for 2017 is:

a. $80,000.

b. $94,000.

c. $98,000.

d. $99,000.

EXPLANATION: Recall that post-retirement benefit expense is similar to pension expense and, under the ASPE approach, includes current and past service cost, interest cost, a reduction (usually) for the actual return on plan assets, and an adjustment for any actuarial gain or loss. Interest cost is the discount rate multiplied by the defined benefit obligation at the beginning of the year. Therefore, the calculation of post-retirement benefit expense for 2017, under the ASPE approach, is:

Current service cost	$80,000
Interest cost (10% × $330,000)	33,000
Actual return on plan assets	(15,000)
Post-retirement benefit expense, 2017	$98,000

(Solution = c.)

Question

11. Assumptions incorporated in the calculation of pension expense should reflect best estimates regarding the effect of future events on the actuarial present value of net defined benefit liability/asset. These assumptions should take into account the following:
    a. Recognition of the past history of the plan; actual experience
    b. Recognition of the long-term nature of the plan; expected long-term future events
    c. Recognition of the fact that best estimates are made at a point in time; recent experience
    d. All of the above

EXPLANATION: Assumptions are a matter of professional judgement and should take into account all of the factors listed above. (Solution = d.)

Question

12. Which of the following would *not* be considered a defined benefit plan?
    a. Benefit is fixed and based on number of service years.
    b. Benefit is based on number of service years and returns earned on plan assets up to date of retirement.
    c. Benefit is based on number of service years and compensation earned by the employee over the entire service period.
    d. Benefit is based on number of service years and compensation earned by the employee over a specified number of years in the service period.

EXPLANATION: Under a defined benefit plan, the benefit is fixed, and usually calculated by a formula. The answer selections are all formulas (versus exact dollar amounts), but selection "b" has an element of benefit uncertainty related to investment returns. If the benefit is based on number of service years and returns earned on plan assets, economic risk is transferred to the employee, which is the essence of a defined contribution plan. (Solution = b.)

Chapter 20

Leases

OVERVIEW

A lease is a contractual agreement between a lessee and a lessor that gives the lessee the right, for a period of time, to use specific property owned by the lessor in exchange for periodic cash payments. A lease provides a flexible source of financing for the lessee and a source of finance revenue for the lessor. Current standards under ASPE and IAS 17 follow a classification approach to accounting for lessees. The new IFRS 16 (effective in 2019) adopts a contract-based approach for lessees. The standards determine whether the lease is accounted for as the acquisition of an asset with a corresponding liability on the statement of financial position (capital or finance lease, or right-of-use asset), or as an expense of the current period (operating lease). From the lessor's perspective, non-operating leases may be sales-type (called "manufacturer" or "dealer leases" under IFRS, and "sales-type leases" under ASPE) or financing-type (called "finance leases" under IFRS, and "direct financing leases" under ASPE). This chapter discusses lease criteria under IFRS 16, classification of leases according to criteria as set out by IAS 17 and ASPE, and accounting procedures under each from both the lessee and the lessor perspective.

STUDY STEPS

Understanding the Nature of Leases

A **lease** is a contractual agreement between a **lessee** and a **lessor** that gives the lessee the right, for a period of time, to use specific property owned by the lessor in exchange for periodic cash payments. Therefore, the lessor gives up use of the leased property over the lease term in exchange for a stream of revenue (cash payments), and the lessee gives up cash payments in exchange for use of the leased property over the lease term.

While **legal title** of the leased property does not transfer to the lessee in a lease, the **economic substance** of the transaction is that benefits from and rights to use the leased property do transfer to the lessee, and further analysis is required to determine appropriate accounting treatment.

Approach to Accounting for Leases

Current accounting standards under ASPE and IAS 17 follow a **classification approach** to lease accounting, under which the lessee classifies a lease as either a finance lease (called a "capital lease" under ASPE) or an operating lease, and the lessor classifies a lease as either a finance lease (called a "non-operating lease" under ASPE) or an operating lease.

If the lease does not transfer **risks and benefits of ownership** of the leased property to the lessee, the lease represents a rental arrangement and is an **operating lease**. For example, if a tenant (lessee) signs a lease to rent a unit in a commercial building for one year, risks and benefits of ownership of the unit do not transfer to the lessee, the lease is an operating lease, and the tenant records the rent portion of lease payments as prepaid rent or rent expense. However, if the lease does transfer risks and benefits of ownership of the leased property to the lessee, the lease represents an in-substance instalment purchase and is a **finance (or capital) lease**. For example, if a lessee signs a "lease-to-own" lease agreement for a new computer, the risks and benefits of ownership of the computer do transfer to the lessee; therefore, the lease is a finance lease. In a finance lease, the lessor is effectively selling the asset and the lessee is effectively buying the asset, even though legal title often remains with the lessor under the lease contract (at least initially).

Because leases often contain a variety of terms and conditions, it may not be clear whether risks and benefits of ownership are transferred. As such, the current IFRS standard (IAS 17) and ASPE followed by most lessees outline criteria for classification of a lease as a finance (or capital) lease. The criteria indicate that if any one or a combination of the criteria is met, there is support for classification of the lease as a finance (or capital) lease. For example, if there is reasonable assurance that the lessee will obtain ownership of the leased property by the end of the lease term, the lease is likely a finance lease. Existence of a **bargain purchase option** (an option for the lessee to purchase the leased asset at a price significantly less than expected fair value at the time the lessee can exercise the option) usually provides reasonable assurance that the lessee will obtain ownership of the leased asset by the end of the lease term, and therefore, reasonable assurance that the lease is a finance lease. A lease agreement may also include a **guaranteed residual value** (a maximum amount the lessor can require the lessee to pay at the end of the lease). A guaranteed residual value effectively requires the lessee to assume the risk associated with the residual amount of the leased property at the end of the lease.

From a lessor's perspective, the criteria to assess whether a lease is operating or non-operating are the same as the criteria applied by the lessee, with the exception that, under ASPE, two additional revenue-recognition-based criteria must also be met in order to classify the lease as non-operating. In effect, ASPE requires that in order for a lessor to classify a lease as non-operating (and therefore remove the asset from its books and recognize revenue related to the sale of the asset), revenue recognition criteria should also be met. In contrast, in an operating lease, the lessor simply records the rent portion of lease payments received as rent revenue, and the leased asset continues to be depreciated on the lessor's books. Non-operating leases are further classified as either **sales-type** (called **manufacturer** or **dealer leases** under IFRS and **sales-type leases** under ASPE) or **financing-type** (called **finance leases** under IFRS and **direct financing leases** under ASPE).

IFRS 16, which comes into effect in January 2019 but can be adopted earlier, replaces the classification approach with a contract-based approach. All leases that convey a right to **control** the use of an **identified asset** for a period of time in exchange for consideration should result in the recognition of assets and liabilities. The exceptions are short-term leases (12 months or less), or leases where the underlying asset is low value.

Becoming Proficient in Related Calculations and Journal Entries

The following discussion covers right-of-use assets (IFRS 16) and finance (or capital) leases from the lessee's perspective under IAS 17 (or ASPE), and non-operating leases from the lessor's perspective.

Lessee—Right-of-Use and Finance (or Capital) Leases

IFRS 16
From the lessee's perspective, if the lease involves the contractual right to use an asset (not transfer) for a period of time in exchange for consideration, it is accounted for as follows:

1. Initial measurement
   Record the right-of-use asset and the lease liability:

Right-of-Use Asset	XX	
Lease Liability		XX
Cash		XX

The asset and liability are recorded at the present value of the lease payments not paid at the commencement date, which include fixed payments, variable payments that depend on an index, amounts expected to be payable by the lessee under residual value guarantees, purchase options reasonably certain to be exercised, and lease termination penalties if the lease term reflects the lessee exercising an option to terminate the lease.

2. Measurement after recognition

(a) Record lease payments:

Lease Liability	XX	
Interest Expense	XX	
Cash		XX

(b) Accrue interest on the lease liability as at the financial statement date:

Interest Expense	XX	
Interest Payable		XX

If the financial statement date falls between lease payment dates, a journal entry is recorded to accrue interest expense incurred up to the financial statement date.

(c) Record depreciation on the right-of-use asset as at the financial statement date:

Depreciation Expense	XX	
Accumulated Depreciation—Right-of-Use Asset		XX

ASPE and IAS 17

From the lessee's perspective, if economic substance of the lease is such that risks and benefits of ownership of the leased property transfer (and the lessee is effectively purchasing the property), the lease is a finance (or capital) lease and is accounted for as follows:

1. Initial measurement

Record the asset and obligation under capital lease:

Assets under Lease	XX	
Obligations under Lease		XX

Assets under Lease and Obligations under Lease are debited and credited, respectively, by an amount equivalent to **present value of minimum lease payments**. Note that the accounts in the above journal entry are similar to the accounts in a journal entry to record purchase and financing of a fixed asset:

Property, Plant, and Equipment Assets	XX	
Notes Payable		XX

2. Measurement after recognition

(a) Record lease payments:

Obligations under Lease	XX	
Interest Expense	XX	
Cash		XX

Each lease payment consists of an interest component and a reduction of lease obligation (principal) component, as broken down in a **lease amortization schedule** prepared based on the effective interest method.

(b) Accrue interest on the lease obligation as at the financial statement date:

Interest Expense	XX	
Interest Payable		XX

If the financial statement date falls between lease payment dates, a journal entry is recorded to accrue interest expense incurred up to the financial statement date.

(c) Record depreciation on the asset under capital lease as at the financial statement date:

Depreciation Expense	XX	
Accumulated Depreciation—Leased Assets		XX

If the **lessee will retain the asset at the end of the lease term**, the depreciable period is the useful life of the asset to the lessee, and the depreciable amount is equal to capitalized asset cost minus estimated residual value (if any) at the end of the asset's useful life to the lessee. Therefore, if the lessee will retain the asset at the end of the lease term, calculation of depreciation is similar to how depreciation would be calculated had the lessee purchased the asset outright.

If the **asset will revert to the lessor at the end of the lease term**, the depreciable period is the lease term; however, the depreciable amount depends on whether or not the lessee guarantees a residual value. If the lessee does not guarantee a residual value, the depreciable amount is equal to the capitalized asset cost. If the lessee does guarantee a residual value, the depreciable amount is equal to the capitalized asset cost minus undiscounted guaranteed residual value.

Calculations

The lessee records the asset under lease (or right-of-use asset) and the corresponding obligation (or lease liability) at an amount equal to the **present value of minimum lease payments** under ASPE or the **present value of lease payments** not paid at the commencement date under IFRS 16.

Minimum lease payments under ASPE (used to calculate present value of minimum lease payments) include minimum rental payments (which exclude executory costs), guaranteed residual value (if any), and bargain purchase option amount (if any, assuming that management would exercise the option to purchase the asset at the end of the lease for a bargain price). Note that whether a purchase option is a bargain or not is sometimes a question of professional judgement. In general, a purchase option would be considered a bargain if the option amount is significantly lower than expected fair value of the asset at the time the lessee can exercise the option.

Lease payments under IFRS 16 include the above elements plus any variable payments that depend on an index and any lease termination penalties if the lease term reflects the lessee exercising an option to terminate the lease. IFRS 16 uses slightly different terminology [purchase options reasonably certain to be exercised (rather than bargain purchase options) and amounts expected to be payable by the lessee under residual value guarantees (rather than guaranteed residual values)].

Under IFRS 16, present value of lease payments is calculated using the **rate implicit in the lease**, unless it is not reasonably determinable, in which case, present value of lease payments is calculated using the **lessee's incremental borrowing rate**.

Under ASPE, present value of minimum lease payments is calculated using the lower of the rate implicit in the lease and the lessee's incremental borrowing rate.

The **rate implicit in the lease** is the lessor's internal rate of return at the beginning of the lease that makes the present value of the lease payments plus any unguaranteed residual value equal to the fair value of the leased asset. It is the rate of return that the lessor needs to receive in order to justify leasing the asset, and is usually based on factors such as the lessee's credit standing, the length of the lease, and the status of the residual value. The **lessee's incremental borrowing rate** is the interest rate that, at the beginning of the lease, the lessee would incur to borrow the funds needed to purchase an asset of similar value, assuming a similar term and using similar security for the borrowing.

Under ASPE the lower of present value of minimum lease payments and fair value of the asset is the capitalized cost of the asset and is included in the lease amortization schedule as the opening lease obligation amount, from which the first reduction of lease obligation (included in the first lease payment) is deducted. The capitalized cost of the asset is also used to calculate the depreciable amount of the asset under capital lease.

Lessor—Sales-Type and Financing-Type Leases

From the lessor's perspective, if the economic substance of the lease is such that risks and benefits of ownership of the leased asset transfer (and the lessee is effectively purchasing the asset), the lease is a finance lease (or a non-operating lease under ASPE). Non-operating leases are further classified as either **sales-type** (called "manufacturer" or "dealer leases" under IFRS and "sales-type leases" under ASPE) or **financing-type** (called "finance leases" under IFRS and "direct financing leases" under ASPE), and are accounted for as follows:

Journal Entries

1. Record the lease transaction:

   In a **sales-type lease**, the net investment in the lease and the gross profit on sale of the asset are recorded:

Cost of Goods Sold	XX	
Lease Receivable	XX	
Sales Revenue		XX
Unearned Interest Income		XX
Inventory		XX

Note that the accounts in the above journal entry are similar to the accounts in the journal entries to record a normal instalment sale of goods:

Accounts Receivable	XX	
Sales Revenue		XX
Unearned Interest Income		XX
Cost of Goods Sold	XX	
Inventory		XX

OR

In a **financing-type lease**, equipment purchased for lease and net investment in the lease are recorded as follows:

Equipment Acquired for Lessee	XX	
Cash		XX
Lease Receivable	XX	
Equipment Acquired for Lessee		XX
Unearned Interest Income		XX

In a financing-type lease, the asset purchased for lease is recorded, and sales revenue and cost of goods sold (and therefore gross profit) are not affected, because the lessor is usually a finance-lease company or financial intermediary that acquires the specific asset required by the lessee for the purpose of leasing the specific asset to the lessee.

2. Record lease payments received:

Cash	XX	
Lease Receivable		XX

3. Record interest income earned:

Unearned Interest Income	XX	
Interest Income		XX

Interest income is earned over time based on the net investment in the lease (lease receivable minus unearned interest income) over the life of the lease, and is calculated in a **lease amortization schedule** prepared based on the effective interest method.

Note that in a non-operating lease (sales-type or financing-type), no depreciation is recorded by the lessor.

Calculations

In both sales-type and financing-type leases, the lessor records a lease receivable and unearned interest income.

Lease receivable. Lease receivable is calculated as undiscounted rental/lease payments (excluding executory costs) plus any guaranteed or unguaranteed residual value that will accrue to the lessor at the end of the lease or any bargain purchase option. **Executory costs** are costs related to actual use of the asset (such as insurance, maintenance, and property taxes), and are therefore excluded from the calculation of rental/lease payments. The **undiscounted rental/lease payment** is the periodic rental/lease payment required to yield the rate implicit in the lease, on the amount to be recovered by the lessor through rental/lease payments. The **amount to be recovered by the lessor through rental/lease payments** is calculated as:

Investment in asset to be recovered (usually the fair value of the asset plus any initial direct lease costs if the lease is not a sales-type lease)	minus	Present value of the amount to be recovered through a bargain purchase option or (guaranteed or unguaranteed) residual value

The calculation under IFRS 16 is similar, but it uses slightly different terminology (for example, IFRS 16 refers to a purchase option reasonably certain of being exercised).

To calculate the undiscounted rental/lease payment, the amount to be recovered by the lessor through rental/lease payments is divided by an annuity factor reflecting the lease term and the rate implicit in the lease. If the rental/lease payment is made at the beginning of each lease year, an annuity due factor is used. If the rental/lease payment is made at the end of each lease year, an ordinary annuity factor is used.

Unearned finance or interest income. At lease inception, unearned finance or interest income is the difference between lease receivable and fair value of the leased property. Over the life of the lease, unearned interest income is amortized to interest income using the effective interest method and the rate implicit in the lease.

In sales-type leases, the lessor also records sales revenue and cost of goods sold.

Sales revenue. As a general rule, sales revenue will be the present value of the lease receivable, minus the present value of any unguaranteed residual value.

Cost of goods sold. As a general rule, cost of goods sold will be the laid-down cost of the asset to the lessor, minus the present value of any unguaranteed residual value. Note that inventory is credited for the full amount of laid-down cost to the lessor.

Note that present value of any unguaranteed residual value is excluded from the sales revenue amount and cost of goods sold amount, but included in the lease receivable amount. An unguaranteed residual value cannot be recognized as revenue (or an increase in gross profit) because realization of the amount is not reasonably assured. However, an unguaranteed residual value is included in the lease receivable amount because it is an estimate of the residual value of the asset that will accrue to the lessor at the end of the lease.

TIPS ON CHAPTER TOPICS

- In accounting for a finance (or capital or right-of-use) lease for a lessee or a non-operating lease for a lessor, consider **drawing a timeline** and entering all expected cash flows associated with the lease from the perspective of the party for whom you are preparing journal entries. For a lessee, expected cash flows will be minimum lease payments under ASPE, or the lease payments not paid at the commencement date under IFRS 16. For a lessor, expected cash flows will be minimum lease payments plus any unguaranteed residual value that will accrue to the lessor at the end of the lease. A timeline will help to determine the amounts to be discounted for calculation of **present value of minimum lease payments**.

- **ASPE minimum lease payments** include the following:
  1. minimum rental payments (the payments that the lessee will make or can be required to make under the lease agreement, excluding contingent rent and executory costs);
  2. amounts guaranteed (any amounts guaranteed by the lessee related to the residual value of the leased asset), if any;
  3. bargain purchase option (an option that allows the lessee to acquire the leased asset at the end of the lease term for an amount considerably below the asset's fair value at that time), if any; and
  4. penalty for failure to renew, if any.

- **IFRS 16 lease payments** include the following payments for the right to use the underlying leased asset during the lease term (IFRS 16 specifically excludes payments made at the commencement date of the lease):
  1. fixed rental payments,
  2. variable payments that depend on an index (such as those under a consumer price index),
  3. other contingent payments expected to be payable by the lessee under residual value guarantees,
  4. purchase options reasonably certain to be exercised, and
  5. lease termination penalties if the lease term reflects the lessee exercising an option to terminate the lease.

- Under an ASPE capital lease, the lessee records an asset under capital lease and a corresponding obligation under capital lease at **present value of minimum lease payments**. However, the amount recorded should not exceed fair value of the asset at lease inception.

(continued)

- Under an IFRS 16 right-of-use lease, the lessee records an asset and a corresponding liability at the **present value of lease payments**.

- Under IFRS 16, present value of lease payments is calculated using the **rate implicit in the lease**, unless it is not reasonably determinable, in which case, present value of lease payments is calculated using the lessee's incremental borrowing rate. Under ASPE, present value of minimum lease payments is calculated using the **lower of the rate implicit in the lease and the lessee's incremental borrowing rate**.

- In calculating and recording depreciation of the asset under capital lease, the lessee's determination of **depreciable period** depends on whether or not the asset will revert to the lessor at the end of the lease term. If the asset will revert to the lessor at the end of the lease term, the depreciable period is the lease term because the lessee will use the asset only for the lease term. If the lessee will retain the asset at the end of the lease term, or if the lease contains a bargain purchase option or a purchase option reasonably certain to be exercised (the assumption is that the lessee will exercise the option), the depreciable period is the useful life of the asset to the lessee.

- Under an **operating lease** under ASPE or IAS 17, the **lessee** records rental payments on a **straight-line basis** over the term of the lease (even if the payments are not payable on a straight-line basis), unless another systematic and rational basis better represents the pattern of the benefits received. The straight-line basis is also used for short-term leases of 12 months or less and for leases where the underlying asset is of low value under IFRS 16. Leases involving lease bonuses, scheduled rent increases, or rent-free periods must also conform to this guideline. For example, if a lessee signs a five-year operating lease that includes free rent for the last 10 months of the lease, total rent payments (for 50 months) are divided by 60 months (the entire lease term) to determine monthly rent expense.

- Under an **operating lease**, the **lessor** also recognizes rent revenue on a **straight-line basis** over the term of the lease (regardless of lease provisions), unless another systematic and rational basis better represents the pattern in which the leased asset provides benefits. If cash is not received in a period rent revenue is recognized, a deferral (or an accrual) type adjustment is required.

- The lessor's **gross investment in lease** is recorded in an account called "Lease Receivable." Gross investment in lease is defined as undiscounted rental/lease payments (excluding executory costs) plus any guaranteed or unguaranteed residual value that accrues to the lessor at the end of the lease, or any bargain purchase option. Thus, any guaranteed portion of residual value or any remaining unguaranteed portion of residual value that will accrue to the lessor at the end of the lease is included in the lessor's gross investment in lease.

- The lessor records **initial direct costs** (costs directly associated with negotiating and arranging a specific lease) based on the matching principle. In an operating lease, the lessor defers and allocates initial direct costs over the lease term in proportion to the amount of rent revenue that is recognized. In a financing-type lease, the lessor also defers and allocates initial direct costs over the lease term. In a sales-type lease, initial direct costs are expensed in the year they are incurred (in the year that gross profit is recognized).

Illustration 20-1   255

- Under an ASPE capital lease, the lessee's **capitalized asset cost and obligation under capital lease** is based on the lower of present value of minimum lease payments and fair value of the asset. In contrast, under IFRS 16, the lessee's **right-of-use asset** and **lease liability** are based on a present value of the lease payments, which include amounts expected to be payable by the lessee under residual value guarantees and purchase options. The initial lease liability should exclude any initial (advance) lease payments.

- Under a financing-type lease, the lessor's **lease receivable** is based on undiscounted rental/lease payments (excluding executory costs) plus any guaranteed or unguaranteed residual value or any bargain purchase option.

- Under ASPE, a lease is classified as a capital lease if any one or more of the following criteria are met: (1) there is reasonable assurance the lessee will obtain ownership (bargain purchase option); (2) lessee will benefit from most of the asset's benefits (length of lease ≥ 75% of economic life); or (3) present value of the minimum lease payments is substantially all (≥ 90%) of the fair value of the leased asset.

- Under IFRS 16, all leases are capitalized and placed on the statement of financial position except where lessees elect not to apply the IFRS 16 present value requirements for (1) short-term leases (12 months or less), or (2) leases where the underlying asset is of low value.

ILLUSTRATION 20-1

Classification of Leases

Classification of Leases by the Lessee

Under the ASPE classification approach to accounting for leases, the lessee classifies a lease as either an operating lease or a capital lease.

Under IFRS 16, "a contract is, or contains, a lease if the contract conveys the right to control the use of an identified asset for a period of time in exchange for consideration" (IFRS 16.9). All leases should be capitalized unless they meet one or both of the two exceptions discussed above (short-term leases or low-value leases).

Under ASPE, if the lease meets **one or more** of the following three criteria, the lessee should account for the lease as a **capital lease**:

1. There is reasonable assurance that the lessee will obtain ownership of the leased property by the end of the lease term. This criterion is considered satisfied if ownership transfers to the lessee at the end of the lease or if there is a bargain purchase option in the lease.

2. The lessee will benefit from most of the property benefits due to the length of the lease term, which is assumed to occur if the lease term is 75% or more of the leased property's economic life.

3. The lessor will recover substantially all of its investment in the leased property and earn a return on that investment, which is assumed to occur if, at lease inception, present value of minimum lease payments equals 90% or more of fair value of the leased property.

Classification of Leases by the Lessor

Under the classification approach to accounting for leases, the lessor classifies a lease as either an operating lease or a non-operating (or finance) lease. A non-operating (or finance) lease is further classified as either **sales-type** (called a "manufacturer" or "dealer lease" under IFRS and a "sales-type lease" under ASPE) or **financing-type** (called a "finance lease" under IFRS and a "direct financing lease" under ASPE).

Under IFRS, if the lease meets **one or more** of the following four criteria there is support for classification of the lease as a **finance lease** by the lessor.

1. There is reasonable assurance that the lessee will obtain ownership by the end of the lease term (e.g., a bargain purchase option).
2. The lease term is for the major part of the economic life of the assets.
3. The lease allows the lessor to recover substantially all of its investment in the leased property and to earn a return on the investment.
4. The leased assets are so specialized that, without major modification, they are of use only to the lessee.

Under ASPE, if the lease meets **one or more** of the three criteria (see previous page) for classification of a lease as a capital lease by the lessee, **and both** of the following revenue-recognition-based criteria are met, the lessor should account for the lease as a non-operating lease:

1. Credit risk associated with collection of lease payments is normal (compared with credit risk associated with collection of similar receivables).
2. Amounts of any unreimbursable costs that are likely to be incurred by the lessor under the lease can be reasonably estimated.

If there is a manufacturer's or dealer's profit (or loss) on the transaction, the lease is classified as a **sales-type lease**. Otherwise, the lease is classified as a **financing-type lease**. In sales-type leases, the lessor is usually a manufacturer or dealer that entered into the lease agreement as a way of facilitating the sale of the leased property. In contrast, in financing-type leases, the lessor is usually a lease-finance company or a financial intermediary that acquired the leased property for the specific purpose of earning finance revenue on the lease.

Under ASPE, a lease recorded as a capital lease by the lessee may or may not be recorded as a non-operating lease by the lessor. This is because the lease must meet both additional revenue-recognition-based criteria in order for the lessor to record the lease as non-operating. If the lease is recorded as a capital lease by

Illustration 20-2 257

the lessee and recorded as an operating lease by the lessor, both parties would report the leased property on their statements of financial position, and both parties would record depreciation on the leased property.

ILLUSTRATION 20-2

Steps in Evaluating and Accounting for a Lease Arrangement for a Lessee

Step 1: Examine the terms and conditions in the lease agreement.

- ASPE: Determine if the lease meets one or more of the criteria for a capital lease. (The criteria are listed in **Illustration 20-1** above.) If the lease is a capital lease, perform the rest of the steps below. If the lease is not a capital lease, account for the lease as an operating lease.

- IFRS 16: Determine if the contract is a lease (refer to **Illustration 20-1** above). If it is, then determine if it may be eligible for exemption from IFRS 16 because either (1) it is a short-term lease (12 months or less), or (2) the value of the underlying assets is low. If a lease exists and it is not eligible for an exemption, then it is a right-of-use lease and you should perform the rest of the steps below. If it is not a lease, or if it is eligible for exemption from IFRS 16, then the lease payments would be accounted for as an expense on a straight-line basis over the lease term, or by another systematic approach.

Step 2: Draw the timeline.

Step 3: Calculate present value of minimum lease payments (ASPE) or present value of lease payments (IFRS 16).

- ASPE minimum lease payments include:
  (a) minimum rental payments,
  (b) guaranteed residual value, if any, and
  (c) bargain purchase option, if any.

- IFRS 16 lease payments include:
  (a) fixed rental payments,
  (b) variable payments that depend on an index (such as those under a consumer price index),
  (c) other amounts expected to be payable by the lessee under residual value guarantees,
  (d) purchase options reasonably certain to be exercised, and
  (e) lease termination penalties if the lease term reflects the lessee exercising an option to terminate the lease.

- Under IFRS, use the **rate implicit in the lease**, unless it is not reasonably determinable, in which case, use the lessee's incremental borrowing rate. Under ASPE, use the **lower of the rate implicit in the lease, and the lessee's incremental borrowing rate**.

Step 4: Determine cost of the asset under capital lease.

- ASPE: Cost is the **lower** of present value of minimum lease payments (calculated in Step 3) and fair value of the asset. If cost is determined to be fair value of the asset, a new effective interest rate must be determined. The new effective interest rate is the interest rate that sets present value of minimum lease payments equal to fair value of the asset, including the effect of time value of money.

- IFRS 16: Cost of the right-of-use asset is the present value of lease payments (calculated in Step 3), plus lease payments made on or before the start date of the lease, in addition to initial direct costs incurred by the lessee and removal and restoration costs.

Step 5: Prepare the lessee's amortization schedule.

The beginning obligation under capital lease (lease liability) balance under ASPE is the amount determined in Step 4. Under IFRS 16, the initial lease liability is equal to the present value of lease payments as determined in Step 3 (excluding any initial (first day of lease or advance) lease payments).

(The interest rate for Step 5 is the rate used in Step 3, unless a new effective interest rate was determined under ASPE in Step 4, which would occur if the fair value of the asset was less than the present value of the minimum lease payments.)

Step 6: Prepare journal entries to record the lease on the lessee's books.

ILLUSTRATION 20-3

Steps in Evaluating and Accounting for a Lease Arrangement for a Lessor

Step 1: Examine the terms and conditions in the lease agreement.

Determine if the lease meets one or more of the criteria for a non-operating lease. (The criteria are listed in **Illustration 20-1**.) If the lease is a non-operating lease, perform the rest of the steps below. If the lease is not a non-operating lease, account for the lease as an operating lease. You should be aware that IFRS 16 largely carries forward the lessor accounting requirements from IAS 17. So, lessors continue to classify their leases as operating leases or finance leases and to account for those two types of leases in a manner that is consistent with how they are accounted for under ASPE.

Step 2: Determine the undiscounted rental/lease payment required to yield the lessor's desired rate of return on the investment (if the rental/lease payment amount is not given).

- The **undiscounted rental/lease payment** is the periodic rental/lease payment required to yield the rate implicit in the lease, on the amount to be recovered by the lessor through rental/lease payments. The **amount to be recovered by the lessor through rental/lease payments** is calculated as:

Investment in asset to be recovered (usually fair value of the asset plus any initial direct lease costs if the lease is not a sales-type lease)	minus	Present value of the amount to be recovered through a bargain purchase option or (guaranteed or unguaranteed) residual value

To calculate the undiscounted rental/lease payment, the amount to be recovered by the lessor through rental/lease payments is divided by an annuity factor reflecting the lease term and rate implicit in the lease. If the rental/lease payment is made at the beginning of each lease year, an annuity due factor is used. If the rental/lease payment is made at the end of each lease year, an ordinary annuity factor is used.

Step 3: Draw the timeline.

Step 4: Calculate net investment in the lease and unearned finance or interest income.

- Net investment in the lease is the present value of gross investment in the lease (calculated using the rate implicit in the lease).

- Gross investment in the lease is calculated as undiscounted rental/lease payments (calculated in Step 2) plus any (guaranteed or unguaranteed) residual value that will accrue to the lessor at the end of the lease or any bargain purchase option.

- Unearned finance or interest income is calculated as gross investment in the lease minus net investment in the lease.

Step 5: Prepare the lessor's amortization schedule.
Net investment in the lease (calculated in Step 4) is the starting point for this schedule. The lessor's implicit interest rate (the rate implicit in the lease) is used to calculate interest income on net investment in the lease.

Step 6: Prepare journal entries to record the lease on the lessor's books.

EXERCISE 20-1

PURPOSE: This exercise illustrates how a lessee and a lessor account for a lease when the lease agreement allows for automatic transfer of title of the leased asset to the lessee at the end of the lease term.

The following facts pertain to a lease between Star Bank Leasing (lessor) and JKL Printers (lessee) for a piece of equipment:

1. The lease is for a six-year term, beginning on January 1, 2017. Remaining economic life of the asset is six years.
2. The lessor's implicit interest rate is 9%; the lessee's incremental borrowing rate is 9%.
3. Fair value of the equipment is $150,000. Cost of the equipment to the lessor is $150,000.
4. The annual lease payment is $32,177.03; the first payment is due on January 1, 2017. This amount includes $1,500 for executory costs.
5. Title to the equipment automatically transfers to the lessee at the end of the lease term. The asset is expected to have a residual value of $12,000 at the end of its useful life.
6. Both the lessee and lessor use the calendar year for their accounting periods and prepare financial statements in accordance with ASPE.

Instructions

(a) Identify the lease type from the standpoint of the (1) lessee and (2) lessor.
(b) Prepare a lease amortization schedule for the lessee and lessor. Explain why they can both use the same schedule in this situation. Also, draw a timeline for the lessor.
(c) Prepare the journal entry to record the inception of the lease on the lessee's books.
(d) Prepare the journal entry to record the inception of the lease on the lessor's books.
(e) Indicate the amount(s) that will appear on the lessee's December 31, 2018 statement of financial position for this lease. Also indicate the portion that will appear in the current liability section and the portion that will appear in the non-current liability section. Explain how to determine these amounts.
(f) Indicate the amount(s) that will appear on the lessor's December 31, 2018 statement of financial position for this lease. Also indicate the portion that will appear in the current asset section and the portion that will appear in the non-current asset section. Show the gross investment in lease (lease receivable) and unearned interest components of each net investment amount. Explain how to determine these amounts.

Solution to Exercise 20-1

(a) The lease is a capital lease for the lessee because title to the equipment automatically transfers to the lessee at the end of the lease term. (The lease also meets the two other criteria for a capital lease.) For the lessor, under ASPE, two additional revenue-recognition-based criteria must be met in order for the lease to be treated as a non-operating lease. Assuming that credit risk associated with the lease is normal and that the amounts of any unreimbursable costs that are likely to be incurred by the lessor are reasonably estimable, the lessor should record the lease as a non-operating lease. Fair value of the equipment ($150,000) is equivalent to cost of the equipment to the lessor ($150,000); therefore, the lease is a direct financing lease.

(b) **Calculations:**

$32,177.03 − $1,500.00 executory costs = $30,677.03 annual lease payment (excluding executory costs)

$30,677.03 × Present value factor for an annuity due of 1 for $n = 6$, $i = 9\% =$ Net investment

$30,677.03 × 4.88965 = $150,000 net investment (rounded)

LEASE AMORTIZATION SCHEDULE

Date	Annual Lease Payment	9% Interest	Reduction of Present Value	Present Value Balance
1/1/17				$150,000.00
1/1/17	$ 30,677.03[a]	$ -0-	$ 30,677.03	119,322.97
1/1/18	30,677.03	10,739.07	19,937.96	99,385.01
1/1/19	30,677.03	8,944.65	21,732.38	77,652.63
1/1/20	30,677.03	6,988.74	23,688.29	53,964.34
1/1/21	30,677.03	4,856.79	25,820.24	28,144.10
1/1/22	30,677.03	2,532.93[b]	28,144.10	-0-
	$184,062.18	$34,062.18	$150,000.00	

[a]$32,177.03 − $1,500.00 = $30,677.03
[b]Includes rounding difference of $0.04

The lessor and the lessee can use the same lease amortization schedule in this situation because they are using the same interest rate to account for the lease (9%), and because there is no unguaranteed residual value that will accrue to the lessor at the end of the lease. For these same reasons, both parties have the same timeline for the lease, which is depicted as follows:

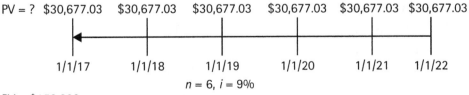

PV = ? $30,677.03 $30,677.03 $30,677.03 $30,677.03 $30,677.03 $30,677.03

1/1/17   1/1/18   1/1/19   1/1/20   1/1/21   1/1/22

$n = 6$, $i = 9\%$

PV = $150,000

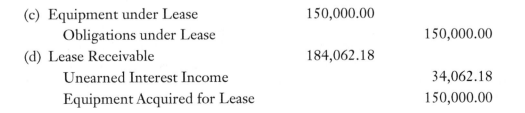

(c) Equipment under Lease   150,000.00
        Obligations under Lease   150,000.00

(d) Lease Receivable   184,062.18
        Unearned Interest Income   34,062.18
        Equipment Acquired for Lease   150,000.00

(e) Equipment under Lease will appear in the property, plant, and equipment section of the lessee's statement of financial position (at $150,000). Accumulated depreciation of $46,000 will also appear in that section. To calculate annual depreciation, residual value is deducted from capitalized cost of the equipment under lease to arrive at depreciable amount, and depreciable amount is depreciated over useful life of the asset (because title to the asset will transfer to the lessee at the end of the lease term). Thus, annual depreciation is calculated as ($150,000 − $12,000) ÷ 6 years = $23,000. The amounts that will appear on the lessee's December 31, 2018 statement of financial position under current liabilities and non-current liabilities are as follows:

Current liabilities

Interest payable	$ 8,944.65
Obligations under lease	21,732.38

Non-current liabilities

Obligations under lease	77,652.63

To determine these amounts, refer to the lease amortization schedule. Find the date on the schedule that is relevant to the statement of financial position date (December 31, 2018). If the reporting date is not on the schedule (as is the case here), find the date that most recently precedes the statement of financial position date (January 1, 2018, in this exercise). As at the statement of financial position date, current liabilities include interest payable to date ($8,944.65 due on 1/1/19) and current obligation under lease ($21,732.38 due on 1/1/19), and non-current liabilities include non-current obligation under lease ($23,688.29 + $53,964.34 = $77,652.63).

(f) Net investment in lease at December 31, 2018, is $108,329.66 ($99,385.01 + $8,944.65 = $108,329.66). This will be reflected on the lessor's December 31, 2018 statement of financial position as follows:

Current assets

Lease receivable	$30,677.03
Unearned interest income	-0-
Net investment in lease	$30,677.03

Non-current assets

Lease receivable	$92,031.09
Unearned interest income	(14,378.46)
Net investment in lease	$77,652.63

To determine these amounts, refer to the lease amortization schedule. Find the date on the schedule that is relevant to the statement of financial position date (December 31, 2018). If the reporting date is not on the schedule (as is the case here), find the date that most recently precedes the statement of financial position date (January 1, 2018, in this exercise). The lease payment on the following line is the amount of gross investment in lease (lease receivable) to be classified as a current asset. The unearned interest portion of that lease payment (as at the statement of financial position date) is deducted to arrive at net investment in lease. In this exercise, no portion of the $8,944.65 interest due on 1/1/19 is unearned as of 12/31/18 because it was all earned during 2018; therefore $0 of unearned interest income is reflected in the current assets section. The total of lease payments (and other receipts) appearing on all subsequent lines of the lease amortization schedule ($30,677.03 + $30,677.03 + $30,677.03 = $92,031.09) is the amount of gross investment in lease (lease receivable) to be classified as a non-current asset. The unearned interest portion of those lease payments (as of the statement of financial position date) is deducted to arrive at net investment in lease. In this exercise, ($6,988.74 + $4,856.79 + $2,532.93 = $14,378.46) is deducted from lease receivable to arrive at non-current net investment in lease.

To check the accuracy of the current and non-current portions, the total of current and non-current net investment in lease ($30,677.03 + $77,652.63 = $108,329.66) should equal present value of the lease at the statement of financial position date, which is true in this case. Present value of the lease at the statement of financial position date equals present value balance ($99,385.01) plus any accrued interest earned to the statement of financial position date ($8,944.65).

EXERCISE 20-2

PURPOSE: This exercise is a comprehensive illustration of the accounting procedures for a lease in which the leased asset reverts back to the lessor and still has some value at the end of the lease term. This exercise illustrates (1) how the lessor determines the amount of the periodic lease payment, (2) the lessor's calculations for recording the transactions associated with the lease, (3) the meaning of the terms "gross investment in lease" and "net investment in lease," (4) the lessee's calculations for recording the transactions associated with the lease, (5) the journal entries on the lessor's books, and (6) the journal entries on the lessee's books.

On January 1, Year 1, Leaseco has a piece of equipment with a cost of $95,000 and a fair value of $95,000. On that date, Leaseco leases the piece of equipment to Rentco for a five-year term at an implicit rate of 10%. The annual lease payment is due at the beginning of each year, and the first payment is due on the lease inception date. The leased equipment will revert back to Leaseco at the end of the lease term; its fair value at that date is estimated to be $10,000. Both Leaseco and Rentco have a calendar-year reporting period, and both companies prepare financial statements in accordance with IFRS. Rentco is aware of Leaseco's implicit rate; Rentco's incremental borrowing rate is 11%.

Instructions

Assuming the lease is a right-to-use lease to the lessee and a finance lease to the lessor:

(a) Calculate the amount of the annual lease payment (excluding executory costs) to be collected by the lessor.

(b) Draw the timeline for the lessor.

(c) For the lessor, calculate (1) gross investment in lease at lease inception, and (2) net investment in lease at lease inception.

(d) Calculate the amount of interest income to be reported by the lessor for (1) Year 1, (2) Year 2, and (3) Year 5.

(e) Prepare the lease amortization schedule for the lessor.

(f) Calculate the cost of the lessee's equipment under right-of-use lease.

(g) Draw the timeline for the lessee.

(h) Calculate the amount of interest expense to be reported by the lessee for (1) Year 1, (2) Year 2, and (3) Year 5.

(i) Prepare the lease amortization schedule for the lessee.

(j) Explain why the lessee's lease amortization schedule is different from the lessor's lease amortization schedule. Under what circumstances would the two parties be able to use the same lease amortization schedule?

(k) Prepare all of the journal entries for the lessor's books for Years 1 and 2.

(l) Prepare all of the journal entries for the lessee's books for Years 1 and 2.

(m) Compare and contrast the journal entries for the lessee [part (l)] with the journal entries for the lessor [part (k)].

Solution to Exercise 20-2

(a) Investment to be recovered	$95,000.00
Less: Present value of unguaranteed residual ($10,000 × 0.62092)[a]	(6,209.20)
Present value of investment to be recovered through lease payments	88,790.80
Present value factor for an annuity due of 1 for $n = 5, i = 10\%$	÷ 4.16986
Annual lease payment to be collected by the lessor	**$21,293.47**

[a]0.62092 is the factor for present value of 1 for $n = 5, i = 10\%$

In this exercise, the lessor's investment is recovered through annual lease payments by the lessee and the equipment's fair value ($10,000) at the end of the lease. Due to the time value of money, today's cash equivalent of $10,000 due in five years is less than $10,000.

(b)   PV = ? $21,293.47 $21,293.47 $21,293.47 $21,293.47 $21,293.47 $10,000

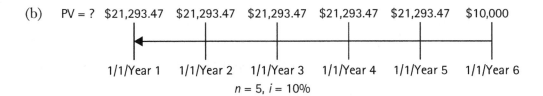

    1/1/Year 1   1/1/Year 2   1/1/Year 3   1/1/Year 4   1/1/Year 5   1/1/Year 6

                        $n = 5, i = 10\%$

PV = $ 6,209.20[a]

PV =   88,790.80[b]

    $95,000.00

[a]$10,000.00 × 0.62092 = $6,209.20
[b]$21,293.47 × 4.16986 = $88,790.80

(c) 1. Periodic rent payment $ 21,293.47

        Number of rent payments in lease term   × 5

        Total rent payments   106,467.35

        Plus bargain purchase option or guaranteed residual   -0-

        Total minimum lease payments   106,467.35

        Unguaranteed residual value   10,000.00

        Gross investment in lease at lease inception $116,467.35

    2. Present value of annual rent payments (annuity due) $ 88,790.80

        Plus present value of bargain purchase option or
        guaranteed residual   -0-

        Present value of minimum lease payments   88,790.80

        Present value of unguaranteed residual value   6,209.20

        Net investment in lease at lease inception $ 95,000.00

(d) Year 1 = $7,370.65, Year 2 = $5,978.37, Year 5 = $909.27

Calculations:

    Net investment in lease at lease inception $ 95,000.00

    First lease payment received, 1/1/Year 1   (21,293.47)

    Net investment in lease after first lease payment
    received, 1/1/Year 1   73,706.53

    Interest income for Year 1 (10% × $73,706.53)   7,370.65

    Net investment in lease at 12/31/Year 1   81,077.18

    Second lease payment received, 1/1/Year 2   (21,293.47)

Net investment in lease after second lease payment received, 1/1/Year 2	59,783.71
Interest income for Year 2 (10% × $59,783.71)	**5,978.37**
Net investment in lease at 12/31/Year 2	65,762.08
Third lease payment received, 1/1/Year 3	(21,293.47)
Net investment in lease after third lease payment received, 1/1/Year 3	44,468.61
Interest income for Year 3 (10% × $44,468.61)	**4,446.86**
Net investment in lease at 12/31/Year 3	48,915.47
Fourth lease payment received, 1/1/Year 4	(21,293.47)
Net investment in lease after fourth lease payment received, 1/1/Year 4	27,622.00
Interest income for Year 4 (10% × $27,622.00)	**2,762.20**
Net investment in lease at 12/31/Year 4	30,384.20
Fifth lease payment received, 1/1/Year 5	(21,293.47)
Net investment in lease after fifth lease payment received, 1/1/Year 5	9,090.73
Interest income for Year 5 ($10,000 − $9,090.73)	**909.27**[a]
Net investment in lease at end of lease term	$ 10,000

[a]Includes a rounding difference of $0.20

- Notice that the interest amount for the last period ($909.27 for Year 5, in this exercise) is a "plug" figure. The difference between the derived amount ($909.27) and the calculated amount of interest ($9,090.73 × 10% = $909.07) is the rounding difference ($909.27 − $909.07 = $0.20).

- Notice that **net investment in lease is a present value (discounted) amount**.

- Interest income is a function of (a) present value balance, (b) interest rate, and (c) time. As time passes, interest income accrues (due to the time value of money). Interest income **increases** the present value balance, whereas lease payments **decrease** the present value balance.

- Notice that there is interest income in Year 5, even though the last lease payment is received at the beginning of Year 5. This is due to the fact that a single sum (unguaranteed residual value, in this exercise) is expected by the lessor at the end of the lease term.

(e) LESSOR'S LEASE AMORTIZATION SCHEDULE

Date	Annual Lease Payment and Residual Value	Interest on Net Investment (10%)	Net Investment Recovery	Net Investment
1/1/Year 1				$95,000.00
1/1/Year 1	$ 21,293.47		$21,293.47	73,706.53
1/1/Year 2	21,293.47	$ 7,370.65	13,922.82	59,783.71
1/1/Year 3	21,293.47	5,978.37	15,315.10	44,468.61
1/1/Year 4	21,293.47	4,446.86	16,846.61	27,622.00
1/1/Year 5	21,293.47	2,762.20	18,531.27	9,090.73
12/31/Year 5	10,000.00	909.27[a]	9,090.73	-0-
	$116,467.35	$21,467.35	$95,000.00	

[a]Includes a rounding difference of $0.20

- Interest income included in a lease payment is interest income for the period that occurs **prior** to the due date of the lease payment. Thus, interest income shown on the 1/1/Year 3 line on the lease amortization schedule is the interest income earned during the Year 2 calendar year.

- The amounts on the lessor's lease amortization schedule can be derived by the calculations shown in part (d) above.

- There is no interest income included in the first lease payment received, because the first lease payment is received on the lease inception date and no time has passed during which interest income was earned.

- The rounding difference is always plugged to the interest column on the last line of the lease amortization schedule. If all calculations are performed correctly and are rounded to the nearest cent, the rounding difference will be small—usually less than $10. A larger rounding difference generally indicates that there are errors in the lease amortization schedule. The lease amortization schedule may contain mathematical errors or more serious procedural errors.

- All items that appear on the timeline in part (b) appear in the "Annual Lease Payment and Residual Value" column of the lease amortization schedule.

- On the lease amortization schedule, the total of the "Net Investment Recovery" column is equal to the beginning amount of the "Net Investment" column.

- The total of the "Annual Lease Payment and Residual Value" column is the initial gross investment in lease amount [see solution to part (c)].

- Notice how the net investment in lease amount at December 31, Year 1, derived from the appropriate numbers on the lease amortization schedule, can be proven by an independent present value calculation as at that date.

(continued)

Calculations:

From the lease amortization schedule:

Net investment in lease balance at 1/1/Year 1	$73,706.53
Interest income for Year 1	7,370.65
Net investment in lease balance at 12/31/Year 1	$81,077.18

Present value calculation:

Present value factor of an annuity due of 1 for
$n = 4, i = 10\% = 3.48685$

Present value factor of 1 for $n = 4, i = 10\% = 0.68301$

$21,293.47 $\times$ 3.48685	$74,247.14
$10,000.00 $\times$ 0.68301	6,830.10
Present value at end of Year 1	$81,077.24

The $0.06 difference between $81,077.18 and $81,077.24 is a
rounding difference.

(f) Annual rental payment $21,293.47

  Present value factor of an annuity due of 1, $n = 5, i = 10\%$ ... $\times$ 4.16986

  Present value of annual rental payments ... 88,790.79

  Present value of bargain purchase option or guaranteed residual ... -0-

  Present value of minimum lease payments ... $88,790.79

- The lessee's cost of the asset is equal to the total of the initial lease liability, any lease payments made at the commencement date, initial direct costs incurred by the lessee, and an estimate of the costs to be incurred by the lessee to dismantle and remove the underlying asset. Under IFRS, the interest rate to be used in determining present value of the minimum lease payments is the rate implicit in the lease whenever it can be reasonably determined; otherwise, the lessee's incremental borrowing rate is used. In this exercise, Rentco is aware of the rate implicit in the lease (10%), which is used to calculate present value of minimum lease payments.

- If the leased asset reverts back to the lessor at the end of the lease term and the lessee does not guarantee a residual value, the residual value of the leased asset (if any) does not affect the lessee's calculations. In this exercise, the leased equipment reverts back to Leaseco at the end of the lease term, and Rentco does not guarantee a residual value; therefore, the $10,000 residual value does not affect Rentco's calculations.

(g)

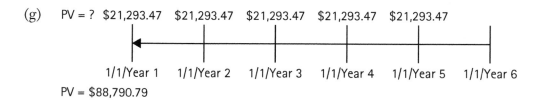

PV = $88,790.79

In this exercise, the lessee's timeline differs from the lessor's timeline because the lessor expects to have an unguaranteed residual value, which is not relevant to the lessee.

(h) Year 1 = $6,749.73, Year 2 = $5,295.36, Year 5 = $0

Calculations:

Present value of obligation at lease inception	$88,790.79
First lease payment, 1/1/Year 1	(21,293.47)
Present value of obligation after first lease payment, 1/1/Year 1	67,497.32
Interest expense for Year 1 (10% × $67,497.32)	**6,749.73**
Present value of obligation at 12/31/Year 1	74,247.05
Second lease payment, 1/1/Year 2	(21,293.47)
Present value of obligation after second lease payment, 1/1/Year 2	52,953.58
Interest expense for Year 2 (10% × $52,953.58)	**5,295.36**
Present value of obligation at 12/31/Year 2	58,248.94
Third lease payment, 1/1/Year 3	(21,293.47)
Present value of obligation after third lease payment, 1/1/Year 3	36,955.47
Interest expense for Year 3 (10% × $36,955.47)	**3,695.55**
Present value of obligation at 12/31/Year 3	40,651.02
Fourth lease payment, 1/1/Year 4	(21,293.47)
Present value of obligation after fourth lease payment, 1/1/Year 4	19,357.55
Interest expense for Year 4 ($21,293.47 − $19,357.55)	**1,935.92**[a]
Present value of obligation at 12/31/Year 4	21,293.47
Fifth lease payment, 1/1/Year 5	(21,293.47)
Present value after last lease payment, 1/1/Year 5	-0-
Interest expense for Year 5 (10% × $0)	**-0-**
Present value of obligation at end of lease term	$ -0-

[a]$21,293.47 − $19,357.55 = $1,935.92 interest expense including rounding difference
$19,357,55 × 10% = $1,935.76 interest expense if there was no rounding difference
$1,935.92 − $1,935.76 = $0.16 rounding difference

In this situation, there is no interest expense for Year 5 because the obligation is fully paid as of the beginning of the fifth year.

(i) LESSEE'S LEASE AMORTIZATION SCHEDULE

Date	Annual Lease Payment	Interest Expense (10%)	Reduction of Principal	Balance of Lease Obligation
1/1/Year 1				$67,497.32
1/1/Year 2	21,293.47	$ 6,749.73	14,543.74	52,953.58
1/1/Year 3	21,293.47	5,295.36	15,998.11	36,955.47
1/1/Year 4	21,293.47	3,695.55	17,597.92	19,357.55
1/1/Year 5	21,293.47	1,935.92[a]	19,357.55	-0-
	$85,173.88	$17,676.56	$67,497.32	

[a]Includes rounding difference of $0.16

The total of the "Annual Lease Payment" column minus the total of the "Interest Expense" column equals the total of the "Reduction of Principal" column, and the total of the "Reduction of Principal" column equals the obligation's present value at lease inception (the beginning balance of lease obligation).

(j) Even though the lessee and the lessor both use the same interest rate in this exercise, the lessee's lease amortization schedule differs from the lessor's lease amortization schedule because the $10,000 unguaranteed residual value must be included only on the lessor's lease amortization schedule. The lessor and the lessee can use the same lease amortization schedule if they are using the same interest rate and if one of the following conditions exists: (1) an automatic transfer of title at the end of the lease term, or (2) a bargain purchase option, or (3) a residual value guaranteed by the lessee to the lessor, or (4) an unguaranteed residual value for the lessor of zero.

(k) 1/1/Year 1	Lease Receivable	116,467.35	
	Equipment Acquired for Lease		95,000.00
	Unearned Interest Income		21,467.35
	Cash	21,293.47	
	Lease Receivable		21,293.47
12/31/Year 1	Unearned Interest Income	7,370.65	
	Interest Income		7,370.65
1/1/Year 2	Cash	21,293.47	
	Lease Receivable		21,293.47
12/31/Year 2	Unearned Interest Income	5,978.37	
	Interest Income		5,978.37

(l)	1/1/Year 1	Right-of-Use Equipment	88,790.79	
		Lease Liability		67,497.32
		Cash		21,293.47
	12/31/Year 1	Interest Expense	6,749.73	
		Lease Liability		6,749.73
		Depreciation Expense	17,758.16	
		Accumulated Depreciation—Leased Equipment		17,758.16

($88,790.79 ÷ 5 years = $17,758.16)

	1/1/Year 2	Lease Liability	21,293.47	
		Cash		21,293.47
	12/31/Year 2	Interest Expense	5,295.36	
		Lease Liability		5,295.36
		Depreciation Expense	17,758.16	
		Accumulated Depreciation—Leased Equipment		17,758.16

(m) 1. At lease inception, the lessor records the total **gross** amount to be received in a receivable account (Lease Receivable), whereas the lessee records the total **present value** amount to be paid in a payable account (Lease Liability). Since receivables and payables are generally reported at present value, the lessor sets up a contra receivable account (Unearned Interest Income) to reduce carrying value of the net receivable to present value of all future cash flows associated with the lease.

   2. The lessor accounts for interest as a **deferral** of income, but the lessee accounts for interest as an **accrual** of expense. Therefore, the lessor records interest income only at the end of an accounting period, with an adjusting entry. The lessee records interest expense when a lease payment is made **and** at the end of an accounting period (with an adjusting entry) if the accounting period ends on a date other than a lease payment date. The lessor's adjusting entry to record recognition of interest earned is never reversed; the lessee's adjusting entry to accrue interest expense can be reversed.

   3. The lessor's entry to record a lease payment received is the same each period. (Debit Cash and credit Lease Receivable for the entire lease payment.) Similarly (under IFRS), the lessee's entry to record the lease payment is the same each period (debit Lease Liability and credit Cash for the entire lease payment). Under ASPE, the lessee's entry to record a lease payment is different each period because the amount attributed to interest expense and the amount attributed to the reduction of lease obligation differ for each lease payment.

   4. Both the lessor and the lessee record interest, but only the lessee records depreciation in this lease arrangement.

Under IFRS, depreciation for a leased asset is recorded by either the lessee (in a right-of-use lease) or the lessor (in an operating lease). However, under ASPE, if a lease classified as a capital lease by the lessee does not meet both additional revenue-recognition-based criteria for recognition as a sales-type lease or a direct financing lease by the lessor, then the lessor classifies the lease as operating, the leased asset is (or remains) capitalized by both the lessee and lessor, and depreciation for the leased asset is recorded by both the lessee and lessor.

EXERCISE 20-3

PURPOSE: This exercise provides an example of (1) accounting procedures for a lessor with a sales-type lease, (2) lease periods that do not coincide with accounting periods, and (3) a lease with a purchase option.

The following facts relate to a lease made by Wormold Company to Marina Corporation:

Inception of lease	May 1, 2017
Annual payment due at beginning of each lease year, first payment due May 1, 2017	$10,000
Lease term	5 years
Remaining economic life of asset	7 years
Estimated fair value at end of lease term	$8,000
Purchase option at end of lease term	$2,000
Lessor's cost	$40,000
Lessor's implicit rate	10%
Annual accounting period	Calendar year

Wormold Company prepares financial statements in accordance with IFRS.

Instructions

(a) Prepare the lease amortization schedule and draw the timeline for the lessor.

(b) Answer the following questions from the standpoint of the lessor:

1. What is the gross investment in lease at lease inception?

2. What is the net investment in lease at lease inception?

3. What amount of gross profit should be reported on the income statement for 2017?

4. What amount of gross profit should be reported on the income statement for 2018?

5. What amount should be reported as interest income on the income statement for 2017?

6. What amount should be reported as interest income on the income statement for 2018?

(c) Prepare the following journal entries for the lessor:
1. Lease inception on May 1, 2017
2. Lease payment received on May 1, 2017
3. Adjusting entry at December 31, 2017
4. Lease payment received on May 1, 2018
5. Adjusting entry at December 31, 2018

(d) If the lessee has an incremental borrowing rate of 9%, could the lessee use the same lease amortization schedule as the lessor in this situation?

(e) Explain how the entry in part (c) (1) would be different for the lessor if there was no purchase option and if the estimated residual value to the lessor (unguaranteed) at the end of the lease term was $2,000. Also, explain whether or not the lessee could use the same lease amortization schedule as the lessor in this situation.

Solution to Exercise 20-3

(a) **LESSOR'S LEASE AMORTIZATION SCHEDULE**

Date	Annual Lease Payment Plus PO[a]	Interest on Net Investment (10%)	Net Investment Recovery	Net Investment
5/1/17				$42,940.44
5/1/17	$10,000.00		$10,000.00	32,940.44
5/1/18	10,000.00	$3,294.04	6,705.96	26,234.48
5/1/19	10,000.00	2,623.45	7,376.55	18,857.93
5/1/20	10,000.00	1,885.79	8,114.21	10,743.72
5/1/21	10,000.00	1,074.37	8,925.63	1,818.09
4/30/22	2,000.00	181.91[b]	1,818.09	-0-
	$52,000.00	$9,059.56	$42,940.44	

[a]PO is an abbreviation for "purchase option reasonably certain to be exercised." The purchase option is reasonably certain to be exercised because the option price is only 25% ($2,000 ÷ $8,000 = 25%) of the asset's estimated fair value at the date the option is exercisable.
[b]Includes a rounding difference of $0.10

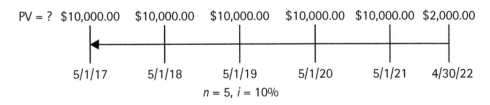

PV = ? $10,000.00 $10,000.00 $10,000.00 $10,000.00 $10,000.00 $2,000.00

5/1/17   5/1/18   5/1/19   5/1/20   5/1/21   4/30/22
                     $n = 5, i = 10\%$

PV = $ 1,241.84[a]
PV =   41,698.60[b]
        $42,940.44

[a]$2,000 × 0.62092 = $1,241.84
[b]$10,000 × 4.16986 = $41,698.60

(b) 1.

Total rent payments: 5 × $10,000	$50,000.00
Purchase option	2,000.00
Minimum lease payments	52,000.00
Unguaranteed residual value	-0-
Gross investment in lease at lease inception	$52,000.00

2.

Present value of rent payments ($10,000 × 4.16986[a])	$41,698.60
Present value of PO ($2,000 × 0.62092[b])	1,241.84
Present value of minimum lease payments	42,940.44
Present value of unguaranteed residual value	-0-
Net investment in lease at lease inception	$42,940.44

[a] Factor for present value of an annuity due for $n = 5, i = 10\%$
[b] Factor for present value of a single sum for $n = 5, i = 10\%$

3.

Sale price	$42,940.44[c]
Cost of goods sold	40,000.00[d]
Gross profit to be recognized during 2017	$ 2,940.44

[c] The sale price is equal to present value of the lease payments receivable minus present value of any unguaranteed residual value for the lessor:

Present value of the lease receivable	$42,940.44
Present value of unguaranteed residual value	-0-
Sale price	$42,940.44

[d] Cost of goods sold is equal to the lessor's cost or carrying value minus present value of any unguaranteed residual value for the lessor:

Lessor's cost	$40,000.00
Present value of unguaranteed residual value	-0-
Cost of goods sold	$40,000.00

4. None. All of the gross profit attributable to a sales-type lease is recognized in the year of lease inception (in this exercise, in the year 2017).

 Do not confuse gross profit attributable to a sales-type lease with profit (gain) on sale of an asset attributable to a sale-leaseback transaction, which is generally deferred and amortized. (In a sale-leaseback transaction, the asset is sold and subsequently leased back to the seller by the purchaser.)

5. $3,294.04 × $\frac{8}{12}$ = $2,196.03 interest for 2017
There are eight months between May 1, 2017, and December 31, 2017. Interest income for those eight months is included on the 5/1/18 payment line of the lease amortization schedule. Interest income of $3,294.04 showing on the 5/1/18 payment line is for the 12-month period preceding 5/1/18. Therefore, interest for the last eight months of 2017 is calculated as $\frac{8}{12}$ × $3,294.04.

6. $3,294.04 \times \dfrac{4}{12}$ $1,098.01

    $2,623.45 \times \dfrac{8}{12}$ <u>1,748.97</u>

    Interest for 2018   <u>$2,846.98</u>

The lease amortization schedule is **always** prepared using the interest dates (which are dictated by the lease agreement). The interest amount appearing on each payment line is then apportioned to the appropriate accounting period(s). Referring to the lease amortization schedule in part (a), the interest appearing on the 5/1/18 line is the interest for 5/1/17 through 4/30/18. Thus, $\dfrac{8}{12}$ of it belongs on the 2017 income statement and $\dfrac{4}{12}$ of it belongs on the 2018 income statement. Likewise, the $2,623.45 appearing on the 5/1/19 line is the interest for 5/1/18 through 4/30/19. Thus, $\dfrac{8}{12}$ of it is reported on the 2018 income statement.

(c) 1. 5/1/17

Lease Receivable	52,000.00	
Cost of Goods Sold	40,000.00	
Unearned Interest Income		9,059.56
Inventory		40,000.00
Sales Revenue		42,940.44

2. 5/1/17

Cash	10,000.00	
Lease Receivable		10,000.00

3. 12/31/17

Unearned Interest Income	2,196.03	
Interest Income		2,196.03

($3,294.04 \times \dfrac{8}{12} = $2,196.03$)

4. 5/1/18

Cash	10,000.00	
Lease Receivable		10,000.00

5. 12/31/18

Unearned Interest Income	2,846.98	
Interest Income		2,846.98

($3,294.04 \times \dfrac{4}{12} = $1,098.01$)

($2,623.45 \times \dfrac{8}{12} = $1,748.97$)

($1,098.01 + $1,748.97 = $2,846.98$)

(d) If the lessee prepares financial statements in accordance with IFRS, the lessee would calculate present value of the lease liability using the implicit rate because it is reasonably determinable in this exercise. Since the lessee would use the same interest rate as the lessor and there is a bargain purchase option (reasonably certain to be exercised) in this lease, the lessee could use the same lease amortization schedule as the lessor. However, if the lessee prepares financial statements in accordance with ASPE, the lessee would use the lower of its incremental borrowing rate and the rate implicit in the lease. If its incremental borrowing rate is 9%, the lessee would calculate present value of the lease obligation and cost of the asset under capital lease using the 9% interest rate, and the lessee would not use the same lease amortization schedule as the lessor.

(e) If there was no purchase option reasonably certain to be exercised, but there was a $2,000 unguaranteed residual value to the lessor at the end of the lease term, the lessor's journal entry at lease inception would be:

Lease Receivable	52,000.00	
Cost of Goods Sold	38,758.16[a]	
Unearned Interest Income		9,059.56[b]
Inventory		40,000.00
Sales Revenue		41,698.60[c]

[a]Cost of the asset	$40,000.00
Present value of unguaranteed residual value	(1,241.84)[(1)]
Cost of goods sold	$38,758.16
[(1)]$2,000.00 × 0.62092 = $1,241.84	
[b]Gross investment in lease	$52,000.00
Net investment in lease	42,940.44[(2)]
Unearned interest income	$9,059.56
[(2)]Present value of minimum lease payments	$41,698.60
Present value of unguaranteed residual value	1,241.84
Net investment in lease	$42,940.44
[c]Present value of lease receivable	$42,940.44[(3)]
Present value of unguaranteed residual value	(1,241.84)
Sales revenue	$41,698.60
[(3)]$52,000.00 − $9,059.56 = $42,940.44	

The entry differs from part (c) (1) in that both Sales Revenue and Cost of Goods Sold are reduced by the cash equivalent value of the $2,000 unguaranteed residual value to be received in five years. In effect, a portion of the asset ($2,000) is **not** considered sold, and the remainder of the asset is considered sold to the lessee.

The lessor's lease amortization schedule would be the same as it appears now in part (a), except that the column heading "Annual Lease Payment Plus PO" would be changed to "Annual Lease Payment Plus Residual Value." However, the lessee's lease amortization schedule would differ, even if both parties were using a 10% interest rate. The lessor's lease amortization schedule would include the

Illustration 20-4   277

$2,000 unguaranteed residual value, whereas the lessee's lease amortization schedule would not. The lessee's lease amortization schedule would start with a beginning balance of lease liability (obligation) of $41,698.60, rather than $42,940.44.

ILLUSTRATION 20-4

Residual Value in Non-operating Leases

In accounting for leases, residual value is the estimated value of the leased asset at a future point in time. Residual value may be the estimated value of the asset at the end of the lease term, or at the end of the asset's useful life, depending on which, if either, is relevant to the party for whom you are preparing journal entries.

Residual value of the leased asset at the end of the lease term is included in the lessor's calculation of periodic lease payment if either of the following is true:

- The asset will revert back to the lessor at the end of the lease and the residual value is guaranteed. (Note: IFRS 16 uses the term amount "expected to be payable by the lessee under residual value guarantees," while ASPE uses the term "guaranteed residual value." We use the two terms interchangeably in our examples.)
- The asset will revert back to the lessor at the end of the lease and the residual value is unguaranteed.

Residual value of the leased asset at the end of the lease term is included in the lessor's calculation of gross investment in lease and net investment in lease if either of the following is true:

- The asset will revert back to the lessor at the end of the lease and the residual value is guaranteed.
- The asset will revert back to the lessor at the end of the lease and the residual value is unguaranteed.

Residual value of the leased asset at the end of the lease term (or any portion thereof) is included in the lessee's calculation of cost of the leased asset and lease liability/obligation, **only** if the following is true:

- The asset will revert back to the lessor at the end of the lease and the residual value (or any portion thereof) is guaranteed by the lessee.

Guaranteed residual value of the leased asset at the end of the lease term, or residual value at the end of the asset's useful life, is used by the lessee in determining periodic depreciation expense if either of the following is true:

- The asset will revert back to the lessor at the end of the lease and the residual value (or a portion thereof) is guaranteed by the lessee. (Use the guaranteed residual value at the end of the lease term.)

- The asset will transfer to the lessee at the end of the lease term either through an automatic transfer clause or a bargain purchase option. (Use the residual value at the end of the asset's useful life.)

CASE 20-1

PURPOSE: This case reviews the lessee's and lessor's accounting procedures for a lease with a guaranteed residual value.

Instructions

Refer to the facts of **Exercise 20-3** above. Assume there is no purchase option at the end of the lease term. Further, assume that the asset reverts back to the lessor at the end of the five-year lease term and that the lessee guarantees the lessor a residual value of $2,000 at that time.

(a) Explain how the lessor's accounting procedures for a lease with a $2,000 guaranteed residual value will differ from the accounting procedures for a lease with a $2,000 bargain purchase option.

(b) Explain how the lessee's accounting procedures for a lease requiring the lessee to guarantee a residual value of $2,000 will differ from the accounting procedures for a lease with a $2,000 purchase option that is reasonably certain to be exercised.

Solution to Case 20-1

(a) From the lessor's standpoint, there is no difference in calculations, timeline, or journal entries between a lease with a $2,000 guaranteed residual value and a lease with a $2,000 purchase option reasonably certain to be exercised. Thus, the **Solution to Exercise 20-3**, parts (a) through (c), would not change if the lease included a $2,000 guaranteed residual value instead of a $2,000 purchase option reasonably certain to be exercised (except that "purchase option" would be replaced with "guaranteed residual value" or "GRV").

(b) From the lessee's standpoint, the timeline, journal entries, and most calculations are the same for a lease with a guaranteed residual value as with a lease with a purchase option reasonably certain to be exercised. However, there is a major difference in the calculation of depreciation:

- If the lease contains a purchase option reasonably certain to be exercised, the cost of the asset under capital lease (reduced by any residual value available to the lessee at the end of the asset's useful life) is depreciated over the remaining useful life of the asset because the lessee is assumed to acquire the asset at the end of the lease term.

- If the lease contains a guaranteed residual value, cost of the asset under capital lease reduced by the guaranteed residual value is depreciated over the lease term because the asset will revert to the lessor.

Thus, using the facts from **Exercise 20-3**, assuming the lessee uses a 10% interest rate to account for the lease and the straight-line depreciation method, annual depreciation expense for the lessee would be as follows:

Assuming a purchase option of $2,000 that is reasonably certain to be exercised:

$$\frac{\$42,940.44 - \$0^a}{7 \text{ years}} = \$6,134.35 \text{ depreciation per year for seven years}$$

[a]Assumes a zero residual value at the end of seven years

Assuming a guaranteed residual value of $2,000:

$$\frac{\$42,940.44 - \$2,000.00}{5 \text{ years}} = \$8,188.09 \text{ depreciation per year for five years}$$

> If the $2,000 is a guaranteed residual value and the lessee uses the same interest rate as the lessor, the lessee's lease amortization schedule is the same as the lessor's lease amortization schedule.

EXERCISE 20-4

PURPOSE: This exercise illustrates how to classify receivables and payables related to leases on the statement of financial position.

The following lease amortization schedule is properly being used by both the lessee and lessor. The lease contains a purchase option (bargain, or reasonably certain to be exercised) (PO). Both the lessee and lessor have a calendar-year reporting period.

Date	Annual Lease Payment Plus PO	Interest (10%)	Reduction of Present Value	Balance of Present Value
5/1/17				$47,731.28
5/1/17	$11,000.00		$11,000.00	36,731.28
5/1/18	11,000.00	$3,673.13	7,326.87	29,404.41
5/1/19	11,000.00	2,940.44	8,059.56	21,344.85
5/1/20	11,000.00	2,134.49	8,865.51	12,479.34
5/1/21	11,000.00	1,247.93	9,752.07	2,727.27
4/30/22	3,000.00	272.73	2,727.27	-0-
	$58,000.00	$10,268.72	$47,731.28	

Instructions

Fill in the blanks that follow. Show your calculations.

(a) The amount of gross investment in lease to be reported in the current asset section of the lessor's statement of financial position at December 31, 2018, is $_____.

(b) The amount of net investment in lease to be reported in the current asset section of the lessor's statement of financial position at December 31, 2018, is $_____.

(c) The amount to be reported in the current liability section of the lessee's statement of financial position at December 31, 2018, by the caption "Interest Payable" is $_____.

(d) The amount to be reported in the current liability section of the lessee's statement of financial position at December 31, 2018, by the caption "Obligations under Capital Leases" (or Lease Liability) is $_____.

(e) The amount to be reported in the non-current liability section of the lessee's statement of financial position at December 31, 2018, by the caption "Obligations under Capital Leases" (or Lease Liability) is $_____.

Solution to Exercise 20-4

(a) The amount of gross investment in lease to be reported in the current asset section of the lessor's statement of financial position at December 31, 2018, is $11,000.

The most recent payment prior to the statement of financial position date (December 31, 2018) was May 1, 2018. The payment line following that line shows a receipt of $11,000 due on May 1, 2019, which is within one year of the statement of financial position date.

(b) The amount of net investment in lease to be reported in the current asset section of the lessor's statement of financial position at December 31, 2018, is $10,019.85.

Gross investment in lease in current assets at December 31, 2018	$11,000.00
Unearned interest income reported as contra-receivable at December 31, 2018	(980.15)[a]
Net investment in lease in current assets at December 31, 2018	$10,019.85

[a]$2,940.44 \times \dfrac{4}{12} = $980.15

The interest portion of the lease payment due to be received on May 1, 2019, is $2,940.44. That amount is for the 12 months that precede May 1, 2019. Thus, at December 31, 2018, four months of the $2,940.44 amount remains unearned.

The net investment reflected in non-current assets (in the non-current investments section) on the lessor's December 31, 2018 statement of financial position would be determined as follows:

Gross investment in lease classified in non-current assets	$ 25,000.00[b]
Unearned interest income classified in non-current assets	(3,655.15)[c]
Net investment in lease classified in non-current assets	$ 21,344.85

[b]Lease payments due 5/1/20 and 5/1/21 plus PO = $11,000 + $11,000 + $3,000 = $25,000
[c]Interest portion of lease payments due 5/1/20 and 5/1/21 plus interest portion of PO = $2,134.49 + $1,247.93 + $272.73 = $3,655.15

(c) The amount to be reported in the current liability section of the lessee's statement of financial position at December 31, 2018, by the caption "Interest Payable" is $1,960.29 under ASPE.

Balance of obligation under capital lease at May 1, 2018	$29,404.41
Interest rate	10%
Interest for 12 months, 5/1/18 to 4/30/19	2,940.44
Fraction of year from 5/1/18 to 12/31/18	× 8/12
Interest for 5/1/18 to 12/31/18, which is a current liability at 12/31/18	$ 1,960.29

Under IFRS, this amount would not be reported separately as Interest Payable, but would be included in the current portion of Lease Liability.

(d) The amount to be reported in the current liability section of the lessee's statement of financial position at December 31, 2018, by the caption "Obligations under Capital Leases" under ASPE is $8,059.56.

The payment line that follows the statement of financial position date (12/31/18) is 5/1/19. The principal portion of the lease payment due on that date ($8,059.56) represents the current portion of the lessee's obligation under capital lease [excluding any accrued interest calculated in part (c)] at 12/31/18.

Under IFRS, the accrued interest payable is added to the balance of the lease liability. When the next payment is received on 5/1/19, the lease liability will be debited for the full $11,000 payment amount. This amount will be reported under current liabilities by the caption "Lease Liability."

(e) The amount to be reported in the non-current liability section of the lessee's statement of financial position at December 31, 2018, by the caption "Obligations under Capital Leases" is $21,344.85. (This figure is the present value balance on the 5/1/19 lease payment line.)

Under IFRS, the amount reported in the non-current liability section by the caption "Lease Liability" is $20,364.70. This is calculated as the present value balance at 5/1/18 plus accrued interest to 12/31/18 less the amount reported as a current liability in part (d) above ($29,404.41 + $1,960.29 − $11,000.00 = $20,364.70).

A summary of the presentations under IFRS and ASPE follows:

	IFRS	ASPE
Current liabilities		
Lease liability	$11,000.00	
Non-current liabilities		
Lease liability	$20,364.70	
Current liabilities		
Interest payable		$ 1,960.29
Obligations under lease, current portion		$ 8,059.56
Non-current liabilities		
Obligations under lease		$21,344.85

The total liability under both IFRS and ASPE represents the present value of the liability at 5/1/18 plus accrued interest from 5/1/18 to 12/31/18 ($29,404.41 + $1,960.29 = $31,364.70).

EXERCISE 20-5

PURPOSE: This exercise reviews the accounting procedures for an operating lease under the classification approach to accounting for leases.

On January 1, 2017, Clarence Corp. leased office space to Montreal Service Corp. The following information applies to the lease:

1. The lease is appropriately classified as an operating lease by both the lessee and lessor. Both companies prepare financial statements under ASPE.
2. The lease term is five years.
3. The lease payment is $50,000 for 2017 and is scheduled to increase by $10,000 each year.
4. Lease payments are due each January 1 and the first one is paid on January 1, 2017.
5. The lessee paid a $5,000 bonus payment to the lessor on January 1, 2017, to obtain the lease.
6. The lessor's cost of the property is $900,000. The lessor uses straight-line depreciation and estimates **that** the property has a useful life of 25 years with no residual value.
7. The lessor paid an $8,000 finder's fee to a leasing agent for their services.
8. Annual insurance and property taxes on the property amount to $7,200 and are paid by the lessor.

Instructions

(a) Calculate rent expense for the lessee for (1) 2017 and (2) 2018.
(b) Calculate the lessor's operating profit (loss) on the leased asset for (1) 2017 and (2) 2018.

Solution to Exercise 20-5

(a) 1. $71,000

    2. $71,000

Calculations:

Average rental	$ 70,000[a]
Amortization of lease bonus	1,000[b]
Rent expense per year	$ 71,000
Rent for 2017	$ 50,000
Rent for 2018	60,000
Rent for 2019	70,000
Rent for 2020	80,000
Rent for 2021	90,000
Total rent	$350,000

[a]$350,000 ÷ 5 years = $70,000 per year
[b]$5,000 bonus ÷ 5 years = $1,000 per year

EXPLANATION: For an operating lease, payments should be expensed by the lessee on a straight-line basis over the lease term, unless another systematic basis better represents the pattern of the benefits received. Thus, the lessee amortizes lease bonus and scheduled rent increases on a straight-line basis over the lease term.

(b) 1. $26,200

    2. $26,200

Calculations:

Average rental		$70,000[a]
Amortization of lease bonus		1,000[b]
Rent revenue		71,000
Less: Depreciation expense	$36,000[c]	
Amortization of initial direct costs	1,600[d]	
Executory costs—insurance and property taxes	7,200	44,800
Operating profit on leased asset		$26,200

[a]Same calculation as in part (a) above
[b]Same calculation as in part (a) above
[c]($900,000 − 0) ÷ 25 years = $36,000 depreciation per year
[d]$8,000 ÷ 5 years = $1,600 amortization per year

EXPLANATION: For an operating lease, an equal (straight-line) amount of rent revenue is recognized in each accounting period regardless of the lease provisions, unless another systematic and rational basis better represents the pattern in which the leased asset provides benefits. Thus, the lessor amortizes the lease bonus and scheduled rent increases on a straight-line basis over the lease term. Initial direct costs paid to independent third parties, such as appraisal fees, finder's fees, commissions, and legal fees, are amortized over the lease term. Executory costs (such as insurance and property taxes) are expensed in the period in which they are incurred.

ANALYSIS OF MULTIPLE-CHOICE QUESTIONS

Question

1. Wellington Ltd. leases an airplane from Kitchener Corp. under an agreement that meets the ASPE criteria for a capital lease for Wellington Ltd. The 12-year lease requires lease payments of $35,000 at the beginning of each year, including $3,000 per year for maintenance, insurance, and taxes. The incremental borrowing rate for the lessee is 11%; the lessor's implicit rate is 9% and is known by the lessee. The present value factor of an annuity due of 1 for 12 years at 11% is 7.20652. The present value factor of an annuity due of 1 for 12 years at 9% is 7.80519. According to ASPE, the lessee should record the leased asset at:
   a. $32,000 × 7.20652 = $230,609.
   b. $32,000 × 7.80519 = $249,766.
   c. $35,000 × 7.20652 = $252,228.
   d. $35,000 × 7.80519 = $273,182.

EXPLANATION: Think through the steps involved in accounting for a lease for a lessee (see **Illustration 20-2**). The lessee should record the leased asset at present value of minimum lease payments (excluding executory costs). Under ASPE, present value of minimum lease payments should be calculated using the lower of the lessee's incremental borrowing rate and the rate implicit in the lease. In this example, the annual $3,000 executory cost is deducted from the $35,000 lease payment to arrive at a $32,000 lease payment excluding executory costs. The lessor's implicit rate of 9% is known by the lessee and is lower than the lessee's incremental borrowing rate of 11%; hence, the 9% implicit rate is used to calculate present value of minimum lease payments. Present value of minimum lease payments is calculated by multiplying the lease payment (excluding executory costs) by the factor for present value of an annuity due of 1 for $n = 12, i = 9\%$. There is no indication that the asset's fair value may be lower than the calculated present value of minimum lease payments; therefore, the asset is recorded at this present value. (Solution = b.)

Question

2. Which item is NOT included in the amount of the lease payment under IFRS 16?
   a. Contingent rentals
   b. Guaranteed residual values
   c. Renewal option
   d. Executory costs

EXPLANATION: Under IFRS 16, the lease liability is initially measured at the present value of the lease payments not paid at the commencement date, including (1) fixed payments, (2) variable (contingent) payments that depend on an index, (3) amounts expected to be payable under residual value guarantees, (4) purchase options reasonably certain to be exercised, and (5) lease termination penalties if the lease term reflects the lessee exercising an option to terminate the lease. Executory costs are not included. (Solution = d.)

Question

3. The following list of items relates to accounting for leases:
    I.   Annual lease payments
    II. Bargain purchase option or a purchase option if the lessee is reasonably certain to exercise that option
    III. Guaranteed residual value
    IV. Unguaranteed residual value

    From a lessee's perspective, minimum lease payments under ASPE and lease payments under IFRS would include items:
    a. I and II only.
    b. I, II, and III only.
    c. I, III, and IV only.
    d. I, II, III, and IV.

EXPLANATION: List the components of minimum lease payments (ASPE) and lease payments (IFRS) and compare with the above selections. From a lessee's perspective, minimum lease payments/lease payments include:

* minimum rental payments,
* guaranteed residual value (if any), and
* bargain purchase option (if any under ASPE) and a purchase option if the lessee is reasonably certain to exercise that option (under IFRS).

Thus, minimum lease payments include only items I, II, and III. (Solution = b.)

> An unguaranteed residual value would affect the lessor's accounting for the lease. For example, the lessor's gross investment in lease consists of undiscounted rental/lease payments plus any guaranteed or unguaranteed residual value or any bargain purchase option, and net investment in lease is the present value of gross investment in lease.

Question

4. On December 31, 2016, Ryan Corporation leased a yacht from François Company for an eight-year period expiring December 31, 2024. Equal annual payments of $80,000 are due on December 31 of each year, beginning on December 31, 2016. Ryan Corporation follows IFRS, and the lease is properly classified as a right-of-use lease on Ryan's books. At December 31, 2016, present value

of the eight lease payments over the lease term discounted at 10% is $469,474. Assuming all payments are made on time, the amount that should be reported by Ryan Corporation as the total lease liability on its December 31, 2017 statement of financial position is:

a. $348,421.

b. $400,063.

c. $436,421.

d. $480,000.

EXPLANATION: Calculate the amounts for the first three lines on the lessee's lease amortization schedule. Remember, the initial liability will not include the payment due at commencement. The schedule would appear as follows: (Solution = a.)

Date	Annual Lease Payment	Interest Expense (10%)	Reduction of Principal	Balance of Lease Obligation
12/31/16				$389,474.00
12/31/17	$80,000.00	$38,947.40	$41,052.60	348,421.40
12/31/18	80,000.00	34,842.14	45,157.86	303,263.54

Question

5. The following facts pertain to a lease:

(1) The lease provides that the asset will revert back to the lessor at the end of the seven-year lease term.

(2) Present value of minimum lease payments is equal to $54,000 and fair value of the asset at lease inception is $60,000.

(3) The remaining economic life of the leased asset is estimated to be 10 years.

(4) For the lessor, credit risk associated with the lease is normal.

(5) The lessor guarantees the asset against obsolescence.

(6) Fair value of the asset exceeds its cost on the lessor's books.

(7) Both the lessee and lessor prepare financial statements in accordance with ASPE.

How should the lease be classified on the books of the lessee and lessor, respectively?

	Lessee	Lessor
a.	Capital	Sales-type
b.	Capital	Operating
c.	Operating	Sales-type
d.	Operating	Operating

EXPLANATION: Review the facts and determine how the lease should be classified on the books of the lessee. Repeat the process and determine how the lease should be classified on the books of the lessor. Refer to **Illustration 20-1**. Present value of minimum lease payments equals 90% or more of the fair value of the asset, which is one of the ASPE criteria for classification of a lease as a capital lease. Thus, the lease should be classified as a capital lease on the books of the lessee. However, the lessor guarantees the asset against obsolescence, which means that the amounts of any unreimbursable costs that are likely to be incurred by the lessor under the lease cannot be reasonably determined, and the lease should be classified as an operating lease on the books of the lessor. Further analysis of the details of the lease is shown below:

(1) The asset will be returned to the lessor at the end of the lease; therefore, the lease does not meet the first criteria for classification of a lease as a capital lease.

(2) Present value of minimum lease payments ($54,000) is equal to 90% of the fair value of the asset at lease inception ($60,000); thus, the lease meets the third ASPE criteria for classification of a lease as a capital lease.

(3) The lease term is seven years, which is only 70% of the remaining economic life of the asset; hence, the lease does not meet the second ASPE criteria for classification of a lease as a capital lease.

(4) The lessor's credit risk associated with the lease is normal; therefore, the lease meets the first revenue-recognition-based ASPE criteria for classification of a lease as a non-operating lease.

(5) The lessor guarantees the asset against obsolescence, which means that the amounts of any unreimbursable costs that are likely to be incurred by the lessor under the lease cannot be reasonably determined. Therefore, under ASPE, the second revenue-recognition-based criteria for classification of a lease as a non-operating lease is not met.

(6) If fair value of the asset exceeds its cost on the lessor's books, the lease would be a sales-type lease on the books of the lessor **if**, under ASPE, the lease meets at least one criteria for classification of a lease as a capital lease on the lessee's books, and **both** revenue-recognition criteria for classification of a lease as a non-operating lease on the lessor's books. (Solution = b.)

In this example, both the lessee and lessor prepare financial statements in accordance with ASPE, which means that ASPE criteria for classification of leases must be applied. ASPE criteria include numerical thresholds, whereas IFRS criteria do not include numerical thresholds. As well, under IFRS, the degree to which the asset is specialized and of use only to the lessee without major expense to the lessor is an additional criterion considered for classification of a lease as a finance lease.

Question

6. Digger Corporation is a lessee with a capital (right-of-use) lease. The asset is recorded at a cost of $195,000 and has a useful life of 10 years. The lease term

is five years. The asset is expected to have a fair value of $70,000 at the end of five years, and a fair value of $25,000 at the end of 10 years. The lease agreement provides for automatic transfer of title of the asset to the lessee at the end of the lease term. What depreciable amount and what service life should the lessee use to calculate depreciation for the first year of the lease?

	Depreciable Amount	**Service Life**
a.	$195,000 – $25,000	5 years
b.	$195,000 – $25,000	10 years
c.	$195,000 – $70,000	5 years
d.	$195,000 – $70,000	10 years

EXPLANATION: Select the option that will provide the best matching of costs with revenues. Because title will automatically be transferred, the lessee is expected to hold and use the asset for 10 years. The benefit to be consumed over the 10 years is the difference between the asset's recorded cost ($195,000) and its expected value at the end of its useful life to the lessee ($25,000). (Solution = b.)

Question

7. Three different lease situations are described below:
    (1) Lessee's incremental borrowing rate is 12%.

    Lessor's implicit rate is 12%.

    Asset will revert to the lessor at the end of the lease term when the asset is expected to have a fair value of $60,000.

    (2) Lessee's incremental borrowing rate is 12%.

    Lessor's implicit rate is 12%.

    Lease requires the lessee to guarantee a residual value of $30,000 to the lessor.

    (3) Lessee's incremental borrowing rate is 12%. Lessor's implicit rate is 14%.

    Lease contains a purchase option that the lessee is reasonably certain to exercise of $20,000.

    Under IFRS, in which of the above cases can the lessor and lessee use the same lease amortization schedule?
    a. 1 and 2 only
    b. 2 and 3 only
    c. 1 and 3 only
    d. 1, 2, and 3

APPROACH AND EXPLANATION: The lessee and lessor can use the same lease amortization schedule when both of the following conditions exist: (1) the lessee and lessor use the same interest rate to account for the lease, and (2) the lessor does **not** have an unguaranteed residual value to account for. The lessee and lessor use the same interest rate in all cases because under IFRS, the lessor uses the implicit rate and the lessee uses the implicit rate whenever it can be reasonably determined (otherwise the incremental borrowing rate is used). In case 1, the asset reverts to the lessor at the end of the lease term when the asset has a fair value of $60,000, which means that an unguaranteed residual value will be reflected in the lessor's lease amortization schedule that will not be reflected in the lessee's lease amortization schedule. Therefore, both parties cannot use the same lease amortization schedule for case 1. In cases 2 and 3, both parties can use the same lease amortization schedule. (Solution = b.)

Question

8. A lessee with a capital (right-of-use) lease containing a bargain purchase option (purchase option that the lessee is reasonably certain to exercise) should depreciate the leased asset over the:

    a.   asset's remaining useful life to the lessee.

    b.   term of the lease.

    c.   useful life of the asset to the lessee or the term of the lease, whichever is shorter.

    d.   useful life of the asset to the lessee or the term of the lease, whichever is longer.

EXPLANATION: Depreciation is a cost allocation process undertaken to comply with the matching principle; that is, to match expenses with revenues. The appropriate depreciation period is the period the asset will be used in operations. If the lease agreement provides for automatic transfer of title of the asset to the lessee at the end of the lease term or for a bargain purchase option (or a purchase option that the lessee is reasonably certain to exercise under IFRS 16), the assumption is that the lessee will use the asset for its remaining useful life to the lessee, which would be the period appropriate for depreciation. If the lease does not provide for automatic transfer of title of the asset or for a bargain purchase option, the assumption is that the lessee will use the asset only for the lease term, which would be the period appropriate for depreciation. The leased asset should be depreciated over either the asset's remaining useful life to the lessee, or the term of the lease, whichever period the asset will be used in operations. The length of the useful life of the asset to the lessee and the length of the term of the lease are not compared to determine the depreciation period. (Solution = a.)

> The cost of leasehold improvements (items such as fences and partitions added to leased premises by a lessee) are amortized over the life of the asset (the improvement) or the term of the lease, whichever is shorter.

Question

9. A lessor has a direct financing lease. The end of the lessor's accounting period does not coincide with a lease payment date. At the end of the lessor's

accounting period, the journal entry to record interest earned since the last rental payment date would be:

a.	Cash	XX	
	Interest Income		XX
b.	Interest Receivable	XX	
	Interest Income		XX
c.	Unearned Interest Income	XX	
	Interest Income		XX
d.	Interest Expense	XX	
	Interest Payable		XX

EXPLANATION: In a non-operating lease, the lessor accounts for interest as a deferral of income. Thus, at date of lease inception, the lessor includes all amounts to be received under the lease (gross investment in lease) in the Lease Receivable account. These amounts include interest to be earned over the term of the lease; hence, a contra account called "Unearned Interest Income" is established in order to reduce the carrying value of Lease Receivable down to the present value of the components of gross investment in lease (called "net investment in lease"). As interest is earned, it is transferred from Unearned Interest Income to an earned interest account (Interest Income). Note that the lessee uses an accrual approach to accounting for interest expense. At lease inception, the lessee records only the present value of the lease obligation in the Obligations under Lease account. Therefore, at a statement of financial position date, an adjusting entry on the lessee's books will include a debit to Interest Expense and a credit to Interest Payable. (Solution = c.)

Question

10. Under ASPE at the inception of a capital lease, a residual value guaranteed by the lessee should be included as part of minimum lease payments on the books of the:

	Lessee	Lessor
a.	Yes	Yes
b.	Yes	No
c.	No	Yes
d.	No	No

EXPLANATION: The components of minimum lease payments are (a) minimum rental payments (excluding executory costs), (b) bargain purchase option, if any, and (c) guaranteed residual value, if any. If the lessor has a guaranteed residual value, it is included in the lessor's calculation of minimum lease payments, regardless of whether the lessee or a third party is the guarantor. The lessee includes a guaranteed residual value in its calculation of minimum lease payments only if the lessee is the party providing the guarantee. (Solution = a.)

Question

11. A lessor has an operating lease with a five-year term that requires lease payments of $100,000 in 2017, $120,000 in 2018, $140,000 in 2019, $160,000 in 2020, and $180,000 in 2021. In 2019, compared with 2018, the lease will cause the following types of revenue/income to increase:

	Rent	Interest
a.	Yes	Yes
b.	Yes	No
c.	No	Yes
d.	No	No

EXPLANATION: In an operating lease, the lessor recognizes rent revenue on a straight-line basis over the lease term, regardless of the lease provisions, unless another systematic and rational basis is more representative of the pattern in which the leased asset provides benefits. In this situation, an average amount of $140,000 would be recognized as rent revenue in each of the five years of the lease. The lessor does not earn interest income in an operating lease. Thus, under an operating lease, the lessor has no increase in rent revenue or interest income from one year to another. (Solution = d.)

The journal entry to record receipt of the lease payment in 2017 would be as follows:

Cash	100,000	
Rent Receivable	40,000	
Rent Revenue		140,000

Question

12. Hanks Leasing Co. has an operating lease. Rents are a constant amount each year. Rent payments collected in 2017 that pertain to use of the leased asset in 2018 should be reported as:

a. rent revenue in 2017.

b. accrued rent revenue on the December 31, 2017 statement of financial position.

c. unearned rent revenue on the December 31, 2017 statement of financial position.

d. rent receivable on the December 31, 2017 statement of financial position.

EXPLANATION: Rent revenue received in advance represents a liability at the December 31, 2017 statement of financial position date. Revenue received in advance is usually called "unearned rent revenue." (Solution = c.)

Question

13. A lessor with a manufacturer or dealer (or sales-type) lease involving an unguaranteed residual value available to the lessor at the end of the lease term will report sales revenue in the period of lease inception at which of the following amounts?

   a. Minimum lease payments plus any unguaranteed residual value

   b. Present value of minimum lease payments

   c. Cost of the asset to the lessor, less present value of any unguaranteed residual value

   d. Present value of minimum lease payments, plus present value of any unguaranteed residual value

EXPLANATION: Unguaranteed residual value is considered a portion of the asset that is not yet sold. Therefore, sales revenue is the present value (today's cash equivalent) of all future cash flows expected to be received by the lessor for the leased asset **except** for the unguaranteed residual value. Therefore, sales revenue is calculated by determining the present value of minimum lease payments. Answer selection "a" describes the gross investment in lease calculation, answer selection "c" describes the lessor's cost of goods sold calculation, and answer selection "d" describes the lessor's net investment in lease amount. (Solution = b.)

Question

14. A lease has an eight-year term and the related asset has a remaining useful life of 10 years. The lease is appropriately classified as a manufacturer or dealer lease on the books of the lessor. Gross profit related to this lease should be:

   a. recognized wholly in the period of lease inception.

   b. amortized evenly over eight years.

   c. amortized evenly over 10 years.

   d. amortized over eight years using the effective interest method.

EXPLANATION: Gross profit related to a manufacturer or dealer lease is recognized wholly in the period of lease inception. The lessor's journal entry at the date of lease inception includes a credit to Sales Revenue (for present value of minimum lease payments) and a debit to Cost of Goods Sold (for the asset's carrying value less present value of any unguaranteed residual value). When these two amounts are reported on the income statement, the resulting difference is the amount of gross profit earned on the lease. (Solution = a.)

Question

15. Tharmarajan Corporation sold a greenhouse to Laventhall Company for $800,000 and realized a gain of $300,000. Laventhall immediately leased the asset back to the seller under a finance lease arrangement for the remainder of

the asset's useful life of 10 years. The lessee uses the straight-line depreciation method. Under IAS 17, profit on the sale of the greenhouse should be:

a. recognized in full in the year of sale.

b. deferred and amortized over the lease term.

c. deferred and recognized in full at the end of the lease term.

d. deferred and amortized on the same basis as the depreciation of the leased asset.

EXPLANATION: The lease meets the criteria to be classified as a finance lease; therefore, the seller-lessee accounts for the transaction as a sale and the lease as a finance lease. In this situation, under IAS 17, any profit on the sale of assets that are leased back is deferred and amortized over the lease term. Note that under ASPE, any profit on the sale of assets that are leased back is deferred and amortized on the same basis as the depreciation of the leased assets. On the statement of financial position, the balance of the deferred gain is reported as Unearned Profit on Sale-Leaseback. (Solution = b.)

Question

16. What type of lease is permitted to be excluded from being recognized as a right-of-use lease under IFRS 16?

a. Short-term lease

b. Vehicle lease

c. Significant value lease

d. Lease including bargain purchase option

EXPLANATION: Under the contract-based right-of-use approach taken by IFRS 16, the general rule is that all leases are recognized as right-of-use assets, but companies can choose to not apply the requirements for right-of-use assets for (1) short-term leases and (2) leases for low-value items (Solution = a.)

Question

17. When can lease payments be recognized as an expense on a straight-line basis over the lease term by the lessee under IFRS 16?

a. If the lease payments are deemed as an expense by the lessor

b. If the lease term is less than one year

c. If the lease doesn't meet the criteria of an operating lease by the lessor

d. If the lessor elects to record the lease as an operating lease and informs the lessee

EXPLANATION: Accounting for the lease by the lessor has no impact on how the lessee should account for the lease. IFRS 16 is based on the view that all lease contracts create assets and liabilities that should be recognized in the financial statements of lessees. As such, all leases are considered capital (right-of-use) unless they are short-term (less than one year) or involve low-value items. (Solution = b.)

Question

18. Under ASPE, leases are either capital or operating to a lessee; under IFRS 16:
    a. leases are treated the same as under ASPE.
    b. leases are treated the same as under IAS 17.
    c. all leases are considered capital (right-of-use).
    d. all leases are considered capital (right-of-use) except when companies apply an exemption for short-term leases and leases of low-value assets.

EXPLANATION: Accounting for leases for lessees differs between ASPE and IFRS. ASPE follows a classification approach, whereas IFRS follows a contract-based approach. Under IFRS, all leases are considered capital (right-of-use) except for short-term leases and leases of low-value assets when companies choose to apply an exemption for these leases. (Solution = d.)

Chapter 21

Accounting Changes and Error Analysis

OVERVIEW

In order for an entity's financial statements to remain comparable between periods, changes in accounting policies, changes in accounting estimates, and correction of a prior period error must be treated in accordance with generally accepted accounting principles. Changes in accounting policies may be required (under GAAP or when a new accounting standard becomes applicable) or voluntary. Changes in accounting estimates are considered a normal part of the accounting process and are usually the result of changed circumstances or new information. A prior period error is a mistake or omission that is not discovered until after the financial statements for the period have been issued. Both IFRS and ASPE limit the types of accounting changes permitted and outline the related reporting and disclosure requirements in order to maintain usefulness and relevance of the financial statements. Approaches to treatment of an accounting policy change or correction of a prior period error are limited to full retrospective application or restatement, partial retrospective application or restatement, and prospective application. This chapter discusses when and how each approach should be applied and the disclosure requirements under each.

STUDY STEPS

Understanding the Nature of Accounting Changes

Changes in Accounting Policies

According to the *CPA Canada Handbook*, changes in accounting policies are changes in the choice of "specific principles, bases, conventions, rules, and practices applied by an entity in preparing and presenting financial statements." Changes in accounting policies may be required under IFRS or ASPE (for example, on initial adoption of a new accounting standard), or they may be voluntary.

Under IFRS, a voluntary change in accounting policy is only permitted if it would result in presentation of **reliable and more relevant** information in the financial statements. For example, a voluntary change in accounting policy would not be permitted if the change would result in presentation of reliable but equally or less relevant information in the financial statements.

Under ASPE, for a voluntary change in accounting policy, the same criteria requiring reliable and more relevant information in the financial statements applies, except within certain specifically identified accounting standards (including, for example, accounting for income taxes). Within these specifically identified accounting standards, a change between or among alternative ASPE methods of accounting and reporting is permitted, even if the new method would not result in presentation of more relevant information in the financial statements. For example, ASPE allows a voluntary change from the future income taxes method to the taxes payable method of accounting for income taxes, even if the change does not result in presentation of more relevant information in the financial statements.

Changes in accounting policies are reflected in the financial statements using (1) full retrospective application if practicable, (2) partial retrospective application if full retrospective application is impracticable, or (3) prospective application if partial retrospective application is impracticable. Accounting standards specifically state that retrospective application is **impracticable** only if one or more of these three circumstances apply:

1. the effects of the retrospective application cannot be determined,
2. assumptions are needed about what management's intentions were in that prior period, or
3. significant estimates must be made that need to take into account circumstances that existed in that prior period, and it is no longer possible to do this.

Full retrospective application requires:

1. **A journal entry to recognize the effects of the new accounting policy that is being applied retrospectively, including any related income tax effects.** This journal entry records the cumulative effect of the change in accounting policy, as of the beginning of the current accounting period, effectively bringing the opening balances of asset, liability, and equity accounts (including

retained earnings and accumulated other comprehensive income) to the correct revised amounts. Note that the current year effect of a change in accounting policy would be recorded in the specific income statement and statement of financial position accounts directly, in the current period.

2. **Restatement of prior period financial statements included alongside the current year's financial statements for comparative purposes.** In the financial statements of the earliest prior period included for comparative purposes, the opening balances of asset, liability, and equity accounts (including retained earnings and accumulated other comprehensive income) are adjusted to reflect the cumulative effect of the change in accounting policy. This is necessary in order to show continuity and reconciliation of statement of financial position accounts between the comparative financial statements presented.

3. **Specific disclosures, as required under IFRS or ASPE.** Under IFRS, retrospective application also requires presentation of the opening statement of financial position for the earliest comparative period included.

Partial retrospective application is similar to full retrospective application, except that the opening balances of asset, liability, and equity accounts are adjusted in the earliest period for which restatement is possible. Thus, the effect of the accounting change is applied to the carrying amounts of assets, liabilities, and affected components of equity at the beginning of the earliest period for which restatement is possible.

Changes in Accounting Estimates

A change in accounting estimate is an adjustment to the carrying amount of an asset or a liability or the amount of an asset's periodic consumption, and results from either an assessment of the present status of or the expected future benefits and obligations associated with the asset or liability. A change in accounting estimate is usually the result of new information or a change in circumstances. For example, a change in the estimated remaining service life of an asset might result from actual experience confirming that the asset's physical life is longer than originally expected. Prior period financial statements were prepared using estimates that were made in good faith, based on available information and known circumstances in those prior periods. Therefore, prior period financial statements are not adjusted to reflect changes in accounting estimates that arise in the current period. A change in accounting estimate is accounted for prospectively: (1) in the current period if the change affects the current year only, or (2) in the current period and in future periods if the change affects both. **Prospective application** simply means that in the current period and going forward, the new estimate is applied to (or used in the calculations related to) the balance(s) of the related asset, liability, and/or equity account(s) as of the date of change.

If it is unclear whether an accounting change is a change in accounting policy or a change in accounting estimate, the accounting change should be treated as a change in accounting estimate.

Correction of a Prior Period Error

A prior period error is a mistake or omission (either intentional or unintentional) that is not discovered until after the financial statements for the period have been issued. Correction of a prior period error is accounted for retrospectively because the relevant prior periods' financial statements are incorrect and/or misleading, and should be adjusted. Retrospective treatment of a correction of a prior period error is called **retrospective restatement**, because amounts that were reported in the relevant prior periods' financial statements are corrected as if the error had never occurred. Retrospective restatement is similar to retrospective application, as described above.

Under IFRS, correction of a prior period error is accounted for using full retrospective restatement if practicable, partial retrospective restatement if full retrospective restatement is impracticable, or prospective application if partial retrospective restatement is impracticable. However, under ASPE, correction of a prior period error must be accounted for using full retrospective restatement.

Be careful to differentiate between changes in accounting estimates and the correction of a prior period error. Changes in accounting estimates are a normal part of the accounting process and a result of routine assessment of present status and future benefits and obligations of assets and liabilities. A prior period error is a mistake or omission or a result of lack of expertise or good faith.

TIPS ON CHAPTER TOPICS

- There are two basic types of **accounting changes:** (1) change in accounting policy, and (2) change in accounting estimate. Correction of a prior period error is not considered an accounting change.

- A change from one generally accepted accounting principle or method to another generally accepted accounting principle or method is a **change in accounting policy**. Therefore, a change from one generally accepted inventory cost formula to another generally accepted inventory cost formula is a change in accounting policy. A change from an accounting principle or method that is **not** generally accepted to a principle or method that is in accordance with GAAP is not an accounting change—it is a correction of a prior period error.

- **Accounting policies** include not only accounting principles and practices but also methods of applying them. Thus, an example of a change in accounting policy is a switch from applying the lower of cost and net realizable value rule to groups of similar or related items (with each group of items relating to the same product line and closely related in terms of their end use) to applying the rule on an individual item-by-item basis.

- A **change in accounting estimate** occurs if an entity changes an estimate made in good faith to another estimate made in good faith. Accounting estimates may change as new events occur, as more experience is acquired, or as new information is obtained. A change in estimate may result from new information or a change in circumstances, but not from oversight or misuse of facts. An error resulting from oversight or misuse of facts would require correction of the prior period error.

- At first, changing from one generally accepted depreciation method to another generally accepted depreciation method might appear to be a change in accounting policy. However, this change is considered a change in accounting estimate because the method of depreciation is based on an estimate of the expected pattern of consumption of the future economic benefits of the related depreciable asset. Examples of a change in accounting estimate also include a change in the estimated useful life of a depreciable asset to the entity and a change in the estimated residual value of a depreciable asset.

- **Errors** include mathematical mistakes, oversight of information available when the related financial statements were completed, misapplication of accounting principles, and misuse of facts.

- Generally, a voluntary change in accounting policy is accounted for with full retrospective application. However, if full retrospective application is impracticable, the change is accounted for with partial retrospective application; and if partial retrospective application is impracticable, the change is accounted for with prospective application. For a change in accounting policy that is the result of adoption of, or change in, a primary source of GAAP, the transitional provision included in the relevant IFRS or ASPE standard may indicate a specific accounting method to apply (either full retrospective, partial retrospective, or prospective application). A change in accounting estimate is accounted for with prospective application. Refer to **Illustration 21-1** for a summary of the relevant reporting requirements.

- Under IFRS, for retrospective application or restatement, or reclassification of items in the financial statements, the entity is also required to present an **opening statement of financial position** for the earliest comparative period reported. There is no similar requirement under ASPE.

- Under IFRS, information about the financial statement effects of **issued standards that are not yet effective** is required to be disclosed in the notes to the financial statements. There is no similar requirement under ASPE.

- Most accounting errors are **counterbalancing**. A counterbalancing error is an error that will be offset or that will self-correct over two periods. A counterbalancing error will often affect two income statements and one statement of financial position (the statement of financial position at the end of the period in which the error occurred). The statement of financial position at the end of the following period will not be affected as the error will "offset" or counterbalance itself by that date.

- A **non-counterbalancing** error will affect two or more income statements and two or more statements of financial position. The error may "reverse" at some point in time, although it may take many years to do so. Conceivably, some non-counterbalancing errors may not "reverse" until, for example, the related asset is disposed of or the business ceases to exist. In the context of error analysis, the terms "offset," "reverse," "self-correct," and "wash out" are synonymous.

(continued)

- If an error causes an **understatement** in revenue, it will cause an **understatement** of net income for that same year; however, if an error causes an **understatement** of expense, it will cause an **overstatement** of net income for that same year.

- All error situations discussed in this chapter maintain balance in the basic accounting equation (often called the balance sheet equation). Thus, when you analyze the effects of these errors, make sure your analysis maintains balance in the balance sheet equation (A = L + SE).

- Many of the errors illustrated in this chapter are the result of using the cash basis of accounting rather than the accrual basis of accounting.

ILLUSTRATION 21-1

Summary of Accounting Methods for Accounting Changes

Accounting Method	When to Use	How to Apply
Full retrospective application or restatement	• Initial adoption of (or change in) a primary source of GAAP, if required by the specific standard, or if no transitional provision is stated in the specific standard • Voluntary change in accounting policy (under IFRS or ASPE, if change in accounting policy would result in presentation of **reliable and more relevant** information; or under ASPE only, within certain specifically identified accounting standards) • Correction of a prior period error	1. Record a catch-up adjustment using the Retained Earnings account (and/or the other affected equity accounts). 2. Restate prior periods' financial statements that are included with the current year's financial statements for comparative purposes. 3. Prepare specific disclosures required under IFRS and ASPE, including a description of the change and its effect on current and prior periods' financial statements.
Partial retrospective application or restatement	• For a change in accounting policy, if full retrospective application is impracticable	1. In the earliest period for which application or restatement is possible, record a

Illustration 21-1   301

Accounting Method	When to Use	How to Apply
	• Under IFRS only, for correction of a prior period error, if full retrospective restatement is impracticable	catch-up adjustment using the Retained Earnings account (and/or the other affected equity accounts). 2. Starting with the earliest period for which application or restatement is practicable, restate financial statements that are included with the current year's financial statements for comparative purposes. 3. Prepare specific disclosures required under IFRS and ASPE, including a description of the change and its effect on current and prior periods' financial statements.
Prospective application	• For a change in accounting policy, if partial retrospective application is impracticable • Under IFRS only, for correction of a prior period error, if partial retrospective restatement is impracticable • For a change in accounting estimate	1. Apply the new policy or estimate (or use in calculations related to) the balance of the related asset, liability, and/or equity account(s) as of the date of change. 2. There is no restatement of prior periods' financial statements. 3. Prepare specific disclosures required under IFRS and ASPE, including a description of the nature and amount of the change.

- It is sometimes difficult to differentiate between a change in estimate and a change in accounting policy. Assume that a company changes from deferring and amortizing certain development costs to recording them as expenses as they are incurred because future benefits associated with these costs have become doubtful. Is this a change in accounting policy or a change in estimate? The definition of a change in estimate clearly includes this scenario. **However, if it is unclear whether a change is a change in accounting policy or a change in accounting estimate, the change should be treated as a change in estimate.** Accounting standards suggest that a change attributed to changed circumstances, experience, or new information should be treated as a change in estimate.

- **Retrospective application or restatement** involves making revisions within previously prepared financial statements before they are republished as comparative financial statements. The accountant will restate only the financial statements of the prior periods that are being published again for readers' use. For example, assume that a company used the LIFO cost formula from the company's inception in 2004 through to 2007. In 2008, because *CICA Handbook* requirements changed to disallow the LIFO cost formula, the company changed to the FIFO cost formula, which meant this was an involuntary change. This change would have been accounted for retrospectively. Thus, if the company normally presents two years of comparative financial statements with current year financial statements, the financial statements previously published for 2006 and 2007 would be restated. That is, they would be changed or revised to reflect the individual amounts that would have been reported in the body of the financial statements in those prior years if the new cost formula (FIFO) had been used. These restated financial statements for 2006 and 2007 would be published with the 2008 financial statements, as comparative financial statements. The effect on the periods prior to the first year being republished (2004 through 2005, in this example) would be shown as an adjustment to the opening balance of Retained Earnings at the beginning of 2006 on the statement of retained earnings for the year ended 2006. Calculations related to this change involve data from several prior years (2004 through 2007), but only two prior years (2006 and 2007) are formally restated because they are the only years being presented as comparative financial statements. Restated financial statements reflect "as-if" amounts in the body of the financial statements.

CASE 21-1

PURPOSE: This case will provide examples of changes in accounting policies, changes in accounting estimates, and corrections of a prior period error, and identify the proper accounting treatment for each.

Instructions

For each item in the list:
(a) Use the appropriate number to indicate if the item is:
   1. a change in accounting policy.
   2. a change in accounting estimate.

3. a correction of a prior period error.

4. none of the above.

(b) Use the appropriate letter to indicate if the item is to receive:

R: retrospective treatment.

PA: partial retrospective treatment.

PR: prospective treatment.

N: none of the above.

For items requiring retrospective treatment, unless otherwise implied or indicated, assume that full retrospective treatment is practicable.

(a)   (b)

_____ _____ 1. Change in estimate of provision for inventory obsolescence.

_____ _____ 2. Change from zero-profit method to percentage-of-completion method of accounting for a long-term construction contract. The zero-profit method was used previously because the outcome of the contract was not determinable. However, due to a change in circumstances related to the contract, the outcome of the contract is now determinable.

_____ _____ 3. Change from straight-line to double-declining-balance depreciation method for all assets held, because management gathered evidence that the assets were being used differently than previously thought.

_____ _____ 4. Change from sum-of-the-years'-digits to straight-line depreciation method for all assets held, because more experience with the assets showed that the expected pattern of consumption of benefits of the assets was different than previously thought.

_____ _____ 5. Change to straight-line depreciation method for all new assets acquired in a new class of assets; double-declining-balance depreciation method will continue to be used for all assets acquired in prior years.

_____ _____ 6. Change in the estimated useful life of a fixed asset.

_____ _____ 7. Change in the estimated residual value of a fixed asset.

_____ _____ 8. Change from FIFO cost formula to weighted average cost formula of inventory costing.

_____ _____ 9. Proposed change from FIFO cost formula to weighted average cost formula of inventory costing, which would not result in presentation of more relevant information in the financial statements.

_____ _____ 10. Change from FIFO cost formula to specific identification method of inventory costing.

_____ _____ 11. Change from weighted average cost formula to FIFO cost formula of inventory costing.

_____ _____ 12. Change to the fair value model from the cost model for measuring investment property, where the full retrospective effects of the change cannot be determined.

_____ _____ 13. Two years ago, did not record a known material change in fair value of a building measured under the revaluation model.

         14. Change from the direct writeoff method to the allowance method of accounting for bad debts, where bad debts have always been (and continue to be) a material amount.

         15. Change from the direct writeoff method to the allowance method of accounting for bad debts, where bad debts have just become a material amount in the current period.

         16. Change from the cash basis to the accrual basis of accounting.

         17. Past service costs of plan amendments that were effective at the beginning of the previous year were not recognized in the previous year's net income. The company prepares financial statements in accordance with IFRS.

         18. Change in interest rate used to calculate pension expense.

         19. Adoption of a new accounting method for a type of transaction that the entity has had no previous experience with.

Solution to Case 21-1

Answers		Explanation and/or Comment
(a)	(b)	
2	PR	1.
2, 4	PR	2. Change in circumstances related to the contract.
2	PR	3. Change in estimate of expected pattern of consumption of benefits of assets.
2	PR	4. Change in estimate of expected pattern of consumption of benefits of assets.
4	N	5. Only note disclosure is required. New method is used only for new assets.
2	PR	6.
2	PR	7.
1	R	8. If changing to new method would result in presentation of information that is reliable and more relevant, this is an acceptable voluntary change in accounting policy.
4	N	9. Under IFRS and ASPE, this change would not be permitted, because it would not result in presentation of more relevant information in the financial statements. (Note: Inventory cost formula is also not included in the group of specifically identified accounting standards under ASPE, within which a voluntary change in accounting policy need not be more relevant.)
1	R	10. If changing to a new method would result in presentation information that is reliable and more relevant, this is an acceptable voluntary change in accounting

Answers		Explanation and/or Comment

		policy. However, if the change is due to a new computer system making a specific identification method feasible where it wasn't before, then (a) = 4 and (b) = PR; that is, it is a change in circumstances.
1	R	11. If changing to a new method would result in presentation of information that is reliable and more relevant, this is an acceptable voluntary change in accounting policy.
1	PA	12. If changing to the fair value model would result in presentation of information that is reliable and more relevant, this is an acceptable voluntary change in accounting policy. For a change in accounting policy, partial retrospective treatment is required if full retrospective application is impracticable. (Note: If partial retrospective treatment is also impracticable, the new policy is applied prospectively.)
3	R	13. Missed recording of a known material change in fair value of a building measured under the revaluation model is an omission in the financial statements of two years ago, caused by failure to use the reliable information that existed when the related financial statements were prepared. (Note: Related depreciation expense that has been recorded since the year of the error should also be corrected as it should be based on the correct fair value of the building.)
3	R	14. Where bad debts are material, the direct writeoff method is not GAAP-compliant. PA or PR would be acceptable if management is unable to put themselves back in a position to assess (without having knowledge of the future) what the balance of the allowance for doubtful accounts would have been in those prior years.
4	PR	15. Change in circumstances.
3	R	16. The cash basis of accounting is not GAAP-compliant.
3	R	17. Under IFRS, past service costs are recognized immediately in net income.
2 or 4	PR	18. Assuming that the previous interest rate was, and the new interest rate is, estimated in good faith, 2 for (a) would be appropriate. If economic conditions have changed and the appropriate interest rate is now higher or lower than before, this would be due to changed circumstances and 4 for (a) would be correct also.
4	PR	19. New circumstances.

EXPLANATION: First determine the nature of the change, then determine how to treat the change. Notice that in most instances, the answer to part (a) determines the answer to part (b). A change in accounting policy is treated retrospectively (unless full retrospective application or restatement is impracticable). A change in accounting estimate is accounted for prospectively. Therefore, an answer of 1 for part (a) requires an answer of R or PA for part (b), an answer of 2 for part (a) requires an answer of PR for part (b), and an answer of 3 for part (a) requires an answer of R or PA for part (b).

ILLUSTRATION 21-2

Calculating and Recording the Effects of a Change in Accounting Policy

A. Calculate and record the effect of a change in accounting policy on income of periods prior to the change, as follows:

1. Determine the cumulative effect of the change on retained earnings (and other affected components of equity) as of the beginning of the current period (the period of change), as follows:

   (a) Identify the revenue and/or expense account(s) and amount(s) that were affected in the prior periods when the previous accounting policy was applied.

   (b) Calculate what the amount(s) of those revenue and/or expense account(s) would have been in the prior periods if the new accounting policy was applied in those periods. Also consider the effect on the amount of income taxes reported.

   (c) Compare the amount(s) in part (a) above with those in part (b) above. The net difference is the (net of tax) effect of the change on income of prior periods.

2. Record the effect of the change on income of prior periods as follows:

   (a) Determine whether the adjustment to retained earnings (and/or other affected components of equity) for the effect on prior periods is a debit or a credit.

   (1) If application of the new accounting policy would have resulted in higher net incomes in prior years, the adjustment to retained earnings (and/or other affected components of equity) is a credit.

   (2) If application of the new accounting policy would have resulted in lower net incomes in prior years, the adjustment to retained earnings (and/or other affected components of equity) is a debit.

   (b) Record the rest of the journal entry so that asset and liability account balances are restated to balances that would have existed at the beginning of the current period had the new accounting policy been applied in all prior periods.

B. Calculate and record the effect of the change in accounting policy on income of the **current** period, as follows:

1. Identify the revenue and/or expense account(s) and amount(s) on the current period income statement calculated as a result of application of the new accounting policy.

2. Calculate the amount(s) of those revenue and/or expense account(s) in the current period if the previous accounting policy was applied in the current period.

3. Compare the amount(s) in (1) above with the amount(s) in (2) above. The net difference is the effect of the change on income of the current period.

> The effect of the change on income of the current period does **not** include the cumulative effect of the change on income of prior periods.

4. Disclose the (net of tax) effect of the change on income of the current period in the notes to the financial statements of the current period.

EXERCISE 21-1

PURPOSE: This exercise will illustrate the following for a change in accounting policy: (1) calculation of effect on prior periods, (2) calculation of effect on the period of change, and (3) calculation of amounts for retrospective application.

In Years 1, 2, and 3, Susan Corporation used weighted average cost to calculate ending inventory and cost of goods sold for book purposes and for tax purposes. In Year 4, Susan changed to FIFO for book purposes, because FIFO would result in presentation of reliable and more relevant information in the financial statements. Assume the weighted average cost formula was used throughout Year 4, and the change in policy was decided on after all adjusting entries were made for Year 4, but before the closing entries were recorded. Susan uses a periodic inventory system and has a tax rate of 30% for all years. Susan prepares financial statements in accordance with IFRS. Cost of goods sold for Years 1 through 4, under each cost formula, is as follows:

Inventory Cost Formula	Cost of Goods Sold			
	Year 1	**Year 2**	**Year 3**	**Year 4**
Weighted average cost	$18,000	$21,000	$23,000	$26,000
FIFO	$16,000	$18,000	$21,000	$24,000

Instructions

(a) Calculate the cumulative effect of the change as of the beginning of the year of change, Year 4.

(b) Prepare the journal entry to record the effect of the change on periods prior to the change.

(c) Calculate the effect of the change on income of the year of change. Indicate the direction of the change (increase or decrease in net income).

(d) Prepare the journal entry to record the effect of the change on the year of change.

(e) Calculate restated net income figures for Years 1–4, assuming the following after-tax amounts were calculated prior to the change in accounting policy:

Net income—Year 1	$52,000
Net income—Year 2	54,500
Net income—Year 3	59,700
Net income—Year 4	66,200

Solution to Exercise 21-1

(a)

	Cost of Goods Sold Using Weighted Average Cost Formula	Cost of Goods Sold Using FIFO Cost Formula
Year 1	$18,000	$16,000
Year 2	21,000	18,000
Year 3	23,000	21,000
	$62,000	$55,000

Cost of goods sold was	$62,000	for Years 1–3 using weighted average cost (previous) formula.
Cost of goods sold would have been	55,000	for Years 1–3 using FIFO cost (new) formula.
Difference is	$ 7,000	cumulative effect on prior periods.
Net-of-tax rate	× 70%	(100% − 30% tax rate)
Cumulative effect, net of tax	$ 4,900	as of Year 4 (beginning of the year of change)

Refer to the guidelines in **Illustration 21-2** to perform the calculations required in this exercise.

EXPLANATION: The current year (year of change) is Year 4. Therefore, the prior years affected are Years 1, 2, and 3. The total amount that was reported as cost of goods sold in Years 1, 2, and 3 (calculated using weighted average cost) is compared with the total amount that would have been reported as cost of goods sold in those same years if FIFO (the new cost formula) was used. The difference is the total effect on the prior periods' income before taxes, which is commonly called the cumulative effect on prior periods. The cumulative effect, net of tax, is calculated by multiplying the cumulative effect on prior periods by the 70% net-of-tax rate (100% minus the 30% tax rate).

(b) Inventory   7,000

    Income Tax Payable (30% × $7,000)   2,100

    Retained Earnings   4,900

EXPLANATION: The new cost formula (FIFO) would have yielded lower cost of goods sold and therefore more net income if it was used in prior periods; therefore, the adjustment to record the cumulative effect of the change as of the beginning of Year 4 is a credit to retained earnings.

    The rest of the journal entry restates the balances of affected asset and liability accounts to balances that would have existed at the beginning of Year 4 had FIFO (the new cost formula) been applied in all prior years. At the end of Year 3, inventory would have been higher by $7,000 if FIFO was used in all prior years. Use of FIFO for tax purposes would have resulted in additional income taxes payable of $2,100 ($7,000 × 30% = $2,100) at the end of Year 3. This is because the same inventory cost formula must be used for tax purposes as is used for financial reporting purposes.

> For tax purposes, the same cost formula is used as the one used for financial reporting purposes, resulting in additional taxes payable on the restatement.

(c) Cost of goods sold Year 4 using previous cost formula $26,000

    Cost of goods sold Year 4 using new cost formula   24,000

    Increase in income before income taxes, Year 4   2,000

    Net-of-tax rate   70%

    Increase in Year 4 income, net of tax $ 1,400

(d) Inventory   2,000

    Cost of Goods Sold   2,000

    Current Tax Expense   600

    Income Tax Payable   600

(e)

	Year 1	Year 2	Year 3	Year 4
Cost of goods sold reported	$18,000	$21,000	$23,000	$26,000
Cost of goods sold using new cost formula	16,000	18,000	21,000	24,000
Increase in income before taxes	2,000	3,000	2,000	2,000
Net-of-tax rate (100% − 30%)	70%	70%	70%	70%
Increase in net income	1,400	2,100	1,400	1,400
Net income reported	52,000	54,500	59,700	66,200
Restated net income	$53,400	$56,600	$61,100	$67,600

ILLUSTRATION 21-3

Accounting for a Change in Accounting Estimate for a Plant Asset

Whenever there is a change in estimated useful life or estimated residual value for a depreciable asset, the following format will aid in the calculation of depreciation.

Original Cost
− Accumulated Depreciation[a]
= Book Value
+ Additional Expenditures Capitalized, if any[b]
= Revised Book Value
− Current Estimate of Residual Value
= Remaining Depreciable Cost to Be Allocated Over Remaining Useful Life of Asset

[a]Total depreciation taken prior to the beginning of the year of change
[b]An additional expenditure is capitalized if future economic benefits are expected to result from the expenditure (assuming that the cost of the expenditure can be measured reliably).

EXERCISE 21-2

PURPOSE: This exercise will illustrate the proper accounting procedures for a change in accounting estimate.

Sock Corporation acquired a plant asset costing $375,000 at the beginning of Year 1. After depreciating it for five years using the straight-line method, a 12-year useful life, and an expected residual value of $15,000, Sock estimated the asset would be useful for a total of 15 years with a residual value of $9,000. The tax rate is 25% for all years. Sock prepares financial statements in accordance with IFRS.

Instructions

(a) Calculate and prepare the journal entry to record depreciation expense for Year 6.
(b) Prepare the journal entry, if any, to record the accounting change. Explain the type of treatment to apply in this situation.
(c) Calculate the effect of the change on the year of change. Explain where it is reported.

Solution to Exercise 21-2

(a) **APPROACH:** Apply the format outlined in **Illustration 21-3** to calculate depreciation where there has been a change in estimated useful life and/or residual value of a plant asset.

Original cost	$375,000
Accumulated depreciation	(150,000)[a]
Book value, beginning of Year 6	225,000
Additional expenditures capitalized	-0-
Revised book value	225,000
Current estimate of residual value	(9,000)
Remaining depreciable cost	216,000
Divided by remaining useful life	÷ 10[b]
Depreciation per year for Year 6 and subsequent years	$ 21,600

[a]($375,000 − $15,000) ÷ 12 years = $30,000 depreciation per year using previous estimates; $30,000 × 5 years = $150,000
[b]15 years total useful life − 5 years depreciated = 10 years of useful life remaining

Journal Entry:

Depreciation Expense	21,600	
Accumulated Depreciation		21,600

An accounting change is always made as of the beginning of the year of change, even though it may not be recorded until the end of the period of change. If depreciation expense has already been recorded in Year 6 under the original assumptions, the adjusting entry brings the depreciation expense to the revised amount.

(b) **No journal entry.** There is no journal entry to record this accounting change because changes in accounting estimates are applied prospectively. For prospective application, there is no calculation of total effect on prior periods and no journal entry to record the effect on prior periods. The total effect on prior periods is spread over the year of change (in this exercise, Year 6) and future periods (Years 7 through 15).

(c)

Depreciation to be reported for Year 6 (part a)	$21,600
Depreciation for Year 6 using previous estimates	30,000
Increase in income before income taxes for Year 6	8,400
Net-of-tax rate	75%
Increase in Year 6 income, net of tax	$ 6,300

The $6,300 effect on the current year is reported in the notes to the financial statements.

ILLUSTRATION 21-4

Common Relationships and Assumptions Inherent in Correcting Error Situations

1. It is assumed that an accrued expense **not** recorded at the end of a period is paid (and recorded as expense) in the following period.
2. It is assumed that an accrued revenue **not** recorded at the end of a period is received (and recorded as revenue) in the following period.
3. It is assumed that a prepaid expense omitted in Year 1 is recorded as expense in Year 1 when the cash was disbursed. Unless otherwise indicated, it is assumed that the related expense is consumed in Year 2 (although not recorded as such, since the prepaid expense was omitted in Year 1).
4. It is assumed that an unearned revenue omitted in Year 1 is recorded as revenue in Year 1 when the cash was received. Unless otherwise indicated, it is assumed that the related revenue is earned in Year 2 (although not recorded as such, since the unearned revenue was omitted in Year 1).
5. Ending inventory of one period is beginning inventory of the following period.
6. If purchases of inventory that are made near the end of Year 1 are not recorded until Year 2, and the merchandise is also omitted from ending inventory for Year 1, there is no net effect on net income of Year 1 or Year 2.
7. Unless otherwise indicated, if depreciation expense for Year 1 is omitted in Year 1, depreciation expense for Year 2 is assumed to be recorded correctly in Year 2 (for the amount related to Year 2 only).

ILLUSTRATION 21-5

Guide to Preparing Correcting Journal Entries

Short Method

Step 1: Adjust current revenue and/or expense (or gain and/or loss) accounts affected by the error.

Step 2: Adjust asset and/or liability accounts to their proper balances (if applicable).

Step 3: Adjust revenue and/or expense items of prior periods with an entry to retained earnings (and/or other affected components of equity).

OR

Long Method

Step 1: Reconstruct the incorrect journal entry that was actually recorded, if any (sometimes no journal entry was recorded, when in fact a journal entry should have been recorded).

Step 2: Reconstruct the journal entry that should have been recorded. Analyze it to determine the impact on each account affected (what was understated, overstated, and so on). Remember: A = L + SE.

Step 3: Record a correcting journal entry to bring affected accounts to their correct current balances. Start with the reconstructed incorrect journal entry that was actually recorded (from Step 1) and the reconstructed journal entry that should have been recorded (from Step 2), and apply three additional steps:

Step 3(a): If the reconstructed journal entries involve any revenue or expense items of prior periods, cross out these account names and replace them with Retained Earnings.

Step 3(b): Clean up the reconstructed journal entries by netting amounts recorded to the same account(s), and record the combined (correcting) journal entry.

Step 3(c): Record an adjusting entry for the current year if necessary.

EXERCISE 21-3

PURPOSE: This exercise will provide an example of the accounting procedures for correction of prior period errors accounted for with full retrospective application.

Build-away Construction Company enters into long-term construction contracts. Gross profit amounts calculated using the completed-contract method and the percentage-of-completion method for Years 1 through 3 are as follows:

	Completed-Contract	**Percentage-of-Completion**
Year 1	$ 40,000	$140,000
Year 2	160,000	280,000
Year 3	270,000	350,000

The company applied the completed-contract method in Years 1 and 2 for both book purposes and tax purposes. In Year 3, the company discovered that the percentage-of-completion method should have been applied for book purposes only. The tax rate is 30% for all years. The company prepares financial statements in accordance with ASPE and applies the future income taxes method of accounting for income taxes.

Instructions

(a) Calculate the effect of the correction on periods prior to the correction.
(b) Prepare the journal entry to record the correction.
(c) Calculate the effect of the correction on the year of change.

Solution to Exercise 21-3

(a)

Total gross profit for Years 1 and 2 using the previous method	$200,000[a]
Total gross profit for Years 1 and 2 using the correct method	420,000[b]
Cumulative effect on prior periods	220,000
Net-of-tax rate	70%
Cumulative effect on prior periods, net of tax	$154,000

[a]$40,000 Year 1 + $160,000 Year 2 = $200,000
[b]$140,000 Year 1 + $280,000 Year 2 = $420,000

(b)

Construction in Process	220,000	
Future Income Tax Liability ($220,000 × 30%)		66,000
Retained Earnings		154,000

If applied in prior periods, the new method would have resulted in higher net income amounts; thus, the adjustment required to record the cumulative effect is a credit to retained earnings.

(c)

Gross profit for Year 3 using the correct method	$350,000
Gross profit for Year 3 using the previous method	270,000
Increase in income before income taxes, Year 3	80,000
Net-of-tax rate	70%
Increase in Year 3 income, net of tax	$ 56,000

EXERCISE 21-4

PURPOSE: This exercise will provide examples of errors and discuss their effect on net income and the statement of financial position.

Mahdi Corporation discovered errors during an audit in 2018. The company has a calendar-year reporting period. The errors are as follows:

Error 1: Accrued interest on notes payable of $3,500 was omitted at the end of 2017.

Error 2: Prepaid insurance of $1,800 was overlooked at the end of 2017. (The premium paid in advance relates to insurance coverage for 2018.)

Error 3: Accrued interest on investments of $5,100 was understated at the end of 2017.

Error 4: Unearned rent revenue of $4,500 was understated at the end of 2017.

Error 5: A truck with a cost of $10,000, a useful life of four years, and a residual value of $4,000 was expensed when it was purchased at the beginning of 2017.

Error 6: Amortization of patent, $700, was omitted in 2017.

Instructions

(a) Assuming net income of $50,000 was reported for 2017, and net income of $72,000 was reported for 2018 (before discovery of the errors), calculate the correct net income figures for 2017 and 2018. Ignore the effect of income taxes.

(b) For each error, describe the following by identifying whether the amounts were overstated or understated (ignore the effect of income taxes):

   1. effect on net income for 2017.

   2. effect on the elements of the basic accounting equation at December 31, 2017.

   3. effect on net income for 2018.

   4. effect on the elements of the basic accounting equation at December 31, 2018.

(c) Prepare the correcting journal entry for each error, assuming the errors are discovered at the end of 2018 before closing. Ignore the effect of income taxes.

Solution to Exercise 21-4

(a)

	2017	2018
Net income as previously reported	$50,000	$72,000
Effect of error 1: failure to accrue interest expense in 2017	(3,500)	3,500
Effect of error 2: failure to defer insurance expense in 2017	1,800	(1,800)
Effect of error 3: failure to accrue interest income in 2017	5,100	(5,100)
Effect of error 4: failure to defer rent revenue in 2017	(4,500)	4,500
Effect of error 5: failure to capitalize truck in 2017 and depreciate	8,500	(1,500)
Effect of error 6: failure to amortize patent in 2017	(700)	-0-
Corrected net income	$56,700	$71,600

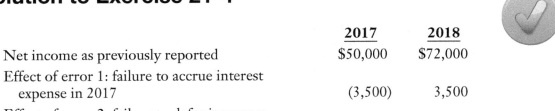

To correct a net income figure that is understated, add the error amount to net income as previously reported; to correct a net income figure that is overstated, deduct the error amount from net income as previously reported.

For each error, the (b) and (c) solution and explanation is presented below.

- Notice how for each error, the net effect on the accounts maintains balance in the basic accounting equation (A = L + SE).

- When you are asked to describe the effects of an error, describe the effects on all periods affected, assuming the error is allowed to run its course (and is not corrected).

APPROACH TO PART (B): Using journal entries, reconstruct what was done and compare that with what should have been done, in order to determine the effects of each.

APPROACH TO PART (C): To prepare correcting journal entries, follow the three steps in the "short method" outlined in **Illustration 21-5**. Refer to the Explanation to the Solution to part (b) to determine the required correcting journal entry.

Error 1

(b) **Effects of Error 1:** Failure to accrue interest expense in 2017:
    1. Net income for 2017 is overstated (because interest expense is understated).
    2. Liabilities are understated, and owners' equity is overstated at 12/31/17.
    3. Net income for 2018 is understated (because interest expense is overstated).
    4. There is no effect on the statement of financial position at 12/31/18.

All income statement accounts are closed to owners' equity at the end of each period; therefore, if net income is affected in the year that an error originates, owners' equity (ending balance) in that same period is misstated in the same direction and by the same amount as net income.

EXPLANATION:

What was done:			What should have been done:		
12/31/17 No Entry			Interest Expense	3,500	
			Interest Payable		3,500
During	Interest Expense	3,500	Interest Payable	3,500	
2018	Cash		3,500	Cash		3,500

An adjusting entry to record accrued interest expense of $3,500 was omitted in 2017. The amount would have been paid and recorded as an expense in 2018. The payment in 2018 should have been recorded as a reduction in Interest Payable (a liability), but an Interest Payable was never reflected on the books.

This is an example of a counterbalancing error. Two successive income statements and the statement of financial position at the end of the first period are affected. The statement of financial position at the end of the second period is unaffected because by that time the error counterbalances (offsets or washes out).

(c) **Correcting journal entry for Error 1 at 12/31/18 before closing:**

Retained Earnings	3,500	
Interest Expense		3,500

Error 1: Explanation for journal entry:

Step 1: Interest Expense in 2018 will be overstated unless a correcting journal entry is made; therefore, Interest Expense for 2018 should be reduced with a credit.

Step 2: No assets or liabilities are affected at 12/31/18.

Step 3: Interest Expense for 2017 was understated. However, the Interest Expense account cannot be debited because all income statement amounts for 2017 were closed to Retained Earnings at the end of 2017. Therefore, a debit to Retained Earnings is required to correct for the error.

Error 2

(b) **Effects of Error 2:** Failure to defer insurance expense in 2017:

1. Net income for 2017 is understated (because insurance expense is overstated).
2. Assets are understated, and owners' equity is understated at 12/31/17.
3. Net income for 2018 is overstated (because insurance expense is understated).
4. There is no effect on the statement of financial position at 12/31/18.

EXPLANATION:

What was done:		What should have been done:		
12/31/17	No Entry	Prepaid Insurance	1,800	
		Insurance Expense		1,800
12/31/18	No Entry	Insurance Expense	1,800	
		Prepaid Insurance		1,800

Insurance premiums for 2018 were paid in advance in 2017. Payment in 2017 must have been recorded with a charge to insurance expense. An adjusting entry at the end of 2017 to record deferral of a portion of the expense to 2018 was omitted. As a result, no portion of the insurance premium was recorded as an expense in 2018 (the year in which some of the benefits of the insurance premium were consumed in the form of insurance coverage).

(c) **Correcting journal entry for Error 2 at 12/31/18 before closing:**

Insurance Expense	1,800	
Retained Earnings		1,800

Error 2: Explanation for journal entry:

Step 1: Insurance Expense in 2018 will be understated unless a correcting journal entry is made; therefore, Insurance Expense for 2018 should be increased with a debit.

Step 2: No assets or liabilities are affected at 12/31/18.

Step 3: Insurance Expense for 2017 was overstated. However, the Insurance Expense account cannot be credited because all income statement amounts for 2017 were closed to Retained Earnings at the end of 2017. Therefore, a credit to Retained Earnings is required to correct for the error.

Error 3

(b) **Effects of Error 3:** Failure to accrue interest income in 2017:

1. Net income for 2017 is understated (because interest income is understated).

2. Assets are understated, and owners' equity is understated at 12/31/17.

3. Net income for 2018 is overstated (because interest income is overstated).

4. There is no effect on the statement of financial position at 12/31/18.

EXPLANATION:

What was done:			What should have been done:		
12/31/17	No Entry		Interest Receivable	5,100	
			Interest Income		5,100
During	Cash	5,100	Cash	5,100	
2018	Interest Income	5,100	Interest Receivable		5,100

An adjusting entry to record accrued interest income of $5,100 was omitted in 2017. The amount would have been received and recorded as income in 2018. The receipt in 2018 should have been recorded as a reduction in Interest Receivable (an asset), but an Interest Receivable was never reflected on the books.

(c) **Correcting journal entry for Error 3 at 12/31/18 before closing:**

Interest Income	5,100	
Retained Earnings		5,100

Error 3: Explanation for journal entry:

Step 1: Interest Income in 2018 will be overstated unless a correcting journal entry is made; therefore, Interest Income for 2018 should be reduced with a debit.

Step 2: No assets or liabilities are affected at 12/31/18.

Step 3: Interest Income for 2017 was understated. However, the Interest Income account cannot be credited because all income statement amounts for 2017 were closed to Retained Earnings at the end of 2017. Therefore, a credit to Retained Earnings is required to correct for the error.

Error 4

(b) **Effects of Error 4:** Failure to defer rent revenue in 2017:

1. Net income for 2017 is overstated (because rent revenue is overstated).
2. Liabilities are understated and owners' equity is overstated at 12/31/17.
3. Net income for 2018 is understated (because rent revenue is understated).
4. There is no effect on the statement of financial position at 12/31/18.

EXPLANATION:

What was done:		What should have been done:		
12/31/17	No Entry	Rent Revenue	4,500	
		Unearned Rent Revenue		4,500
12/31/18	No Entry	Unearned Rent Revenue	4,500	
		Rent Revenue		4,500

In 2017, some rent revenue was collected in advance. (It is assumed that the revenue was earned in 2018 or there would have been a description of another error.) Receipt in 2017 must have been recorded with a credit to revenue. An adjusting entry at the end of 2017 to record deferral of a portion of the revenue to 2018 was omitted. As a result, no portion of the rent collected was recorded as revenue in 2018 (the year in which the rent revenue was earned).

(c) **Correcting journal entry for Error 4 at 12/31/18 before closing:**

Retained Earnings	4,500	
Rent Revenue		4,500

Error 4: Explanation for journal entry:

Step 1: Rent Revenue in 2018 will be understated unless a correcting journal entry is made; therefore, Rent Revenue for 2018 is increased with a credit.

Step 2: No assets or liabilities are affected at 12/31/18.

Step 3: Rent Revenue for 2017 was overstated. However, the Rent Revenue account cannot be debited because all income statement accounts for 2017 were closed to Retained Earnings at the end of 2017. Therefore, a debit to Retained Earnings is required to correct for the error.

Error 5

(b) **Effects of Error 5:** Failure to capitalize truck in 2017 and depreciate:
1. Net income for 2017 is understated by $8,500.
2. Net assets are understated by $8,500, and owners' equity is understated by $8,500 at 12/31/17.
3. Net income for 2018 is overstated by $1,500.
4. Net assets are understated by $7,000, and owners' equity is understated by $7,000 at 12/31/18.

EXPLANATION:

	What was done:			What should have been done:		
Beginning of 2017	Expenses	10,000		Trucks	10,000	
	Cash		10,000	Cash		10,000
12/31/17	No Entry			Depreciation Expense	1,500	
				Accumulated Depreciation— Trucks		1,500
				[($10,000 − $4,000) ÷ 4 = $1,500]		
12/31/18	No Entry			Depreciation Expense	1,500	
				Accumulated Depreciation— Trucks		1,500

In 2017, acquisition of a truck for $10,000 was incorrectly recorded as an expense. The truck should have been depreciated with an annual charge of $1,500 to depreciation expense, beginning in 2017. This means that the income statements for 2017, 2018, 2019, and 2020 are affected by the error, as are the statements of financial position at the end of each of those four years. This error would eventually offset in the period of disposal of the truck. (A gain would be overstated in that period, and only then would the error offset on the statement of financial position.)

(c) **Correcting journal entry for Error 5 at 12/31/18 before closing:**

Trucks	10,000	
Depreciation Expense	1,500	
Accumulated Depreciation—Trucks		3,000
Retained Earnings		8,500

Error 5: Explanation for journal entry:

Step 1: Depreciation Expense in 2018 will be understated unless a correcting journal entry is made; therefore, Depreciation Expense of $1,500 should be recorded with a debit.

Step 2: Trucks will be understated at 12/31/18 by a cost of $10,000 unless a correcting journal entry is made. Likewise, Accumulated Depreciation—Trucks will be understated by two years' worth of depreciation unless a correcting journal entry is made. Therefore, Trucks should be debited for $10,000 and Accumulated Depreciation—Trucks should be credited for $3,000.

Step 3: Expenses for 2017 were overstated by $10,000 and Depreciation Expense for 2017 was understated by $1,500. However, all income amounts for 2017 were closed to Retained Earnings at the end of 2017. Therefore, a credit to Retained Earnings of $8,500 (that is, the amount by which Retained Earnings is understated at the beginning of 2018) is required to correct for the error.

Error 6

(b) **Effects of Error 6: Failure to amortize patent in 2017:**

1. Net income for 2017 is overstated by $700 (because patent amortization is understated).
2. Net assets are overstated by $700, and owners' equity is overstated by $700 at 12/31/17.
3. Net income for 2018 is not affected.
4. Net assets are overstated by $700, and owners' equity is overstated by $700 at 12/31/18.

EXPLANATION:

What was done:		What should have been done:		
12/31/17	No Entry	Amortization Expense	700	
		Accumulated Amortization—Patents		700

Failure to record amortization of a patent is **not** a counterbalancing error. This error will eventually offset in the period when the patent is fully amortized (it will be amortized one year after it should have been fully amortized) or when the patent is disposed of (through sale or abandonment and written off). There is no mention of a similar omission in 2018 so the assumption is that 2018 amortization expense was recorded properly. Therefore, this error affected the income statement of 2017 and will affect the income statement of the period of disposal (or of the last period of amortization) and every statement of financial position prepared in between these two periods.

(c) **Correcting journal entry for Error 6 at 12/31/18 before closing:**

Retained Earnings	700	
Accumulated Amortization—Patents		700

Error 6: Explanation for journal entry:

Step 1: Amortization Expense for 2018 is apparently correctly recorded.

Step 2: Accumulated Amortization—Patents will be understated at 12/31/18 unless a correcting journal entry is made. Therefore, Accumulated Amortization—Patents should be increased with a credit.

Step 3: Amortization Expense for 2017 was understated. However, the Amortization Expense account cannot be debited because all income statement amounts for 2017 were closed to Retained Earnings at the end of 2017. Therefore, a debit to Retained Earnings is required to correct for the error.

- If amortization or depreciation expense for 2017 is omitted in 2017, amortization or depreciation expense for 2018 is assumed to be recorded correctly in 2018, unless otherwise indicated. Thus, carrying value of the long-lived asset will remain overstated on the statement of financial position until a correcting journal entry is recorded, the asset is disposed of (through sale or abandonment and written off), or the asset is completely amortized.

- It may be preferable to take a more detailed approach to preparing correcting journal entries. The following pairs of journal entries are alternative answers to some of the correcting entries presented in this exercise. For each error, both journal entries must be included to be equivalent to the correcting journal entries shown in this exercise.

Error 2:	Prepaid Insurance	1,800	
	Retained Earnings		1,800
	Insurance Expense	1,800	
	Prepaid Insurance		1,800
Error 4:	Retained Earnings	4,500	
	Unearned Rent Revenue		4,500
	Unearned Rent Revenue	4,500	
	Rent Revenue		4,500
Error 5:	Trucks	10,000	
	Accumulated Depreciation—Trucks		1,500
	Retained Earnings		8,500
	Depreciation Expense	1,500	
	Accumulated Depreciation—Trucks		1,500

EXERCISE 21-5

PURPOSE: This exercise will illustrate the effects of various errors involving purchases and ending inventory.

Jones Sports Equipment Company sells sporting goods. By taking a physical count and pricing its inventory using the FIFO cost formula, inventory was determined to be $475,000 and $617,000 at December 31, 2017, and December 31, 2018, respectively. Net income was reported to be $227,000 and $253,000 for 2017 and 2018, respectively. The following errors occurred in accounting for inventory transactions.

Error 1: Purchases of $40,000 made near the end of 2017 were shipped f.o.b. shipping point by the vendor on December 29, 2017; they were not received by Jones until January 3, 2018. These purchases were omitted from the physical count at December 31, 2017, and were not recorded as purchases until January 3, 2018.

Error 2: Merchandise costing $23,000 was on the premises but overlooked during the physical inventory count at December 31, 2017.

Error 3: Merchandise costing $30,000 was double-counted during the physical inventory count at December 31, 2018.

Error 4: Sales made near the end of 2018 were shipped f.o.b. destination by Jones on December 28, 2018; they were not received by customers until January 4, 2019. These items, costing $18,000, were omitted from the inventory sheets of the physical count taken on December 31, 2018, and were treated as sales of $29,000 in 2018.

Instructions

Calculate the correct net income amounts for 2017 and 2018.

Solution to Exercise 21-5

	2017	**2018**
Net income as previously reported	$227,000	$253,000
Effect of error 1: both purchases and ending inventory for 2017 understated	—	—
Effect of error 2: ending inventory for 2017 understated	23,000	(23,000)
Effect of error 3: ending inventory for 2018 overstated	—	(30,000)
Effect of error 4: ending inventory for 2018 understated	—	18,000
sales for 2018 overstated	—	(29,000)
	$250,000	$189,000

EXPLANATION: Analyses of effects of errors on cost of goods sold:

Error 1:	2017	2018
Beginning inventory	No effect	Under by $40,000
+ Net cost of purchases	Under by $40,000	Over by $40,000
= Cost of goods available for sale	Under by $40,000	No effect
− Ending inventory	Under by $40,000	No effect
= Cost of goods sold	No effect	No effect

Error 2:	2017	2018
Beginning inventory	No effect	Under by $23,000
+ Net cost of purchases	No effect	No effect
= Cost of goods available for sale	No effect	Under by $23,000
− Ending inventory	Under by $23,000	No effect
= Cost of goods sold	Over by $23,000	Under by $23,000

Error 3:	2017	2018	2019
Beginning inventory	No effect	No effect	Over by $30,000
+ Net cost of purchases	No effect	No effect	No effect
= Cost of goods available for sale	No effect	No effect	Over by $30,000
− Ending inventory	No effect	Over by $30,000	No effect
= Cost of goods sold	No effect	Under by $30,000	Over by $30,000

Error 4:	2017	2018	2019
Beginning inventory	No effect	No effect	Under by $18,000
+ Net cost of purchases	No effect	No effect	No effect
= Cost of goods available for sale	No effect	No effect	Under by $18,000
− Ending inventory	No effect	Under by $18,000	No effect
= Cost of goods sold	No effect	Over by $18,000	Under by $18,000

Also:

Sales revenue	Over by $29,000	Under by $29,000

● An error involving purchases and/or beginning inventory and/or ending inventory should be analyzed in terms of its effect on components of the cost of goods sold calculation in order to determine its effect on net income. The cost of goods sold calculation is:

> Beginning inventory
>
> + Net cost of purchases
> _____
>
> = Cost of goods available for sale
>
> − Ending inventory
> _____
>
> = Cost of goods sold

● Ending inventory for Year 1 is beginning inventory for Year 2. Thus, if ending inventory for Year 1 is overstated, net income for Year 1 will be overstated and net income for Year 2 will be understated. Retained earnings at the end of Year 1 will also be overstated because net income for Year 1 (which is overstated) is closed to retained earnings. However, retained earnings at the end of Year 2 will be unaffected by the error because net income for Year 2 (which is understated by the same amount as retained earnings was overstated at the end of Year 1) is closed to retained earnings. (Therefore, the error counterbalances at the end of Year 2.) Working capital at the end of Year 1 is overstated (because inventory is a current asset), but working capital at the end of Year 2 is unaffected because the inventory figure at the end of Year 2 is determined by a physical inventory count and inventory cost formula. It should be noted that the preceding analysis assumes that no other new errors occurred in the process.

● If ending inventory for Year 1 is understated, net income for Year 1 will be understated and net income for Year 2 will be overstated. Retained earnings and working capital at the end of Year 1 will also be understated. However, assuming that no other new errors occur in Year 2, retained earnings and working capital will be unaffected at the end of Year 2.

● If purchases in Year 1 are understated by the same amount as an understatement of Year 1 ending inventory, there will be no net effect on net income of Year 1 and no net effect on net income of Year 2. However, the statement of financial position at the end of Year 1 will have errors because both assets (inventory) and liabilities (accounts payable) will be understated.

● When more than one error affects net income for a given year, analyze each error separately and write down each error's effect on net income before attempting to summarize the overall effect on net income.

● When analyzing an error involving inventory, assume the company uses a periodic inventory system, unless otherwise indicated.

EXERCISE 21-6

PURPOSE: This exercise will allow you to practise analyzing the effects of errors on net income.

Billington Corporation calculated net income of $28,000 and $37,000 for Years 1 and 2, respectively. The following errors were later discovered:

Error 1: Depreciation on computers was omitted in Year 1, $850.
Error 2: Deferred (prepaid) expenses were understated at the end of Year 1, $350.
Error 3: Accrued revenues were omitted at the end of Year 1, $780.
Error 4: Deferred (unearned) revenues were understated at the end of Year 1, $900.
Error 5: Accrued expenses were overlooked at the end of Year 1, $625.

Instructions

Calculate the correct net income amounts for Year 1 and Year 2.

Solution to Exercise 21-6

	Year 1	Year 2
Net income as previously reported	$28,000	$37,000
Effect of error 1: depreciation omitted—Year 1	(850)	—
Effect of error 2: deferred expenses understated—Year 1	350	(350)
Effect of error 3: accrued revenues understated—Year 1	780	(780)
Effect of error 4: deferred revenues understated—Year 1	(900)	900
Effect of error 5: accrued expenses understated—Year 1	(625)	625
Corrected net income	$26,755	$37,395

It is assumed that benefits of the prepaid expense (in error 2) are consumed in Year 2, and that the unearned revenue (in error 4) is earned in Year 2, because there is no mention of other new errors existing at the end of Year 2.

ANALYSIS OF MULTIPLE-CHOICE QUESTIONS

Question

1. A manufacturing company changes from the FIFO cost formula to the weighted average cost formula for all inventory held, in order to present information that is reliable and more relevant in the financial statements. In general, under IFRS, how should this change be accounted for?

    a. With full retrospective restatement
    b. With full retrospective application, if practicable
    c. With partial retrospective application
    d. With prospective application

EXPLANATION: This is a voluntary change in accounting policy and in general, under IFRS and ASPE, changes in accounting policies are accounted for with full retrospective application, if practicable. If full retrospective application is not practicable, the change is accounted for with partial retrospective application. If partial retrospective application is not practicable, the change is accounted for with prospective application. (Solution = b.)

Question

2. Under ASPE, a change from one generally accepted accounting method to another generally accepted accounting method is usually accounted for:
   a. with full retrospective restatement.
   b. with full retrospective application, if practicable.
   c. with partial retrospective application.
   d. with prospective application.

EXPLANATION: Under ASPE, a voluntary change from one generally accepted accounting method to another is considered an acceptable change in accounting policy if the change meets one of the following three criteria:

1. the change is required by a primary source of GAAP;
2. the voluntary change results in the financial statements presenting reliable and more relevant information about the effects of transactions, events, or conditions on the entity's financial position, financial performance, or cash flows; or
3. the voluntary change is within certain specifically identified accounting standards, within which a voluntary change in accounting policy need not meet the "reliable, but more relevant" test required in criterion 2 above.

If the voluntary change is considered an acceptable change in accounting policy, it would be accounted for with full retrospective application, if practicable. Note that under IFRS, in order for a voluntary change from one generally accepted accounting method to another to be considered an acceptable change in accounting policy, the change must meet either of the first two criteria stated above. (The third criterion applies only under ASPE.) (Solution = b.)

Question

3. A change from a non-generally accepted accounting method to a generally accepted accounting method should be accounted for:
   a. with full retrospective restatement.
   b. with full retrospective application, if practicable.
   c. with partial retrospective application.
   d. with prospective application.

EXPLANATION: A change from a non-GAAP method to a method that is GAAP-compliant is considered a correction of a prior period error and should be accounted for with full retrospective restatement. However, under IFRS, if full retrospective restatement of financial statements is impracticable, partial retrospective restatement is permitted, and if partial retrospective restatement is impracticable, prospective application is permitted. Under ASPE, only full retrospective restatement of financial statements is permitted in accounting for correction of a prior period error. Note that the term "retrospective restatement" is used to describe retrospective treatment of correction of a prior period error, whereas the term "retrospective application" is used to describe retrospective treatment of a change in accounting policy. (ASPE Solution = a.; IFRS Solution = b.)

Question

4. Middleton Corporation purchased a computer system on January 1, 2015, for $300,000. The company used the straight-line depreciation method and a residual value of zero to depreciate the asset for the first two years of its estimated five-year useful life. In 2017, Middleton changed to the double-declining-balance depreciation method for the asset. The following facts pertain:

	2015	2016	2017
Straight-line	$ 60,000	$60,000	$60,000
Double-declining-balance	120,000	72,000	43,200

Middleton is subject to a 28% tax rate. In the journal entry to record this change, Retained Earnings should be:
a. credited.
b. debited.
c. unaffected.
d. closed.

EXPLANATION: A change in depreciation method is considered a change in the expected pattern of benefits to be received from the related asset, and therefore considered a change in accounting estimate (accounted for prospectively). As a result, no correcting journal entry should be recorded for this change, and retained earnings should not be affected. (Solution = c.)

Question

5. Refer to the facts in Question 4 above. The amount that Middleton should report for depreciation expense on its 2017 income statement is:
a. $120,000.
b. $115,200.
c. $72,000.
d. $43,200.

APPROACH AND EXPLANATION: Depreciation expense for the year of change is calculated using the new depreciation method, current balances of the related asset and contra-asset accounts, and remaining depreciation period of the asset. Calculation of depreciation expense for 2017 is as follows:

Computer system, original cost		$300,000
Depreciation expense for 2015	$60,000	
Depreciation expense for 2016	60,000	
Accumulated depreciation, Jan. 1, 2017		(120,000)
Computer system, book value, Jan. 1, 2017		180,000
Multiplied by double-declining-balance rate		66.67%[a]
Depreciation expense for 2017		$120,000

[a](100% ÷ 3 years remaining useful life) × 2 = 66.67%

(Solution = a.)

> Unless otherwise indicated, it is assumed that the original estimate of useful life of the asset has not changed.

Question

6. Refer to the facts of Question 4 above. If Middleton prepares comparative financial statements in 2017, the income statement for 2016 included therein will reflect depreciation expense of:
   a. $75,000.
   b. $72,000.
   c. $60,000.
   d. none of the above.

EXPLANATION: A change in depreciation method is considered a change in accounting estimate and is applied prospectively. Under prospective application, the effect of a change in estimate is included in net income or comprehensive income, as appropriate, in (1) the period of change if the change affects that period only, or (2) the period of change and future periods if the change affects both. Therefore, the change in depreciation method in 2017 will not affect 2016 depreciation expense as previously reported. (Solution = c.)

Question

7. During 2017, a construction company changed from the completed-contract method to the percentage-of-completion method for accounting purposes but not for tax purposes. The company had discovered that the percentage-of-completion method should have been applied for book purposes only. Gross

profit amounts under both methods for the history of the company appear below:

	Completed-Contract	Percentage-of-Completion
2015	$172,000	$ 312,000
2016	237,000	377,000
2017	266,000	406,000
	$675,000	$1,095,000

The company prepares financial statements in accordance with ASPE. Assuming an income tax rate of 30% for all years, the effect of this accounting change on prior periods should be reported with a credit of:

a. $196,000 on the 2017 income statement.

b. $294,000 on the 2017 income statement.

c. $196,000 on the 2017 statement of retained earnings.

d. $294,000 on the 2017 statement of retained earnings.

EXPLANATION: Identify the type of accounting change and required treatment. This is a correction of a prior period error and is accounted for using full retrospective restatement, if practicable. Therefore, the total effect on prior periods (net of tax) should be recorded as an adjustment to the beginning balance of retained earnings in the current year (2017), and be reported on the 2017 statement of retained earnings. The effect of the change on prior years is calculated as follows:

	Previous Method	New Method	Difference
2015	$172,000	$312,000	$140,000
2016	237,000	377,000	140,000
	$409,000	$689,000	280,000
Net-of-tax rate			70%
Effect on net income, net of tax			$196,000

(Solution = c.)

Question

8. A change in accounting estimate should be accounted for:

   a. as an adjustment to the beginning balance of retained earnings.

   b. by restating the relevant amounts in the financial statements of prior periods.

   c. in the period of change or in the period of change and future periods, if the change affects both.

   d. by reporting restated amounts for all periods presented.

EXPLANATION: Think about the accounting treatment of a change in accounting estimate. A change in accounting estimate is applied prospectively; therefore, it is accounted for by including it in net income or comprehensive income, as appropriate, in (1) the period of change if the change affects that period only, or (2) the period of change and future periods if the change affects both. (Solution = c.)

Question

9. If a change in accounting estimate creates a need for a change in accounting policy (such as when a manufacturing company changes from a policy of deferring and amortizing pre-production costs to a policy of expensing such costs because the estimate of the number of periods that will benefit has changed, and any future benefits now appear doubtful), the change should be accounted for:

   a. with full retrospective restatement.

   b. with full retrospective application, if practicable.

   c. with partial retrospective application.

   d. with prospective application.

EXPLANATION: A change in an accounting estimate that creates a need for a change in accounting policy is accounted for as a change in accounting estimate. Furthermore, in cases where it is unclear whether a change is a change in accounting policy or a change in accounting estimate, the change is treated as a change in accounting estimate. Changes in accounting estimates are accounted for prospectively. (Solution = d.)

Question

10. A machine was purchased at the beginning of 2014 for $75,000. At the time of purchase, the machine's estimated useful life was six years, with a residual value of $9,000. The machine was depreciated using straight-line depreciation through to 2016. At the beginning of 2017, the machine's estimated useful life was revised to a total useful life of eight years, with a revised estimate of residual value of $7,000. The amount to be recorded for depreciation for 2017 is:

    a. $4,375.

    b. $5,250.

    c. $7,000.

    d. $8,450.

EXPLANATION: Write down the model to calculate depreciation if there is a change in estimated useful life and/or residual value of a plant asset. Fill in the data given and solve:

Original cost	$75,000
Accumulated depreciation	(33,000)[a]
Book value	42,000
Additional expenditures capitalized, if any	-0-
Revised book value	42,000
Current estimate of residual value	(7,000)
Remaining depreciable cost	35,000
Remaining years of useful life at 1/1/17	÷ 5[b]
Depreciation expense for 2017	$ 7,000 (Solution = c.)

[a]Original cost	$75,000
Original estimate of residual value	(9,000)
Original depreciable cost	66,000
Original estimate of useful life in years	÷ 6
Original depreciation per year	11,000
Number of years used	3
Accumulated depreciation, 1/1/17	$33,000
[b]Estimated total useful life in years (revised)	8
Number of years asset has been in use	(3)
Remaining years useful life at 1/1/17	5

Question

11. If merchandise inventory was overstated at December 31, 2017, how would 2017 net income, 2018 net income, working capital at December 31, 2017, and owners' equity at December 31, 2017, be affected?

	2017 Net Income	2018 Net Income	Working Capital 12/31/17	Owners' Equity 12/31/17
a.	Overstated	Understated	Overstated	Overstated
b.	Understated	Overstated	Understated	Understated
c.	Overstated	No effect	No effect	Overstated
d.	Overstated	Understated	Understated	Understated

EXPLANATION: Overstatement of ending inventory is a counterbalancing error. Overstatement of 2017 ending inventory will cause 2017 net income to be overstated (due to the understatement of cost of goods sold) and 2018 net income to be understated (due to the overstatement of beginning inventory). The overstatement of 2017 net income will cause owners' equity to be overstated. Inventory is a current asset; therefore, working capital at December 31, 2017, will also be overstated. (Solution = a.)

Question

12. An adjustment to accrue interest expense of $7,500 was omitted at December 31, 2016. In addition, an adjustment to accrue interest expense of $10,000 was omitted at December 31, 2017. The net effect of these errors on net income for 2017 is:

    a. an overstatement of $10,000.

    b. an understatement of $2,500.

    c. an understatement of $7,500.

    d. an overstatement of $2,500.

EXPLANATION: Analyze each error separately, then summarize the effects. (If necessary, for each error, draft the journal entry that was made and the journal entry that should have been made, and compare both to analyze their effect on interest expense, and therefore net income.)

Error 1: Interest expense for 2016 is understated by $7,500.

Net income for 2016 is overstated by $7,500.

Interest expense for 2017 is overstated by $7,500.

Net income for 2017 is understated by $7,500.

Error 2: Interest expense for 2017 is understated by $10,000.

Net income for 2017 is overstated by $10,000.

Interest expense for 2018 is overstated by $10,000.

Net income for 2018 is understated by $10,000.

Net effect on 2017 net income:

Effect of error 1: understatement	$ 7,500
Effect of error 2: overstatement	10,000
Net effect on 2017 net income (overstatement)	$ 2,500

(Solution = d.)

Question

13. Under IFRS and ASPE, a change in accounting policy would not be acceptable if the change is made:

    a. to conform with industry practice.

    b. to avoid breaking a debt covenant.

    c. to conform to a new accounting standard.

    d. to conform to legislative requirements.

EXPLANATION: A change in accounting policy may be implemented to conform with industry practice, to conform to a new accounting standard, or to conform to legislative requirements. A voluntary change in accounting policy is only permitted if it results in reliable and more relevant presentation of information in the financial statements (or, under ASPE, if the policy change is within certain specifically identified accounting standards). These guidelines are in place to prevent manipulation of financial statements to suit objectives such as meeting debt covenants. (Solution = b.)

Question

14. Gus Incorporated discovered a statement of financial position classification error in its prior year's financial statements. The error does not materially affect financial statement presentation. The company is now in the process of preparing its current year financial statements. What adjustment(s) should be made, if any?

   a. No adjustment is required because current year and prior year net income are not affected.

   b. Prior year financial statements should be adjusted. Comparative numbers should be reclassified and the change should be disclosed in the notes to the financial statements.

   c. No adjustment is required because the error is not material.

   d. Prior year financial statements should be adjusted. Comparative numbers should be reclassified but the change should not be disclosed in the notes to the financial statements because the error is not material.

EXPLANATION: Materiality is an overriding concept in recording adjustments; any item that is not material should not be adjusted. (Solution = c.)

If the classification error was material, reclassification of the related items would be considered a change in presentation only (and not a change in accounting policy). In addition, under IFRS, if an entity reclassifies items in its financial statements, an opening statement of financial position must be presented for the earliest comparative period reported. (A similar requirement does not exist under ASPE.)

Chapter 22

Statement of Cash Flows

OVERVIEW

Under both IFRS and ASPE, a complete set of basic financial statements includes a statement of cash flows for each period for which results of operations are provided. The primary purpose of a statement of cash flows is to provide relevant information about an entity's sources (receipts) and uses (payments) of cash during a period. When analyzed in conjunction with related disclosures and information contained in the other financial statements, the statement of cash flows helps investors, creditors, and others to assess: (a) the entity's ability to generate positive future net cash flows; (b) the entity's ability to meet its obligations and to pay dividends; (c) the entity's need for external financing; (d) the reasons for the difference between net income and cash flow from operating activities; and (e) the effects of both cash and non-cash investing and financing transactions during the period on the entity's financial position. This chapter discusses preparation of a statement of cash flows, and related presentation, disclosure, and analysis issues.

STUDY STEPS

Understanding the Value of the Statement of Cash Flows

The primary objective of the statement of cash flows is to provide relevant information about a company's sources of cash (such as operating activities, sale of assets, and external financing) and uses of cash (such as operating activities, purchase of assets, and repaying debt). The statement of cash flows focuses on a company's liquidity and solvency. A company may report positive net income on the income statement, but have negative cash flow from operating activities. This relationship would be highlighted on the statement of cash flows.

A key number on the statement of cash flows is net cash flow from operating activities, or net cash provided by (used in) operating activities. In general, companies that perform better generate higher positive net cash flow from operating activities. These internally generated funds can be used to finance other activities such as business expansion, repayment of debt, and payment of dividends. If a company internally generates high positive net cash flow from operating activities, it may not have to rely heavily on external financing from creditors or shareholders. This is an advantage because external financing often carries with it commitments to pay a return to its providers (such as interest) and to repay principal, which can put an undue strain on the company's cash flows.

The statement of cash flows is valuable to users because it provides cash basis information, whereas measurement of net income on the income statement is affected by estimates and the preparers' choice of accounting principles and procedures.

Becoming Proficient in Related Calculations

In this section, we will discuss the preparation and interpretation of the statement of cash flows.

The statement of cash flows shows changes in cash and cash equivalents, sources of cash, and uses of cash during the period. On the statement of cash flows, this information is divided into the following three categories:

1. Cash flow from operating activities
2. Cash flow from investing activities
3. Cash flow from financing activities

Operating activities are the enterprise's principal revenue-producing activities and all other activities that are not investing or financing activities.

Investing activities involve the acquisition and disposal of long-term assets and other investments that are not included in cash equivalents or acquired for trading purposes.

Financing activities result in changes in the size and composition of the enterprise's equity capital and borrowings.

There are two approaches to the preparation of the statement of cash flows:

1. manual analysis, or
2. the work sheet approach.

To prepare the statement of cash flows following a **manual** approach, the following steps are involved:

1. Determine the change in cash (and cash equivalents).
2. Net income (from the income statement) is the starting point for calculating cash flows from operating activities.
    a. Under the **direct method**, amounts reported on the income statement are transferred line by line to the heading that comes closest to representing the type of cash flow, until all components of net income have been transferred.
    b. Under the **indirect method**, the bottom line net income number is transferred and is then adjusted for items where the actual operating cash flow and the amount reported on the income statement are different. Examples include differences related to receivables, payables, and other working capital accounts; expenses for which there is no associated cash flow, such as depreciation and amortization expense; and gains or losses reported on the income statement that do not pertain to operating transactions, such as those resulting from disposal of long-term assets and on the early retirement of long-term debt.
3. Analyze the change in **each** statement of financial position account, identify all cash flows associated with the changes in the account balance, and record the effect on the statement of cash flows.
4. Complete the statement of cash flows.

The **work sheet approach** is an alternative way to perform the analysis required to produce a statement of cash flows. This approach involves the following steps:

1. Enter the statement of financial position accounts and their beginning and ending balances in the appropriate statement of financial position accounts section of the work sheet.
2. Enter the debits and credits from the summary entries that explain the changes in each statement of financial position account (other than cash). Identify all entries that affect cash, and enter these amounts in the reconciling columns at the bottom of the worksheet.
3. After the analysis is complete and the changes in all statement of financial position accounts have been reconciled, enter the increase or decrease in cash on the statement of financial position cash line (or lines, if cash equivalents) and at the bottom of the worksheet. The totals of the reconciling columns should balance.

Defining Cash and Cash Equivalents

Cash includes cash on hand and demand deposits.

Cash equivalents are short-term, highly liquid investments that are readily convertible to known amounts of cash and have an insignificant risk of change in value. Therefore, cash equivalents include short-term investments that are acquired with short maturities (generally three months or less from the date of acquisition). Under IFRS, preferred share investments acquired close to their maturity date may be included in cash equivalents. However, under ASPE, all equity investments are excluded from cash equivalents because they are not readily convertible to known amounts of cash, and because the risk of change in their value is significant.

Identifying Transactions

Which transactions should be included on the statement of cash flows, and how do we know that all relevant transactions have been included? The work sheet (in the work sheet approach described more fully in Appendix 22A of the textbook) is a particularly helpful tool in answering these questions.

Theoretically, all transactions ultimately affect the statement of financial position, because all income statement accounts are closed out to retained earnings at the end of each year, and retained earnings is a statement of financial position account. Therefore, analyzing the change in each statement of financial position account (from one period to the next) should ensure that all relevant transactions are identified and included in the statement of cash flows. Note that the net change in an account (for example, Land) usually does not provide enough information about individual transactions that affected the account. (For instance, an increase of $100,000 in the Land account may be due to one transaction, such as a purchase of land costing $100,000, or multiple transactions, including offsetting purchases and disposals of land.) Therefore, full *analysis* of the change in each statement of financial position account, together with analysis of other information including disclosures and the other financial statements, is required to ensure that all relevant transactions are identified and included on the statement of cash flows.

Classifying Transactions

The definitions of operating activities, investing activities, and financing activities may be used to classify transactions. Another way to classify transactions is to divide the statement of financial position into quadrants as follows:

I	II
Current assets (excluding cash)	Current liabilities (except current long-term debt)
III	IV
Long-term assets	Long-term debt and equity (including current portion of long-term debt)

In general, transactions that affect quadrant I and quadrant II are classified as operating activities, transactions that affect quadrant III are classified as investing activities, and transactions that affect quadrant IV are classified as financing activities. Purchase of land affects quadrant III; therefore, it is an investing activity. Borrowing of money on a long-term basis affects quadrant IV; therefore, it is a financing activity. Intuitively, the process of earning net income is an operating activity; however, it can also be noted that sales and purchases affect current assets (such as Accounts

Receivable and Inventory) and current liabilities (such as Accounts Payable), which affect quadrant I and quadrant II, respectively.

There are some exceptions to the quadrant approach described above, for instance:

1. **Current portion of long-term debt** is included in current liabilities on the statement of financial position; however, current portion of long-term debt is classified as a financing cash flow since it relates to the company's borrowings.

2. The effect of **interest received** may be included in an interest receivable account (typically a current asset). Under IFRS, interest received may be classified as either an operating or investing cash flow; however, under ASPE, interest received is classified as an operating cash flow.

3. The effect of **interest paid** may be included in an interest payable account (typically a current liability). Under IFRS, interest paid may be classified as either an operating or financing cash flow; however, under ASPE, interest paid is classified as an operating cash flow if recognized in net income. (If charged directly to retained earnings, interest paid is classified as a financing cash flow.)

4. The effect of **dividends received** may be included in a dividend receivable account (typically a current asset). Under IFRS, dividends received may be classified as either an operating or investing cash flow; however, under ASPE, dividends received are classified as an operating cash flow.

5. The effect of **dividends paid** may be included in a dividend payable account (typically a current liability). Under IFRS, dividends paid may be classified as either an operating or financing cash flow; however, under ASPE, dividends paid are classified as an operating cash flow if recognized in net income. (If charged directly to retained earnings, dividends paid are classified as a financing cash flow.)

In summary, **under IFRS, interest and dividends received may be classified as either operating or investing cash flows, and interest and dividends paid may be classified as either operating or financing cash flows**. Note that under IFRS, once the choice of classification is made (for each of interest and dividends received and paid), it is applied consistently from period to period. **Under ASPE, interest and dividends received and paid are generally classified as operating cash flows (unless interest and/or dividends paid are charged directly to retained earnings, in which case they are classified as financing cash flows).**

A statement of cash flows that balances is not necessarily correct; for example:

1. All transactions may not have been identified. (That is, there may be some transactions that offset each other that have not been identified.)

2. Transactions may be classified incorrectly. (For example, an operating cash flow may have been classified as an investing cash flow in error.)

3. The statement may not include sufficient detail, or may include presentation errors.

Presentation

The direct method and the indirect (or reconciliation) method are two different ways of presenting cash flows from operating activities. Given the same information, both methods arrive at the same amount of net cash provided by (used in) operating activities. Both methods are acceptable, although IFRS and ASPE encourage (but do not require) use of the direct method. In practice, many companies use the indirect method.

The direct method shows the following amounts under "Cash flows from operating activities":

Cash receipts from customers

Cash receipts from other revenue sources

Cash payments to suppliers for goods and services

Cash payments to and on behalf of employees

Cash interest paid

Cash dividends paid (if classified as operating cash flows under IFRS)

Cash payments of income tax

The indirect method (also called the reconciliation method) adjusts for the same items included in cash flows from operating activities under the direct method. However, the indirect method begins with net income (per the income statement) and adds or deducts cash and non-cash items and changes in working capital, resulting in reconciliation of net income to net cash provided by (used in) operating activities.

Interpreting the Statement of Cash Flows

The final, and perhaps the most important, study step is learning how to interpret a statement of cash flows. When analyzing a company's financial position, it may be best to start with the statement of cash flows, because its focus is on cash flow from operating activities (or cash from continuing operations). Analysis of cash flow from operating activities often reveals the strength of the company, whether or not the company's operating cash flow is sustainable, and whether or not the company will be able to pay dividends and interest and repay debt from internally generated funds. As previously discussed, the statement of cash flows also provides information regarding the company's sources and uses of cash during the period.

TIPS ON CHAPTER TOPICS

● Homework and examination problems related to the statement of cash flows very often involve comparative statement of financial position data. Although sometimes the earlier year's information is listed first (so that the data are shown in chronological order), it is also common to list the current year's information first. Before beginning work on a problem, carefully note the order of the data so that increases or decreases in accounts are correctly identified.

- Additional information is often provided with comparative statements of financial position. If no additional information is provided for a particular account, but the account balance has changed, assume that (1) only one transaction is responsible for the change in the account balance; (2) the most common transaction for the particular account occurred, which changed the account's balance; and (3) cash was involved in the transaction.

- In studying this chapter and doing homework questions, you will encounter transactions for which you may not recall the proper accounting procedures. This chapter draws on your knowledge of all preceding chapters. Use this opportunity to look up accounting procedures you don't recall, and to refresh your memory. The accounting procedures you review will likely be easier to recall the next time you need to use them.

- Every transaction affecting the Cash account is reflected as either an inflow (receipt) or outflow (payment) on the statement of cash flows. Furthermore, receipts and payments are classified by activity. The three activity classifications are (1) operating; (2) investing; and (3) financing.

- To determine if a cash transaction is related to an operating activity, investing activity, or financing activity, first determine if the transaction meets the definition of an investing activity. If not, determine if the transaction meets the definition of a financing activity. If not, then the transaction is related to an operating activity. (Refer to **Illustration 22-1** below for definitions and examples of operating activities, investing activities, and financing activities.)

- For investing activities and financing activities, cash receipts and payments are reported **gross (not net)**. Thus, if issuance of long-term debt results in proceeds of $2 million, and principal repayments of the same long-term debt total $300,000 in the same period, the two amounts *cannot* be netted to show only a net cash inflow of $1.7 million. Instead, the cash inflow of $2 million and the cash outflow of $300,000 must be shown separately in the financing section of the statement of cash flows. Similarly, if there are acquisitions and disposals of plant assets in the same period, the related cash payments and receipts must be reported gross (not net).

- **Cash** includes currency on hand and demand deposits with banks or other financial institutions. **Cash equivalents** are short-term, highly liquid investments that are readily convertible to known amounts of cash and have an insignificant risk of change in value. Examples of items that are cash equivalents include treasury bills, commercial paper, and money market funds. Cash equivalents may be included in the cash amount presented on the statement of financial position and on the statement of cash flows.

- Under IFRS, income taxes paid are required to be disclosed. However, under ASPE, income taxes paid are encouraged (but not required) to be disclosed.

- Cash flows related to investments and loans that are acquired **specifically for trading purposes** are operating cash flows, whereas investments and loans that are acquired for other purposes are investing cash flows.

- If a homework or exam problem requires use of the indirect method but does not give the net income figure, the amount of net income (or net loss) can usually be determined by analyzing the change in retained earnings (which will contain net income or net loss, in addition to other items).

ILLUSTRATION 22-1

Operating, Investing, and Financing Activities

Definitions:

Operating activities are the enterprise's principal revenue-producing activities and other activities that are not investing or financing activities. Operating cash flows generally involve the cash effects of transactions that determine net income.

Investing activities involve the acquisition and disposal of long-term assets and other investments that are not included in cash equivalents or acquired for trading purposes. Investing cash flows are generally the result of (a) making and collecting loans and (b) acquiring and disposing of investments and productive long-lived assets.

Financing activities result in changes in the size and composition of the enterprise's equity capital and borrowing. Financing cash flows are generally the result of (a) obtaining capital from owners and providing them with a return on, and a return of, their investment; and (b) obtaining cash from issuing debt and repaying amounts borrowed.

Examples:

Operating activities

Cash inflows:

From cash sales and collections from customers on account

From returns on loans (interest) and equity securities (dividends)[a]

From receipts for royalties, rents, and fees

Cash outflows:

To suppliers on account

To, and on behalf of, employees for services

To governments for taxes

To lenders for interest[b]

To others for expenses

Investing activities

Cash inflows:

From proceeds on sale of property, plant, and equipment

From proceeds on sale of debt or equity securities of other entities

From collection of principal on loans to other entities

Cash outflows:

For purchases of property, plant, and equipment[c]

For purchases of debt or equity securities of other entities

For loans to other entities

Financing activities

Cash inflows:

From proceeds on issuance of equity securities (company's own shares)

From proceeds on issuance of debt (bonds and notes)

Cash outflows:

For payments of dividends to shareholders[d]

For repayments of long-term debt or reacquisitions of share capital

For reductions of capital lease obligations

[a]Under IFRS, interest and dividends received may be classified as either operating or investing cash inflows. Under ASPE, interest and dividends received are generally classified as operating cash inflows.

[b]Under IFRS, interest paid may be classified as either operating or financing cash outflows. Under ASPE, interest paid is generally classified as an operating cash outflow.

[c]If as part of a purchase of a plant asset, the company incurs debt owed directly to the seller, the transaction is considered a significant non-cash transaction that will not appear on the statement of cash flows, but will be disclosed elsewhere in the financial statements.

[d]Under IFRS, dividends paid may be classified as either operating or financing cash outflows. Under ASPE, dividends paid are classified as financing cash outflows if charged to retained earnings.

> The statement of cash flows summarizes all transactions that occurred during the period and had an impact on the cash balance.

EXERCISE 22-1

PURPOSE: This exercise will give you practice in classifying transactions by activity category.

The Wolfson Corporation prepares financial statements in accordance with ASPE, and had the following transactions during 2017:

1. Issued common shares for $100,000 in cash.
2. Issued $22,000 worth of common shares in exchange for equipment.
3. Sold services for $52,000 cash.
4. Purchased securities as a long-term investment for $18,000 cash.
5. Collected $9,000 of accounts receivable.
6. Paid $14,000 of accounts payable.
7. Declared and paid a cash dividend of $12,000.
8. Sold a long-term investment in securities with a cost of $18,000 for $18,000 cash.
9. Purchased a machine for $35,000 in exchange for a long-term note.
10. Exchanged land costing $20,000 for equipment costing $20,000.
11. Paid salaries and wages of $6,000.
12. Paid $1,000 for advertising services.
13. Paid $8,000 for insurance coverage for a future period.
14. Borrowed $31,000 cash from the bank.

15. Paid $11,000 interest.

16. Paid $31,000 cash to the bank to repay loan principal.

17. Issued $40,000 of common shares upon conversion of bonds payable having a face value of $40,000.

18. Paid utilities of $4,000.

19. Loaned a vendor $6,000 cash.

20. Collected interest of $2,000.

21. Collected $6,000 loan principal from a borrower.

22. Purchased treasury shares for $4,000.

23. Sold treasury shares for $6,000 (cost was $4,000).

24. Paid taxes of $20,000.

Instructions

Analyze each transaction above and indicate whether it results in a(n):

(a) inflow of cash from operating activities,

(b) outflow of cash from operating activities,

(c) inflow of cash from investing activities,

(d) outflow of cash from investing activities,

(e) inflow of cash from financing activities,

(f) outflow of cash from financing activities, or

(g) non-cash investing and/or financing activity.

Solution to Exercise 22-1

1. (e)	5. (a)	9. (g)	13. (b)	17. (g)	21. (c)
2. (g)	6. (b)	10. (g)	14. (e)	18. (b)	22. (f)
3. (a)	7. (f)	11. (b)	15. (b)	19. (d)	23. (e)
4. (d)	8. (c)	12. (b)	16. (f)	20. (a)	24. (b)

APPROACH: Write down the definitions for operating activities, investing activities, and financing activities. (Refer to **Illustration 22-1** above.) Analyze each transaction to determine its classification. Watch for any transactions that do not result in cash flow; they are non-cash items. Most non-cash items are disclosed elsewhere in the financial statements.

EXPLANATION:

1. Issuance of share capital for cash results in an inflow of cash from financing activities.

2. Issuance of share capital in exchange for equipment (a plant asset) does not involve cash; the transaction is a non-cash investing and financing activity.

3. Sale of services is a revenue transaction. Sale of services for cash results in an inflow of cash from operating activities.

4. Cash purchase of a long-term investment results in an outflow of cash from investing activities.

5. Collection of accounts receivable is a cash inflow from customers for revenues already recorded. Cash inflow from customers is an inflow of cash from operating activities.

6. Payment of accounts payable is a cash outflow to suppliers for inventory or expenses already recorded. Cash outflow to vendors is an outflow of cash from operating activities.

7. Under ASPE, cash payment of dividends to shareholders is an outflow of cash from financing activities.

8. Sale of a long-term investment results in an inflow of cash from investing activities.

9. Acquisition of a machine (a plant asset) is an investing activity. Issuance of debt is a financing activity. Purchase of a machine plant asset by issuance of a note payable does **not** involve cash. Hence, the transaction is a non-cash investing and financing activity.

10. Acquisition of land (a plant asset) is an investing activity. Sale (disposal) of equipment (also a plant asset) is also an investing activity. Exchange of one plant asset for another plant asset does **not** involve cash; the transaction is a non-cash investing activity.

11. Payment of salaries and wages is payment to employees for services rendered, and results in an outflow of cash from operating activities.

12. Payment for advertising services is payment to a supplier for services used in operations, and results in an outflow of cash from operating activities.

13. Payment for insurance coverage for a future period is payment to a supplier for services to be used in operations in a future period. The related expense will be recognized in the future period covered by the insurance; however, the payment (cash flow) occurred during 2017, and results in an outflow of cash from operating activities in 2017.

14. Borrowing cash from a bank results in issuance of debt (that is, note payable), which is an inflow of cash from financing activities.

15. Under ASPE, payment of interest is an outflow of cash from operating activities.

16. Repayment of loan principal (debt) is an outflow of cash from financing activities.

17. Issuance of common shares is a financing activity and liquidation (redemption) of bonds payable is a financing activity. Redemption of bonds by issuance of shares is a **non-cash** financing activity because no cash is exchanged.

18. Payment of utilities is payment to a supplier for services used in operations, and results in an outflow of cash from operating activities.

19. Lending cash to another entity is an outflow of cash from investing activities.

20. Under ASPE, cash interest received is an inflow of cash from operating activities.

21. Collection of loan principal is an inflow of cash from investing activities.

22. Cash payment to reacquire a company's own shares (treasury shares) is an outflow of cash from financing activities.

23. Sale of treasury shares for cash results in an inflow of cash from financing activities.
24. Payment of taxes is an outflow of cash from operating activities.

- To determine if a cash transaction should be classified as operating, investing, or financing, it is usually helpful to reconstruct the journal entry that recorded the transaction, and apply the following observations:

    1. The journal entry to record a cash transaction that is an operating activity will generally involve (1) Cash and (2) a revenue account or an expense account; or, a prepaid expense account or an unearned revenue account; or, an account receivable or an account payable.

    2. The journal entry to record a cash transaction that is an investing activity will generally involve (1) Cash and (2) an asset account other than Cash, such as Investments (that are not included in cash equivalents or acquired for trading purposes), Land, Building, Equipment, or Patent.

    3. The journal entry to record a cash transaction that is a financing activity will generally involve (1) Cash and (2) a liability account (such as Bonds Payable, Notes Payable, or Dividends Payable), or a shareholders' equity account (such as Common Shares, Contributed Surplus, or Treasury Shares).

- If Wolfson prepares financial statements in accordance with IFRS, answers to items 7, 15, and 20 may differ. Item 7 involves dividends paid, which may be classified as either an operating or financing cash outflow under IFRS. Items 15 and 20 involve interest received and paid. Under IFRS, interest received may be classified as either an operating or investing cash inflow, and interest paid may be classified as either an operating or financing cash outflow.

EXERCISE 22-2

PURPOSE: This exercise will provide an opportunity to prepare a statement of cash flows using the indirect method.

A comparative balance sheet for Hummingbird Pictures appears below:

| | | December 31 | |
Assets	2017	2016	Change
Cash	$ 58,000	$ 47,000	$ 11,000
Accounts receivable	65,000	52,000	13,000
Inventory	127,000	83,000	44,000
FV-OCI investments	101,000	61,000	40,000
Equipment	165,000	95,000	70,000
Accumulated depreciation	(33,000)	(19,000)	(14,000)
	$483,000	$319,000	$164,000

Liabilities and Shareholders' Equity

Accounts payable	$ 33,000	$ 37,500	$ (4,500)
Notes payable	75,000	50,000	25,000
Bonds payable	90,000	—	90,000
Common shares	35,000	17,500	17,500
Contributed surplus	170,000	170,000	—
Retained earnings	80,000	44,000	36,000
	$483,000	$319,000	$164,000

Additional information:

1. New equipment costing $85,000 was purchased for cash.
2. Old equipment was sold at a loss of $3,000.
3. Bonds were issued for cash.
4. An equity investment costing $40,000 was acquired in exchange for a long-term note payable. Hummingbird Pictures intends to hold the equity investment for the long term. As at December 31, 2017, the fair value of the equity investment is $40,000.
5. Cash dividends of $8,750 were declared and paid during the year.
6. Depreciation expense for 2017 was $19,000.
7. Accounts payable relate to operating expenses.

Instructions

Prepare a statement of cash flows for 2017 using the indirect method, assuming Hummingbird Pictures applies ASPE.

In this exercise, you must analyze the changes in the Retained Earnings account balance to determine the net income figure for 2017.

Solution to Exercise 22-2

HUMMINGBIRD PICTURES
Statement of Cash Flows
For the Year Ended December 31, 2017

Cash flows from operating activities

Net income		$ 44,750
Adjustments to reconcile net income to net cash provided by operating activities		
Depreciation expense	$ 19,000	
Loss on sale of equipment	3,000	

Increase in accounts receivable	(13,000)	
Increase in inventory	(44,000)	
Decrease in accounts payable	(4,500)	(39,500)
Net cash provided by operating activities		5,250
Cash flows from investing activities		
Purchase of equipment	(85,000)	
Sale of equipment	7,000	
Net cash used by investing activities		(78,000)
Cash flows from financing activities		
Payment on long-term note payable	(15,000)	
Issuance of bonds	90,000	
Issuance of share capital	17,500	
Payment of dividends	(8,750)	
Net cash provided by financing activities		83,750
Net increase in cash		11,000
Cash at beginning of period		47,000
Cash at end of period		$ 58,000

Non-cash investing and financing activities

Acquisition of equity investment by issuance of long-term debt	$ 40,000

Examine the statement of cash flows and notice the major sources and uses of cash during the period.

APPROACH: Glance through the balance sheet data and additional information to get a sense of the facts given. Set up the format for the statement of cash flows by placing the major classification headings approximately where they should be. Leave space between the headings to fill in details later. (Allow about a one-half page for operating activities, one-quarter page for investing activities, and one-quarter page for financing activities.) Then take each fact in order and process it by placing it where it belongs on the statement of cash flows.

1. Find the net change in cash by comparing the balance of Cash at the end of the period with the balance of Cash at the beginning of the period. Net change in cash should equal net increase in cash (or net decrease in cash), which should reconcile beginning and ending cash balances.

2. Analyze every change in every balance sheet account other than Cash. Reconstruct the journal entries for the transactions that caused each balance sheet account to change. Examine each journal entry to identify (a) if there is an inflow of cash (debit to Cash) or an outflow of cash (credit to Cash) or no effect on cash; (b) if the transaction involves an operating, investing, or financing activity.

3. To help identify the activity classification for each transaction, write down the definitions for operating activities, investing activities, and financing activities. Analyze each transaction to see if it meets one of these definitions. (Refer to **Illustration 22-1** above.)

4. To help identify transactions involving operating activities, recall that operating activities typically result in recording of revenues or expenses at some point in time. Thus, if the journal entry to record the transaction involves revenue earned, expense incurred, a receivable, a prepaid expense, a payable, or an unearned revenue, the transaction likely involves an operating activity. When the indirect method is used, the net income figure is used as a starting point for calculation of "net cash flows provided by operating activities." The net income figure must then be converted from an accrual basis to a cash basis amount. To help identify the transactions requiring an adjustment to net income, find the transactions that affect an income statement account and a balance sheet account other than Cash (such as depreciation), or that affect Cash and result in accruals or deferrals of revenues or expenses (such as payment of expense in advance of consumption of related benefits).

5. To help identify investing activities, recall that transactions involving investing activities typically cause changes in non-current asset accounts (or changes in certain current asset accounts such as short-term investments that are *not* included in cash equivalents and are *not* acquired specifically for trading purposes, and non-trade receivables).

6. To help identify financing activities, recall that transactions involving financing activities typically cause changes in non-current liability accounts or shareholders' equity accounts (or changes in certain current liability accounts such as short-term non-trade notes payable, and current portion of long-term debt).

7. If the reason for change in a balance sheet account is not fully explained in the additional information given, assume the most common reason for the change in the particular account. Assume purchases and sales of assets are for cash unless otherwise indicated.

8. When more than one transaction is responsible for the net change in an account balance, it may be helpful to draw a T account for the account, and to include all transactions that occurred during the period.

EXPLANATION:

1. There was an increase of $11,000 in the Cash account. This net increase in cash goes near the bottom of the statement of cash flows and reconciles the $47,000 beginning cash balance with the $58,000 ending cash balance.

2. The journal entry to record the increase in Accounts Receivable is reconstructed as follows:

Accounts Receivable	13,000	
Sales Revenue		13,000

Net income increases but Cash is not affected; thus, under the indirect method, this increase in accounts receivable is deducted from net income to arrive at net cash provided by operating activities. An increase in accounts receivable indicates that sales revenue for the period exceeded cash collections from customers during the period; therefore, net income is greater than net cash provided by operating activities.

3. The journal entry to record the increase in Inventory is reconstructed as follows:

Inventory	44,000	
Cash		44,000

Payments to suppliers are an operating cash outflow. This cash outflow is not reflected in the net income figure; thus, under the indirect method, this increase in inventory is deducted from net income to arrive at net cash provided by operating activities. An increase in inventory indicates that cost of goods sold expense was less than cash payments to suppliers; therefore, net income is greater than net cash provided by operating activities.

4. The journal entry to record the increase in FV-OCI Investments is reconstructed as follows:

FV-OCI Investments	40,000	
Notes Payable (Long-Term)		40,000

Acquisition of an equity investment is an investing activity, and issuance of debt is a financing activity; however, in this transaction, there is no effect on cash. This non-cash investing and financing transaction is not reported in the body of the statement of cash flows, but must be disclosed elsewhere in the financial statements.

5. The T accounts for Equipment, Accumulated Depreciation, and Loss on Sale of Equipment are reconstructed as follows:

Equipment

Jan. 1, 2017 Balance	95,000	Unexplained transaction	
Acquisition during 2017	85,000	during 2017	15,000
Dec. 31, 2017 Balance	165,000		

Accumulated Depreciation—Equipment

Unexplained transaction		Jan. 1, 2017 Balance	19,000
during 2017	5,000	Depreciation for 2017	19,000
		Dec. 31, 2017 Balance	33,000

Loss on Sale of Equipment

Sale of equipment during 2017	3,000	

The additional information given states that Equipment costing $85,000 was purchased. Depreciation expense amounted to $19,000, and old equipment was sold at a loss of $3,000. We can solve for the missing data (an unexplained credit of $15,000 to Equipment and an unexplained debit of $5,000 to Accumulated Depreciation—Equipment). The most common reason for a credit to the Equipment account is disposal of an asset. That transaction would also explain the $5,000 reduction in Accumulated Depreciation—Equipment and the $3,000 loss on sale of equipment. Thus, it appears that an asset with a cost of $15,000 and book value of $10,000 ($15,000 − $5,000 = $10,000) was sold at a loss of $3,000. This means cash proceeds on the disposal amounted to $7,000 ($10,000 book value − $3,000 loss = $7,000 cash proceeds).

The journal entries to record the transactions discussed above are reconstructed as follows:

Equipment	85,000	
Cash		85,000

Purchase of plant assets is an investing activity. Therefore, this cash outflow is reported as an investing activity.

Depreciation Expense	19,000	
Accumulated Depreciation—Equipment		19,000

This journal entry does not affect cash, but does reduce net income. Under the indirect method, depreciation expense is added back to net income to calculate net cash provided by operating activities.

Cash	7,000	
Loss on Sale of Equipment	3,000	
Accumulated Depreciation—Equipment	5,000	
Equipment		15,000

Disposal of plant assets is an investing activity. Therefore, this inflow of cash is reported as an investing activity. Under the indirect method, the loss on sale of equipment must also be added back to net income, as there was no corresponding outflow of cash.

6. The journal entry to record the decrease in Accounts Payable is reconstructed as follows:

Accounts Payable	4,500	
Cash		4,500

Payment to suppliers for goods and services consumed in operations is an operating activity. Under the indirect method, this decrease in Accounts Payable must be deducted from net income because a decrease in Accounts Payable indicates that expenses incurred were less than cash payments to suppliers; therefore, net income was greater than the net cash provided by operating activities.

7. The T account for Notes Payable (Long-Term) is reconstructed as follows:

Notes Payable (Long-Term)

		Jan. 1, 2017 Balance	50,000
Unexplained transaction		Purchase of equity	
during 2017	15,000	investment in 2017	40,000
		Dec. 31, 2017 Balance	75,000

The most common reason for a debit to a liability account is a payment. The journal entries to record these transactions are reconstructed as follows:

FV-OCI Investments	40,000	
Notes Payable (Long-Term)		40,000

This transaction was discussed and analyzed in point 4 (above).

Notes Payable (Long-Term)	15,000	
Cash		15,000

This cash outflow of $15,000 was due to payment of a non-trade note payable, which is a financing activity.

8. The journal entry to record increase in Bonds Payable is reconstructed as follows:

Cash	90,000	
Bonds Payable		90,000

This cash inflow of $90,000 was due to the issuance of bonds, which is a financing activity.

9. The most common reason for an increase in Common Shares is the issuance of shares for cash. The journal entry to record this transaction is reconstructed as follows:

Cash	17,500	
Common Shares		17,500

This cash inflow of $17,500 was due to the issuance of common shares, which is a financing activity.

10. The Retained Earnings T account is reconstructed as follows:

Retained Earnings

		Jan. 1, 2017	44,000
Declaration of cash		Unexplained transaction	
dividends during 2017	8,750	during 2017	44,750
		Dec. 31, 2017 Balance	80,000

The most common reason for a credit to Retained Earnings is net income. Since the indirect method is being applied in this exercise, the net income figure is needed as the starting point for calculation of net cash provided by operating activities.

The journal entries to record the declaration and payment of cash dividends are reconstructed as follows:

Retained Earnings	8,750	
Dividends Payable		8,750
Dividends Payable	8,750	
Cash		8,750

Providing owners with a return on their investment is classified as a financing activity under ASPE, or as an operating or financing activity under IFRS. Declaration of dividends has no effect on cash; however, payment of a previously declared dividend reduces cash. Thus, payment of cash dividends is reported as a financing activity under ASPE, or as an operating or financing activity under IFRS.

The last step in the preparation of the statement of cash flows is to subtotal each of the three activity classifications. Inflows are shown as positive amounts; outflows are shown as negative amounts. An excess of inflows over outflows within a classification results in a net inflow; an excess of outflows over inflows within a classification results in a net outflow. Subtotals of the three activities are then totalled to determine net change in cash during the year. This net change must agree with your calculation of the change in the Cash account balance (Step 1); otherwise, one or more errors exist and must be corrected in order to balance the statement of cash flows.

CASE 22-1

PURPOSE: This case will help you practise classifying transactions as operating, investing, or financing.

Four different situations are described below:

1. A company purchased a machine priced at $100,000 by issuing a cheque for $100,000.

2. A company purchased a machine priced at $100,000 by giving a down payment of $20,000 and by issuing a note payable to the seller for $80,000. During the same year, the company made principal payments of $12,000 on the note and interest payments of $7,000.

3. A company purchased a machine for $100,000. Of that amount, $80,000 was borrowed from a local bank. During the same year, principal payments of $12,000 and interest payments of $7,000 were paid to the bank for this loan.

4. A company acquired a machine under a capital lease agreement. The present value of minimum lease payments at inception was $100,000. The first lease payment of $2,000 was paid on the date of lease inception. During the year, additional lease payments of $24,000 were made, which included interest of $15,000.

Instructions

Explain how each situation would be reflected in a statement of cash flows. For each situation, indicate the amount that would be included in the operating, investing, and/or financing section of the statement of cash flows, or indicate the amount that would be separately disclosed as a non-cash investing and/or financing transaction.

Solution to Case 22-1

1. Investing outflow of $100,000

2. Investing outflow of $20,000

   Financing outflow of $12,000

   Operating outflow of $7,000. (Under IFRS, interest paid may be classified as either an operating or financing activity; under ASPE, interest paid is required to be classified as an operating activity.)

   Disclosure of issuance of a note payable for $80,000 as part of this transaction to acquire machinery would be included elsewhere in the financial statements as a non-cash investing and financing activity.

3. Financing inflow of $80,000

   Investing outflow of $100,000

   Financing outflow of $12,000

   Operating outflow of $7,000. (Under IFRS, interest paid may be classified as either an operating or financing activity; under ASPE, interest paid is required to be classified as an operating activity.)

4. Financing outflow of $11,000 ($2,000 + $24,000 − $15,000)

   Operating outflow of $15,000. (Under IFRS, interest paid may be classified as either an operating or financing activity; under ASPE, interest paid is required to be classified as an operating activity.)

Illustration 22-2   3 5 5

Disclosure of the capital lease obligation related to this acquisition of machinery for $100,000 would be included elsewhere in the financial statements as a non-cash investing and financing activity.

APPROACH: Refer to **Illustration 22-1** above for a description of the three classifications of activities.

Note that repayments of principal on seller-financed debt are classified as financing cash outflows.

ILLUSTRATION 22-2

Conversion from Accrual Basis to Cash Basis

ACCRUAL BASIS	CASH BASIS
Revenues Earned	Cash Received from Operations
− Expenses Incurred	− Cash Paid for Operations
= Net Income	= Net Cash Provided by Operating Activities

DIRECT METHOD

To calculate net cash provided by operating activities:

Cash Received from Customers	**EXPLANATION:** The major types of cash receipts and cash payments from operating activities (for which selected calculations are shown below) are listed and summarized on the face of the statement of cash flows when the direct method is used.
+ Interest and Dividends Received[a]	
+ Other Operating Cash Receipts	
− Cash Paid for Merchandise Inventory and Operating Expenses	
− Interest Paid[b]	
− Other Operating Cash Payments	
= Net Cash Provided by Operating Activities	

[a]Under IFRS, interest and dividends received may be classified as either operating or investing activities; under ASPE, interest and dividends received are classified as operating activities.

[b]Under IFRS, interest paid may be classified as either an operating or financing activity; under ASPE, interest paid is required to be classified as an operating activity.

To convert revenues earned to cash received from customers:

Revenues Earned

− Increase in Accounts Receivable

+ <u>Increase in Unearned Revenues</u>

= Cash Received from Customers

EXPLANATION: An increase in Accounts Receivable from one statement of financial position date to the next indicates that revenues earned exceeded cash collections from customers during the period; hence, the increase in Accounts Receivable should be subtracted from Revenues Earned to calculate Cash Received from Customers. (A decrease in Accounts Receivable would indicate that cash collections exceeded revenues earned during the period, and would be added to Revenues Earned to calculate Cash Received from Customers.) An increase in Unearned Revenue indicates that cash collections from customers exceeded Revenues Earned; hence, the increase in Unearned Revenue should be added to Revenues Earned to calculate Cash Received from Customers. (A decrease in Unearned Revenue would be subtracted from Revenues Earned.)

OR

Revenues Earned

+ Beginning Accounts Receivable

− Ending Accounts Receivable

− Beginning Unearned Revenue

+ <u>Ending Unearned Revenue</u>

= Cash Received from Customers

EXPLANATION: The balance of Accounts Receivable at the beginning of the period represents revenues earned in a prior period that were collected in the current period. The balance of Accounts Receivable at the end of the period represents revenues earned in the current period that are not yet collected. Beginning Unearned Revenue represents cash collected in a prior period for revenues earned in the current period. Ending Unearned Revenue represents cash collected in the current period for revenues that will be earned in a future period.

Illustration 22-2 357

To convert cost of goods sold to cash paid for merchandise inventory:

Cost of Goods Sold

+ Increase in Inventory

− Increase in Accounts Payable

= Cash Paid for Merchandise Inventory

EXPLANATION: An increase in Inventory indicates that purchases for the period exceeded cost of goods sold. An increase in Accounts Payable indicates that purchases for the period exceeded cash payments for merchandise. (Decreases indicate opposite relationships.)

OR

Cost of Goods Sold

− Beginning Inventory

+ Ending Inventory

+ Beginning Accounts Payable

− Ending Accounts Payable

= Cash Paid for Merchandise Inventory

EXPLANATION: Beginning Inventory represents items purchased in a prior period that were consumed (sold) in the current year. Ending Inventory represents items purchased in the current period that are not reported in Cost of Goods Sold (because they are on hand at the statement of financial position date). Beginning Accounts Payable represents items purchased in a prior period that require cash payments in the current period. Ending Accounts Payable represents items purchased in the current period that will require cash payments in the next period.

To convert operating expenses to cash paid for operating expenses:

Operating Expenses Incurred (excluding depreciation and bad debt expense)

+ Increase in Prepaid Expenses

− Increase in Accrued Liabilities

= Cash Paid for Operating Expenses

EXPLANATION: An increase in Prepaid Expenses indicates that cash payments for prepaid expenses in the current period exceed prepaid expenses consumed in the current period. Therefore, an increase in Prepaid Expenses is added to Operating Expenses Incurred to calculate Cash Paid for Operating Expenses. An increase in Accrued Liabilities indicates that accrued expenses consumed in the current period exceed cash payments for accrued expenses in the current period. Therefore, an increase in Accrued Liabilities is deducted from Operating Expenses Incurred to calculate Cash Paid for Operating Expenses. (Decreases indicate opposite relationships.)

OR

Operating Expenses Incurred (excluding depreciation and bad debt expense)

− Beginning Prepaid Expenses

+ Ending Prepaid Expenses

+ Beginning Accrued Liabilities

− Ending Accrued Liabilities

= Cash Paid for Operating Expenses

EXPLANATION: Beginning Prepaid Expenses represents cash payments in a prior period for expenses to be consumed in the current period. Ending Prepaid Expenses represents cash payments in the current period for expenses to be consumed in the next period. Beginning Accrued Liabilities represents expenses consumed in a prior period, to be paid for in the current period. Ending Accrued Liabilities represents expenses consumed in the current period, to be paid for in the next period.

To convert interest expense to interest paid:

Interest Expense

− Increase in Interest Payable

− Amortization of Discount on Debt

+ Amortization of Premium on Debt

= Interest Paid

EXPLANATION: An increase in an accrued payable indicates that the related expense consumed exceeds cash payments for the related expense in the current period. Amortization of Discount on Debt increases total interest expense but does not cause a cash outflow; Amortization of Premium on Debt decreases total interest expense but does not cause a cash inflow.

OR

Interest Expense

+ Beginning Interest Payable

− Ending Interest Payable

− Amortization of Discount on Debt

+ Amortization of Premium on Debt

= Interest Paid

EXPLANATION: Beginning Interest Payable represents interest expense accrued in a prior period and paid in the current period. Ending Interest Payable represents interest expense accrued in the current period, to be paid in a future period. Amortization of Discount on Debt increases total interest expense but does not cause a cash outflow; Amortization of Premium on Debt decreases total interest expense but does not cause a cash inflow.

Illustration 22-2   3 5 9

**To convert income tax expense
to income tax paid:**

Income Tax Expense

+ Increase in Income Tax Receivable

− Increase in Income Tax Payable

+ Increase in Deferred Tax Asset

− <u>Increase in Deferred Tax Liability</u>

= Income Tax Paid

EXPLANATION: An increase in Income Tax Receivable and/or an increase in Deferred Tax Asset indicates that the amount paid for income taxes during the period exceeds income tax expense. An increase in Income Tax Payable and/or an increase in Deferred Tax Liability indicates that income tax expense exceeds the amount paid for income taxes during the period.

OR

Income Tax Expense

− Beginning Income Tax Receivable

+ Ending Income Tax Receivable

+ Beginning Income Tax Payable

− Ending Income Tax Payable

− Beginning Deferred Tax Asset

+ Ending Deferred Tax Asset

+ Beginning Deferred Tax Liability

− <u>Ending Deferred Tax Liability</u>

= Income Tax Paid

EXPLANATION: Beginning Income Tax Receivable represents income taxes paid in a prior period and expensed in the current period. Ending Income Tax Receivable represents income taxes paid in the current period to be expensed in the next period. Beginning Income Tax Payable represents current income taxes expensed in a prior period and paid in the current period. Ending Income Tax Payable represents current income taxes expensed in the current period to be paid in the next period. Changes in the balances of Deferred Tax Asset or Deferred Tax Liability cause Deferred Tax Expense to change without a corresponding effect on cash. Treatment of Deferred Tax Asset in this reconciliation is the same as for Income Tax Receivable, and treatment of Deferred Tax Liability in this reconciliation is the same as for Income Tax Payable.

For all of the calculations above, a decrease in an account balance is treated in a manner opposite to the way an increase in an account balance is treated.

INDIRECT METHOD

To calculate net cash provided by operating activities:

Net income

Add non-cash charges (such as depreciation expense and amortization of intangibles)

Add non-cash losses (such as losses due to writedown of assets and unrealized losses)

Add losses on sale of assets, settlement of debt, and discontinued operations

Deduct gains on sale of assets, settlement of debt, and discontinued operations

Deduct non-cash gains (such as unrealized gains)

Deduct non-cash credits (such as amortization of premium on bonds payable and income recognized under equity method in excess of dividends received)

Add (deduct) decrease (increase) in net accounts receivable

Add (deduct) decrease (increase) in accrued receivables

Add (deduct) decrease (increase) in inventory

Add (deduct) decrease (increase) in prepaid expenses

Add (deduct) decrease (increase) in deferred tax asset

Add (deduct) increase (decrease) in accounts payable

Add (deduct) increase (decrease) in accrued liabilities

Add (deduct) increase (decrease) in unearned revenue

Add (deduct) increase (decrease) in deferred tax liability

Add (deduct) increase (decrease) in pension liability

= Net Cash Provided by Operating Activities

EXPLANATION: Non-cash charges (such as depreciation) and non-cash losses (or gains) are **added** to (or deducted from) net income because they are expense or loss (or gain) items that do not require an outlay of cash (or result in an inflow of cash). Losses (or gains) on sale of assets, settlement of debt, and discontinued operations are **added** to (or deducted from) net income because they relate to transactions for which cash flows should be classified as investing or financing activities. Non-cash credits (such as amortization of premium on bonds payable and income recognized under the equity method) are **deducted** from net income because they increase net income without resulting in an inflow of cash. An increase in accounts receivable indicates that revenues earned **exceeded** cash inflows; therefore, net income **exceeds** net cash provided by operating activities. An increase in inventory or prepaid expenses indicates that expenses were less than cash outflows; hence, net income **exceeds** net cash provided by operating activities. Increases in accounts receivable, accrued receivables, inventory, and prepaid expenses must therefore be **deducted** from net income to calculate net cash provided by operating activities. On the other hand, an increase in accounts payable or accrued liabilities indicates that expenses incurred **exceeded** cash outflows for payment of merchandise inventory and operating expenses; hence, net income is **less** than net cash provided by operating activities. An increase in unearned revenue indicates that cash received **exceeds** revenue earned; hence, net income is **less** than net cash provided by operating activities. Therefore, increases in accounts payable, accrued liabilities, and unearned revenue must be **added** to net income to calculate net cash provided by operating activities.

Illustration 22-3   361

ILLUSTRATION 22-3

Treatment of Accruals and Deferrals

Treatment of increases in deferred (unearned) revenues, deferred (prepaid) expenses, accrued liabilities, and accrued receivables can be summarized as follows:

	Direct Method		**Indirect Method**
	Revenues	**Expenses**	**Net Income**
Increase in Deferred Revenues	+		+
Increase in Deferred Expenses		+	−
Increase in Accrued Liabilities		−	+
Increase in Accrued Receivables	−		−
	Cash Provided by Operating Activities	**Cash Used in Operating Activities**	**Net Cash Provided by (Used in) Operating Activities**

- In examining the summary above, notice the mathematical signs are the **same** for both the direct method and indirect method for changes in deferred revenues and changes in accrued receivables. This is because (1) changes in deferred revenues and accrued receivables explain the difference between revenues earned during the period and cash received from operating activities during the period; and (2) revenues earned are a **positive** component of net income, and cash received from operating activities is a **positive** component of net cash provided by operating activities.

- Also notice that the mathematical signs are **different** for the direct method and the indirect method for changes in deferred expenses and changes in accrued liabilities. This is because (1) changes in deferred (prepaid) expenses and accrued liabilities explain the difference between expenses incurred during the period and cash paid for operating activities during the period; and (2) expenses incurred are a **negative** component of net income, and cash paid for operating activities is a **negative** component of net cash provided by operating activities.

- "(Net) cash provided by operating activities" (or "cash provided by operations") is another name for "net income on a cash basis."

EXERCISE 22-3

PURPOSE: This exercise will test your ability to convert accrual basis information to cash basis information.

The First Corporation reported the following on its income statement for 2017:

Sales revenue	$625,000
Cost of goods sold	412,000
Salaries and wages expense	42,500
Insurance expense	3,300
Depreciation expense	47,000
Other operating expenses	63,200
Income tax expense	14,000
Net income	43,000

The comparative statements of financial position reported the following selected information:

	12/31/17	12/31/16	Increase (Decrease)
Cash	$24,300	$14,700	$9,600
Accounts Receivable	36,000	40,500	(4,500)
Inventory	79,300	67,400	11,900
Prepaid Insurance	4,500	4,100	400
Accounts Payable	29,500	26,600	2,900
Salaries and Wages Payable	700	900	(200)
Income Tax Payable	21,500	14,400	7,100
Deferred Tax Liability	6,000	4,000	2,000

All of the operating expenses included in "other operating expenses" were paid in cash during 2017. Accounts payable relate to purchases of merchandise inventory.

Instructions

Calculate the following amounts for 2017:

(a) Cash received from customers
(b) Cash paid for merchandise inventory
(c) Cash paid to employees
(d) Cash paid for insurance
(e) Cash paid for income taxes
(f) Net cash provided by operating activities

Solution to Exercise 22-3

(a) Sales revenue $625,000

    Decrease in accounts receivable   4,500

    Cash received from customers $629,500

OR

Sales revenue $625,000

Beginning accounts receivable   40,500

Ending accounts receivable   (36,000)

Cash received from customers $629,500

(b) Cost of goods sold $412,000

    Increase in inventory   11,900

    Purchases   423,900

    Increase in accounts payable   (2,900)

    Cash paid for merchandise inventory $421,000

OR

Cost of goods sold $412,000

Beginning inventory   (67,400)

Ending inventory   79,300

Purchases   423,900

Beginning accounts payable   26,600

Ending accounts payable   (29,500)

Cash paid for merchandise inventory $421,000

(c) Salaries and wages expense $ 42,500

    Decrease in salaries and wages payable   200

    Cash paid to employees $ 42,700

OR

Salaries and wages expense $ 42,500

Ending salaries and wages payable   900

Beginning salaries and wages payable   (700)

Cash paid to employees $ 42,700

(d) Insurance expense $ 3,300

    Increase in prepaid insurance   400

    Cash paid for insurance $ 3,700

OR

Insurance expense	$ 3,300
Beginning prepaid insurance	(4,100)
Ending prepaid insurance	4,500
Cash paid for insurance	$ 3,700

(e) Income tax expense	$ 14,000
Increase in income tax payable	(7,100)
Increase in deferred tax liability	(2,000)
Cash paid for income taxes	$ 4,900

OR

Income tax expense	$ 14,000
Beginning income tax payable	14,400
Ending income tax payable	(21,500)
Beginning deferred tax liability	4,000
Ending deferred tax liability	(6,000)
Cash paid for income taxes	$ 4,900

(f) Cash received from customers	$629,500
Cash paid for merchandise inventory	(421,000)
Cash paid to employees	(42,700)
Cash paid for insurance	(3,700)
Cash paid for income taxes	(4,900)
Cash paid for other operating expenses	(63,200)
Net cash provided by operating activities	$ 94,000

The change in the cash balance ($9,600 increase) had no effect on the calculations. Net cash provided by (used in) operating activities, plus net cash provided by (used in) investing activities, plus net cash provided by (used in) financing activities should net to the $9,600 increase in the cash balance.

Refer to **Illustration 22-2** above for explanations for the above calculations.

EXERCISE 22-4

Purpose: This exercise will help you practise classifying transactions on a statement of cash flows using the direct method.

Pepper Corporation uses the direct method for preparation of the statement of cash flows. Pepper prepares financial statements in accordance with IFRS, and classifies dividends paid as a financing activity, and interest paid and received and dividends received as operating activities. The following summarized transactions took place in 2017:

Collected cash from customers on account	$84,000
Paid interest on debt	2,500
Paid principal of note payable	27,000
Sold services for cash	22,000
Paid salaries and wages	32,000
Paid other operating expenses	45,000
Recorded depreciation expense	8,000
Paid dividends	7,500
Purchased machinery	55,000
Sold equipment for book value	13,000
Issued common shares in exchange for cash	40,000
Issued long-term debt	57,000
Amortized patents	1,500
Purchased treasury shares	5,500
Accrued salaries and wages	750
Purchased a long-term investment	31,000
Acquired a computer in exchange for Pepper common shares	12,000
Received dividends from investee	900
Paid income taxes	7,000
Sold a long-term investment (and recognized a gain of $3,500)	36,500

Instructions

(a) Calculate the following:
1. Net cash provided by (used in) operating activities
2. Net cash provided by (used in) investing activities
3. Net cash provided by (used in) financing activities
4. Net increase (decrease) in cash for the period

(b) If any transactions are **not** used in the required calculations in part (a), explain why.

(c) Based on the information given, prepare a statement of cash flows using the direct method. Assume the cash balance at the beginning of the year was $21,500.

Solution to Exercise 22-4

(a) 1. Collected cash from customers on account · · · · · · · · $ 84,000

Sold services for cash · 22,000

Received dividends from investee · · · · · · · · · · · · · · · · · 900

Paid interest on debt · (2,500)

Paid salaries and wages · (32,000)

Paid other operating expenses · · · · · · · · · · · · · · · · · (45,000)

Paid income taxes · (7,000)

Net cash provided by operating activities · · · · · · · · $ 20,400

2. Purchased machinery · $(55,000)

Sold equipment for book value · · · · · · · · · · · · · · · · · 13,000

Purchased a long-term investment · · · · · · · · · · · · · · (31,000)

Sold a long-term investment · · · · · · · · · · · · · · · · · · · 36,500

Net cash used in investing activities · · · · · · · · · · · · · $(36,500)

3. Paid principal of note payable · · · · · · · · · · · · · · · · · $(27,000)

Paid dividends · (7,500)

Issued common shares · 40,000

Issued long-term debt · 57,000

Purchased treasury shares · (5,500)

Net cash provided by financing activities · · · · · · · · · $ 57,000

4. Net cash provided by operating activities · · · · · · · · $ 20,400

Net cash used in investing activities · · · · · · · · · · · · · (36,500)

Net cash provided by financing activities · · · · · · · · · 57,000

Net increase in cash · $ 40,900

(b) 1. Recorded depreciation expense, $8,000, was not used because it is a non-cash charge to income. It is an expense that did not require a cash payment this period. (The cash outlay occurred at time of payment for acquisition of the related depreciable assets.)

2. Amortized patents, $1,500, was not used because it is a non-cash charge against income. It is an expense that did not require a cash payment in this period. (The cash outlay occurred at time of payment for acquisition of the related intangible assets.)

3. Accrued salaries and wages, $750, was not used because it relates to an expense recognized in this period, to be paid in the next period.

4. Acquired a computer in exchange for shares, $12,000, was not used because this is a non-cash investing and financing activity.

If the indirect method were used: (1) the depreciation of $8,000 and the amortization of $1,500 would be added back to net income, (2) the increase of $750 in accrued salaries and wages would also be added to net income, and (3) the $3,500 gain on sale of long-term investment would be deducted from net income, in the process of reconciling net income to net cash provided by operating activities.

(c)

PEPPER CORPORATION
Statement of Cash Flows
For the Year Ended December 31, 2017
(Direct Method)

Cash flows from operating activities		
Cash receipts from customers	$106,000[a]	
Dividends received from investee	900	
Interest paid	(2,500)	
Cash paid to employees	(32,000)	
Cash paid for operating expenses	(45,000)	
Income taxes paid	(7,000)	
Net cash provided by operating activities		$20,400
Cash flows from investing activities		
Purchase of machinery	(55,000)	
Sale of equipment	13,000	
Purchase of long-term investment	(31,000)	
Sale of long-term investment	36,500	
Net cash used in investing activities		(36,500)
Cash flows from financing activities		
Payment of note payable	(27,000)	
Payment of dividends	(7,500)	
Issuance of common shares	40,000	
Issuance of long-term debt	57,000	
Purchase of treasury shares	(5,500)	
Net cash provided by financing activities		57,000
Net increase in cash		40,900
Cash at beginning of period		21,500
Cash at end of period		$62,400[b]
Non-cash investing and financing activities		
Acquired a computer in exchange for common shares		$12,000

[a]$84,000 + $22,000 = $106,000

[b]$40,900 net increase in cash + $21,500 beginning cash balance = $62,400 ending cash balance

When using the direct method, an additional schedule reconciling net income to net cash provided by operating activities should be provided as a supplementary disclosure. The information given in this exercise is insufficient to prepare a similar reconciliation (for Pepper Corporation).

EXERCISE 22-5

PURPOSE: This exercise will provide examples of transactions on a statement of cash flows using the indirect method.

CODE FOR FORMAT OF STATEMENT OF CASH FLOWS FOR USE WITH EXERCISE 22-5
(Read instructions for use below)

Item Code	Format of Statement of Cash Flows
	Cash flows from operating activities:
	Net income (loss).
A	Add non-cash expenses (charges), losses, and changes in certain accounts needed to convert net income to cash basis.
D	Deduct non-cash revenue (credits), gains, and changes in certain accounts needed to convert net income to cash basis.
	Net cash provided by (used in) operating activities.
	Cash flows from investing activities:
II	Add amount for an **investing** activity that produced a cash **inflow**.
IO	Deduct amount for an **investing** activity that resulted in a cash **outflow**.
	Net cash provided by (used in) investing activities.
	Cash flows from financing activities:
FI	Add amount for a **financing** activity that produced a cash **inflow**.
FO	Deduct amount for a **financing** activity that resulted in a cash **outflow**.
	Net cash provided by (used in) financing activities.
	Net increase (decrease) in cash and cash equivalents.
	Cash and cash equivalents at beginning of year.
	Cash and cash equivalents at end of year.
NI	Use this code for a transaction that is an operating activity and a component of net income, and has the same effect (positive or negative) on cash as it does on net income (thus, this transaction is included in net income and no adjustment to net income is required for this item).

NC	Use this code for a non-cash financing and/or investing activity to be reported elsewhere in the financial statements.
C	Use this code to refer to a transaction that affects only cash and cash equivalents.
X	Use this code for a transaction or event that is not reported or otherwise reflected on the statement of cash flows.

Instructions

For each of the following transactions and events, indicate how it should be reported in a statement of cash flows using the indirect approach. Use the code from the table above for shorthand notations for your responses. Include the appropriate dollar amount with each code. A transaction or event may require more than one code for a complete answer.

___ $ _____ 1. Borrow $50,000 by issuance of a short-term note payable.

___ $ _____ 2. Sell land used in operations: selling price, $15,000; cost, $3,500.

___ $ _____ 3. Exchange long-term mortgage note receivable for shares in another company: carrying value of receivable, $38,000; fair value of the shares, $36,000. The investment in shares is intended to be long-term and accounted for under the FV-OCI model.

___ $ _____ 4. Repay short-term non-trade note payable, $5,100.

___ $ _____ 5. Declare and distribute 10% stock dividend. Fair value, $18,000.

___ $ _____ 6. Pay administrative salaries and wages for the current period, $56,000.

___ $ _____ 7. Accrue interest expense, $1,500.

___ $ _____ 8. Accrue rent revenue, $1,800.

___ $ _____ 9. Collect magazine subscription revenue in advance, $9,000.

___ $ _____ 10. Recognize income of $5,000 from significant influence investment. Collect $1,800 in dividends from that associate.

___ $ _____ 11. Acquire machinery by transfer of treasury shares: cost of treasury shares, $18,000; fair value of treasury shares, $22,000.

___ $ _____ 12. Acquire machinery by issuance of long-term note payable to the seller: face amount of note, $50,000; stated interest rate, 2%; fair value of machinery, $40,000.

___ $ _____ 13. Amortize premium on bonds payable, $200.

___ $ _____ 14. Record increase in deferred tax asset, $1,000.

___ $ _____ 15. Use $1,000 cash to purchase a 90-day treasury bill.

___ $ ___   16. Record bad debt expense of $7,000.

___ $ ___   17. Settle long-term debt by transfer of an FV-OCI investment: carrying value of debt, $77,000; fair value of investment, $70,000; book value of investment, $70,000.

___ $ ___   18. Amortize deferred service revenue of $600.

___ $ ___   19. Sell a piece of equipment for $1,000: cost, $7,000; accumulated depreciation—equipment, $4,000.

___ $ ___   20. Exchange old truck for new truck and pay cash of $11,000: cost of old truck, $10,000; book value of old truck, $3,000; fair value of old truck, $2,200; list price of new truck, $14,500.

___ $ ___   21. Recognize temporary decline of $7,000 in fair value of investment in equity securities classified as trading securities and accounted for under the FV-NI model.

___ $ ___   22. Sell merchandise for $400 cash.

___ $ ___   23. Pay advertising fees of $1,600 for the current period.

___ $ ___   24. Purchase treasury shares: cost, $7,500; original issuance price, $7,000.

___ $ ___   25. Pay accounts payable, $5,700.

___ $ ___   26. Acquire equipment by a capital lease: present value of minimum lease payments at inception, $75,000; first annual payment made at lease inception, $10,000.

___ $ ___   27. Redeem long-term debt (bonds) prior to maturity by cash payment of $78,000: carrying value of debt, $88,000.

Solution to Exercise 22-5

1.	FI	$50,000
2.	II	$15,000; and D $11,500
3.	NC	$36,000; and A $2,000
4.	FO	$5,100
5.	X	$18,000
6.	NI	$56,000
7.	A	$1,500
8.	D	$1,800
9.	A	$9,000
10.	D	$5,000; and A $1,800
11.	NC	$22,000
12.	NC	$40,000
13.	D	$200
14.	D	$1,000

15.	C	$1,000
16.	A	$7,000
17.	NC	$70,000; and D $7,000
18.	D	$600
19.	II	$1,000; and A $2,000
20.	IO	$11,000; and A $800; and NC $2,200
21.	A	$7,000
22.	NI	$400
23.	NI	$1,600
24.	FO	$7,500
25.	D	$5,700
26.	NC	$75,000; and FO $10,000
27.	FO	$78,000; and D $10,000

Approach:

1. Reconstruct the journal entry for each transaction. Examine each journal entry to determine if there is an inflow of cash, an outflow of cash, or no effect on cash.

- The journal entry to record a cash transaction that is an investing activity will generally involve (1) Cash and (2) an asset account other than Cash, such as Investments, Land, Building, Equipment, or Patent.

- The journal entry to record a cash transaction that is a financing activity will generally involve (1) Cash and (2) a liability account (such as Bonds Payable, Notes Payable, or Dividends Payable), or a shareholders' equity account (such as Common Shares, Contributed Surplus, or Treasury Shares).

2. Write down the definitions for investing activities and financing activities (see below). Analyze each transaction to see if it fits one of these definitions:

   Investing activities involve the acquisition and disposal of long-term assets and other investments that are not included in cash equivalents or acquired for trading purposes. Investing cash flows are generally the result of (a) making and collecting loans and (b) acquiring and disposing of investments and productive long-lived assets.

   Financing activities result in changes in the size and composition of the enterprise's equity capital and borrowings. Financing cash flows are generally the result of (a) obtaining capital from owners and providing them with a return on, and a return of, their investment; and (b) obtaining cash from issuing debt and repaying amounts borrowed.

3. Identify the items requiring adjustments to net income in order to convert net income to net cash provided by operating activities, by identifying the reconstructed journal entries that involve (a) an income statement account and a statement of financial position account other than Cash (for example, the journal entry to record depreciation); or (b) the Cash account and a non-cash

asset or liability account that relates to operating activities (accounts receivable, inventory, accounts payable, etc.); or (c) a gain or loss that has no cash effect or a gain or loss from a transaction that is classified as an investing or financing activity.

4. Identify the items that are non-cash financing and investing activities by identifying transactions that fit the definitions of investing activities and/or financing activities, but do not affect Cash.

EXPLANATION: The journal entries for each transaction are reconstructed and analyzed below:

1. Cash	50,000	
Notes Payable (Short-Term)		50,000

This is a cash inflow due to a financing activity.

2. Cash	15,000	
Land		3,500
Gain on Sale of Land		11,500

Cash proceeds of $15,000 from sale of a plant asset should be reported as an investing cash inflow. The $15,000 represents recovery of the asset's book value of $3,500 and a gain of $11,500. The gain of $11,500 was included in net income. Using the indirect method, the gain must be deducted from net income in reconciling net income with net cash provided by operating activities, so that the $11,500 gain is not included in the statement of cash flows twice. (The entire $15,000 cash proceeds will be reported as an investing cash inflow.)

3. FV-OCI Investments	36,000	
Loss on Investments	2,000	
Notes Receivable		38,000

Cash is not affected. This exchange of one non-cash asset for another non-cash asset is a non-cash investing activity that must be disclosed elsewhere in the financial statements. The loss on investment in mortgage note receivable was deducted from net income. Therefore, using the indirect method, the loss is added back to net income in reconciling net income with net cash provided by operating activities.

4. Notes Payable (Short-Term)	5,100	
Cash		5,100

This is a cash outflow due to a financing activity.

5. Retained Earnings	18,000	
Common Stock Dividend Distributable		18,000
Common Stock Dividend Distributable	18,000	
Common Shares		18,000

Cash is not affected. A stock dividend is not a financing and/or investing activity, and therefore, is not required to be reported on the statement of cash flows. A stock dividend would be reflected on other financial statements or in notes to the financial statements, because it changes shareholders' equity.

6. Salaries and Wages Expense	56,000	
Cash		56,000

This is a cash outflow due to an operating activity. This $56,000 salaries and wages expense amount was deducted from net income at the time of expense recognition. Therefore, using the indirect method, no adjustment is needed for this amount because it reduces both net income and cash.

7. Interest Expense	1,500	
Interest Payable		1,500

Cash is not affected. Accrued interest expense was deducted from net income at the time of expense recognition. Therefore, using the indirect method, accrued interest expense is added back to net income in reconciling net income with net cash provided by operating activities.

8. Rent Receivable	1,800	
Rent Revenue		1,800

Cash is not affected. Accrued rent revenue was added to net income at the time of revenue recognition. Therefore, using the indirect method, accrued rent revenue is deducted from net income in reconciling net income with net cash provided by operating activities.

9. Cash	9,000	
Unearned Subscription Revenue		9,000

This is a cash inflow due to an operating activity. This $9,000 unearned subscription revenue amount was not included in net income. Therefore, using the indirect method, unearned subscription revenue is added back to net income in reconciling net income with net cash provided by operating activities.

10. Investment in Associate	5,000	
Investment Income or Loss		5,000
Cash	1,800	
Investment in Associate		1,800

This transaction includes a non-cash journal entry to record income from an investment in associate accounted for using the equity method, and an operating cash inflow of $1,800. (Under IFRS, dividends received are permitted to be classified as operating cash inflows; under ASPE, dividends received are classified as operating cash inflows.) The non-cash journal entry increases net income, but not cash. The journal entry to record dividends received increases cash but does not affect net income. Therefore, using the indirect method, the $5,000 investment income amount is deducted from net income, and the $1,800 dividends received amount is added to net income, in reconciling net income with net cash provided by operating activities. On a net basis, $3,200 in undistributed earnings of the associate is deducted from net income.

11. Machinery	22,000	
Treasury Shares		18,000
Contributed Surplus		4,000

Cash is not affected. This is a significant investing activity (acquisition of equipment) and financing activity (disposal of treasury shares) that must be disclosed elsewhere in the financial statements or in a schedule of non-cash investing and financing activities.

| 12. Machinery | 40,000 | |
| Notes Payable (Long-Term) | | 40,000 |

A note payable is issued at an unreasonably low interest rate in exchange for a non-cash asset; this transaction should be recorded at the fair value of the asset received. Cash is not affected. This is a significant investing and financing activity that must be disclosed elsewhere in the financial statements or in a schedule of non-cash investing and financing activities.

| 13. Bonds Payable | 200 | |
| Interest Expense | | 200 |

Cash is not affected. A credit to interest expense was added to net income. Therefore, using the indirect method, the credit to interest expense is deducted from net income in reconciling net income with net cash provided by operating activities.

| 14. Deferred Tax Asset | 1,000 | |
| Deferred Tax Benefit | | 1,000 |

Cash is not affected. A credit to deferred tax benefit was added to net income. Therefore, using the indirect method, the credit to deferred tax benefit is deducted from net income in reconciling net income with net cash provided by operating activities.

| 15. Cash Equivalents | 1,000 | |
| Cash | | 1,000 |

This is a decrease in cash and an increase in cash equivalents. Therefore, there is no change in total cash and cash equivalents.

| 16. Bad Debt Expense | 7,000 | |
| Allowance for Doubtful Accounts | | 7,000 |

Cash is not affected. Bad debt expense was deducted from net income at the time of expense recognition. Therefore, using the indirect method, bad debt expense is added back to net income in reconciling net income with net cash provided by operating activities.

17. Long-Term Debt	77,000	
FV-OCI Investments		70,000
Gain on Extinguishment of Debt		7,000

Cash is not affected. This is a non-cash investing and financing activity that must be disclosed elsewhere in the financial statements or in a schedule of non-cash investing and financing activities. Using the indirect method, the gain on extinguishment of debt must be deducted from net income because it relates to a (non-cash) financing activity.

18. Unearned Revenue	600	
Service Revenue		600

Cash is not affected. Cash related to unearned revenue was collected in a previous period. Therefore, using the indirect method, a decrease in unearned revenue is deducted from net income in reconciling net income with net cash provided by operating activities.

19. Cash	1,000	
Accumulated Depreciation—Equipment	4,000	
Loss on Disposal of Equipment	2,000	
Equipment		7,000

This transaction includes a cash inflow of $1,000 related to an investing activity. Using the indirect method, the loss must be added back to net income in reconciling net income with net cash provided by operating activities. (The $1,000 cash proceeds will be reported as an investing cash inflow.)

20. Trucks ($11,000 + $2,200)	13,200	
Accumulated Depreciation—Trucks ($10,000 − $3,000)	7,000	
Loss on Disposal of Trucks ($3,000 − $2,200)	800	
Trucks		10,000
Cash		11,000

This transaction includes a cash outflow of $11,000 related to an investing activity. Using the indirect method, the loss must be added back to net income in reconciling net income with net cash provided by operating activities. The exchange of one non-cash asset (book value of $2,200 after the writedown for impairment) for another must be disclosed as a non-cash investing activity.

21. Unrealized Gain or Loss	7,000	
FV-NI Investments		7,000

Cash is not affected. The unrealized holding loss was deducted from net income at the time of recognition of the temporary decline in fair value of investment. Therefore, using the indirect method, the unrealized holding loss is added back to net income in reconciling net income with net cash provided by operating activities.

| 22. Cash | 400 | |
| Sales Revenue | | 400 |

This is a cash inflow due to an operating activity. This $400 sales revenue amount was added to net income at the time of revenue recognition. Therefore, using the indirect method, no adjustment is needed for this amount because it increased both net income and cash.

| 23. Advertising Expense | 1,600 | |
| Cash | | 1,600 |

This is a cash outflow due to an operating activity. This $1,600 advertising expense amount was deducted from net income at the time of expense recognition. Therefore, using the indirect method, no adjustment is needed for this amount because it reduced both net income and cash.

| 24. Treasury Shares | 7,500 | |
| Cash | | 7,500 |

This is a cash outflow due to a financing activity (return of investment to owner).

| 25. Accounts Payable | 5,700 | |
| Cash | | 5,700 |

This is a cash outflow due to an operating activity. This $5,700 decrease in accounts payable was not included in net income. Therefore, using the indirect method, the decrease in accounts payable paid is deducted from net income in reconciling net income with net cash provided by operating activities.

26. Equipment Under Lease	75,000	
Obligations Under Lease		75,000
Obligations Under Lease	10,000	
Cash		10,000

A capital lease is a transaction that qualifies as a non-cash investing and financing activity that must be disclosed elsewhere in the financial statements or in a schedule of non-cash investing and financing activities. The first lease payment results in a cash outflow due to a financing activity.

27. Bonds Payable	88,000	
Cash		78,000
Gain on Redemption of Bonds		10,000

Payment of $78,000 to the creditor is a cash outflow due to a financing activity. Using the indirect method, the gain of $10,000 must be deducted from net income because it relates to a non-cash financing activity.

ANALYSIS OF MULTIPLE-CHOICE QUESTIONS

Question

1. At the end of 2017, a company acquired a hotel by paying a portion of the purchase price in cash and issuing a mortgage note payable to the seller for the balance. On the statement of cash flows for 2017, what amount is included in financing activities for this transaction?

   a. Zero

   b. Cash payment

   c. Mortgage amount

   d. Acquisition price

EXPLANATION: The cash down payment should be reported as a cash outflow due to an investing activity. Issuance of the mortgage note payable to the seller (that is, seller-financed debt) is a non-cash investing and financing activity, which should be disclosed elsewhere in the financial statements. Payments of principal on the debt are financing cash outflows, although none have occurred yet because the purchase happened at the end of the period. (Solution = a.)

Question

2. Smith Corporation had the following transactions occur in the current year:

   (1) Cash sale of merchandise inventory

   (2) Sale of delivery truck at book value

   (3) Sale of Smith Corporation common shares for cash

   (4) Issuance of a note payable to a bank for cash

   (5) Sale of a security held as a long-term investment

   (6) Collection of a note receivable

In a statement of cash flows, how many of the above items are reported as a cash inflow from investing activities?

   a. All six items

   b. Five items

   c. Four items

   d. Three items

EXPLANATION: Define "investing activities." Compare each transaction above with the definition. Investing activities involve the acquisition and disposal of long-term assets and other investments that are not included in cash equivalents or those acquired for trading purposes. Investing cash flows are generally the result of (a) making and collecting loans and (b) acquiring and disposing of investments and productive long-lived assets. The sale of a delivery truck (regardless of the difference between selling price and carrying value), the sale of a long-term investment, and the collection of a note receivable are three items that produce cash inflows from investing activities. The cash sale of merchandise inventory results in a cash inflow from operating activities. The sale of the corporation's own common shares and the issuance of the note payable both produce cash inflows from financing activities. (Solution = d.)

 Recall that transactions classified as investing activities involve assets (delivery truck, equity investments, and note receivable in this example), whereas transactions classified as financing activities involve liabilities (note payable in this example) or shareholders' equity (common shares in this example).

Question

3. A corporation had the following transactions occur during the current year:
   (1) Reclassification of debt from long-term liabilities to current liabilities
   (2) Payment of principal on mortgage note payable
   (3) Payment of interest on mortgage note payable
   (4) Purchase of treasury shares
   (5) Payment of cash dividend
   (6) Payment of property dividend
   (7) Distribution of stock dividend

   Under ASPE, on a statement of cash flows, how many of the above items are reported as a cash outflow from financing activities?
   a. Six items
   b. Five items
   c. Four items
   d. Three items

   EXPLANATION: The payment of principal on a note payable, the purchase of treasury shares, and the payment of a cash dividend are the three items that result in cash outflows from financing activities. Reclassification of debt does not affect cash. (It may be included in a schedule of non-cash investing and financing activities.) Under ASPE, the payment of interest is reported as a cash outflow from operating activities. (Under IFRS, the payment of interest may be classified as either operating or financing activities.) Payment of a property dividend is a non-cash activity to be disclosed elsewhere in the financial statements. Neither declaration nor distribution of a stock dividend affects cash. (Solution = d.)

Question

4. During 2017, Pinto Inc. had the following activities related to its financial operations:

Proceeds from sale of treasury shares (on books at cost of $95,000)	$113,000
Carrying value of convertible preferred shares in Pinto, converted into common shares of Pinto	130,000
Distribution in 2017 of cash dividend declared in 2016 to preferred shareholders	67,000
Payment for early retirement of long-term bonds payable (carrying amount $707,000)	712,000

Pinto prepares financial statements in accordance with ASPE. The amount of net cash used in financing activities to appear in Pinto's statement of cash flows for 2017 should be:

   a. $679,000.

   b. $666,000.

   c. $545,000.

   d. $469,000.

EXPLANATION: Net cash used in financing activities is calculated as follows:

Proceeds from sale of treasury shares	$ 113,000
Payment of cash dividends	(67,000)
Retirement of bonds payable	(712,000)
Net cash used in financing activities	$(666,000)

The conversion of preferred shares to common shares is a non-cash transaction and would be disclosed elsewhere in the financial statements. (Solution = b.)

The $5,000 loss on retirement of bonds payable ($712,000 retirement price exceeds carrying value of $707,000 by $5,000) would be a component of net income. If the indirect method is used to present the net cash provided (used) by operations, the $5,000 loss would be added to net income in this calculation.

Question

5. During 2017, Vaudry Corporation had the following activities related to its financial operations:

   (1) Purchased equipment for cash, which was borrowed from a bank.

   (2) Acquired treasury shares for cash.

(3) Declared a cash dividend payable in 2018.

(4) Appropriated retained earnings for possible loss from a lawsuit.

(5) Purchased a two-month guaranteed investment certificate.

(6) Acquired a five-year guaranteed investment certificate from a bank.

(7) Made interest payments on bonds payable.

(8) Converted preferred shares to common shares.

(9) Received dividends from an investment in equity of another corporation.

In a statement of cash flows prepared under ASPE, how many of the above transactions would be reported as a cash outflow from investing activities?

  a. Two

  b. Three

  c. Four

  d. Five

EXPLANATION: Identify each transaction as one of the following:

- A cash inflow from operating activities
- A cash outflow from operating activities
- A cash inflow from investing activities
- A cash outflow from investing activities
- A cash inflow from financing activities
- A cash outflow from financing activities
- An investing and/or financing activity not affecting cash

Refer to the definitions in **Illustration 22-1** above if necessary.

Item 1:   Purchase of equipment for cash is an investing outflow. Borrowing of cash from a bank is a financing inflow.

Item 2:   Acquisition of treasury shares for cash is a financing outflow.

Item 3:   Declaration of a cash dividend is a transaction not affecting cash and is not reported on a statement of cash flows. Subsequent payment of the cash dividend will be a financing cash outflow.

Item 4:   Appropriation of retained earnings is a transaction not affecting cash and is not reported on a statement of cash flows.

Item 5:   Purchase of a two-month guaranteed investment certificate is an exchange of cash for a cash equivalent and is not reported on a statement of cash flows.

Item 6:   Acquisition of a five-year guaranteed investment certificate is an investing cash outflow.

Item 7:   Under ASPE, interest payments are an operating cash outflow. (Under IFRS, interest payments may be classified as either operating or financing cash outflows.)

Item 8: Conversion of preferred shares to common shares is a financing activity that does not affect cash; this transaction would be disclosed elsewhere in the financial statements.

Item 9: Under ASPE, dividends received are cash inflows from operating activities. (Under IFRS, dividends received may be classified as either operating or investing cash inflows.)

Transactions 1 and 6 are reported as cash outflows from investing activities. (Solution = a.)

Question

6. Refer to the facts of Question 5 above. In a statement of cash flows prepared under ASPE, how many of the transactions would be reported as a cash outflow from financing activities?
   a. One
   b. Two
   c. Three
   d. Four

EXPLANATION: Refer to the explanation for Question 5 above. Only Item 2 is reported as a cash outflow from financing activities. (Solution = a.)

Question

7. Which of the following may be classified as a financing activity on a statement of cash flows?
   a. Declaration and distribution of a stock dividend
   b. Deposit to a bond sinking fund
   c. Sale of a note receivable
   d. Payment of income taxes

EXPLANATION: Write down the definitions for operating, investing, and financing activities. Analyze each transaction and determine if it meets the definition of an operating, investing, or financing activity. Declaration and distribution of a stock dividend does not meet any of the definitions; it is not reported on a statement of cash flows. Although a journal entry to record a deposit to a bond sinking fund results in an increase in the fund, which is often classified as a long-term investment, a deposit to a sinking bond fund is usually classified as a financing activity because its purpose is to pay for amounts borrowed. Sale of a note receivable is an investing activity, and payment of income taxes is an operating activity. (Solution = b.)

Question

8. The following information was taken from the 2017 financial statements of Lincoln Corporation:

Bonds payable, January 1, 2017	$300,000
Bonds payable, December 31, 2017	750,000

During 2017
- Bonds payable with a face amount of $80,000 were issued in exchange for equipment.
- A $220,000 payment was made to retire bonds payable with a carrying amount of $200,000.

In its statement of cash flows for the year ended December 31, 2017, what amount should Lincoln report as proceeds from the issuance of bonds payable?
  a. $450,000
  b. $570,000
  c. $170,000
  d. $630,000

EXPLANATION: Draw a T account for Bonds Payable. Enter the data given and solve for the unknown.

Bonds Payable			
Retired	200,000	300,000	Bal., Jan. 1, 2017
		80,000	Issued for equipment
		570,000	Issued for cash
		750,000	Bal., Dec. 31, 2017
			(Solution = b.)

Question

9. In a statement of cash flows, using the indirect method, which of the following are subtracted from net income to determine net cash provided by operating activities?
  I. Amortization of premium on bonds payable
  II. Loss on sale of equipment
  III. Depreciation expense
     a. I only
     b. II only
     c. I and II
     d. I and III

EXPLANATION: Think about how each item (1) affects net income and (2) affects cash. Determine the adjustment needed (if any) to reconcile net income to net cash provided by operating activities. Amortization of premium on bonds payable increases net income (because it reduces interest expense), but does not affect cash; thus it is deducted from net income in reconciling net income to net cash provided by operating activities. Loss on sale of equipment reduces net income but does not affect cash and is not an operating activity, and is therefore added to net income in reconciling net income to net cash provided by operating activities. Depreciation expense reduces net income but does not affect cash and is therefore added to net income in reconciling net income to net cash provided by operating activities. (Solution = a.)

Question

10. Stone Corporation had net income for 2017 of $4 million. Additional information is as follows:

Depreciation of plant assets	$1,500,000
Amortization of intangibles	350,000
Increase in accounts receivable	620,000
Increase in accounts payable	740,000

Stone's net cash provided by operating activities for 2017 was:
a. $2,380,000.
b. $5,730,000.
c. $5,850,000.
d. $5,970,000.

EXPLANATION: The depreciation and amortization amounts are items that reduce net income but do not cause a decrease in cash. The increase in accounts receivable indicates that sales revenue earned for the period exceeded cash collected from customers, and therefore net income exceeded net cash provided by operating activities. The increase in accounts payable indicates that expenses incurred exceeded cash payments for expense-type items, which caused net income to be less than net cash provided by operating activities. The solution is as follows:

Net income	$4,000,000
Depreciation of plant assets	1,500,000
Amortization of intangibles	350,000
Increase in accounts receivable	(620,000)
Increase in accounts payable	740,000
Net cash provided by operating activities	$5,970,000

(Solution = d.)

Question

11. Net cash flow from operating activities for 2017 for Ginger Corporation was $82,000. The following items are reported on the financial statements for 2017:

Depreciation	7,000
Cash dividends paid on common shares	10,000
Increase in accounts receivable	3,000

Ginger prepares financial statements in accordance with ASPE. Based only on the information above, Ginger's net income for 2017 was:
   a. $72,000.
   b. $69,000.
   c. $86,000.
   d. $78,000.

EXPLANATION: Write down the format for reconciliation of net income to net cash flow from operating activities. Fill in the information given. Solve for the unknown.

Net income	$ X
Depreciation	7,000
Increase in accounts receivable	(3,000)
Net cash flow from operating activities	$82,000

Solving for X, net income = $78,000.

Cash dividends paid on common shares have no effect on this calculation because cash dividends paid are not a component of net income and they are classified as financing cash outflows under ASPE. (Solution = d.)

Question

12. Change in accounts receivable is used to convert sales revenue to cash receipts from customers when the direct method is used. Change in accounts receivable is also used to convert net income to net cash from operating activities when the indirect method is used. Under each method, is change in gross accounts receivable or net accounts receivable used?

	Direct	**Indirect**
a.	Gross	Gross
b.	Net	Net
c.	Net	Gross
d.	Gross	Net

EXPLANATION: Change in net accounts receivable includes the change in the Accounts Receivable account and the change in the Allowance for Doubtful Accounts account. The Accounts Receivable account changes as a result of credit sales, writeoffs of individual accounts, cash collections, and reinstatement of accounts previously written off. The allowance account changes as a result of recognition of bad debt expense, writeoffs of individual accounts, and reinstatement of accounts previously written off.

When the direct method is used, only the change in gross receivables is used to convert sales revenue to cash receipts from customers. The change in the allowance account is not a factor because the related bad debt expense was not included in sales revenue. When the indirect method is used, the change in net receivables is used to convert net income to net cash provided by operating activities because it includes the effect of the bad debt expense that was recorded as well as the difference between the accrual basis revenue amount and cash collections from customers. (Solution = d.)

Question

13. Venice Company reported salaries and wages expense of $109,000 for 2017. The following data were extracted from the company's financial records:

	12/31/16	12/31/17
Prepaid Salaries and Wages	$20,000	$25,000
Salaries and Wages Payable	66,000	79,000

On a statement of cash flows for 2017, using the direct method, cash payments for salaries and wages should be:
a. $91,000.
b. $101,000.
c. $117,000.
d. $127,000.

EXPLANATION: Think of the relationship between salaries and wages expense and cash payments for salaries and wages when there is (1) an increase in prepaid salaries and wages, and (2) an increase in salaries and wages payable. Convert the expense amount to a cash-paid figure.

Salaries and wages expense	$109,000
Increase in prepaid salaries and wages	5,000
Increase in salaries and wages payable	(13,000)
Cash payments for salaries and wages	$101,000

(Solution = b.)

Question

14. The following information was taken from the 2017 financial statements of Gardner Corporation:

Inventory, January 1, 2017	$ 30,000
Inventory, December 31, 2017	40,000
Accounts payable, January 1, 2017	25,000
Accounts payable, December 31, 2017	40,000
Sales revenue	200,000
Cost of goods sold (COGS)	150,000

If the direct method is used in the 2017 statement of cash flows, what amount should Gardner report as cash payments for goods to be sold?

a. $165,000

b. $155,000

c. $145,000

d. $125,000

EXPLANATION:

Cost of Goods Sold		Inventory			Accounts Payable	
		Beg. Bal. 30,000			25,000	Beg. Bal.
150,000		Purchases ?		150,000 Cash		
				COGS Payments ?	?	Purchases
		End. Bal. 40,000			40,000	End. Bal.

Solve for the amount of purchases. Assume all purchases of inventory are on account and solve for the amount of cash payments for goods to be sold (assuming all accounts payable arise from purchases of inventory).

Inventory			
Beg. Bal.	30,000		
Purchases	160,000	150,000	COGS
End. Bal.	40,000		

Accounts Payable			
		25,000	Beg. Bal.
Cash Payments	145,000	160,000	Purchases
		40,000	End. Bal.

(Solution = c.)

Question

15. Selected information for 2017 for Barriage Company follows:

Total operating expenses (accrual basis) (includes depreciation and amortization)	$225,000
Beginning prepaid expenses	9,000
Ending prepaid expenses	13,000
Beginning accrued liabilities	15,000
Ending accrued liabilities	21,000
Depreciation of plant assets	27,000
Amortization of intangible assets	6,000
Payment of cash dividends	9,000

Barriage Company prepares financial statements in accordance with IFRS and classifies interest and dividends received as operating cash inflows, interest paid as operating cash outflows, and dividends paid as financing cash outflows. The amount of cash payments made during 2017 for operating expenses is:

a. $185,000.
b. $190,000.
c. $194,000.
d. $256,000.

EXPLANATION: Use one of the relevant formats in **Illustration 22-2** above to convert operating expenses to cash paid.

Total operating expenses (accrual basis)	$225,000
Increase in prepaid expenses	4,000
Increase in accrued liabilities	(6,000)
Depreciation of plant assets	(27,000)
Amortization of intangibles	(6,000)
Cash paid for operating expenses	$190,000

(Solution = b.)

Notice that the amount given in the question for "total operating expenses" includes depreciation and amortization, whereas the format requires exclusion of these items. Depreciation expense and amortization expense are both expense items that do not require a cash outlay at the time the expense is recorded. Thus, they are deducted from total operating expenses to arrive at cash paid for operating expenses.

Question

16. The following information was taken from the 2017 financial statements of Keewatinowi Corporation:

Income tax payable, January 1, 2017	$ 50,000
Income tax payable, December 31, 2017	40,000
Deferred tax liability, January 1, 2017	15,000
Deferred tax liability, December 31, 2017	30,000
Income tax expense	200,000

If the direct method is used to prepare the 2017 statement of cash flows, what amount should Keewatinowi report as cash payments for income taxes?
   a. $210,000
   b. $205,000
   c. $195,000
   d. $190,000

EXPLANATION: Draw T accounts. Enter the information given and solve for the missing amounts.

Income Tax Expense

Curr. Tax Exp. (2)	185,000		
Def. Tax Exp. (1)	15,000		
End. Bal.	200,000		

Income Tax Payable

		50,000	Beg. Bal.
Taxes Pd. (3)	195,000	185,000	Cur. Tax Exp. (2)
		40,000	End. Bal.

Deferred Tax Liability

		15,000	Beg. Bal.
		15,000	Def. Tax Exp. (1)
		30,000	End. Bal.

(1)	$ 30,000	Deferred tax liability, 12/31/17
	(15,000)	Deferred tax liability, 1/1/17
	$ 15,000	Deferred tax expense for 2017

(2)	$200,000	Total income tax expense for 2017
	(15,000)	Deferred tax expense for 2017
	$185,000	Current income tax expense for 2017

(3) $ 50,000   Income tax payable, 1/1/17
     185,000   Current income tax expense for 2017
     235,000
     (40,000)   Income tax payable, 12/31/17
     $195,000   Income tax paid in 2017   (Solution = c.)

The use of T accounts is a good approach because it requires only that you recall the normal balance of relevant accounts and the transactions that affect those accounts. Picturing the accounts helps you determine the amounts of any debits or credits that affected each account. Another approach that requires more analysis of the relationship between the accounts appears as follows:

Income tax expense for 2017	$200,000
Increase in deferred tax liability (deferred tax expense)	(15,000)
Current income tax expense for 2017	185,000
Decrease in income tax payable	10,000
Income taxes paid during 2017	$195,000

Question

17. The following facts are available for Pace Company:

Sales revenue for 2017	$450,000
Accounts receivable, January 1, 2017	35,000
Accounts receivable, December 31, 2017	29,000
Allowance for doubtful accounts, January 1, 2017	5,000
Allowance for doubtful accounts, December 31, 2017	3,500
Bad debt expense for 2017	42,000
Writeoff of accounts receivable during 2017	43,500

The amount of cash collections from customers during 2017 was:
a. $498,000.
b. $496,500.
c. $487,500.
d. $412,500.

EXPLANATION: The amount of cash collections from customers is calculated as follows:

Sales revenue	$450,000
Decrease in accounts receivable	6,000
Writeoff of accounts receivable	(43,500)
Cash collections from customers	$412,500

(Solution = d.)

- An alternative solution is as follows:

Sales revenue	$450,000
Decrease in accounts receivable	6,000
Decrease in allowance for doubtful accounts	(1,500)
Bad debt expense	(42,000)
Cash collections from customers	$412,500

- Another way of solving for the above is as follows:

Sales revenue	$450,000
Decrease in net accounts receivable	4,500[a]
Bad debt expense	(42,000)
Cash collections from customers	$412,500

[a]$35,000 − $5,000 = $30,000 Beginning net accounts receivable
$29,000 − $3,500 = $25,500 Ending net accounts receivable
$30,000 − $25,500 = $4,500 Decrease in net accounts receivable

- Draw T accounts for Sales Revenue, Accounts Receivable, Allowance for Doubtful Accounts, and Bad Debt Expense. Enter the information given and solve for the missing amount. The T accounts would appear as follows:

Sales Revenue

450,000	
450,000	

Accounts Receivable

Beg. Bal.	35,000		
		43,500	Writeoffs
Sales Revenue	450,000		
		412,500	Cash collections
End. Bal.	29,000		

Allowance for Doubtful Accounts

		5,000	Beg. Bal.
Writeoffs	43,500	42,000	Bad Debt Expense
		3,500	End Bal.

Bad Debt Expense

42,000
42,000

- Assume all sales were on account. Even if some sales were cash sales, the answer would be the same for total cash collections.

Question

18. The activities of a discontinued operation should be presented on the face of a statement of cash flows as follows:

   a. in one net amount, under cash flows from operating activities.

   b. in one net amount, under cash flows from investing activities.

c. in one net amount, under cash flows from financing activities.

d. separately, with a net amount attributed to operating activities, a net amount attributed to investing activities, and a net amount attributed to financing activities.

EXPLANATION: Net cash flows attributable to operating, investing, and financing activities of a discontinued operation are presented separately on a statement of cash flows. (Solution = d.)

Question

19. Both ASPE and IFRS allow either the direct or the indirect method of presenting the statement of cash flows; however, use of the direct method is preferred. Which of the following statements is true?

   a. Cash flow from operating activities is higher under the direct method than it is under the indirect method.

   b. Cash flow from operating activities is lower under the direct method than it is under the indirect method.

   c. Presentation of information under cash flow from investing activities and cash flow from financing activities is different under the direct method than it is under the indirect method.

   d. Under both the direct and indirect methods, the statement of cash flows is the same except for the presentation of information under cash flow from operating activities.

EXPLANATION: The only difference between the direct and indirect methods is the presentation of information under cash flow from operating activities. The direct method gives more detail about operating cash inflows and outflows, which is why it is the preferred method. (Solution = d.)

Chapter 23

Other Measurement and Disclosure Issues

OVERVIEW

Often, more detail relating to amounts shown in the financial statements is provided in the notes to the financial statements and/or other supplementary disclosures in order to provide users with more useful information. Disclosure issues involving accounting policies, illegal acts, segmented reporting, and interim reporting are discussed in this chapter. Other measurement issues, including related-party transactions and subsequent events, are also discussed in this chapter. An overview of financial statement analysis techniques, including ratio analysis and horizontal and common-size analyses, is also provided in this chapter, with an emphasis on examining the relationships between items on the financial statements and identifying trends in these relationships.

STUDY STEPS

Understanding the Importance of Disclosures

The **full disclosure principle** requires that any financial facts that are significant enough to influence the judgement of an informed reader should be reported. This is a very broad guideline, and therefore professional judgement is required in applying it. More disclosure is generally better than less disclosure; for example, if the financial statements contain unexpected results or events, more disclosure of the related transactions is preferred. However, the full disclosure principle does provide that if a financial fact is not significant enough to influence the judgement of an informed reader, it need not be reported.

Disclosure requirements, especially for public companies, have increased substantially. Accounting standard-setting bodies have issued many disclosure-related standards in the recent past, due to the increasing complexity of business transactions and increasing necessity for timely information. As well, other regulatory bodies (such as securities exchange commissions) have become involved in financial reporting by mandating their own disclosures that must be included in the financial statements of any company whose shares are listed on a stock exchange.

A financial statement user should not analyze financial statements without reading the notes to the financial statements. The notes are considered part of a basic set of financial statements and often incorporate additional valuable information. However, it is important to note that note disclosure is not a substitute for proper financial statement presentation.

Accounting errors are unintentional mistakes, whereas irregularities are intentional misstatements of financial information. If errors or irregularities are discovered, they should be corrected in the financial statements. If irregularities and/or illegal acts are discovered, the accountant or auditor must also evaluate the adequacy of related disclosures in the financial statements and assess whether the related item(s) should be recognized in the statement of financial position and/or the income statement.

Accounting Policies

A key financial statement note is the note disclosing the entity's accounting policies, which are the specific accounting principles and methods that are currently used and considered most appropriate to present the entity's financial statements fairly. All significant accounting policies should be disclosed in this note, especially those that were selected from among different policies. This note is usually the first note to the financial statements, and is sometimes presented before the financial statements to encourage users to read it first.

Segmented Reporting

Segmented reporting is not addressed by ASPE. However, under IFRS, separate information is required to be presented for **reportable segments** including information about each segment's revenues, profits and loss, and assets and liabilities.

A **reportable segment** is a significant **operating segment**. Operating segments and reportable segments, and their related disclosures, are discussed further in the Solution to **Case 23-2** below. Segmented reporting is required under IFRS because different operating segments in an enterprise are often exposed to different business risks.

Interim Reporting

Interim financial reports cover periods of less than one year. Interim reporting is also not addressed by ASPE, and IFRS does not mandate that entities should provide interim reports. However, IFRS does provide guidance for interim reporting, which entities are encouraged to follow if interim financial reports are prepared. In general, IFRS recommends that each interim period be considered a discrete (separate) period and that deferrals and accruals follow the same principles that are used for annual reports. Interim reporting is discussed further in the Solution to **Case 23-3** below.

Understanding the Significance of Other Measurement Issues

Related-Party Transactions

A **related-party transaction** arises when an enterprise engages in a transaction in which one of the transacting parties has the ability to significantly influence the policies of the other, or in which a non-transacting party has the ability to significantly influence the policies of the two transacting parties. Related-party transactions must be analyzed carefully because they are not necessarily based on arm's-length exchange values, terms, and/or conditions. Under both IFRS and ASPE, related-party transactions should be disclosed so that users are informed of the transactions, their accounting treatment, and their effect on the financial statements.

Under ASPE, certain related-party transactions that are (1) not in the normal course of business; (2) without substantive change in ownership; and/or (3) exchanged at an amount that is not supported by independent evidence are remeasured to the **carrying amount** of the underlying assets or services that were exchanged. In recording these transactions at carrying amount (the amount of the item transferred as recorded on the books of the transferor), no gain or loss is recorded on the exchange, and any difference between the carrying amounts of the items exchanged is booked directly to equity.

The following disclosures are recommended for related-party transactions:

- the nature of the relationships involved
- a description of the transactions
- the recorded amounts of transactions
- the measurement basis that was used
- amounts due from or to related parties and the related terms and conditions
- contractual obligations with related parties
- contingencies involving related parties

- under IFRS, management compensation and the name of the entity's parent company as well as its ultimate controlling entity or individual

See **Illustration 23-1** below for a summary of measurement issues.

Subsequent Events

Subsequent events occur after the statement of financial position date, but before the financial statements are complete. Under IFRS, the date the financial statements are complete is the date the financial statements are considered authorized for issue. Under ASPE, the date the financial statements are complete is a matter of professional judgement, taking into account management structure and procedures followed in completing the financial statements.

Subsequent events that provide additional evidence about conditions that existed at the statement of financial position date, and affect the estimates used in preparing financial statements, should be adjusted (reflected) in the financial statements.

Subsequent events that provide evidence about conditions that did not exist at the statement of financial position date but arose subsequent to that date do not require adjustment of the financial statements. However, they may have to be disclosed in order to prevent the financial statements from being misleading.

Understanding the Auditor's Report

An independent **auditor** is an accounting professional who conducts an independent examination of the accounting data presented by an entity, and expresses an opinion as to the fairness of the entity's financial statements in presenting the financial position, results of operations, and cash flows of the entity in accordance with generally accepted accounting principles.

In most cases, the auditor issues a standard **unmodified (or clean) opinion**. However, in some situations, the auditor is required to express a **qualified opinion**, which contains an exception to the standard unmodified opinion. A qualified opinion is issued in situations where, except for the effects of the matter related to the qualification, the financial statements present fairly, in all material respects, the financial position, results of operations, and cash flows in conformity with generally accepted accounting principles. The auditor is required to express an **adverse opinion** in situations where the exceptions to fair presentation in the financial statements are so pervasive that, in the independent auditor's judgement, a qualified opinion is not justified.

Overview of Financial Statement Analysis

Relationships between the amounts presented in financial statements may be analyzed to help identify strengths, weaknesses, and possible trends in the entity's financial position, results of operations, and cash flows.

Ratio analysis begins with an expression of the relationship between two numbers from the financial statements, and facilitates a more in-depth analysis of the entity's financial position and performance, including comparison of the company's position and performance with those of its competitors in the same industry. Liquidity, activity, profitability, and coverage or solvency ratios are calculated to help analyze the entity's position and performance in each of these categories.

For **horizontal analysis**, the change in an amount (the current year amount less the previous year amount) is expressed as a percentage of the previous year amount. For **vertical analysis**, amounts on a statement of financial position are often expressed as a percentage of total assets, and amounts on an income statement are often expressed as a percentage of net sales. Reducing all dollar amounts to a percentage of a base amount is frequently called **common-size analysis**.

TIPS ON CHAPTER TOPICS

- Information regarding the company's **accounting policies** is given either as one of the first notes or as a separate summary of significant accounting policies.

- **Notes to the financial statements** are an integral part of a set of basic financial statements.

- **Related-party transactions** require separate, **detailed** disclosures because transactions involving related parties cannot be presumed to be carried out on an arm's-length basis (because these transactions may not have been carried out under competitive, free-market conditions). The financial statements should reflect the economic substance of these transactions rather than the legal form.

- **Subsequent events** can be classified into two categories: those that provide additional **evidence** about conditions that existed at the statement of financial position date, which require an adjustment to the financial statements; and those that result from new information that financial statement users may find useful, which would normally be disclosed in the notes to the financial statements. Note that some subsequent events may not fit into either category, and therefore would not be accrued or disclosed.

- In general, the same accounting principles used for the preparation of annual reports should be used in the preparation of interim reports. In preparing an interim report, **an interim period is treated as a separate accounting period**. Therefore, accruals and deferrals should follow the principles used for annual reports (accounting transactions should be recorded using accrual accounting).

- In preparing an interim report, income tax expense for the interim period is calculated using an **annual estimated tax rate**. Specifically, interim taxable income and temporary differences are estimated, and the estimated annual effective tax rate is applied, to arrive at an estimate of income tax expense for the interim period.

- **Bankruptcy** is a legal process that occurs when a company is unable to pay its debts. This may involve the company making a proposal to pay their creditors a percentage of what is owed, or requesting an extension on the amount of time allowed to pay their debts (or both).

(continued)

● **Receivership** is a process typically initiated by a secured creditor (or group of secured creditors) if a company defaults on a loan. An appointed "receiver" will act on behalf of the creditors during the receivership process.

● If a company is in receivership or bankruptcy, the going-concern assumption of the conceptual framework may no longer be met. In such a case, a liquidation approach would likely be more appropriate for the financial statements than continued use of the historical cost principle.

● Although ratio, horizontal, and common-size analysis are useful in helping to identify the strengths, weaknesses, and possible trends in the entity's position and performance, a deeper analysis of the entity's business environment, financial statements, and notes to the financial statements is required to better evaluate the entity's financial position, results of operations, and cash flows.

CASE 23-1

PURPOSE: This case will review the meaning or significance of a number of terms used in this chapter.

Instructions

Select the letter of the item that most directly relates to the numbered statements. Use the letter to identify your response.

(a) summary of significant accounting policies
(b) related-party transactions
(c) segmented reporting
(d) subsequent events
(e) errors
(f) interim reports

(g) full disclosure principle
(h) notes to the financial statements
(i) auditor's report
(j) management discussion and analysis
(k) financial statement analysis
(l) limitation of financial statement analysis

_____ 1. Calls for reporting of any financial information significant enough to influence the judgement of an informed reader.

_____ 2. Information that is an integral part of the financial statements and serves as a means of amplifying or explaining the items presented in the body of the financial statements.

_____ 3. Disclosure of the accounting methods used in the preparation of the financial statements.

_____ 4. A business enterprise engages in transactions in which one of the transacting parties has the ability to significantly influence the policies of the other, or in which a non-transacting party has the ability to influence the policies of the two transacting parties.

_____ 5. Unintentional mistakes.

_____ 6. When analyzing financial statements, it should be considered that management is responsible for determining the accounting policies and methods used to prepare the financial statements, and that users may suspect that management's choices may be motivated by a need to "manage earnings."

_____ 7. Information related to revenues, operating profit or loss, and identifiable assets of different components of an entity.

_____ 8. Reports that cover periods of less than one year.

_____ 9. Section of an annual report that covers three financial aspects of an enterprise's business: liquidity, capital resources, and results of operations.

_____ 10. Information related to events occurring after the statement of financial position date but before the date financial statements are completed.

_____ 11. A report that states whether or not the financial statements are presented in accordance with IFRS or ASPE (referred to collectively as generally accepted accounting principles).

_____ 12. Evaluation of the relationships between the amounts presented in the financial statements, using ratio, horizontal, and common-size analysis.

Solution to Case 23-1

1. (g)	4. (b)	7. (c)	10. (d)
2. (h)	5. (e)	8. (f)	11. (i)
3. (a)	6. (l)	9. (j)	12. (k)

CASE 23-2

PURPOSE: This case will review the tests applied in determining the reportable segments of an entity.

Diversified Galore Inc. has several reportable industry segments that account for 80% of its operations. Diversified Galore Inc. prepares financial statements in accordance with IFRS.

Instructions

(a) Explain the term "operating segment" as it applies to an entity diversified in its operations.

(b) Explain when information about two or more operating segments may be aggregated.

(c) Explain the criteria used to determine Diversified's reportable segments.

(d) Indicate what information is to be disclosed for each reportable segment.

Solution to Case 23-2

(a) An **operating segment** is a component of an enterprise that has all of the following characteristics:

1. It engages in business activities from which it earns revenues and incurs expenses.

2. Its operating results are regularly reviewed by the company's chief operating decision-maker to assess segment performance and allocate resources to the segment.

3. Discrete financial information is available for it.

(b) Information about two or more operating segments may be aggregated only if the segments have the same basic characteristics in all of the following areas:

1. The nature of the products and services provided

2. The nature of the production process

3. The type or class of customer

4. The methods of product or service distribution

5. If applicable, the nature of the regulatory environment

(c) After an entity identifies its operating segments for possible disclosure, a quantitative materiality test is applied to determine whether each operating segment is significant enough to be a **reportable segment** (and therefore reported separately). An operating segment is regarded as significant, and therefore identified as reportable, if it satisfies **one or more** of the following quantitative thresholds:

1. Its **reporting revenue** (including both sales to external customers and intersegment sales or transfers) is 10% or more of the combined revenue of all the enterprise's operating segments.

2. The absolute amount of its reported **profit or loss** is 10% or more of the greater, in absolute amount, of:

- the combined operating profit of all operating segments that did not incur a loss, and

- the combined reported loss of all operating segments that did report a loss.

3. Its **assets** are 10% or more of the combined assets of all operating segments.

In applying these tests, three additional factors must be considered:

1. Segment data must explain a significant portion of the company's business. Specifically, the segmented results must equal or exceed 75% of the combined sales to unaffiliated customers for the entire enterprise. This test prevents a company from providing limited information on only a few segments and grouping the rest into one category.

2. Entities are required to disclose at most 10 reportable segments.

3. If an operating segment does not meet any of the tests but management believes separate information would be useful to users, then the segment may be presented separately.

(d) IFRS requires that an enterprise report the following:

1. **General information about its reportable segments.** This includes factors that management considers most significant in determining the company's reportable segments, and the types of products and services from which each operating segment derives its revenues.

2. **Segment revenues, profit and loss, assets, liabilities, and related information for each reportable segment.** In addition, the following specific information about each reportable segment must be reported if the amounts are regularly reviewed by management:

   - revenues from external customers (revenues from customers attributed to individual material foreign countries should be separately disclosed)
   - revenues from transactions with other operating segments of the same enterprise
   - interest income
   - interest expense
   - depreciation and amortization
   - unusual items
   - equity in the net income of investees and joint ventures that are accounted for using the equity method
   - income tax expense or benefit
   - significant non-cash items other than depreciation and amortization expense

3. **Reconciliations.** An enterprise must provide a reconciliation of the total of the segments' revenues to total revenues; a reconciliation of the total of the operating segments' profits and losses to its income before income taxes and discontinued operations; and a reconciliation of the total of the operating segments' assets and liabilities to total assets and liabilities. Reconciliations for other significant items that are disclosed should also be presented and all reconciling items should be separately identified and described for all of the above.

4. **Products and services.** The amount of revenues from external customers.

5. **Geographic areas.** Revenues from external customers (Canada versus foreign), and capital assets and goodwill (Canada versus foreign) should be stated. Foreign information must be disclosed by country if the amounts are material.

6. **Major customers.** If 10% or more of the revenues are derived from a single customer, the enterprise must disclose the total amount of revenues from each of these customers by segment.

CASE 23-3

PURPOSE: This case will review the reporting requirements for interim financial statements.

Sally's Sweater Shop is located in Burnaby, B.C. It sells sweaters, jackets, and other related merchandise. Some shareholders have asked management to distribute quarterly financial statements to shareholders. Sally's Sweater Shop prepares financial statements in accordance with IFRS.

Instructions

(a) Discuss the accounting principles that should be used for interim reports.

(b) Indicate whether or not it is a requirement to include a statement of cash flows in an interim report. Also list the minimum data to be disclosed in an interim report.

Solution to Case 23-3

(a) **IFRS indicates that the same accounting principles used for annual reports should be used for interim reports**. Assets and liabilities should be recognized at the interim period reporting date on the same basis as they would be recognized at year end. Therefore, revenues and costs directly associated with revenues (product costs) such as materials, labour and related fringe benefits, and manufacturing overhead should be treated in the same manner for interim reports as they are for annual reports.

   Generally, companies should use the same inventory pricing methods (FIFO, weighted average cost) for both interim reports and annual reports. However, an exception is provided for planned variances under a standard cost system that are expected to be absorbed by year end. These should ordinarily be deferred.

   Costs and expenses other than product costs, often referred to as period costs, are often charged to the interim period as incurred. However, they may be allocated to interim periods based on estimated time to expiry, benefits received, or activities associated with each interim period.

(b) At a minimum, a condensed statement of financial position, statement of comprehensive income, statement of changes in equity, statement of cash flows, and notes to financial statements are required. Comparative financial statements are also required.

   Regarding disclosure, the following interim data should be reported as a minimum:

   1. Whether the statements comply with IFRS
   2. A statement that the company follows the same accounting policies and methods as the most recent annual financial statements, including a description of new or changed policies
   3. A description of any seasonality or cyclicality of interim period operations
   4. The nature and amount of any unusual items
   5. The nature and amount of changes in estimates
   6. Issuances, repurchases, and repayments of debt and equity securities
   7. Dividends paid

Illustration 23-1 403

8. Information about reportable segments, including revenues from external customers, intersegment revenues, segment profit or loss, total assets for which there is a material change, a description of differences from the last annual statements in the basis of segmentation, and reconciliation of segment profit or loss to the entity's total profit or loss before taxes and discontinued operations

9. Events subsequent to the interim period

10. Specific information about changes in the composition of the entity

11. Any other information that is required for fair presentation and/or is material to an understanding of the interim period

ILLUSTRATION 23-1

Related-Party Transactions—Decision Tree (ASPE)[1]

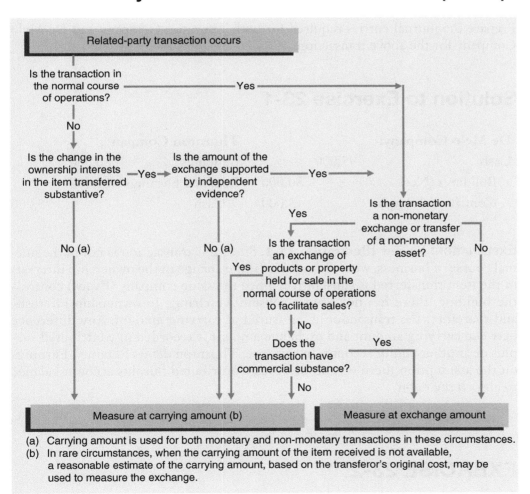

(a) Carrying amount is used for both monetary and non-monetary transactions in these circumstances.

(b) In rare circumstances, when the carrying amount of the item received is not available, a reasonable estimate of the carrying amount, based on the transferor's original cost, may be used to measure the exchange.

[1] Note that for related-party transactions, IFRS deals only with disclosure requirements, whereas ASPE requires that some related-party transactions be remeasured according to the decision tree above.

EXERCISE 23-1

PURPOSE: This exercise will allow you to practise accounting for related-party transactions.

Evans and Associates is a large multinational company with related companies all over the world. During 2017, De Melo Company (a subsidiary company fully owned by Evans) sold a building to Thornton Company (a different subsidiary company fully owned by Evans). The building has a fair value of $120,000 and a net book value of $80,000. Thornton Company paid De Melo Company $95,000 in cash for the building. You may assume that this transaction is outside the normal course of business. Both Thornton Company and De Melo Company prepare financial statements in accordance with ASPE.

Instructions

Prepare the journal entries required for both Thornton Company and De Melo Company for the above transaction.

Solution to Exercise 23-1

De Melo Company:			Thornton Company:		
Cash	95,000		Buildings	80,000	
Buildings (Net)		80,000	Retained Earnings	15,000	
Contributed Surplus		15,000	Cash		95,000

EXPLANATION: Review **Illustration 23-1**. Since this transaction is not in the normal course of business, we must consider if the change in the ownership interests in the item transferred is substantive. Since the same company (Evans) controls the building, there has not been a substantive change in ownership interests, and therefore, the transaction is measured at carrying amount. Any difference between carrying amount and exchange amount is recorded in contributed surplus or another equity account. In this case, Thornton debits Retained Earnings on the assumption there was no previous Contributed Surplus account balance to absorb the debit.

EXERCISE 23-2

PURPOSE: This exercise will provide you with examples of subsequent events.

Instructions

Analyze the following subsequent events and determine the correct accounting treatment.

(a) Fire destroys an office building that is fully covered by insurance.

(b) A significant customer declares bankruptcy.

(c) A major contract is lost.

(d) The union decides to go on strike.

(e) Fair value of FV-NI investments drops by a material amount.

(f) A new business segment is purchased.

(g) A lawsuit outstanding for two years is finally settled.

(h) The company issues new common shares.

(i) A new company president is appointed.

Solution to Exercise 23-2

(a) Since the condition did not exist at the statement of financial position date, this event would not require an adjustment to the financial statements. Whether or not to disclose the transaction would be a matter of professional judgement. Factors to consider would include the significance of the event to the overall operations.

(b) Assuming there is an amount owing at year end, this event would likely require an adjustment to the financial statements, because it provides additional evidence about conditions that existed at the statement of financial position date. A situation leading up to bankruptcy does not happen all of a sudden, but develops over a long period of time. The allowance for doubtful accounts on the year-end financial statements would be adjusted to take this into account.

(c) Loss of a major contract would likely be treated as an event of the subsequent year. It would be neither adjusted nor disclosed on the current year's financial statements. Instead, it would likely be communicated through the financial press.

(d) Since the condition did not exist at the statement of financial position date, there would be no adjustment to the financial statements. However, this too would be covered by the financial press.

(e) Similar to (a) above, with the decision based on the significance of the loss.

(f) Similar to (a) above, with the decision based on the significance of the transaction to its existing assets and liabilities and the company's future operations.

(g) As the lawsuit was outstanding at year end, the settlement provides additional evidence about conditions (the company's potential liability) that existed at the reporting date. The financial statements should be adjusted to reflect the settlement liability and loss amount.

(h) Similar to (a) above, with the decision based on the significance of the additional shares issued.

(i) Similar to (d) above.

ILLUSTRATION 23-2

A Summary of Financial Ratios

Ratio	Formula	What It Measures
I. Liquidity		
1. Current ratio	$\dfrac{\text{Current assets}}{\text{Current liabilities}}$	Short-term debt-paying ability
2. Quick or acid-test ratio	$\dfrac{\text{Cash, marketable securities, and receivables (net)}}{\text{Current liabilities}}$	Immediate short-term liquidity
3. Current cash debt coverage ratio	$\dfrac{\text{Net cash provided by operating activities}}{\text{Average current liabilities}}$	Company's ability to pay off its current liabilities in a specific year from its operations
II. Activity		
4. Receivables turnover	$\dfrac{\text{Net sales}}{\text{Average trade receivables (net)}}$	Liquidity of receivables
5. Inventory turnover	$\dfrac{\text{Cost of goods sold}}{\text{Average inventory}}$	Liquidity of inventory
6. Asset turnover	$\dfrac{\text{Net sales}}{\text{Average total assets}}$	How efficiently assets are used to generate sales
III. Profitability		
7. Profit margin on sales	$\dfrac{\text{Net income}}{\text{Net sales}}$	Net income generated by each dollar of sales
8. Rate of return on assets	$\dfrac{\text{Net income}}{\text{Average total assets}}$	Overall profitability of assets
9. Rate of return on common share equity	$\dfrac{\text{Net income minus preferred dividends}}{\text{Average common shareholders' equity}}$	Profitability of owners' investment
10. Earnings per share	$\dfrac{\text{Net income minus preferred dividends}}{\text{Weighted average shares outstanding}}$	Net income earned on each common share
11. Price earnings ratio	$\dfrac{\text{Market price of shares}}{\text{Earnings per share}}$	Ratio of the market price per share to earnings per share
12. Payout ratio	$\dfrac{\text{Cash dividends}}{\text{Net income}}$	Percentage of earnings distributed as cash dividends
IV. Coverage		
13. Debt to total assets	$\dfrac{\text{Total debt}}{\text{Total assets}}$	Percentage of total assets provided by creditors
14. Times interest earned	$\dfrac{\text{Income before interest charges and taxes}}{\text{Interest charges}}$	Ability to meet interest payments as they come due
15. Cash debt coverage ratio	$\dfrac{\text{Net cash provided by operating activities}}{\text{Average total liabilities}}$	Company's ability to repay its total liabilities in a specific year from its operations
16. Book value per share	$\dfrac{\text{Common shareholders' equity}}{\text{Number of common shares outstanding at SFP date}}$	Amount each share would receive if the company were liquidated at the amounts reported on the balance sheet

EXERCISE 23-3

PURPOSE: This exercise will allow you to practise analyzing ratios and results of horizontal analysis.

The following ratios and percentages were calculated using amounts from the 2015 to 2017 financial statements of Fall Corporation, as at and for the years ended December 31:

	2015	2016	2017
Current ratio	1.65	1.92	2.02
Quick or acid-test ratio	1.14	1.01	0.77
Inventory turnover	6.44	6.02	5.42
Change in sales as a % of previous years' sales	0.2%	1.1%	3.7%

Instructions

Analyze the ratios and percentages provided, and comment on the financial position of Fall Corporation in the three-year period from 2015 to 2017.

Solution to Exercise 23-3

Fall Corporation's current ratio is increasing, while its quick or acid-test ratio is declining. The quick or acid-test ratio is the current ratio without including inventory and prepaid expenses in current assets (although prepaid expenses are generally insignificant relative to inventory). Any divergence in trend between these two ratios would therefore be explained by the inventory account. Inventory turnover has declined sharply in the three-year period, from 6.44 to 5.42. During the same period, total sales have continually increased. The decline in the inventory turnover is therefore not due to a decline in sales. Investment in inventory has increased at a faster rate than sales, and this has accounted for the divergence between the quick or acid-test and current ratios. These are signs that Fall Corporation's liquidity is deteriorating.

The ratios and percentages provided may be used to comment on the liquidity of Fall Corporation, one aspect of the company's overall financial position. To comment on the overall financial position and performance of Fall Corporation, additional activity ratios (such as receivables turnover and asset turnover) and coverage ratios (such as debt to total assets and cash debt coverage ratio) should be calculated and analyzed. As well, the company's financial position should be compared with the financial position of competitors in the same industry, and an in-depth analysis of the company's business environment and accounting policies and methods should be completed.

ANALYSIS OF MULTIPLE-CHOICE QUESTIONS

Question

1. Which of the following should be disclosed in the summary of significant accounting policies?

	Depreciation Method	Composition of Property, Plant, and Equipment
a.	Yes	Yes
b.	Yes	No
c.	No	Yes
d.	No	No

EXPLANATION: The depreciation method for plant assets should be disclosed in the summary of significant accounting policies. Composition of plant assets should not be disclosed in the summary of significant accounting policies because that information is provided elsewhere in the notes to the financial statements. Disclosures in the summary of significant accounting policies should not duplicate information already presented.

Examples of accounting policies to be disclosed include:
- inventory pricing method
- depreciation and amortization methods
- revenue recognition policies   (Solution = b.)

Question

2. Keswick Corporation has six operating segments:

Segments	Total Revenue	Operating Profit (Loss)	Assets
A	$25,000,000	$ 4,700,000	$ 55,000,000
B	23,000,000	4,445,000	49,000,000
C	19,500,000	2,300,000	36,000,000
D	8,500,000	2,150,000	10,000,000
E	30,000,000	8,725,000	39,000,000
F	7,200,000	1,015,000	8,880,000
	$113,200,000	$23,335,000	$197,880,000

Under IFRS's quantitative guidelines, for which of the operating segments should separate information be presented?

a. Segments A, B, C, and D
b. Segments A, B, C, and E
c. Segments A, B, C, D, and E
d. All six segments

EXPLANATION: An operating segment is regarded as significant and therefore identified as reportable if it satisfies one or more of the following quantitative thresholds:

1. Its **reporting revenue** (including both sales to external customers and intersegment sales or transfers) is 10% or more of the combined revenue of all the enterprise's operating segments.
2. The absolute amount of its reported **profit or loss** is 10% or more of the greater, in absolute amount, of:
   - the combined operating profit of all operating segments that did not incur a loss, and
   - the combined reported loss of all operating segments that did report a loss.
3. Its **assets** are 10% or more of the combined assets of all operating segments.

Segments A, B, and E pass the operating profit test, but A, B, C, and E pass the revenue and asset tests. Since an operating segment need only pass one of the three 10% tests to be considered a reportable segment, Keswick Corporation has four reportable segments: A, B, C, and E. (Solution = b.)

Question

3. Which of the following does the IASB require an enterprise to report about its reportable segments?
   a. Reconciliations including reconciliation of the segments' revenues to total revenues
   b. Factors that management considers most significant in determining the company's reportable segments, and the types of products and services from which each operating segment derives its revenues
   c. Information about major customers (if 10% or more of the revenues are derived from a single customer, the enterprise must disclose the total amount of revenues from each of these customers by segment)
   d. All of the above

EXPLANATION: The IASB requires that an enterprise report the following information about its reportable segments: general information about its reportable segments; segment revenues, profit and loss, assets, liabilities, and related information; reconciliations; products and services; geographic areas; and major customers. (Solution = d.)

Question

4. For interim reporting, a company's income tax expense for the second quarter should be calculated using the:
   a. statutory tax rate for the year.
   b. effective tax rate expected to be applicable for the second quarter.
   c. annual estimated tax rate estimated at the end of the first quarter.
   d. annual estimated tax rate estimated at the end of the second quarter.

EXPLANATION: In preparing an interim report, income tax expense for the interim period is calculated using an annual estimated tax rate. Specifically, interim taxable income and temporary differences are estimated, and the estimated annual effective tax rate is applied, to arrive at an estimate of income tax expense for the interim period. (Solution = d.)

Question

5. IFRS recommends that interim reporting be viewed as:
   a. reporting for a separate accounting period.
   b. reporting for an integral part of an annual period.
   c. a "special" type of reporting that need not conform to generally accepted accounting principles.
   d. requiring a cash basis approach.

EXPLANATION: Under IFRS, each interim period is considered a discrete (separate) period. Generally, preparation of interim reports should be based on the same accounting principles used in preparation of annual reports. However, certain principles and practices used in preparation of annual reports may require modification in preparation of interim reports. (Solution = a.)

Question

6. Events that occur after the December 31, 2017 statement of financial position date (but before the financial statements are completed) that provide additional evidence about conditions that existed at the statement of financial position date and affect the net realizable value of accounts receivable should be:
   a. discussed only in the MD&A (Management Discussion and Analysis) section of the annual report.
   b. disclosed only in the notes to the financial statements.
   c. used to record an adjustment to Bad Debt Expense for the year ended December 31, 2017.
   d. used to record an adjustment directly to the Retained Earnings account.

EXPLANATION: Notes to the financial statements should explain any significant financial events that took place after the statement of financial position date, but before the financial statements are issued. These events are referred to as **subsequent events** or **events after the reporting period**. Two types of events or transactions occurring after the statement of financial position date that may have a material effect on the financial statements, or may need to be considered to interpret the financial statements accurately, are as follows:

- events that provide additional evidence about conditions that existed at the statement of financial position date, which affect the estimates used in preparing the financial statements, and therefore require adjustment of the financial statements; and

- events or information about conditions that did not exist at the statement of financial position date, but are significant enough to require disclosure.

The subsequent event described in the question provides additional evidence about conditions that existed at the statement of financial position date. This information would have been recorded in the accounts if it was known at the statement of financial position date. Therefore, this subsequent event requires adjustment of the financial statements before they are issued. (Solution = c.)

Question

7. The following amounts are from the 2015 to 2017 financial statements of Boardwalk Corporation for the years ended December 31:

	2015	2016	2017
Cash dividends	$ 15,000	$ 15,000	$ 15,000
Net sales	600,000	627,000	693,000
Net income	72,000	68,000	51,000

Which of the following statements is true?
a. Boardwalk's payout ratio remained unchanged between 2015 and 2017.
b. Boardwalk's payout ratio increased between 2015 and 2017.
c. Boardwalk's profit margin on sales improved between 2015 and 2017.
d. Boardwalk's profit margin on sales between 2015 and 2017 cannot be determined from the information given.

EXPLANATION: Payout ratio is calculated as cash dividends divided by net income, and profit margin on sales is calculated as net income divided by net sales. Boardwalk's profit margin on sales deteriorated between 2015 and 2017; however, Boardwalk's payout ratio increased between 2015 and 2017. (Solution = b.)

Question

8. Under ASPE, a related-party cash transaction in the normal course of business is measured at the following amount:

    a. exchange amount.

    b. fair value.

    c. carrying amount.

    d. replacement cost.

EXPLANATION: Refer to **Illustration 23-1**. Recall that related-party transactions can only be recorded at exchange amount or carrying amount. If a related-party cash transaction is in the normal course of business, it is recorded at the exchange amount. (Solution = a.)

Question

9. Under ASPE, a related-party cash transaction that is not in the normal course of business, and is without a substantive change in ownership interests, is measured at the following amount:

    a. exchange amount.

    b. fair value.

    c. carrying amount.

    d. replacement cost.

EXPLANATION: Refer to **Illustration 23-1**. Recall that a related-party transaction can only be recorded at its exchange amount or carrying amount. If a related-party cash transaction is not in the normal course of business and there is no substantive change in ownership interests, it is recorded at the carrying amount of the assets exchanged. Any difference between the exchange amount and carrying amount is recorded in equity. (Solution = c.)

Question

10. Which of the following would not be considered a related party to A Company?

    a. B Company, where A Company controls B Company

    b. A major shareholder of A Company (owns 55%)

    c. Management of A Company

    d. C Company, where C Company is a 15% shareholder of A Company

EXPLANATION: Related parties include but are not limited to the following: (1) companies or individuals who control, or are controlled by, or are under common control with the reporting enterprise; (2) investors and investees where there is significant influence or joint control; (3) company management; (4) members of immediate family of the above; and (5) the other party when a management contract exists. (Solution = d.)

Question

11. Jutland Company is in the process of having its financial statements audited. The audit partner has called a meeting to discuss the fact that the company has not followed generally accepted accounting principles in accounting for advertising costs. The impact on net income is fairly significant but not so material that it renders the financial statements invalid as a whole. This situation, if not fixed, could result in which type of audit opinion?

    a. An unmodified opinion
    b. A qualified opinion
    c. An adverse opinion
    d. A denial of opinion

EXPLANATION: A qualified opinion would be issued because there is an exception to the standard opinion. The problem is not significant enough that it affects the usefulness of the rest of the financial statements taken as a whole. Therefore, an adverse opinion would not be issued, and a denial of opinion would not be issued. (Solution = b.)

Question

12. Jefferies Company is a clothing manufacturer in its fifth year of operations, and is seeking a short-term bank loan to fund planned expansion of its manufacturing operations in 2018. Sara Sherwin is a loan officer at Jefferies Company's bank, and is analyzing the company's financial statements for the years ended December 31, 2015, 2016, and 2017. In particular, Sara is concerned about Jefferies Company's short-term debt-paying ability. Which ratios should Sara calculate and consider in her assessment of Jefferies Company's liquidity?

    a. Asset turnover
    b. Quick or acid-test ratio
    c. Times interest earned
    d. Cash debt coverage ratio

EXPLANATION: Asset turnover is a measure of how efficiently assets are used to generate sales, and is not a measure of short-term debt-paying ability or liquidity. Times interest earned is a measure of the company's ability to meet interest payments as they come due, and cash debt coverage ratio is a measure of the company's ability to repay its total liabilities in a specific year from its operations. The times interest earned and cash debt coverage ratios are coverage ratios, and are not specific measures of short-term debt-paying ability or liquidity. The quick or acid-test ratio is a measure of immediate short-term liquidity. (Solution = b.)